The Trotsky Reappraisal

'In 1937 there were trials in Moscow. In one ... my father [Leonid Petrovich Serebriakov] was accused. From that time I only could dream about the possibility of his rehabilitation. It was even impossible after the 20th Party Congress [in 1956] ...

It is [only] now ... [that] we begin to feel free. We can read what we want. The truth returns to us.'

Zorya Leonidovna Serebriakova, speaking to Grampian Television in Aberdeen, 2 August 1990. Her contribution to the conference 'Trotsky after fifty years' gave it a true sense of history.

'Finally, after the longest, darkest nights of this century, a light is illuminating the scene of history ... '

Esteban Volkov (Seva), grandson of Trotsky, speaking at a symposium 'Leo Trotsky, 1879-1940 - Kritiker und Verteidiger der Sowjetgesellschaft', Wuppertal, Germany, 29 March 1990.

The Trotsky Reappraisal

edited by
TERRY BROTHERSTONE AND PAUL DUKES

translations by
BRIAN PEARCE, JENNY BRINE AND ANDREW DRUMMOND

EDINBURGH UNIVERSITY PRESS

© Edinburgh University Press, 1992

Edinburgh University Press
22 George Square, Edinburgh

Typeset in Linotron Goudy
by Koinonia Ltd., Bury, and
printed in Great Britain by
The University Press, Cambridge

A CIP record from this book is
available from the British Library

ISBN 0 7486 0317 4

Contents

Notes on Contributors

VALERY BRONSTEIN, a political prisoner in the Stalin years, is now a geophysicist in the Committee on Geology of the Russian Republic in Moscow.

TERRY BROTHERSTONE lectures in History at the University of Aberdeen.

PIERRE BROUÉ is President and Scientific Director of the Leon Trotsky Institute, Grenoble.

V. P. BULDAKOV is Vice-chair, Department of the History of Revolutions in Russia of the Academy of Sciences in Moscow.

ROBERT V. DANIELS is Professor of History at the University of Vermont.

RICHARD B. DAY is Professor of Political Science at the University of Torornto in Mississauga.

PAUL DUKES is Professor of History and Director of the Centre for Soviet and East European Studies, University of Aberdeen.

UDO GEHRMANN lectures in History at the University of Halle.

AGOTA GUEULLETTE is director of the section concerned with the institutions and economy of the countries of Eastern Europe and the former Soviet Union at the Institute for Comparative Research on Institutions and Law, Ivry-sur-Seine.

BARUCH HIRSON, a former political prisoner in South Africa, now edits *Searchlight South Africa* in London.

GEORGE L. KLINE is Professor of Philosophy at Bryn Mawr College, Pennsylvania.

SERGEI KUDRIASHOV is editor of the Russian journal *Rodina*.

ALEC NOVE is Emeritus Professor of Economics and Honorary Senior Research Fellow at the University of Glasgow.

PHILIP POMPER is Professor of History, Wesleyan University, Connecticut.

MICHAEL REIMAN worked at the Institute of Political Science in Prague until the crushing of the 'Prague Spring' in 1968; and is now Professor of Political Science at the Free University of Berlin.

BORIS STARKOV is a Doctor of History from St Petersburg.

N. S. TARKHOVA researches at the Archive of the Soviet Army in Moscow.

HILLEL TICKTIN lectures in Soviet Studies at the Institute of Soviet and East European Studies, University of Glasgow; and edits the journal, *Critique*.

A. VATLIN is an editor of the Russian journal *Kriminal*.

Preface and Acknowledgements

The Trotsky Reappraisal is intended as a major contribution and encouragement to the development of discussion about one of the most important and talented – and, arguably, one of the least understood – figures in twentieth-century world history. Its title does not mean that the book is a definitive statement: on the contrary, its aim is to excite controversy, criticism and further research.

The book is based on papers delivered at, or submitted to, the conference entitled 'Trotsky after fifty years', held at King's College, University of Aberdeen, Scotland, from 31 July to 4 August 1990 – close to the fiftieth anniversary of Trotsky's assassination at Coyoacán, Mexico, on 20 August 1940, by the Stalinist agent Jaime Ramón Mercader del Río. The conference was organised jointly by the University's Department of History and its newly formed Centre for Soviet and East European Studies, of which Paul Dukes is director.

Our first thanks must go to Brian Pearce. He is the translator from the Russian of the articles by Bronstein, Vatlin, Starkov, Kudriashov and Buldakov. But he has also acted well beyond the call of duty as in effect a co-editor of much of what follows. The book would have many more flaws were it not for him; but he bears no responsibility for those which remain nor for any opinions expressed by the editors.

Our thanks also to Jenny Brine who translated the articles by Tarkhova and Reiman, from Russian originals; to Andrew Drummond who translated Gehrmann's article from the German; and to Youssef-al-Khatib who took time away from his Edinburgh translation agency to attend part of the conference, and to give advice on, and make translations of, background materials.

The conference, without which this book would not have been possible, received indispensable financial support from a number of sources, to all of which we wish to express gratitude here. A grant from the Nuffield Foundation allowed us to run a special series of seminars and discussions on economic questions, reflected most directly in this volume in the articles by Nove, Gueullette and Ticktin. *The Scotsman* newspaper provided a grant at a vital moment and we thank its editor, Magnus Linklater, for taking time in a busy schedule to talk about our problems. An article by Terry Brotherstone discussing the conference appeared in the paper on 20 August 1990.

Our other funding came from the University of Aberdeen Faculty of Arts; the University's Research Committee, which provided assistance towards the preparation of *The Trotsky Reappraisal*; the Ford Foundation working through the British Association for Soviet, Slavonic and East European Studies; the British Academy; Grampian Regional Council and the City of Aberdeen District Council. We should also like to thank Grampian's convenor, Robert Middleton, and Aberdeen's Lord Provost, R. A. Robertson, for their hospitality to our international guests; and for the care they put into their welcoming speeches.

We also acknowledge, with gratitude, material support and assistance from British Rail; the Wild Boar Restaurant, Aberdeen; Morrison Bowmore Distillers Ltd; Arthur Watson of Peacock Printmakers; Tom Spiers; Pat Carlos; Helen Forsås-Scott and Bill Scott; Michael Kulyk; and John Biggart. To all those charged with providing back-up services for conferences in the University thanks are also due.

Greatly to our regret it has not been possible to include in this volume all the excellent papers at our disposal. We should like to thank everyone who participated: by contributing to the success of the conference, they have made possible the book. Particular thanks must go to those who assisted their less linguistically prepared colleagues by translating during the seminars. Several have essays in the book but, of those who do not, Alexander Kan deserves special mention. Jo Forsyth of the University Russian Department was also very helpful. The participation of Galeena Alekseeva – whose opening paper helped to establish the contemporary relevance of Trotsky's writings on culture – along with her colleagues from the Institute of the History of Russia of the Academy of Sciences in Moscow, made firmer the already welcome links between our two institutions. The historical connections established by Zorya Serebriakova's contribution on her father's relationships with Trotsky was an important element in the conference. Regrettably it was not of a suitable length to publish here, but we hope it will soon be available elsewhere, and we thank Zorya Leonidovna for making the journey to Aberdeen – and for her hospitality in Moscow.

This is perhaps the point at which to comment on the problems of transliteration and citation. We have sought to achieve the greatest possible consistency in rendering names, in particular from the cyrillic, but without being pedantic. To be consistent with usage elsewhere in the book, for example, we would have used 'Bronshtein' rather than 'Bronstein', but felt that this would only cause needless confusion. No doubt undetected inconsistencies remain despite the best efforts of the book's copy-editor, but not, we hope, to the extent that they get in the way of clarity. As to citations, thanks in no small measure to Brian Pearce references to English editions of works available in this language, but which the author has used in Russian, German or French versions, are often given.

The organisation of the conference and the production of this book would not have been possible without help and encouragement in large and small ways from many more individuals than can be mentioned here. Several of our students at the time assisted and we thank them all; but the most dedicated helpers were Cath

Brennan, Jim Phillips and David Swanson. They probably did more than either of us even now realises.

Our colleagues in the History Department and the Centre for Soviet and East European Studies at Aberdeen provide the constant stimulation that encouraged us to launch and carry through a venture which, when it was conceived, might have attracted high odds against its success. We were fortunate in having one of them, Roy Bridges, to conduct the official opening of the conference, deputising for the then Principal who was out of town. We are grateful too for the careful and efficient work done both for the book and the conference by our colleagues in the Faculty of Arts Secretariat. The assistance given in the History Department by Moira Buchan and Ann Gordon went far beyond what we had any right to expect. Ann's husband, the late David Gordon, also lent his distinctively Scottish persona to part of our conference proceedings, and those who met him, even briefly, will regret his sad death in 1991.

A special word of thanks must go to David King, builder and possessor of the most splendid Trotsky photo-library. The picture of Trotsky's train which graces our cover comes from this collection and is gratefully acknowledged.

Finally, Terry Brotherstone would like personally to acknowledge Jenny Brotherstone, Charles Campbell, James Cornford, the late John Dinkel, Andrew Drummond, Peter Fryer, Frank Girling, Hilary Horrocks, Tom Kemp, Youssef-al-Khatib, John Mathieson, Michael McInnes, Brian Pearce, Cyril Smith and Hillel Ticktin. In carrying out his role in this project he has appreciated in different ways their help, encouragement and even criticism. But they bear no responsibility for the use he has made of any of these things.

Paul Dukes wishes, as always, to thank Rosie Dukes, on this occasion most particularly for her help with his part in organising our conference.

T. B.

P. D.

Aberdeen

July 1991

Editors' Note: The editorial content of this book was prepared before the un-successful August 1991 *coup*, and the dissolution of the Soviet Union.

Part I

Introduction

1

Introductory Essay

PAUL DUKES

Nearly a hundred years ago, Lev Davidovich Trotsky set out on the political path that was to lead to his death on 21 August 1940. Making use of the half century that has elapsed since his assassination, the essays in this book examine his career in that perspective from a number of points of view: Trotsky the man and his family; his significance for the Russian Revolution and its aftermath; approaches to him and his work; and his contribution to the recently revived economic debates of the 1920s.

The essays in this volume, it may be confidently asserted, need no introduction. Each is self-contained at the same time as forming an integral part of the collection as a whole. Nevertheless, there may be a case for setting out one possible framework into which they can all be fitted.

Certainly, it is difficult to separate Trotsky from his life's work: his personal characteristics are virtually inseparable from his public positions. My *Life* is just one of many attempts to justify himself and his policies, and right up to the end he was concerned to demonstrate to the world that there was no stain on his revolutionary honour.

At least one accident of birth may have been of great influence – the fact that he was born a Jew. A key moment was just after the success of the October Revolution, when Lenin asked him to become Commissar of the Interior, arguing that the most important task at that juncture was to oppose counter-revolution. Later, Trotsky himself asserted: 'If, in 1917 and later, I occasionally pointed to my Jewish origin as an argument against some appointment, it was simply because of political considerations.' His Jewishness 'never played a leading part – not even a recognised one – in the list of my grievances'. But he did concede that national inequality probably was one of the underlying causes of his dissatisfaction with the order then existing, even if it was lost among all the other aspects of social injustice. According to his own account, his Marxist education deepened such an attitude as it changed it to one of active internationalism.[1]

Possibly, then, Trotsky's world outlook, like that of Marx, owed something to his racial origins. It was also the consequence, no doubt, of formative experiences in childhood and adolescence. Unfortunately for the psycho-historian, there was no dramatic conversion, and his own description of his first years gives some reinforcement to Tolstoy's observation that 'All happy families resemble each other, each unhappy family is unhappy in its own way.' While Trotsky's evocation of childhood is as compelling as any other, he gives us little further clue to the emergence of the stance that he was later to assume. There was no elder brother executed for an attempt on the life of the tsar, as in the case of Lenin; no drunken father, smallpox or other difficulties such as were experienced by the youthful Stalin. Life with the Bronsteins may not have been all plain sailing, but Trotsky appears to number himself among those avoiding 'a dark cave' even if missing out on ' a sunny meadow'.

He is not, then, the most helpful subject for psycho-history. Throughout adolescence, nevertheless, his 'subconscious strivings were tinged by a spirit of opposition', which came to the surface in 1896, when Tolstoyan tendencies towards pacifism were dying down among the intelligentsia and 'Marxism was marching upon the populist movement'. Soon, he made the choice of the political path that he wanted to follow.[2]

This is not the place to chart the successive stages in Trotsky's subsequent political career through 1905 to 1917, 1929 and 1940. But there may be a case for a brief consideration of his mature world outlook, most concisely summarised in the phrase 'permanent revolution'. This concept, applied most closely to the history of his own lifetime, has a symbiotic relationship with the concept that he applied to the history of the centuries before his birth, that of 'uneven and combined development'. The fifty years since his death, along with the great changes that have occurred during them, provide a sufficient pause for a clearer consideration of that relationship than might once have been possible.

The most succinct exposition of 'uneven and combined development' is to be found in the first chapter of *The History of the Russian Revolution*, beginning: 'The fundamental and most stable feature of Russian history is the slow tempo of her development, with the economic backwardness, primitiveness of social forms and low level of culture resulting from it.' In comparison with the leading countries of the West in particular, Russia would be numbered among those backward countries which revealed with the greatest sharpness and complexity in their destiny the most general law of the historic process – unevenness. From that law derived another involving 'a drawing together of the different stages of the journey, a combining of separate steps, an amalgam of archaic with more contemporary forms', a law which was to be called 'the law of combined development'.

Thus, medieval Russia lacked cities as centres of commerce and craft, with significant social consequences. And so when it came to the Pugachev Revolt of the late eighteenth century, there could be no conversion into revolution because of the lack of an ingredient most apparent in France – a Third Estate. A century later, however, the Europeanisation and modernisation of Russia were especially noticeable in industry, which went on to double its production between 1905 and 1914. Now, the law of combined development revealed itself most forcibly in this economic sphere. While more than 80 per cent of the people were involved in an agriculture, which still often used seventeenth-century methods, Russian industry in some aspects had caught up with and even outstripped its advanced rivals – for example, in the number of large-scale enterprises and in the confluence of industrial with financial capital. Indeed, this latter circumstance meant the subjection of much of Russian industry to the Western European money market.[3]

As with capitalism, so with socialism, and the concept of permanent revolution about which Trotsky wrote in 1930, revising his first formulation of 1906. In 1905, he argued, revolutionary Russia had revealed to the world the most advanced form of proletarian organisation, the soviet, moving on from the sansculottes and even the Communards of Paris to proletarians at a higher level of consciousness. In 1917 the soviet forces had achieved a great victory in combination with the peasants, for whom the proletarians had provided leadership. However, there were other lessons to be drawn from 1905 and 1917. For backward countries, the road to democracy was by way of the dictatorship of the proletariat. Consequently, a permanent state of revolutionary development was established between the democratic revolution and the socialist reconstruction of society. At the same time, indefinitely and constantly, all social relations were undergoing transformation, with attendant periods of war and peace, scientific and moral adaptations, never allowing the achievement of equilibrium. A final aspect of permanent revolution was its international character. The socialist revolution might have begun on national foundations, but it could not continue in such a manner without falling victim through isolation to internal and external contradictions:

> The way out for it lies only in the victory of the proletariat of the advanced countries. Viewed from this standpoint, a national revolution is not a self-contained whole; it is only a link in the international chain. The international revolution constitutes a permanent process, despite temporary declines and ebbs.[4]

As the 1930s unfolded, Trotsky saw little necessity to make fundamental changes in his overall theory. Considering the isolation of the Soviet Union in the contradictions of 'socialism in one country', he came to the conclusion that:

> the crushing of Soviet democracy by an all-powerful bureaucracy and the extermination of bourgeois democracy by fascism were produced by one and the same cause: the dilatoriness of the world proletariat in solving the problems set for it by history. Stalinism and fascism, in spite of a deep difference in social foundations, are symmetrical phenomena. In many of their features they show a deadly similarity.

At the same time, he emphasised that the Soviet Union even under Stalin was separated from Hitler's Germany and Mussolini's Italy by 'the difference between a workers' state and a capitalist state'. And until the violent end, he strove to keep the Fourth International along such lines as set out at the foundation congress in 1938.[5]

The split that occurred with the Hitler–Stalin pact of 1939 underlined the difficulty of ideological consistency, yet this remains Trotsky's greatest legacy to his followers today. In different ways (for the splits continue), they revere Trotsky for his avoidance of the over-simplifications and distortions of Stalinist 'Marxism-Leninism'. As early as 1923, Lunacharsky had argued that Trotsky 'takes revolutionary Marxism and draws from it the conclusions applicable to a given situation. He is as bold as can be in opposing liberalism and semi-socialism, but he is no innovator.' If this view has a certain validity, to it must certainly be added the observation that Trotsky had a most profound understanding of revolutionary Marxism and a much closer acquaintance with European culture as a whole than his rivals, especially Stalin. But, in combination with various personal failings and tactical errors, it was arguably his very sophistication that led to his defeat in the great struggle of 1923 and after. Great orator and dynamic figure though he was, Trotsky did not have Stalin's understanding of a Party which itself calculated that fewer than 10 per cent of its members were fully literate, albeit that Stalin was a man of narrower outlook in virtually every respect. Even Trotsky perhaps never acquired a world-view in all senses of the word (for example, he had little understanding of Africa, even of American Blacks), but his outlook was as broad as the circumstances of the 1930s allowed.[6]

Today, more than fifty years after his death, the world has changed so much (not necessarily for the better) that it is difficult not to take a global view in a sense only approached by Trotsky. But this does not mean that his ideas have lost all relevance. Beyond all doubt, uneven and combined development is still with us, as markedly as ever. As for permanent revolution, we must certainly accept that all social relations are still undergoing transformation, indefinitely and constantly, with attendant periods of war and peace, scientific and moral adaptations, never allowing the achievement of equilibrium. On the other hand, there is little sure sign that the Soviet Union constituted a workers' state. Socialism is widely discerned as on the retreat throughout the world, whose new order, as Fukuyama has alleged, will have no room for any ideology developed after Hegel. In reply to this, several of the contributors to this volume would want to assert that appearances can be deceptive as well as misrepresented, and that the course of human history still has some way to run. All the contributors would agree that, among activists and ideologues of the past, none has been so maligned and caricatured as Lev Davidovich Trotsky, and they have collaborated here in an attempt to help set the record straight.[7] The extent of their success will be estimated by their readers.

Notes

1. Leon Trotsky, My Life, New York, 1960, pp. xvi, 340–1; Victor Danilov, 'We are starting to learn about Trotsky', History Workshop, no. 29, 1990, pp. 142–5. On Marx as Jew, see Edmund Wilson, To the Finland Station, London, 1962, pp. 114–16, 121–2.
2. Trotsky, My Life, pp. 1, 90, 96. For an interesting attempt at psycho-history, see Steven Englund and Larry Ceplair, 'Un essai de psycho-histoire: portrait d'un jeune révolutionnaire, Léon Trotsky', Revue d'histoire moderne et contemporaine, 1977, pp. 524–43. See also Philip Pomper, 'Trotsky and Martov', below, Ch. 14.

3. Leon Trotsky, *The History of the Russian Revolution*, London, 1965, pp. 25–37.

4. Leon Trotsky, *The Permanent Revolution and Results and Prospects*, New York, 1969, pp. 132–3.

5. Leon Trotsky, *Stalin*, New York, 1970, p. 336; *The Revolution Betrayed: What is the Soviet Union and where is it going?*, London, 1973, pp. 278–9.

6. A. V. Lunacharsky, *Revolutionary Silhouettes*, London, 1967, pp. 66–7. On literacy in the Bolshevik Party, see *Pravda*, 27 January 1923, cited by A. V. Pantsov, 'Lev Davidovich Trotskii', *Voprosy istorii*, no. 5, 1990, p. 80.

7. For an interesting and useful survey, se Ian D. Thatcher, 'Recent Soviet writings on Leon Trotsky', *Coexistence*, no. 27, 1990, pp. 141–67. See also Pantsov, 'Lev Davidovich Trotskii' and K. K. Shirinia, 'Trotskii i Komintern', *Novaia i noveishaia istoriia*, no. 1, 1991. The main Trotsky bibliographies are W. Lubitz, *Trotsky bibliography: a classified list of published items about Leon Trotsky and Trotskyism*, Munich and New York, 1988; and L. Sinclair, *Leon Trotsky: a bibliography*, Stanford, 1972, with supplements published by the Hoover Institute in 1978 and 1980.

2

Stalin and Trotsky's relatives in Russia

VALERY BRONSTEIN

In the spring of 1879 the family of David Leontevich Bronstein, which consisted of his wife Anneta and two children, nine-year-old Aleksandr and five-year-old Elizaveta, were living in the village of Yanovka, near the town of Kherson in Odessa province, in the south of the Ukraine, where the father of the family rented several hundred *desyatinas* of land. Here, in October 1879, another son was born, Lev, and in 1883 a younger daughter, Olga.

Work on the land brought in a certain income which, to be sure, was not particularly large, but was enough to ensure the family a comfortable existence and to enable the children to receive a decent education. The question of his children's schooling worried the father greatly: not having had much education himself, he appreciated rightly that only learning and respectable professions would make it possible for them to look to the future with confidence. Consequently, he spared no expense in the education of his children, and, given the restrictions to which Jews were subject in Russia, this expense was considerable. As a rule, Jewish children, after getting their secondary schooling in Russia, went abroad for their higher education. In the event, the eldest son became an agronomist, while Elizaveta qualified as a physician specialising in stomatology. Olga completed the higher courses for women which were available in Russia. It was intended that Lev should become a mechanical engineer, but, to his father's great chagrin, after leaving modern school he quitted the family home and chose the path of a professional revolutionary.

The father took hard his son's departure into the unknown, all the more because the boy had shown himself a brilliant student and carried great hopes. Consequently, until 1907 he broke off all contact with his son, and met him again only in a courtroom to which he and his wife went at the time of the trial of the members of the first Petersburg Soviet of Workers' Deputies. The trial made Trotsky famous, and this reconciled the father to his son to some degree, though it did not bring them close together. In fact Trotsky never managed to revisit Yanovka, where he was born and spent his childhood. He loved the place and frequently mentioned it in conversation. He remembered it, too, when he went illegally to Petersburg in 1905, taking 'Yanovsky' as his cover-name and in this way paying tribute to the memory of his birthplace. Trotsky's two daughters from his first marriage, Nina and Zina, were brought up there, as were the children of Aleksandr and Elizaveta. Yanovka was abandoned only when the civil war began, the last to leave being David Leontevich, who walked 200 kilometres from Kherson to Odessa across devastated country. He later reached his sons Aleksandr and Lev in Moscow.

David Leontevich expressed his opinion concerning the revolution in a well-known sentence: 'Fathers work and work so as to provide for their old age, and then their children go and make a revolution.' For a time he lived with Aleksandr's family at 10 Bolshoi Gnesdovsky Pereulok, then he acquired a flat in the Vorobiev Hills district. He died in Moscow in 1922. His wife Anneta had died earlier, in 1910, at Yanovka.

Trotsky's influence on his family was very great, despite his parents' conservatism and their resistance to his influence. Aleksandr left home to work for hire as an agronomist. Olga and Aleksandr's elder son Boris, who was brought up by his grandfather at Yanovka, both chose the path of revolutionary struggle and also left home.

However, Trotsky's fate was tragically interwoven with that of all the members of his family. After Trotsky was exiled in 1929 there remained in the USSR eighteen of his close relatives and also his first wife, Aleksandra Lvovna Sokolovskaya. Eleven of them were adults and eight were children. Practically all were subjected to repressive measures, regardless of sex or age. Seven were shot (Trotsky's son Sergei Sedov, Aleksandr, Olga, Aleksandr's elder son Boris Bronstein, Olga's children Aleksandr and Yuri Kamenev, and also A. L. Sokolovskaya). Matilde Menkes, Aleksandr's elder daughter, died in a camp, while Lev Bronstein, Aleksandr's younger son, died in doubtful circumstances just after he had returned to Moscow from a camp. The rest experienced prisons, camps and exile to the remote parts of the country.

The 'iron roller' of repression rolled over the member of Lev Davidovich's family, crushing not only his relatives in the first and second generations, but also those in the third. The children of Trotsky's younger daughter Nina – Lev and Volina Nevelson – disappeared without trace. His granddaughter Aleksandra Molina, through his elder daughter Zina, and Aleksandr Davidovich's grandson, through his son Boris, Valery Bronstein, experienced prison and exile.

Who were these people? Relatives of L. D. Trotsky, or persons who constituted a danger to the state and were therefore subject to extermination or isolation? Of them all, only three engaged in political activity during their lives – Aleksandra Lvovna Sokolovskaya, Trotsky's first wife; Olga Davidovna Kameneva, his younger sister; and his nephew Boris Aleksandrovich Bronstein, the elder son of his brother Aleksandr. The rest of his relatives were remote from politics and never took part in political activity.

Aleksandra Lvovna Sokolovskaya (Party cover-name 'Vonskaya'), who was Lev Davidovich's first wife and may be considered his first instructor in the foundations of Marxism when he was living in Nikolaev, was born in 1872. Together with Trotsky she joined the South Russia Workers' Union, in the southern Ukraine, and upheld Marxist views within it. After the destruction of the Union and the arrest of its members in 1898, in Butyrki transit prison in Moscow, on the way to exile, she married Lev Bronstein. She went into exile with him at Ust-Kut. After she had become the mother of his two daughters, Zina and Nina, she approved of his plan to escape from exile and helped him to carry it out. She then sent the children to her husband's parents and devoted herself completely to revolutionary activity. She was arrested more than once by the Tsarist secret police. In the Soviet period she supported Trotsky's ideas and worked actively in Leningrad Party organisations. After the death in 1928 of her daughter Nina she brought up Nina's children, Lev and Volina Nevelson.

Although her marriage with Trotsky broke up in 1902, she maintained friendly relations with him and his new wife, Natalya Ivanovna Sedova (1882–1962). She was arrested in Leningrad in 1935 and exiled to Siberia. In 1937 she was again arrested and, by sentence of the Military Collegium of the USSR Supreme Court, she was shot in 1938. Her grandchildren through her younger daughter Nina Lvovna Bronstein – Lev (born 1921) and Volina (1925) Nevelson – were brought up, after her arrest, by her sister in the Ukraine, and their subsequent fate is unknown. The first and second husbands of her elder daughter Zinaida – Zakhar Moglin and Platon Volkov – and also the husband of her younger daughter Nina were also shot.

Both Trotsky's daughters loved their father very much, and were fanatically devoted to his ideas. Zinaida Lvovna Bronstein (by marriage, Volkova), his elder daughter and a teacher by profession, followed her father abroad in 1930. In 1932 Zinaida was deprived, along with her father, of Soviet citizenship. Having gone to Berlin in order to be treated for tuberculosis (of which disease her sister had died), on 11 January 1933, threatened with expulsion from the country and suffering from deep depression, she killed herself.

Her son, Vsevolod (Esteban) Platonovich Volkov (born 1926) was taken abroad with her and was in Berlin when she died. Following his mother's death he went to live with Trotsky's elder son by his second marriage, Lev Lvovich Sedov (died in Paris, 1938), who had no children of his own, and after Sedov's death he went to his grandfather in Mexico, where he is now living. He has four daughters (Veronika, Nora, Natalya and Patritsiya) and two grandchildren.

Aleksandra Zakharovna Moglina (married name, Bakhvalova), the daughter of Zinaida Lvovna and Zakhar Moglin, was born in 1923 and remained in the USSR. Until her mother went abroad she lived with the Volkovs, and thereafter with her father. After his arrest she was brought up by Moglin's second wife. In 1949 she was arrested under Article 7–35 of the RSFSR Criminal Code (as a socially dangerous element) and, as Trotsky's granddaughter, was exiled to Kazakhstan, where she remained until rehabilitated in 1956. She died in Moscow in 1989. Presently living in Moscow are her daughter, Olga Anatolevna Bakhvalova (born 1958), and her grandson Denis Bakhvalov (born 1983).

Sergei Lvovich Sedov, Trotsky's younger son from N. I. Sedova, was born in 1908 and, unlike his brother, made himself deliberately remote from politics. As a boy he practised gymnastics and dreamt of becoming an athlete and circus performer, but later he was attracted to technology, graduating from Moscow's Higher Technical Institute (MVTI). A talented engineer and the author of several scientific works on thermodynamics and the theory of engines, he became when still young a professor at one of the technical colleges in Moscow. He married early and lived apart from his parents in one room of a communal flat. He did not follow his father and brother into exile at Alma-Ata, and he also declined to go abroad, which proved to be a fatal decision. In 1933 he divorced his wife, but they went on living together in one room because there was nowhere else to live. At the beginning of 1935, in connection with the so-called 'Kremlin case',[1] he was sentenced to five years' exile in the Krasnoyarsk territory. In 1937, however, he was rearrested, and on 29 October he was shot at the age of twenty-nine. He was posthumously rehabilitated in 1988.

While in exile S. L. Sedov got married again, to Henrietta Rubinstein in 1935, about whose parents or relatives in Russia nothing is known. Of this marriage a daughter, Yulia, was born in 1936. Yulia Sergeevna Sedova (married name, Akselrod) now lives in the USA, and her son David and three small grandchildren live in Israel. Her mother, H. M. Rubinstein, served ten years' imprisonment and subsequent exile, and died in 1987 in Tallinn.

Aleksandr Davidovich Bronstein, Trotsky's elder brother, was born in 1870. He attended the *gymnasium* in Omsk and went to university in Switzerland. He spent his whole life working as a cattle-breeder and agronomist in various sugar-works. Although not indifferent to his brother's ideas, he was by nature remote from politics and did not engage in revolutionary activity. For this reason, apparently, he did not object when his elder son Boris became attracted to Marxism and left home.

During the revolution and the Civil War which followed, he and his family, fleeing from the Whites, managed to get away from his birthplace and move to Moscow for a time (1918–20). When the fighting was over he returned home and continued his work in sugar-making enterprises. His last employment was as manager of a farm (a fattening centre) belonging to the Deriuginsk sugar-works, in Kursk region. Here, in March 1937, he was arrested, and after a brief period in Kursk prison he was sent to Moscow. His case was examined by the Military Collegium of the USSR Supreme Court and, on the basis of Articles 58–6, 58–8 and 58–11 of the RSFSR Criminal Code, 'for maintaining connections with his brother Trotsky and the latter's son Sedov, for contact with the spy Blair, and for anti-Soviet activity at the Deriuginsk fattening centre, expressed in sympathy with the participants, since executed, in the Trotskyist-Zinovievist centre', he was sentenced to be shot. The sentence was carried out on the same day, 25 April 1938.

The elder son of Aleksandr Davidovich, Boris Aleksandrovich Bronstein, was closely connected with Trotsky not only through family ties, but also through his ideas and in his career. Born at Yanovka in 1897, he attended the *gymnasium* in Nikolaev, from which he was expelled in 1912 for active participation in a May Day demonstration and other 'illegal acts'. In that same year he went abroad to join Trotsky, with whom he spent two years. In 1914 he returned to Russia 'to work among the masses', joining the Bolshevik wing of the RSDLP in Ekaterinoslav. In 1916 he was working for the Party among the soldiers. He helped to form Red Guard units in the Ukraine, where he fought against the Haidamaks.

During the Civil War he was a member of the Supreme Military Inspectorate, and also a military commissar with engineer forces, motor-car units, artillery and supply organisations on the Eastern, and later on the Southern and Western Fronts. In 1920 he was appointed deputy chairman of the extraordinary plenipotentiary Council of Labour and Defence, which was headed by Trotsky. He also served as office manager of the People's Commissariat of Foreign Affairs (1921) and military attaché in Austria (1925). He kept up an illegal connection with Trotsky after the latter's expulsion from the Party, until his uncle was deported. Arrested in May 1937 and condemned by the Military Collegium, under articles 58–7, 58–8 and 58–11 for having, 'as a relative of Trotsky's, become a member of an anti-Soviet organisation in the Civil Air Fleet', he was shot in October 1937 along with Sergei Sedov. He was posthumously rehabilitated in 1956.

His wife, Rufina Vasilevna Kepanova-Bronstein, sentenced to seventeen years' imprisonment, was rehabilitated in 1956 and died in Moscow in 1975.

Aleksandr Davidovich's other children – he had four – experienced camps and exile. The younger of his sons, Lev Aleksandrovich Bronstein, was a documentary cameraman in the Mosfilm studios. After spending ten years in the Vorkuta camps, he died suddenly, two days after his return to Moscow in 1947. The cause of his death is not known.

The eldest daughter, Maltilda Aleksandrovna Bronstein (married name, Menkes), died in a camp. She was married to one of the heads of TASS, who was also shot.

Aleksandr's two younger daughters, Evgenia and Anna, were also subjected to repressive measures of one kind or another. Only one of them is still living – Anna Aleksandrovna Kasatikova (born 1912), resident in Moscow.

Boris Aleksandrovich's son, Valery Borisovich Bronstein, Trotsky's greatnephew – the only one of the surviving men of the family who lives in Russia – was born in 1924. After the arrest of his father, and then of his mother, he was sent to a children's home. Later he was brought up by his grandmother (the mother of R. V. Kepanova-Bronstein). He served in the war against fascist Germany in 1942–5 and was awarded twelve decorations by the government. In 1948 he was arrested and put in the Lubyanka internal prison until sentenced to exile by the Special Board, under article 7–35, 'as Trotsky's grandson and the son of an enemy of the people'. He was sent to Kolyma, where he remained until 1958. He now lives in Moscow where he works, in accordance with his qualifications, as a geologist and geophysicist in one of the organisations of the USSR Ministry of Geology. He has a daughter, Elena Valerevna Bronstein (married name, Kudasheva), born in 1956, and in 1979 he became a grandfather, with the birth of Maksim Kudashev. They also live in Moscow.

Elizaveta Davidovna Bronstein (Meilman), Trotsky's elder sister, was born in 1875. By profession she was a physician specialising in stomatology. In 1898 she married a doctor, Naum Meilman, and thereafter lived in Nikolaev. She did not engage in political activity. In 1900 she had a son, named Lev. In 1924 she died from an illness in the Crimea, and was followed in 1934 by her husband.

Her son, Lev Naumovich Meilman, was quite a well-known architect, the author of the project for the Aquatic Sports Stadium on Leningradsky Prospekt in Moscow. He was arrested, spent some time in prison, and after his release was sent to reside compulsorily in Kazakhstan (in Balkhash), where he died in 1960. He had no children.

Olga Davidovna Bronstein (Kameneva), Trotsky's younger (and favourite) sister, was born at Yanovka in 1883. As a student following the Higher Courses for Women, she was active in revolutionary work and was consequently arrested. In 1905 she joined the Party and married the well-known Bolshevik L. B. Kamenev. In the Soviet period O. D. Kameneva held a number of leading posts in state and public organisations, carrying on cultural and educational work. Her last appointment was as chair of the All-Union Society for Cultural Relations with Foreign Countries. In 1927 she publicly denounced her brother's activity and repudiated his ideas, and later those of her husband. She told her relatives that ideological differences with her husband were the reason why she divorced him. Nevertheless, she was arrested in 1935 and six years later, in the autumn of 1941, she was shot.

Aleksandr (Liutik) Lvovich Kamenev, her elder son, was born in 1907, and her other son, Yury, was born in 1916. Aleksandr, a test-pilot by profession, was very remote from politics. Yury was still a student when they were both arrested in 1936 and shot in the same year. Left alive and not subjected to repressive measures were Aleksandr's wife Galina Kravchenko, a well-known film actress in her day, and their son Vitaly. This was due to a rapid remarriage by Kravchenko and the adoption of Vitaly by her new husband. Vitaly worked as a script-writer for Mosfilm, fell gravely ill and committed suicide at the beginning of 1970.

Thus, a substantial section not only of the close but also of the more distant relatives of Trotsky were killed, and practically all were victims of repressive measures. Their fate confirmed the prophecy uttered by G.L. Piatakov when he said to Lev Davidovich after a session of the Politburo in 1926: 'He [Stalin] will never forgive you for that – neither you, nor your children, nor your grandchildren'. (The reference was to Trotsky's statement at the Politburo session that Stalin had finally presented his candidacy for the role of 'gravedigger of the Party and the revolution'.) It did not confirm Trotsky's own prognosis: 'Blows against persons close to me in Russia cannot give him [Stalin] the necessary "satisfaction", and at the same time they cause serious political inconveniences.' He had, after all, underestimated certain features of Stalin's character: 'The greatest delight is to mark one's enemy, prepare everything, avenge oneself thoroughly, and then go to sleep.'[2]

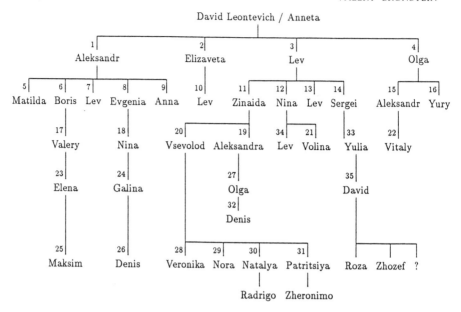

David Leontevich / Anneta

1. Aleksandr   2. Elizaveta   3. Lev   4. Olga

5. Matilda 6. Boris 7. Lev 8. Evgenia 9. Anna 10. Lev 11. Zinaida 12. Nina 13. Lev 14. Sergei 15. Aleksandr 16. Yury

17. Valery 18. Nina 20. Vsevolod 19. Aleksandra 34. Lev 21. Volina 33. Yulia 22. Vitaly

23. Elena 24. Galina 27. Olga 35. David

32. Denis

25. Maksim 26. Denis 28. Veronika 29. Nora 30. Natalya 31. Patritsiya Roza Zhozef ?

Radrigo Zheronimo

1. Aleksandr Davidovich Bronstein, b.1870, arrested in Kursk province 1937, shot in Moscow 25th April 1938.

2. Elizaveta Davidovna Meilman (Bronstein), b.1875, died in Crimea 1924(?) from illness.

3. Lev Davidovich Bronstein (Trotsky), b.1879, d.1940, in Mexico.

4. Olga Davidovna Bronstein (Kameneva), b.1883, arrested 1935, shot autumn 1941.

5. Matilda Aleksandrovna Menkes (Bronstein) b.1895, d. in Potura concentration camp, p.o. Yavas, Mordovian A.S.S.R., 1952.

6. Boris Aleksandrovich Bronstein, b.1897, shot 25th October 1937.

7. Lev Aleksandrovich Bronstein, b.1902, d. in Moscow immediately after return from imprisonment (Vorkuta), cause of death unknown (1947).

8. Evgenia Aleksandrovna Uspenskaya (Bronstein), b. 1908, d. 1985 in Moscow, from illness. In 1946 exiled to Kazakhstan.

9. Anna Aleksandrovna Kasatikova (Bronstein), b.1912. Lives in Moscow. In 1946 arrested and exiled to Kazakhstan.

10. Lev Naumovich Meilman, b.1900, d.1960 in Balkhash, Kazakoh S.S.R., after release from imprisonment.

11. Zinaida Lvovna Volkova (Bronstein), b.1900, d.1933 in Berlin (suicide).

12. Nina Lvovna Nevelson (Bronstein), b.1902, d. in Moscow 1927.

13. Lev Lvovich Sedov (Bronstein), b.1906, d. in Paris 1938.

14. Sergei Lvovich Sedov (Bronstein), b.1908, arrested 1935, sentenced to 5 years exile. Shot 1937.

15. Aleksandr (Liutik) Lvovich Kamenev, b.1907, shot 1936.

16. Yury Lvovich Kamenev, b.1916, shot 1936.

17. Valery Borisovich Bronstein, b.1924, arrested 1948, sentenced to exile in Kolyma. Lives in Moscow.

18. Nina Petrovna Uspenskaya, b.1928, lives in Moscow.

19. Vsevolod (Esteban) Platonovich Volkov, b.1926, lives in Mexico.

20. Aleksandra Zakharovna Bakhvalova (Moglina), b.1923, arrested 1949 and exiled to Kazakhstan. Died in Moscow 1989.

21. Volina (daughter of Nina Lvovna Nevelson-Bronstein), b.1925, fate unknown.

22. Vitaly (son of Aleksandr Lvovich Kamenev and Galina Kravchenko), d. in Moscow (suicide) in 1970s.

23. Elena Valerevna Kudasheva (Bronstein), b.1956, lives in Moscow.

24. Galina Borisovna Denisova (Uspenskaya), b.1960, lives in Moscow.

25. Maksim Valerevich Kudashev, b.1979, lives in Moscow.

26. Denis Vladimirovich Denisov, b.1982, lives in Moscow.

27. Olga Anatolevna Bakhvalova, b.1958, lives in Moscow.

28. Veronika Volkova, b.1954, lives in Mexico.

29. Nora Volkova, b.1955, lives in U.S.A.

30. Natalya Volkova, b.1956, lives in U.S.A.

31. Patritsiya Volkova, b.1956, lives in Mexico.

32. Denis Bakhvalov, b.1983, lives in Moscow.

33. Yulia Sergeevna Akselrod, b. 1936, lives in U.S.A.

34. Lev Nevelson, b. 1921, fate unknown.

35. Yulia Akselrod's son David, lives in Israel.

Notes

1. *Izvestiya TsKKPSS*, no. 7, 1989, pp. 86–93.
2. Leon Trotsky, *Dnevniki i pisma* [Diaries and Letters] Leningrad, 1990, pp. 94 and 97; *Diary in Exile 1935*, London, 1959, pp. 66 and 67.

3

Trotsky: A biographer's problems[1]

PIERRE BROUÉ

I must begin with the sources. Many people – for the most part, they were not familiar with the subject – told me that they were surprised at my attempt to write a biography of Trotsky without access to the Soviet archives. My answer was: (1) that the Trotsky papers in the Western world, particularly at Harvard, were rich and complete enough for such an attempt; and (2) that I was sure that the publication of my book would constitute an incentive for the publication of other works and eventually for the opening of the relevant Soviet archives.

I want to underline, however, that I knew I was writing not *the* Trotsky biography, but the Trotsky biography before the complete opening of the Soviet archives. I was conscious that my work could not be definitive. I am glad, therefore, to take this chance of summing up not only my past difficulties and the gaps in my work, but also of assessing the contribution made by Soviet investigators during the years of *glasnost*.

Let me first acknowledge two circumstances which have been of great help to me and have at the same time raised some serious problems. The first is the fact that Trotsky wrote his autobiography, *My Life*. The second is the existence of a famous biography of him, Isaac Deutscher's trilogy.

On the period of Trotsky's childhood, we have, for practical purposes, various materials at our disposal: Trotsky's autobiography; the memoirs of his former friend, Ziv; some chapters of Deutscher's brilliantly written first volume; and the beginning of the biography by the American, Max Eastman.[2]

The problem of the reliability of the autobiography is not exactly the same for Trotsky's childhood as it is for his adult political life. Trotsky, for this first period, had to rely upon his own recollections, always more or less unconsciously distorted as we know, and impossible to check seriously against documents.

Ziv had been a good friend of Trotsky, but he became, at the time of the First World War and the revolution, his political enemy. He was very hostile when he wrote his book, as is perfectly clear to every reader. Deutscher, using the technique of a good novelist, borrowed material from Ziv and used it purged of the worst signs of this hostility. Fortunately, Max Eastman interviewed Trotsky during the early 1930s and visited people who knew him as a boy – the Spentzer cousins, at least one of his fellow students and some of his first comrades-in-arms in the underground Union for the Liberation of the Working Class.

In my own work I did my best not to fall into the traps of self-justification, political enmity, and even literary talent, set by my sources. I tried to arrive at a balanced assessment.

It is improbable that Soviet archives will be of much help for the period of Trotsky's childhood. Today it is not as important as it was in the 1930s and during the Stalin era to know that Trotsky's father was a 'kulak' and an 'oppressor', employing wage labour; and that his second wife Natalia Sedova was born into the nobility. Yet these two facts still seemed very important in 1987 to one of the specialists in the struggle against Trotskyism, Professor V. M. Ivanov.[3]

The problem of the sources takes a different form for the next period, the pre-revolutionary period. There remains the autobiography. There are a small number of memoirs of contemporary co-workers. But there is now the important contribution of Natalia Ivanovna Sedova to Victor Serge's *The Life and Death of Leon Trotsky*.[4]

In addition, we have at our disposal the bulk of Trotsky's writings, articles and pamphlets to 1914, either in the original papers and magazines or in his complete *Works* published in the Soviet Union; and his speeches at the Congresses of the International or to the Russian Party. But we do not have access to any archives, correspondence or contemporary manuscripts.

This lacuna is all the more important since it was this period that Stalin used extensively to get ammunition with which to discredit Trotsky and present him as an 'anti-Leninist'. Professor V. M. Ivanov found here the substance of his main slanders in the article already mentioned: the term 'Little Judas' (Yudushka) applied to Trotsky by Lenin was written during their violent quarrel about Lenin's use of the name of the *Pravda* of Vienna (edited by Trotsky) for his newspaper in Petrograd.

For Trotsky's biographer, the more striking feature of this period is his constant striving at any price for conciliation and for the unity of the Russian Party. For Trotsky at that time, Lenin was sectarian and even secessionist, fully responsible for the Party split. The outcome of this line was the constitution of the 1912 August Bloc, in practice the regroupment of every current of the Party against Lenin and several so-called Party Mensheviks.

Curiously enough the 'conciliationist' Trotsky is very sharp in his polemics. The pamphlets *Report of the Siberian Delegation* (1903) and *Our Political Tasks* (1904) are written in a needlessly aggressive tone – not really suitable for a conciliator – and some of the best-known evaluations by Trotsky of Lenin's policy are greatly exaggerated. At the time of *Our Political Tasks*, the dictatorship of Lenin did not involve the expulsion of opponents, far less their assassination. There is here a surprising discordance between what we know of Trotsky's ends and the means he employed.

We may say something similar about the fact that, in the 1907 Congress,

Lenin's proposal to discuss 'The present moment in the revolution' was defeated by the Mensheviks with Trotsky's help. Did he believe that a practical step towards reunification was more important than a theoretical debate about 'permanent revolution'? We do not know and to this day there has been no satisfactory answer.

Writing these chapters of the biography, I gained a sense of the international importance of Trotsky – very well known in the International and even in the world press, and probably more important than Lenin in the eyes of many observers. To this day no inkling of this has been given in the Soviet historical literature.

In the sovietology of the cold war period, which Stephen Cohen calls 'countercommunist', great use was made of Trotsky's attacks to discredit Lenin, while the Stalinists used Lenin's attacks to discredit Trotsky. But in more recent years, these episodes of the pre-revolutionary period have not attracted the attention of Soviet historians.

I came to the conclusion that Trotsky was right in his explanations concerning his own position on the October uprising. He was not opposed to it, as Lenin believed for a while, and as was repeated later *ad nauseam* by the Stalinists. He favoured co-ordinating the uprising with the meeting of the Congress of Soviets, because he thought that the uprising ought to be carried out in the name of the soviets. Such an interpretation seems to be far from the conception of present Soviet historians: Yuri Afanasiev himself repeats the Stalinist interpretation that Trotsky was hostile to the uprising.[5]

Western historiography in general understood long ago that the main event of the year 1917 was the coming together of Lenin and Trotsky under the pressure of the war and the revolution, which they interpreted in the same way, and tried together to resolve by demanding 'all power to the soviets'. Even now, I find in the new Soviet historiography no consciousness of such a coming together. Nor does there seem to be an awareness of the extraordinary variety of the currents which constituted the rejuvenated Bolshevism of 1917.

Finally, I have been told that the first Trotsky archives confiscated by the Austrian police in Vienna in 1914 and returned to him during the Brest-Litovsk negotiations as a diplomatic gesture, have recently been located in Moscow. If this is true, it will be very helpful in the completion of this part of the biography. Perhaps we will be able to answer the as yet unanswered questions.

We now come to the most studied period, from the revolution to Trotsky's expulsion from the USSR. Too often studies of these years have been made by journalists or politicians in search of analogies, precedents and illustrations for present political ends. In effect this is the only period seriously studied in the Soviet Union recently. It is a period all too briefly reported in the autobiography, and one which Deutscher is too inclined to interpret in the light of his own conceptions. In sum, there remain many open questions about the role of Trotsky during these key years.

We have at our disposal not only *My Life*, Deutscher's second volume and Natalia's recollections, but also the Trotsky Archives in Harvard – official Party documents, circulars, Central Committee minutes, text of speeches and reports, declarations of the Left Opposition, part of the correspondence between the oppositionists, etc. – mainly, however, public rather than personal documents.

Let me begin with the basic discussion. Was the conflict between Stalin and Trotsky – or, as I prefer, between the apparatus and the bureaucracy on one side and the Left Opposition on the other – a conflict of ideas and of social contradictions? Or was it the struggle between two would-be oppressors and hangmen, two 'bears' equally ruthless towards ordinary Soviet people? For years Western 'counter-communist' sovietology defended the second interpretation, presented as the 'struggle for power', the 'succession war', etc. And the great majority of recent writers in the Soviet Union seem to have adhered to this counter-communist point of view.

For the first time since before the period of Stalin's distortions, the Brest-Litovsk peace negotiations have been presented without distortions and slanders, by the historian A. V. Pantsov. And Vasetsky's work on Trotsky and foreign affairs gives the latter's interpretation of his own positions during the Brest debate.[6]

Several military historians are at work on the topic of Trotsky and the Civil War. Volkogonov has already published extracts entitled 'Trotsky at the front' where the commander first of the Red Guards, then of the Red Army, is properly portrayed.[7]

The Kronstadt Rising is often invoked as one of the biggest crimes of Bolshevism, but without any explanation. For instance, nothing has been produced to confront the current anarchist/counter-communist interpretation in the West, which makes Trotsky principally, if not solely, responsible for a repression he did not lead. For some, Makhno's rehabilitation has been an occasion for new attacks on Trotsky – putting on his shoulders the responsibility for the armed struggle against the anarchist partisans in Ukraine.

Like Stalin in the past, many authors today make use of the militarisation of the unions to depict Trotsky as the 'patriarch of the bureaucrats' or, to use the more fashionable phrase, as the theoretician of 'barracks socialism'. To this end, some authors make great use of his own 'terrorist' utterances of the period of the Civil War, a period during which he exaggerated once more, not only in the tone but even in the content of his fighting speeches.

In my Trotsky biography, I explain at length the Panteleev case,[8] involving the Communist commissar who was summarily tried before Kazan by a military court, on Trotsky's orders. He was sentenced to death and shot for having fled with some of his panic-stricken soldiers. Such an episode – of which plenty are to be found in every war, and which are settled sometimes more ruthlessly than this one was by Trotsky – was the centre of the attacks against Trotsky's behaviour as the head of the Red Army during the Civil War. Today the same tales are repeated without adding anything new. The Leningrad historian V. I. Billik notes that Stalin would have publicised other episodes if they had happened, or if some document in the archives suggested they might have happened.[9]

Discussion of the Civil War and the trade union question gives ammunition for an offensive against Trotsky, notably by Stalin's new biographer, General Volkogonov.[10] The theory according to which Stalin and Trotsky were two rival wild beasts is useful for historians serving those in power: the establishment of an equivalence between Stalinism and Trotskyism aids the idea of a continuity from Bolshevism and Leninism to Stalinism and strengthens a regime which fears revolutionary sentiments. Moreover, the struggle of opposites loses interest if it results merely from personal rivalries, with ideas reduced to the cover for such rivalries. From this point of view, Soviet rewriting of this history up to now has only reinforced the central theme of counter-communism.

Fortunately, there are other sides to the story. For instance, an interview in *Pravda* by the historians Zhuravlev and Nenarokov brought a glaring confirmation of what Trotsky had already asserted concerning the Georgian case in 1922: namely, Lenin's sympathetic attitude and his proposal to Trotsky of a bloc against Stalin in defence of the Georgians.[11]

The 'Letter of the 46' of 15 October 1923, which began the debate, has now been published. Articles and documents by A. M. Podshchekoldin about the 1923 crisis illustrate accurately the nature of the debate on the New Course, which was a conflict between Party bureaucracy and democracy.[12] We have also learnt that the results of the votes in the Moscow organisation, decisive for the general vote in the Party, were in favour of the opposition and were deliberately falsified by the apparatus. Anton Antonov-Ovseenko, using the testimony of one of his father's aides-de-camp, tells us that several military commanders, Antonov himself and Muralov, as well as the Chekist Tsintsadze, suggested to Trotsky a limited military coup, which they could have accomplished, and the aim of which would have been to sweep away Stalin's clique and restore Party democracy. But Trotsky was opposed to the use of force and of illegal means inside the Party.[13]

Concerning Trotsky's absence at Lenin's funeral, the same Antonov-Ovseenko tells us that in archives in Moscow he was able to read correspondence between Stalin and the secretary of the Abkhazian Party, Nestor Lakoba, reflecting the efforts of Stalin to induce Lakoba to keep Trotsky in Sukhumi.

About the literary discussion opened up around *Lessons of October*, Krupskaya's correspondence shows clearly that Trotsky was right when he wrote that his preface was only a pretext for an attack against him long before decided by the triumvirate of Stalin, Kamenev and Zinoviev.[14] Everybody, including myself, used to believe that Trotsky abstained during the discussion about the fate of Lenin's 'Testament'. We now know that he voted in the Politburo in favour of its publication inside the Party and that his abstention in the Central Committee was only the effect of the discipline he observed at that time in respect of the decisions of the higher organ of the Party.

The publication – for the first time in the Soviet Union – of *Our Differences*, written in December 1924, shows the real motivation of Trotsky, who abstained from any gesture which could be interpreted as pursuing personal motives and who was prepared to wait long enough to reveal the real motivation of his adversaries and the social forces supporting them.

Apart from the routine estimation by M. S. Gorbachev of Trotsky's alliance with Zinoviev and Kamenev, nothing new has emerged to illuminate its making, except some details about differences inside the Zinovievist current in a work by Vasetsky.[15]

We still lack elementary information on the differences between the leaders of the United Opposition which seriously weakened their coalition from the beginning. We also lack such information about the differences inside the leadership, which were expressed in the open clash during the Central Committee of August 1927 between Stalin and Ordzhonikidze. We have nothing at all on Stalin's use of GPU provocation in the case of Wrangel's officer, whose real name is still secret.

We know that two sets at least of the Left Opposition's archives, prepared and classified by Trotsky's collaborators, were hidden for years before being finally discovered – one in the Marx-Engels Institute, where they had been entrusted to Riazanov, and the other in Smolensk, about which I have been informed by Viktor Dallin through Miklos Kun. I personally think that historians today will get much more information about political development at the end of the 1920s from the KGB and Stalin archives than from Party ones.

Trotsky's working hypothesis – that of the existence and development, after Lenin's death, of a bureaucracy whose political power was invested in the apparatus and then taken over by Stalin personally – gave a vital theoretical lead. But while there has been a debate between sociologists about the bureaucracy, with the participation of one historian, no real debate between historians on this specific theme has taken place.[16]

Among Mikhail Gefter's many illuminating remarks, I wish to mention one about the fact that Stalinism was not, properly speaking, a necessity in 1923, but that Stalin made it more and more necessary by a deliberate policy in the following years. Gefter also reached a sort of belated and unconscious agreement with Trotsky: the latter speaks of a 'preventive civil war' on the part of Stalin and his apparatus, whereas Gefter uses the term 'permanent civil war'.[17]

Ideas are not lacking to fuel this debate. What is badly needed is new archival material.

For the last period of Trotsky's life, his final exile, we have access to all the information possible about his personal life and personal intervention in the political field, thanks to the Harvard, Amsterdam and Stanford archives. We also have the testimonies of his collaborators in exile.

There are, however, numerous gaps in the history of Trotsky in the Soviet Union. For example, when Podshchekoldin and Elena Kotelenets tried to give a popular summary of Trotsky's real history,[18] they had to reduce the exile to some dates and an account of Trotsky's murder. If something new is to be written on the blank pages of Soviet history at that time, even well-worked Trotsky archives could gain a new value.

Despite the great quantity of new materials brought to light in recent years in the Soviet Union, the use being made of them remains disappointingly unbalanced.

At last we have good information about the Ryutin case and his arrest in 1932. Before now, we only knew the content of rumours circulating in Moscow through Nikolaevsky, Victor Serge and Sedov's correspondence. We know now who constituted the Ryutin group – which won over several real Trotskyists, despite Trotsky's denial. We are also able to read some of the programmatic texts of the group and extracts from the others.

We also have some scraps of information concerning what happened behind the scenes of the Moscow trials. For instance, we know that Rakovsky, Trotsky's friend who was sentenced to prison in 1938, was finally shot in September 1941 in the prison of Orel, together with others. We know that his friend Sosnovsky, who capitulated in 1934 with Rakovsky, was broken through interrogation; that he confessed and denounced some of the defendants who were later shot. But the GPU was not able to put him on display in a public trial and he had to be shot before it. Among the few Old Bolsheviks who did not yield under torture and were shot, two were former members of the United Opposition, of the Left Opposition and finally of the Opposition Bloc – E. A. Preobrazhensky and I. T. Smilga.

N. A. Vasetsky, who is, in effect, an official historian for the Central Committee, was the first to confess that Trotsky's murder by Mercader had been ordered by Stalin in person and carefully prepared. Such a confession does not add much to our knowledge, but takes on a certain importance after fifty years of official denial. The curious article in *Moscow News* according to which Trotsky and Mercader were both Stalin's victims may perhaps be explained, psychoanalytically, by the fact that the author's father worked for Stalin's action service.[19]

It must be said, then, that for the period of Trotsky's exile we still have too many blank pages – far more pages are still blank, indeed, than those which have recently been filled in.

The problem of the Opposition Bloc of 1932 has been left untouched, despite the discovery of several conclusive documents in the Harvard and Stanford archives. We have not heard of any attempt to explain Stalin's famous cable on 'the four years of delay' of the GPU in 1936, or the testimony of Safarov at the first Zinoviev trial on the semi-public activity of the Bloc, which corroborates all the information found in Trotsky's and Sedov's archives. There has been no study of Ivan Nikitich Smirnov, the key man of the Bloc, the circumstances of his arrest, or his confession on the eve of his trial after months of resistance. We await patiently the Saratov University edition of the complete minutes of the first Moscow trial, on which I have written a paper, 'Trotsky and the first Moscow trial', which includes all that we know about the Bloc.[20]

For the first time since Khrushchev's famous speech at the 22nd Congress, it has been stated publicly in the Soviet Union that Kirov was killed on Stalin's orders. The documents of the Investigation Commission seem to have been more or less put into limited circulation, but many problems remain. Who was the important person at the top who used Dr Levin to contact Sedov and inform himself about Trotsky's intentions? Kirov, it is widely supposed. But why not Ordzhonikidze, whose death in 1937 was no accident?

What about the ferocious struggle at the top in 1936 at the beginning of the Spanish Civil War, when Radek (who had no importance of his own) was able to criticise openly the non-intervention policy and explain that the revolution in Spain spelt danger for the British imperialists? Every foreign diplomat in Moscow at that time saw a crisis about which nobody speaks today. We badly need more information on the political life of the USSR than we have at our disposal, if we are to sketch in the new periodisation suggested by Gefter.[21]

It is quite possible, even highly probable, that the necessary documents are kept carefully under lock and key in the KGB and Stalin archives. The explanation for many mysteries can no doubt be found there – such as the open opposition of people like Piatnitsky; the murders ordered by Stalin in Spain; the cases of Landau, Berneri (about which what we already knew has now been published in the USSR) and above all Nin; the trial in the Soviet Union of the last Trotskyists accused of a plot in the prisons; and also the circumstances of the preparation of Trotsky's murder, about which also nothing has been revealed which was not already known in the West.

To conclude, I started by saying that I was conscious of having only produced the biography of Trotsky which could be written on the basis of archives in the Western world, and that we had to look for a new biography on the basis of the Soviet archives.

Three years after the publication of my book, six years after the beginning of *perestroika* and *glasnost*, it seems that we must still look for the first real sign of a willingness of those in power to help in the creation of a scientific history by opening the archives – particularly the KGB and Stalin collections – to scholars, independently of their political views.

The fate of history in the Soviet Union is closely linked to the political battle being waged in that country. It depends on the outcome of that struggle.

Notes

1. Pierre Broué, *Trotsky*, Paris, 1988.
2. Max Eastman, *Leon Trotsky: The portrait of a youth*, New York, 1925. I have been rightly criticised by Philip Pomper for not having used Eastman's archives at the University of Indiana. My only excuse is that, having written twice and received no answer at all, I did not risk a trip which could have been unfruitful.
3. V. M. Ivanov, 'Perekrashivaiut iudushku', *Sovetskaia Rossiia*, 27 September 1987.
4. Victor Serge, *The Life and Death of Leon Trotsky*, London, 1975.
5. Iu. N. Afanasiev in a dialogue with Shatrov, *Moskovskie novosti*, no. 45, 8 November 1987.

6. A. V. Pantsov, 'Lev Davidovich Trotskii', *Voprosy istorii*, no. 5, 1990;
   N. A. Vassetsky, 'Trotsky commissaire du peuple aux affaires étrangères',
   Cahiers Léon Trotsky, no. 44, December 1990.
7. D. A. Volkogonov, 'Trotskii na fronte', *Literaturnaia gazeta*, 30 May and
   13 June 1990.
8. Pierre Broué, *Trotsky*, p. 258.
9. V. I. Billik, 'V puti pravdy', *Sobesednik*, no. 39, August 1989.
10. Dmitry Volkogonov, *Stalin: Triumph and tragedy*, London, 1991.
11. V. V. Zhuravlev and A. N. Nenarokov, *Pravda*, 12 August 1988.
12. A. Podshchekoldin, 'Novyi kurs: prolog tragedii', *Molodoi kommunist*, no.
   8, 1989.
13. Antonov-Ovseenko's paper at the symposium, 'Leo Trotsky, 1879–1940
   – Kritiker und Verteidiger der Sowjetgesellschaft', Wuppertal, Germany,
   April 1990.
14. Krupskaya's correspondence, *Izvestiia TsKKPSS*, no. 2, 1989.
15. N. A. Vasetsky, *Likvidatsiia*, Moscow, 1989, pp. 111, 120.
16. A report on the debate may be found in *Voprosy istorii KPSS*, no. 2, 1989.
17. Mikhail Gefter, 'Staline est mort hier', *L'homme et la société*, vol. 2, no. 3,
   1988.
18 *Druzhba*, vol. 3, no. 14, May 1990.
19. The paper by Juan Cobo is in *Moskovskie novosti*, vol. 3, 15 January 1989.
20. Pierre Broué, 'Party opposition to Stalin, 1930–1932, and the first Moscow trial', in *Essays on Revolutionary Culture and Stalinism*, ed. J. W.
   Strong, Columbus, Ohio, 1990; 'Trotsky et le Bloc des Oppositions',
   Cahiers Léon Trotsky, no. 5, January–March 1980.
21. See note 17.

Part II

Trotsky, the Russian Revolution and its outcome

4

Trotsky's train: an unknown page
in the history of the Civil War

N. S. TARKHOVA

The history and itinerary of this train have long been hidden from view. It is not hard to guess that the reason for this lies with the man who gave his name to the train. For many decades, Trotsky's name and his activity in the highest military positions in the Republic were either presented in a tendentious way or were depersonalised by expressions such as 'the People's Commissar for War' or 'the Chairman of the Revolutionary Military Council of the Republic'. A vacuum of silence enclosed these years, and included the history of the train serving the Chairman of the Revolutionary Military Council, the train in which Trotsky travelled to the front, the base for his campaigning life on wheels. Such a long silence has resulted in many false rumours and fables about Trotsky himself, and about his train. Unfortunately, it is still widely thought that Trotsky used to travel to the front on this train and mete out justice right and left.

The time has come when historians are beginning to discuss objectively many of the 'white' and 'black' spots of history; the time has come when it is possible to bring into the light, out from the shadows of the past, one small page from the history of the Civil War, intimately linked with L. D. Trotsky, the People's Commissar for War and Chairman of the Revolutionary Military Council of the Republic. It concerns the Train of the Chairman of the Revolutionary Military Council of the Republic, better known as 'Trotsky's train'.

The train was formed during the night of 7–8 August 1918 as a campaign facility for the People's Commissar for War, but its role in the life of the Red Army during the Civil War was more important than that. By the end of the war, it was an independent military unit with its own battle record and military traditions. After starting its journey from the platform of the Kazan Station in Moscow on the morning of 8 August 1918, the train completed thirty-six trips during the Civil War, travelling about 100,000 versty (over 100,000 kilometres).[1] The map of the train's journeys amounts to a map of Trotsky's journeys. He always aimed to be where help was required, where his organisational and oratorical abilities were needed, where he could give support in word and deed. The map of Trotsky's journeys is a map of the front lines of the Republic. Where there was the greatest danger, there sped Trotsky's train. Towns, villages, hamlets on the train's route flashed past, like telegraph poles seen through carriage windows.

1918 – the Eastern Front: Sviyazhsk, Kazan; the Southern Front: Kozlov, Liski, Bobrov, Voronezh, Tambov Province. 1919 – the Southern Front: Kursk, Valuiki, Balashov; the Petrograd Front: Yamburg; the Eastern Front: Samara, Penza, Simbirsk, Kazan, Vologda, Vyatka; the Southern Front: Kozlov, Kupyansk, Izyum, Boguchar, Kharkov, Lozovaya, Kremenchug, Mirgorod, Konotop, Tula, Orel; the Western Front: Petrograd. 1920 – the Eastern Front: Samara, Ekaterinburg; the Western Front: Smolensk, Zhlobin, Mogilev; the Southern Front: Kharkov. Of course, this is not a complete record of towns visited; those listed are the major milestones on the train's journey. Later, recalling his nomadic life, L. D. Trotsky wrote:

> For two and a half years, except for comparatively short intervals, I lived in a railway-coach ... There I received those who brought reports, held conferences with local military and civil authorities, studied telegraphic despatches, dictated orders and articles. From it I made long trips along the front in automobiles with my co-workers.[2]

Initially, the train was made up of one unit of fifteen carriages, but its structure constantly grew more complex as it was reorganised in accordance with the needs of the army. As it fulfilled the function of a 'mobile command post', the train included a secretariat, printing works, a telegraph station, a radio station, an electricity generator, a library, a garage and a bath-house. Some of the carriages were covered with iron cladding, for defensive purposes. All this made the train heavy and required the use of two steam engines. When the train itself was stationary, one engine was used for carrying messages; the other engine was kept in steam and ready to move off. After a while, the train was split into two units.

What sort of train was this, and why should we discuss its history? What were the aims of Trotsky's lengthy journeys to the fronts? Trotsky's answer, which, in my view, is correct, would have been: to organise the army, to educate it, to improve morale, and to ensure the supply of all essentials. He himself described the train's activities thus: 'the train linked the front with the base, solved urgent problems on the spot, educated, appealed, supplied, rewarded and punished'.[3] However, there is an alternative evaluation of the train's activities during the war, and for many years this was the only one presented in our historical literature. Thus, in the memoirs of K. Kh. Danishevsky, a member of the Republic's Revolutionary Military Council and also a member of the Revolutionary Military Council for the Eastern Front, a different point of view is given. In his opinion, the presence of Trotsky's train at the front caused dissatisfaction among the commanders, it 'created a situation of dual power, and confused actions and plans, for Trotsky often informed neither the commanders nor the Revolutionary Military Council of his orders and actions'.[4]

We cannot reject Danishevsky's assertions out of hand, as we have no proof. Historians have yet to study the archives and uncover documents on the history of Trotsky's train which would assist in the reconstruction of an objective picture of its journeys and activities.

The train's story is, above all, one of efficient and well-organised work by all its components, geared to servicing the activities of the People's Commissar for War and Chairman of the Revolutionary Military Council of the Republic. Of course, Trotsky's journeys were not restricted to sections of the railway network; he used cars to travel for dozens of kilometres in the front line. The train's technical facilities corresponded to the tasks they had to fulfil. The telegraph office maintained a permanent link with Moscow, with the central military authorities and with Trotsky's Deputy, E. M. Skliansky. In its turn, this ensured a very rapid solution to problems relating to the organisation and supply of the army in the localities. The train's telegraph office transmitted telegrams and reports from the field to Lenin and members of the government.

The train's radio station had links with thirteen stations abroad. Radio messages brought information about world events, including the reactions of foreign governments to current developments. Through the radio station, the train received information about the activities of 'White' governments within the country. The most important telegrams were printed in the newspaper published by the train's crew, and were commented on in articles, leaflets and orders by Trotsky.

The garage on the train, which housed several lorries and cars and a petrol tank, facilitated Trotsky's numerous journeys to military units and also maintained a continuous link with the headquarters of the army groups and armies. These three communications links on the train – the telegraph office, the radio station and the garage – fulfilled the same, most important function: they kept Trotsky in touch with the outside world, with the centre and with the localities. Without its communications, the train would have been but a lifeless corpse. Communications gave it life, animated it. The effectiveness of the work of the People's Commissar for War depended on the efficient and well-organised functioning of the train's communications team. An equally important role in the life and work of the train was played by its other components.

Trotsky's current correspondence was the responsibility of the field office, which was housed in the restaurant car. The registration of incoming and outgoing documents, the preparation of materials for the daily morning briefings to Trotsky, typing his spoken orders, his replies to requests from the army and his speeches, maintaining an archive – all this was the responsibility of the field office. The office worked unceasingly, both when the train was stopped, when there would be very many visitors, and when the train was on the move. Work started early in the morning and finished late at night. On days when there were decisive events at the front, or, on the contrary, when 'vacillation was shown in military units, work on the train became exceptionally intensive' recalled R. Peterson, the train's commander. 'Then the telegraph machines and typewriters clattered throughout the night, the telephones jangled, the printing press printed military orders. People were completely absorbed in their work, feeling no tiredness, completely forgetting about rest and sleep.'[5]

There were also unforeseen incidents in the life of the train, which disrupted the rhythm of its work. Such a mishap was the train crash which happened in May

1919 at Gorki station. It was caused by incorrectly set points. Fortunately, at the time the train was travelling at only 30 kilometres per hour. One of the train's crew recalled:

> Our office was in a terrible mess: everything was muddled up – the wood from the carriage, glass, office equipment, our archives – unfiled telegrams flew all over the carriage. In addition, everything was soaked in ink and in water from the tank in the restaurant-car kitchen. Working at night, by candle-light, we laboured to pick up all the intact documents. But most of them looked as if they had just been pulled out of a bucket of water or ink.[6]

Two carriages of the train housed the field printing press. It printed efficiently Trotsky's orders, proclamations and broadsheets for the soldiers; it also printed the newspaper *V puti* (*En Route*), issued by the train's crew.

It is worth pausing to consider Trotsky's orders in more detail. Their content was often closer to an appeal, rather than to the military or operational document we associate with the word 'order'. Roy Medvedev, introducing a translation of a chapter from Isaac Deutscher's book on Trotsky, evaluated Trotsky's achievements in the post of Chairman of the Revolutionary Military Council of the Republic and stressed the organisational and civilian aspects of his work. In Medvedev's opinion, 'Trotsky did not aim to become a military leader in the strict sense of the word. He remained a civilian. He was in fact the People's Commissar, not the commander of the Red Army.'[7] One might add that when he travelled around the front, Trotsky put himself across as the tribune of the revolution, inspiring the masses and explaining the ideas and goals of the revolution.

Many of Trotsky's orders appeared as a result of his visits to the front – to where a difficult situation had developed, to where the troops had lost their ability to fight and had begun to retreat, to where forces had to be mobilised. For this reason, his orders are often addressed to particular armies and divisions. Examples of such orders from the Chairman of the Revolutionary Military Council of the Republic include his orders/appeals to the 10th Army (November 1918), to the rebellious soldiers of the Nikolaev Division (January 1919), to the soldiers of the Northern Army, defending the approaches to Petrograd (February 1919), to the commissars of the 3rd Army (April 1919), to the 28th Rifle Division, parts of which had been in retreat for several months (May 1919), to the armies on the Southern Front and the 13th Army in connection with Grigorev's uprising (June 1919), to the 9th Army (July 1919), to the Tula military district (October 1919), and to the 7th Army, defending the approaches to Petrograd (October 1919). These orders, printed as proclamations on the train's printing press, were delivered to the units and distributed among the commanders and soldiers. In this way, they were of great benefit to morale.

The words of the Chairman of the Revolutionary Military Council of the Republic, set out as a proclamation/appeal, inspired, bolstered confidence and helped to overcome confusion in the face of the enemy's attack. Here are just some of these revolutionary words from Trotsky:

> Comrade communists of the Third Army! It is up to you to save the

revolutionary honour of the Third Army and, along with that, to save the Revolution. In the situation which has been created for the Third Army and for the country, communists cannot have doubts or hesitations; there can be for them no looking back, no indulgence in criticism, but one slogan only: Forward! (From Order No. 9, dated 22 April 1919 issued by the Chairman of the Revolutionary Military Council).[8]

When I visited you … I convinced myself through talking with your riflemen, gunners, troopers, armoured car crews, sailors, commanders and commissars, that the temporary retreat has not broken your spirit … Warriors of the 28th Division! An end to retreating! Not a step back! Long live the courageous 28th Division! (From Order No. 95, dated 6 May 1919, from the Chairman of the Revolutionary Military Council to the 28th Division).[9]

Trotsky's words were addressed not only to the Red Army. Thus, after the rout of Yudenich's forces before Petrograd in November 1919, the train's printing press printed an order from the Chairman of the Revolutionary Military Council 'to the North-Western White Army'. The order stated:

All units without exception of the so-called North-Western White-Guard Army of General Yudenich [there followed a list of the units] are to be disbanded … All soldiers of the North-Western Army are released from military service and required to return to their homes … The following payments will be made in full for weapons brought by demobilized soldiers of Yudenich's North-Western Army, to one of the Red Army's Headquarters: for a rifle – 600 roubles; for a machine-gun – 2,000 roubles; for separate parts – according to valuation; for a gun – 15,000 roubles.[10]

The orders of the Chairman of the Revolutionary Military Council for 1919 include two appeals to railway workers (Order No. 84) and to the peasants (Order No. 85). They share the same date – 18 March 1919. The reason for their appearance was the upsurge in anti-Soviet attacks in the localities, which had led to the destruction of the permanent way, disrupting the normal work of the railways. Both appeals contain exhortations not to surrender to counter-revolutionary agitation and to redouble vigilance. In the appeal to the peasants, he said:

Pointless revolts and damage to the railway network will only drag out the war, disrupt the country and cause more and more disasters for the peasants and the workers. Comrade peasants, be on your guard! Do not let yourselves be fooled! Help the Red Army and the town workers to strangle the counter-revolution. Soviet power is your power. It will do everything to better the peasants' position, to help agriculture.[11]

Simultaneously with these appeals, on the same day, Trotsky published an order directed at the soldiers of the Red Army. It said:

Comrades, soldiers! Sometimes complaints come from the peasantry about the Red Army. This shouldn't happen. The Red Army must put a stop to it. It is the kulak who is our enemy. But the middle peasant, the working cultivator, ought to be our friend and brother. To harm him is an unforgiveable crime.[12]

In Trotsky's words about the work of the train, quoted above, the verb 'educated' appeared alongside the verb 'appealed'. What did Trotsky have in mind when he spoke of the 'educational' work of the train? Probably the role of the newspaper V puti, issued by the train's crew. The newspaper was printed on the train's printing press and distributed to the local population along the train's route, and to the headquarters of the armies, divisions, brigades and regiments; it was given directly to Red Army soldiers at railway stations and during Trotsky's visits to military units. Material from the newspaper was reprinted in the army and local press. In the conditions prevailing during the Civil War, when the printed word was worth its weight in gold, issuing such a newspaper was of great political and, of course, educational importance. In this instance, education meant constantly informing Red Army soldiers and the population at large about the situation in the outside world, within the country and on the Republic's front lines.

The first issue of the newspaper appeared on 6 September 1918. Thereafter it was published every few days – at intervals of one to four days. It is hard now to establish how many issues were printed because there is no complete run of this newspaper in the archives and libraries of Moscow, and because of the restrictions placed on access to the newspaper on account of Trotsky's name. (This ban is still in force.) I have managed to establish, however, that during the period September 1918 to December 1919 104 issues appeared, during the first nine months of 1920 129 issues were published, and during the same period of 1921 there were 145 issues. The number of copies printed is even harder to establish. This information does not appear on copies of the newspaper itself. Nevertheless, archival sources help provide an answer to this question.

It is known that from 8 to 16 September 1920 thirty-four thousand copies of the newspaper V puti (nos. 122–9) were distributed from the train.[13] Simple arithmetic helps us to establish an approximate print-run for the newspaper – 4,500 copies. Is this many or few? Compared to the print-run of a newspaper circulating all over Soviet Russia in that period, it is, of course, small. But if one takes into account the fact that the area in which the newspaper was distributed was restricted to that around the train, then it is not insignificant.

It is equally interesting, I think, to find out about the ways in which the newspaper was distributed, and those to whom it was addressed. Archival sources provide some assistance on this question too. During the first half of September 1921 individual issues of the newspaper were distributed to the following institutions, units and organisations: the All-Ukraine Publishing House in Kiev (50 copies), the Army Catering School for the Kiev Military District (10 copies), the main railway station in Kiev (55 copies), the railway station hospital in Kiev (10 copies), the Odessa Provincial Commissariat (100 copies), for distribution on the Romanian frontier (450 copies), a hospital train (43 copies), armoured train no. 15 'Lieutenant Schmidt' (15 copies), the agitational bases at the stations in Kiev

(650 copies), Orel (36 copies) and Fastov (140 copies), and the agitational points at the stations in Vapnyarka, Zhmerinka, Kursk and Razdelnaya (489 copies).[14] While the train was stopped at Birzula station, issues of the newspaper were distributed through the local executive committee, the agitational point, the military commissar for that sector of the railway, the military supply centre and also the Komsomol club. The newspaper was not only distributed to institutions and units, but was also put up on display. For instance, during these same two weeks in September 1921, over thirty thousand copies of the newspaper *V puti* were stuck up on display at stations or given out to individuals.

Let us leaf through the yellowed pages of this newspaper, slightly smaller in size than ordinary newspaper sheets. The bulk of the information was divided up into short items only a few lines long. They were convenient for visual comprehension and easy to read, particularly for those who had only just started to read or who read with difficulty. And, of course, during the Civil War period many soldiers and peasants fell into this category. The news items carried information about events in the outside world, within the country and at the fronts. For convenience, they were grouped under headings: 'On the front line of the Revolution', 'The red front', 'Telegrams', 'Operational summaries', 'Soviet power', 'Abroad', 'The world revolution has begun', 'Comments', 'In the enemy camp', 'In the counter-revolutionary camp', and so on. Under each heading, clear and legible, each item was provided with its own subheading, summarising its content: 'In the Far East', 'On the Ussuri Front', 'What the White Guard has done', 'Ufa will soon be ours', 'The revolution in Berlin has started', 'Revolution in Austria is inevitable'. The subheadings reflect the drama and revolutionary pathos of the times: 'The fire of world revolution is flaring up' or 'The peoples have arisen, the gods have fallen and thrones are being overturned'.[15]

The train's newspaper had its own editorials, and its own special articles. The editorials, as one might expect, explained the business of the day. The majority were articles by Trotsky, or orders and appeals issued by him. There was much that needed explaining to the Red Army men and to the former soldiers in the old army – why Tsarist officers, who had been stripped of their rank not so long ago, were now being invited to return to command the Red Army; why the Red Army was now repudiating the former elected committees, which had been the highest achievement of democracy in the Russian army; why mechanical parade-ground drill, which had been so detested in the old army, had now been replaced in the Red Army by military training. There were many such questions, and each needed an answer.

The pages of the newspaper carried replies to many questions – how to organise Party work at the front, who should be defined as a deserter, how to treat defectors from the other side, and so on. For example, the reply on defectors was as follows: 'Greet them in a friendly way, as comrades who have escaped from Kolchak's grip or as repentant adversaries; in no circumstances should enemies who have given themselves up or repented be shot.'[16] The newspaper did not merely reply to questions posed; it also gave practical advice. A series of issues of the newspaper for October 1918 carried articles under the heading 'For every Red Army man', signed by the initials B. K.[17] One of them states: 'It is clear that victory must be won with little bloodshed, i.e. troops must be commanded in battle so that they do not suffer unnecessary losses. How is this to be done?'[18] The answer was provided in these articles. In one case, the author described the fighting methods of their opponents, particularly the Cossacks on the Southern Front; in another, advice was given on what a scout, a telephone operator, a soldier on sentry duty and so on should do in a tactical situation, how they could win victory. Practical advice was not restricted to the conduct of battle. The same issues in October 1918 included articles on wounds and how to treat them.

It was not only Trotsky who wrote articles for the newspaper. On his journeys to the front line, he was accompanied by government and local officials, political workers and military specialists. They too could be the authors of articles. The work of the train attracted the attention of foreign revolutionaries, journalists and writers. The train's passengers included the French revolutionary Jacques Sadoul, the poet Demyan Bednyi, the *Izvestiya* journalist G. Ustinov and the ROSTA correspondent comrade Manych. The list could be expanded by including the names of those who visited the train during its many halts. These included the poet Larissa Reisner, who visited the train in 1918 and dedicated her poem 'Sviyazhsk' to it.

Visits to the train by writers, poets and journalists resulted in articles, sketches and poems which were published in the newspaper. Jacques Sadoul published several articles reviewing the revolutionary movement in the West; poems by Demyan Bednyi appeared in the newspaper several times; G. Ustinov's journey led to a small pamphlet, dedicated to Trotsky and his train.[19] In time, literary feature articles became a tradition in the newspaper; publications included travel sketches, tales of Red Army life and notes on life aboard the train.

The educational work of the train was not limited to the publication of its newspaper. There was a library aboard the train which distributed political, agitational, educational, technical and other forms of literature along the route. The literature given out was varied; including social science and politics, fiction and drama, military and agricultural manuals, works of reference and textbooks. It included collections of decrees, orders and instructions from the War Department, and various army regulations. In addition, the train distributed a variety of broadsheets, posters and appeals.

Thus, during the visit to the Western Front in the autumn of 1920, 141,000 items of literature of this sort were posted up or given out between 8 and 16 September alone,[20] and the total amount of literature distributed during this period amounted to 290,382 copies.[21] It is interesting how these figures break down. A total of 112,382 items was given out, excluding broadsheets and newspapers, and these included 3,500 field and artillery regulations, etc.; 437 copies of Lenin's book *Left-Wing Communism: An infantile disorder*, Bukharin and Preobrazhensky's *ABC of Communism* and Trotsky's *Terrorism and Communism*; 600 copies of the *Red Commander's Vade-Mecum*; 1,000 copies of collections of decrees, orders and regulations from the War Department; 77,445 political pamphlets; 15,000 military items; 1,200 novels, books of poetry, etc.; 1,750 books and pamphlets on farming; 600 calendars; and 650 portraits.[22]

The record of this same journey allows us to establish where and to whom this literature was distributed. The ninety-four recipients included: the political administration for the Western Front; political sections in the army; groups of political workers heading for the front; Communist Party cells in civilian organisations; agitational centres at main-line stations; clubs, cells and cultural and educational centres at railway stations; branches of the Central Press Agency; military units, organisations and institutions, including armoured trains, air-force units, infantry divisions, engineering units and troop trains; and civilian institutions, such as Belorussia's Commissariat of Justice and Council for National Economy, polytechnical colleges and a city education department. The example given of only a few days' work by the train during its visit to the Western Front demonstrates the range of the train's educational activities. And there were many such visits and halts in the life of the train.

Trotsky's train did not only supply the front line with literature. The train held a stock of uniforms, weapons and quartermaster's supplies. Of course, the material resources of the train were insignificant in comparison with the needs of the army. But in emergencies, when it was essential to stabilise and urgently improve the battle readiness of particular units, the train's reserves were brought into play. Recalling such situations later, Trotsky himself evaluated them thus: 'Tens and hundreds of times, they [the train's resources] played the part of the shovelful of coal that is necessary at a particular moment to keep the fire from going out.'[23]

In civil war conditions, moving about on the railways was fraught with difficulty. Many memoirs and fictional accounts of the Civil War describe this. Indeed, travel to other cities within the country often took weeks, even months. Troop trains as well as civilian trains got stuck. But there were no obstacles for Trotsky's train. For hundreds and thousands of kilometres along its route, the train was met with green signal lights. During the Civil War, the unique potential of the express train was frequently utilised. Trucks with equipment, teams of Red Army soldiers, commanders, political workers and military specialists for the Red Army were all sent to the front with this train.

Here are some examples from 1918. In August, two aircraft with their pilots and mechanics were sent to the front with Trotsky's train, and this air detachment had a 30 cwt truck.[24] In September, the train's load included a team of 40 men from the Simonovsko-Rogozhskii infantry regiment, 30 men from the Second Latvian Soviet Rifles and 14 men from the Moscow Flying Armoured Detachment.[25] In November, the train pulled trucks of equipment which had to be covered with eight tarpaulins.[26] It was the same in 1919 and 1920.

Government officials also utilised Trotsky's train for express journeys. Those who travelled on Trotsky's train included members of the peace delegation, headed by A. A. Ioffe, and representatives of the People's Commissariat for Foreign Affairs, Comintern activists and well-known foreign revolutionaries,

Soviet officials travelling to the Urals, metallurgical industry specialists, and representatives of central and local organisations. It was not unusual for the number of additional passengers attached to the train to be as high as fifty or more. After the war ended, the train's crew estimated that during the war up to three thousand senior political and official figures had been transported on the train.[27]

During 1919–21 the train was also utilised several times on the labour front, fulfilling tasks such as transporting food to workers in Moscow and the Urals and bringing timber and coal from distant regions. In March 1920 the train's crew participated in organising the All-Urals subbotnik, and took part in the work. During the war years, the sum total of foodstuffs brought from the regions to the hungry central areas amounted to 2,027,592 pud (about 33,200 tonnes), and the distance travelled on missions for the labour front was 138,737 versty (about 147,000 km).[28]

But Trotsky's train did not only 'educate, appeal and supply' on its travels around the country. In Trotsky's words, it also 'rewarded and punished'. It is well known that Trotsky was always a supporter of firm discipline. He played a great part in transforming the Red Army into a regular and sufficiently disciplined military machine. But the methods through which he achieved this discipline were frequently based on force and repression. Trotsky himself thought that 'An army cannot be built without punitive measures. Masses of men cannot be led towards death unless the army command has the death penalty in its arsenal.'[29]

On his orders, those who showed insubordination and disobedience were dealt with mercilessly and harshly. For example, A. M. Shchastny, commander of the Red Baltic Fleet, was punished mercilessly for his intractability, the SR revolt in Rybinsk was suppressed harshly, 'to set an example', and the Don Cossack insurgents were dealt with equally cruelly. The disobedient were lashed by the full force of Trotsky's words, and these were the words of a judge, not of an agitator. Here are just a few examples. In May 1919 he addressed the expeditionary force sent against the Don Cossacks:

> Soldiers and commanders of the punitive forces! You have formed up your ranks. Now, at the command – Forward! The nests of these dishonoured traitors and betrayers must be destroyed. The Cains must be annihilated. Against the helpers of Kolchak and Denikin – lead, steel and fire![30]

Trotsky's words were equally pitiless when dealing with those who would not obey the orders of the Red Army leadership. For instance, when the Don Cossack F. K. Mironov, commander of the Cavalry Corps then being created and a former Cossack lieutenant-colonel, refused to subordinate himself to the orders of the Southern Front Command, Trotsky declared him to be 'an outlaw', 'a traitor and betrayer'. An order from the Chairman of the Revolutionary Military Council of the Republic dated 19 September 1919 made this appeal: 'Any honourable citizen who encounters Mironov is obliged to shoot him like a mad dog. Death to the traitor!'[31]

In Trotsky's train, as it travelled along the front, an Extraordinary Military Tribunal was in operation. This not only pronounced its own judgements, but also dealt with many appeals for the review of pitiless verdicts. Such appeals were frequent, written by the wives, relatives and colleagues of those convicted, asking for help and sympathy for their friends and dear ones. I do not know to what extent the train's crew participated in punitive measures, as no evidence on this has so far come to light in the archives. But I believe that the calls to be merciless and harsh, which resound in the orders of Trotsky, the Chairman of the Revolutionary Military Council, and appear in the pages of V *puti*, provide a justification for referring to the punitive function of Trotsky's train.

Good and bad always run alongside each other in life. So it was in the work of the train, which simultaneously 'punished' and 'rewarded'. Along with clothing, weapons and literature, the train's trucks brought rewards to the front. One of the carriages operated as a field commission called 'The Red Present', under the auspices of the All-Russian Executive Committee. At a time of destruction, hunger, lack of everyday comforts and a shortage of uniforms, any item could serve as a present for a Red Army soldier, a reward for his valiant service to the revolutionary cause. And when the award was presented near the battlefield, it became doubly valuable, a distinctive decoration conferred by the Republic. Today probably even the most fertile imagination could not guess at the items used to reward soldiers and their commanders. Here are just some: watches (gold, silver or other metal), watch-straps and watch-chains, binoculars and telescopes, cigarette cases and waterproof cloaks, paper and envelopes, razors and shaving tackle, Finnish knives and sabres, daggers and dirks, scarves and felt boots, pencils and pens, pocket torches and mugs.[32] This list is far from complete, and could be extended to include the leather jackets, red trousers and calf-leather boots and so on, already familiar from the literature. In mentioning the leather jackets, it is worth adding that all the crew of Trotsky's train had their own uniform – a black leather suit (jacket and breeches), which made them, in Trotsky's words 'look heavily imposing'. On the left arm, just below the shoulder, each wore a conspicuous metal badge, which became very popular in the army. This badge was specially made in the mint, and its picture appeared on the masthead of V *puti*.

Concern for outward effect was characteristic of Trotsky both in his speeches and in his appearance. His own looks were striking – a thick shock of black hair, blue eyes and an aquiline nose. He paid great attention to his dress, and aimed to make those around him look equally striking. The carriage in which Trotsky lived was also unusual in its appearance and internal furnishings. According to eyewitness accounts, the carriage was distinctive because of its length and its blue décor. The carriage had previously belonged to a minister of communications and had been well equipped for ministerial comforts, but, in Trotsky's words, 'it was scarcely adapted to work'.[33]

The story of Trotsky's train also includes episodes of fighting. The train's crew received their baptism of fire near Kazan in 1918, when a cavalry detachment under the command of Poznansky was formed from the train's personnel. This detachment fought heroically on the approaches to Kazan, and took part in the liberation of the city. The train's crew demonstrated their heroism and courage near Sviyazhsk in the autumn of 1918, when the train was nearly surrounded. They took part in military action near Balashov in October 1918, in the sector occupied by forces of the 9th Army, where they 'defended the positions entrusted to them and raised the spirits of the neighbouring units'.[34] In December 1918 a detachment under the command of R. Peterson (later to become the train's commander) successfully carried out missions for the 8th Army command, when 'their behaviour elicited the enthusiastic approval of comrade Yakir, member of the army's Revolutionary Military Council', to quote from an official letter of thanks sent to Trotsky's train.[35]

In September 1919, on the Petrograd Front, two detachments were formed from the train's personnel, and took part in the fighting. One reinforced the armoured train 'Lenin' and the other was merged with Red Army active service units in the Ligovo area. The tradition of creating detachments of volunteers from the train's crew to be sent to the front continued thereafter. Armoured vehicle detachments, manned by staff from the train, saw action on both the Western and Southern fronts in the summer and autumn of 1920.

The train's work at the front during the Civil War earned several awards. On 1 January 1919 the crew of the train were given a banner of honour, and in November 1919 they were accorded the Order of the Red Banner. The citation in the Revolutionary Military Council's Order No. 309, dated 17 November 1919, read: 'For fighting before Kazan in 1918, before Petrograd and in other places on the front line of the Soviet Republic'.[36]

There is a curious story about the circumstances in which the banner of honour was presented to the train, and about the origin of the banner itself. At midnight precisely on 31 December 1918, when the train was travelling near Liski station, where the train's crew had recently fought so bravely, the battle alarm was sounded. The New Year did not prevent the fighting men from being ready for action within a few minutes. When the train stopped at Liski station, the train's crew was marshalled, and then Trotsky addressed them. 'Comrade fellow-workers! Let me give you New Year greetings!' It was in this unusual setting that Trotsky presented the banner of honour to the train's crew, after explaining its origin to them:

> To mark the first anniversary of the October Revolution, the Saratov railway workers gave two banners of honour to me, asking me to present them to a unit which had shown courage and resolution in battle. Allow me to award one of these banners to you, our crew, and to present it to the train's commander, comrade Peterson.[37]

As this account of the history of the train of the Chairman of the Revolutionary Military Council draws to a close, let us say a few words about the people whose activities created the history of Trotsky's train. The train's crew was multinational, but its core were Latvians, who at that time were reckoned to be the most devoted to the revolutionary cause. They included Rudolf Peterson, the train's commander, who replaced V. Ukhenberg in this post, the train's commandants Irbe Vilus and Skuya Jakob, the train's librarian Jan Berzin, regimental commander Ans Opits and section commander Karl Rudzit. Mention must also be made of Stepan Orlovsky, who initiated the creation of a communist cell on the train, acted as its first secretary, and perished at the Southern Front in autumn 1920; V. G. Fedorov, in charge of the train's garage, who fought on the Western and Southern fronts in the train's armoured-car unit; the Estonian Pyuvi, who was Trotsky's personal driver; M. Glazman, who was Trotsky's personal secretary; and the artist Peter Kiselis, who made many journeys with the train and was wounded before Petrograd in 1919. There are many names, and each is worthy of attention. For some, military service ended with the Civil War, but for others it became their profession. Thus, P. Ya. Kiselis, for example, became a well-known artist after the war and joined AKhRR – The Association of Revolutionary Russian Artists; R. A. Peterson was awarded the Order of the Red Banner in 1922 for his part in the battle at Povorino station in December 1918, and after the end of the Civil War he remained in the Red Army and became the Commander of the Moscow Kremlin.

The first attempt to write the history of Trotsky's train goes back to 1923, on the fifth anniversary of the founding of the Red Army. At an exhibition to mark the anniversary, held in the former Hunters' Club, one room was devoted to the activities of Trotsky's train. Displays included maps of the train's journeys, with charts of the distance it travelled each year and over the five years, and diagrams demonstrating its activities in the military, agitational and economic/labour spheres. Exhibits in the room included collections of literature published by the train's printing press – broadsheets, orders, issues of the newspaper *V puti* and pamphlets.[38]

At the same time, there were plans to publish a small pamphlet, to include reminiscences from the train's commanders, soldiers and passengers. The majority of these memoirs were drawn from the journal *Na strazhe* (*On Guard*), which the train's crew issued from May 1922 to replace *V puti*.[39] It is not certain whether this particular publication ever saw the light of day, but a draft of it has been preserved in the Central State Archive of the Soviet Army, along with many other documents describing the work of L. D. Trotsky and his train during the Civil War. They are awaiting their readers and researchers.

Notes

1. *Tsentralny gosudarstvenny arkhiv sovetskoi armii* (*TsGASA*), f. 63, op. 1, d. 176, 1. 147.
2. Trotsky, *Moya zhizn*, Berlin, 1930, ch. 2, p. 143. [Translation from *My Life* (N.Y., 1930), ch. xxxiv, p. 413.]
3. *ibid.*, p. 141. [Translation from *ibid.*, p. 411.]
4. *Vospominaniya o V. I. Lenine*, vol. 3, Moscow, 1979, p. 446.
5. *TsGASA*, f. 63, op. 1, d. 176, 1. 151.
6. *ibid.*, 1. 178.
7. R. Medvedev, 'Trotsky: shtrikhi k politicheskomu portretu', *Inostrannaya literatura*, no. 3, 1989, p. 171.
8. *TsGASA*, f. 33988, op. 2, d. 8, 1. 63. [Translation from *How The Revolution Armed*, vol. 2, p. 505.]

9. *ibid.*, l. 70. [Translation from *ibid.*, p. 526.]

10. *ibid.*, l. 145. [Translation from *ibid.*, pp. 601–2.]

11. *ibid.*, 1. 58.

12. *ibid.*, 1. 54.

13. TsGASA, f. 33987, op. 2, d. 127, 1. 24ob.

14. TsGASA, f. 4, op. 7, d. 68, 11. 559–61.

15. *ibid.*, 1. 561.

16. TsGASA, f. 33988, op. 2, d. 8, 1. 67.

17. *V puti*, no. 11, 14 October 1918; no. 12, 16 October 1918; no. 16, 24 October 1918.

18. *V puti*, no. 16, 24 October 1918.

19. G. Ustinov, *Tribun revoliutsii*, Moscow, 1920.

20. TsGASA, f. 33987, op. 2, d. 127, 1. 24ob.

21. *ibid.*, 1. 24.

22. *ibid.*, 1. 24ob.

23. Trotsky, *Moya zhizn*, p. 145. [Translation from *My Life*, p. 415.]

24. TsGASA, f. 25883, op. 1, d. 88, 1. 44.

25. TsGASA, f. 4, op. 7, d. 1, 1. 11.

26. *ibid.*, 1. 90.

27. TsGASA, f. 63, op. 1, d. 176, 1. 147.

28. *ibid.*, 1. 147.

29. Trotsky, *Moya zhizn*, p. 141. [Cf. *My Life*, p. 411.]

30. TsGASA, f. 33988, op. 2, d. 8, 1. 75.

31. TsGASA, f. 33988, op. 2, d. 8, 1. 128.

32. TsGASA, f. 33987, op. 1, d. 85, 1. 9.

33. Trotsky, *Moya zhizn*, p. 143. [Translation from *My Life*, p. 413.]

34. TsGASA, f. 33988, op. 2, d. 8, 1. 36.

35. *ibid.*, 1. 36.

36. TsGASA, sbornik prikazov RVSR za 1919.

37. *V puti*, no. 20, 9 January 1919.

38. *Yubileinaya vystavka Krasnykh Armii i Flota, 1918–1923: putevoditel*, Moscow, 1923.

39. TsGASA, f. 63, op. 1, d. 176, 1. 138–83.

5

Trotsky and the struggle for 'Lenin's heritage'

MICHAL REIMAN

Western historiography in recent years has devoted much attention to the issue of why Trotsky was unsuccessful in the struggle for supremacy in the Bolshevik Party during the period of Lenin's illness and subsequent withdrawal from political life. Most of the authors who have discussed the topic have come to the conclusion that Trotsky was insufficiently active. Indeed, this is not contradicted by Trotsky's own statements. Trotsky spoke of his own passivity, giving several different reasons for it, including his own illness, which did not allow him to take a full part in political and governmental activity,[1] and his unwillingness to appear as a pretender to the seat vacated by the ailing Lenin.[2] In his speech at the Plenum of the TsKRKP (Central Committee of the Russian Communist Party) in October 1923, which has now been published by V. Danilov, Trotsky also spoke of how he felt he had no right to take the highest state and Party posts, since for political reasons such posts in Russia should not be occupied by people of Jewish nationality. He had informed Lenin of his arguments several times, and Lenin had eventually taken account of them.[3]

It is not my aim to cast doubts on these or other personal motives for Trotsky's passivity. They undoubtedly played some role in events. However, the fundamental reason was the position which Trotsky occupied in the leadership of the Bolshevik Party.

I have already discussed, on several occasions, the issue of Trotsky's position in the Bolshevik Party in the early 1920s.[4] Here, therefore, I want to refer to only some of the salient points.

The position of Trotsky in the Bolshevik Party

Trotsky joined the Bolshevik Party relatively late, after the July Days in 1917, which ended with the partial but nevertheless very tangible defeat of the Bolsheviks in the conflict with the government and the then leadership of the soviets. The reasons for Trotsky's late membership of the Bolsheviks are given varying interpretations in the literature. Depending on the author of the work and his or her aims, Trotsky is sometimes depicted as a principled opponent of Lenin and Bolshevism, or, on the other hand, as a man who was ideologically and politically close to Lenin. Therefore it would clearly be a mistake not to stress at this point that Trotsky was ideologically and politically an independent person, who did not belong to the small circle of 'Lenin's pupils'. He was, in particular, the author of the theory of 'permanent revolution', and a critic of Lenin's course within the social-democratic movement.

Trotsky's misfortune, if one sets aside the question of his personal qualities, was that he, as a representative of the left wing of Russian socialism, appeared on that wing when it was already occupied by Lenin and his supporters. Therefore Trotsky did not succeed in scraping together any sort of significant party or grouping. He relied on a relatively small circle of like-minded people yearning for a compromise between the two basic tendencies within the Russian social-democratic movement – the Bolsheviks and the Mensheviks. A united party created more favourable conditions for their political activity than closed factionalist groups, with their own hierarchy and discipline, which rejected 'outsiders'.

In 1917, as is well known, the positions of Lenin and Trotsky grew significantly closer.[5] They were both directing themselves towards the socialist revolution. The Bolshevik Party gave Trotsky the opportunity not only to have a greater influence on events, but also to work towards actually seizing power, which would have been difficult for him and his political friends to achieve outside that party. For the Bolsheviks, the arrival in the party of Trotsky and his supporters undoubtedly strengthened the general balance of leadership forces and was a factor in the further growth of its political power. Nevertheless, Trotsky's joining the Bolsheviks did not much alter the situation on the left wing of Russian socialism. Even within the Bolshevik Party, Trotsky retained his political individuality. Therefore, unlike Lenin, he could not rely on the Party, its organs and apparatus to support his activities. His strength as a politician lay in his work in the soviets and in the role of tribune of the people, able to affect the thoughts and emotions of large groups of the capital's population. This left a clear imprint on the tactical differences between Lenin and Trotsky in October 1917.[6]

In October 1917 Trotsky's role was exceptionally important. The Bolshevik victory in the October Revolution would have been just as unthinkable and unrealisable without Trotsky as it would have been unthinkable and unrealisable without Lenin. Trotsky's popularity and his influence in Bolshevik circles grew significantly. Nevertheless, the Bolshevik Party remained the party of Lenin, and in that sense Trotsky's position within it was insecure. It did not give him enough scope for political independence. This independence led to clashes and conflicts with Lenin and his circle, in which Trotsky inevitably suffered defeat. There was not enough room in the Bolshevik Party for two independent leaders of the make-up of Lenin and Trotsky.

A certain tension in relations between Lenin and Trotsky did not play an important role at the beginning since, initially, the conflicts within the nucleus of the 'Leninist guard' were too great: Lenin together with Trotsky had to rebuff Zinoviev, Kamenev, Rykov and others who opposed the Bolsheviks' governing independently. On the issue of the Peace of Brest-Litovsk, Lenin was opposed by a radical group of 'Left Communists', headed by a younger generation of Bolshevik

leaders, which attracted the support of a significant section of the Party organisations. In this conflict, Trotsky adopted a central position. He opposed Lenin, but
kept his distance from the Left Communists. At the decisive moment, Lenin was
only able to win a majority at the highest levels in the Party because Trotsky
abstained from voting. In the subsequent two years of Civil War, Trotsky, as the
strongest member of the Party leadership alongside Lenin, was placed at the head of
the new Red Army then being created. He played an extremely important part in
ensuring its military preparedness and, in the long run, in ensuring its victory in the
war. This strengthened Trotsky's position significantly. The old Leninist guard –
Zinoviev, Stalin and Kamenev – could hardly accept such a situation. Their
intrigues poisoned the atmosphere in the Party leadership.[7] Despite this, there can
be little doubt that this guard was closer to Lenin than Trotsky was. Nevertheless,
Lenin valued Trotsky's political talents, and well understood that during the war it
would have been difficult to replace Trotsky as army organiser. Lenin's relationship
with Trotsky continued to be one of co-operation, which paralysed the intrigues.

I mention all these factors in some detail because they made Trotsky's position
in the Party and its leadership appear strong. At the end of the war, Trotsky's
position had indeed strengthened considerably. He had concentrated in his hands
the leadership of the army and, from spring 1920, added transport, which was the
life-blood of the economy. At that time the army was the only organisation in
Soviet Russia capable of effective action. In it, as in transport, were concentrated
the most able and authoritative Party workers. Furthermore, Trotsky exercised a
strong ideological and political influence over the leading activists in the Party,
including the central Party secretariat, which headed the Party apparatus then
coming into existence. In conflicts, he could rely on considerable support. This
potentially created a strong link between Lenin and his guard. Therefore a clash
was inevitable sooner or later.

The trade union debate of 1920 and Lenin's and Zinoviev's coup d'état

The denouement came at the end of 1920. At the heart of the conflict now
coming to a head lay the consequences of the policy of 'War Communism' and the
overall militarisation of economic and social life. The end of the war brought no
weakening in this policy; rather, it became deeper and more severe, with the aim
of ensuring the transition to post-war economic construction. A new wave of
nationalisation and trade victimisation swept over the land. In the villages,
'requisitioned' produce was harshly confiscated. Measures to regiment peasant
production were expected.

Throughout the country, dissatisfaction with the existing socio-political system grew. With the end of the war, military measures had lost their authority.
Dissatisfaction also penetrated the ruling party, merging with opposition from
some of the active workers to bureaucratism and command methods, to the
privileges and corruption in the top party echelons. This refers in particular to the
so-called Workers' Opposition of Shliapnikov, Medvedev, Kollontai and others.[8]

Lenin was worried, and so were other members of the Party leadership. At the end of September 1920, the Bolshevik Party Conference adopted a wide-ranging resolution aimed at democratising Party life, proposed by Preobrazhensky, then one of the Central Committee secretaries. This resolution allowed more opportunities for criticism, but at the same time resolved none of the urgent matters. The root of the problem lay in the system of War Communism as a whole, but the Bolshevik leadership was blind to this.

Increasingly, Trotsky was at the centre of the criticism. As People's Commissar for Military Affairs and for Communications, he embodied the policy of militarisation, which was supported and defended by the Party leadership as a whole.[9]

Trotsky defended himself. At the meeting of the Communist faction of the 5th All-Russian Conference of Trade Unions in early November 1920, he subjected the trade unions to harsh criticism, and suggested merging them with the industrial authorities. On the one hand, this would have given the trade unions greater opportunities to satisfy their members' demands; on the other, it would have improved the leadership in both the industrial authorities and the trade unions. In Trotsky's opinion, it was essential to 'shake up' the trade unions, after ridding them of unnecessary 'chatterboxes'. Trotsky defended militarisation, which had been criticised by part of the trade union leadership, and opposed its replacement by civilian methods.[10]

Immediately after the meeting, Tomsky informed Lenin. Lenin was greatly alarmed. He was not at all attracted by the prospect of conflict in the trade unions, as it might open the door to the organised expression of dissatisfaction. At the same time, Lenin did not see much sense in Trotsky's proposals, and judged them to be yet another bureaucratic notion, one of the many fruitless attempts at 'reconstruction' in that period.

It is not my task to discuss the trade union problem as such. Undoubtedly, from Lenin's point of view, the vital issue was the desire to limit militarisation. The policy of War Communism as a whole was not involved, although in the context of my topic, it is the important issue. Lenin raised the matter at the Politburo, and then at the Central Committee of the Russian Communist Party. The Bolshevik leadership was not, however, ready for a sudden change of direction: the policy which Trotsky had defended was, until the very last moment, the policy of the whole Bolshevik hierarchy. Lenin did not manage to win a clear majority in the Central Committee. Even Zinoviev and Kamenev hesitated initially. True, the matter was delegated to a commission chaired by Zinoviev, whose work was governed by Lenin's suggestions. On the other hand, however, the Central Committee did not permit Lenin to make an open statement against Trotsky. This was a compromise which did not fully satisfy either side. Trotsky suffered most, as he could not openly defend his position.[11]

The conflict which had arisen was of very great significance, as the Bolshevik 'old guard' clearly soon understood. The rift in relations between Lenin and Trotsky provided the first opportunity for a long time for a frontal attack on Trotsky, undermining his position in the leadership. At the same time, Trotsky's position was further weakened by the end of the Civil War and the expected general demobilisation of the army.

It is therefore not surprising that the conflict soon intensified. The pretext was the claim that Trotsky had not fulfilled the Central Committee's decision to transfer the transport unions to a civilian regimen, or had not done so fast enough. On 7 December, the trade union issue was raised once again at the Central Committee Plenum. And once again, despite the protest of Lenin and Zinoviev, the Central Committee compromised, aiming to prevent an outburst of conflict and its spread beyond the Party leadership.

This, however, made it even more obvious that Lenin could not command a reliable majority against Trotsky in the Central Committee.[12] Events were show-ing a definite trend – the changes in intra-party positions and the balance of power were now affecting not only the Bolshevik old guard, but also Lenin himself. This, incidentally, is reasonably clear from some of Zinoviev's statements. He, for instance, is reported to have stated that Trotsky's supporters had seized power in the Party and that the 'Leninists' had been driven 'underground'.[13]

At this same Central Committee meeting, Lenin, with Zinoviev's assistance, pushed through the decision to call a Party Congress immediately. However, this meant that the trade union problem – despite its apparent urgency – was pushed into the background: the issue was not how to deal with the trade unions, but the Party and fundamental changes in its leadership.

Events unfolded very rapidly. Only a few days after the Central Committee meeting, Zinoviev, speaking for himself and for Lenin, called on Trotsky to publish his theses on the trade union issue: the discussion, he said, was already 'leaking out at every point'. Zinoviev later made no attempt to conceal this.[14]

On 24 December the Central Committee – again under pressure from Lenin and Zinoviev – decided to permit open discussion. On 25 December Trotsky published his theses, in accordance with the wishes of Lenin and Zinoviev.[15] Opposition communist groups, particularly the Workers' Opposition mentioned earlier, joined in the debate. In reality, however, there was only one important development: the start of an open struggle to change the composition of the leading Party organs, to change the balance of power within the Party.

Open conflict between Trotsky, supported by Bukharin, and Lenin and Zinoviev took place at the meeting of the Communist faction of the 8th Congress of Soviets on 30 December 1920. Both sides set out their views on the trade union problem. This, however, was only the outward appearance. Only three days later, the Petrograd Party organisation, led by Zinoviev (or, to be more precise, a meeting of selected Party workers), passed an appeal 'To the Party'. This appeal not only expressed their solidarity with Lenin and Zinoviev, but also put forward a demand that delegates to the forthcoming Party Congress be selected by 'platform': that is, according to membership of Party factions.

This open call to factionalism met with amazement and opposition within the Party. Lenin and Zinoviev, however, continued to group their supporters. Under pressure from them, on 12 January 1921 the Central Committee adopted new decisions: to provide complete freedom of discussion and to allow elections to the Congress by platform.[16] On 14 January, i.e. two days after these decisions, a pamphlet appeared containing the so-called 'Platform of the ten' – Lenin, Stalin, Zinoviev, Tomsky, Rudzutak, Kalinin, Kamenev, Petrovsky, Artem and Lozovsky. It later appeared in *Pravda*, with the addition of V. Shmidt, G. Tsiperovich and V. Miliutin. The nucleus of the group aspiring to mastery within the Party thus presented itself to the public.

There is no need to discuss in more detail the progress of the intra-party discussion. The initiative continued to lie with the group around Lenin and Zinoviev. Not only were the methods used in the debate sometimes dirty; in addition the discussion was frequently detrimental to the situation in the country and to the resolution of vitally important matters. The ruling party was too late in registering the rapidly developing catastrophe in supplies to the two capitals – Moscow and Petrograd; it also did not notice in time the rapid rise of the peasant insurrections affecting large parts of the country.

The discussion and factional warfare unleashed, as we have seen, by Lenin and Zinoviev, had to be cut short immediately. Lenin spoke of the 'luxury' which the Party could not permit itself in the future. Zinoviev, though, tried to justify the discussion. At the 10th Congress of the Russian Communist Party in March 1921 he claimed that the discussion anticipated the urgent need to adopt the New Economic Policy (NEP).[17] In reality, however, it was not only Trotsky's proposals for the trade unions which were firmly rooted in War Communism; so were those of Lenin and Zinoviev. The discussion as a whole distracted attention from the basic problems of the socio-economic conception of the period of War Communism.

Lenin considered the discussion a mistake, as mentioned earlier.[18] This, of course, applied to the methods, rather than the goal – to change the composition of the Party leadership. At the 10th Party Congress Trotsky called on the delegates not to deepen the wounds caused to the Party by the trade union discussion, saying that positive decisions on the trade union movement were not worth that, as they would not last until the next Party Congress.[19] (Trotsky was absolutely right about that.) Such appeals, however, could not succeed. The grouping around Lenin and Zinoviev had achieved their main goal – to gain an overwhelming majority in the decisive Party institutions – and, of course, had no desire to relinquish the fruits of their costly victory. In addition, they used the negative consequences of the discussion to achieve the ban on factions. Formally, the ban was not aimed at Trotsky and his backers, who supported the ban at that time, but at the Workers' Opposition and other groups expressing popular dissatisfaction with the Party's policies.[20] However, as future developments showed, the ban had the greatest effect on opposition within the ruling organs of the Party: that is, on Trotsky. The losers were deprived of all opportunities to get a review of the decisions of the 10th Party Congress or make changes in the composition of the Party leadership by legal means.

What happened at the 10th Party Congress was the equivalent of a *coup d'état*: the composition of Party organs was radically altered, and the grouping around Trotsky, which had formed during the Civil War, found that all paths to genuine participation in power had been blocked.[21] This is the real reason why the 10th Party Congress was accorded such an important place in Stalinist historiography.

In the past, the revolution carried out at the 10th Party Congress was often justified by the argument, on the one hand, that Trotsky was the embodiment of War Communism, or, on the other, that Trotsky was the source of the Bonapartist tendency. There can scarcely be any doubt about the part which Trotsky played in carrying out the policy of War Communism. However, it must not be exaggerated. Trotsky did not oppose the adoption of NEP, and right up to 1925 his views on many aspects of NEP were very broad. As to the charge of Bonapartism, the clash with Trotsky took place at a time when the army was being demobilised and had greatly reduced in size. Trotsky himself, well aware of the experience of the French Revolution, to which the Bolsheviks constantly referred at that time, not only did not aspire to the role of a Russian Bonaparte, but was afraid of such a role. Particularly taking into account its subsequent costs, the *coup d'état* at the 10th Party Congress, in the form and on the scale achieved by Lenin and Zinoviev, can hardly be reckoned as a positive factor in Soviet history.

The events of that time also provide an answer to the question of why Trotsky did not engage in any serious struggle for 'Lenin's inheritance' at a later stage: Trotsky had already lost the material resources for such a struggle at the 10th Party Congress.

On the question of the Lenin-Trotsky bloc in 1922

In recent years, the issue of Trotsky's position in the Bolshevik Party has also frequently been discussed in connection with the so-called Lenin-Trotsky bloc in 1922. This topic too is very wide ranging. Therefore I want to discuss only some aspects of it.

Above all, the issue of the intra-party struggle in 1922–3 cannot be viewed in isolation from the results of the 10th Party Congress. This struggle proceeded when the group which had formed around Lenin and Zinoviev at the 10th Congress was fully in power within the Russian Communist Party. Its starting point was not the actions of Trotsky and his supporters, but the situation within the ruling group itself.

Since the autumn of 1921, Lenin's continued illness had been a significant factor in the situation in the Russian Communist Party and in the country, as it prevented him from systematically engaging in regular work. Everyday leadership passed into the hands of the nucleus of the Leninist faction: that is, Zinoviev, Stalin and Kamenev. Thus, the famous 'Troika' did not come into existence after Lenin's second stroke at the end of 1922 and the beginning of 1923, but rather a year earlier, in response to the new situation in the RKP leadership resulting from Lenin's illness.

It is not surprising that, when Lenin was absent for a lengthy period, the ruling nucleus should have taken independent decisions and worked out certain courses of action, which later were found not to coincide with Lenin's intentions on a number of matters. Nevertheless, sooner or later these discrepancies inevitably affected the basis of relations between Lenin and his colleagues in the leadership. This became completely obvious in the autumn of 1922, when Lenin made his final attempt to resume his duties. During his brief return, Lenin rapidly realised that not only were there strongly held views within the Central Committee which did not coincide with his own on at least two major issues (the issue of a federation of Soviet republics and the issue of a monopoly on foreign trade), but also that the new leading group in the Party was definitely in no hurry to bring its behaviour into line with Lenin's views. To some extent, Lenin was faced with a situation analogous to that which had been resolved at the 10th Party Congress: he did not have a guaranteed majority in the Central Committee over the new ruling nucleus of the Party. Nevertheless, in at least one way this situation was fundamentally different to that pertaining in 1922. At the 10th Congress of the RKP Lenin, as we have seen, opposed Trotsky while leading the Bolshevik old guard; now, however, it was he who had to deal with opposition from the old guard.

In this connection, it is important to note substantive changes in the Leninist faction itself during Lenin's absence. Even at the 10th Congress, it had been the faction of Lenin and Zinoviev. Indeed, Zinoviev had been extremely active in the intra-party struggle. However, during Lenin's absence it became clear that Zinoviev on his own was unable to maintain a dominant position in the Party. In reality, this position passed to Stalin. In the autumn of 1922, Lenin was dealing not with Zinoviev, who was dependent on him and therefore inclined to compromise, but with Stalin, who was aiming to shape his own course regardless of Lenin's objections. Lenin's widely known complaint that Stalin had concentrated 'unlimited power' in his own hands therefore seems in no way fortuitous.[22]

Lenin, however, was an experienced enough politician to know that the new situation could not be corrected by compromises and deals on individual issues. From his point of view, a new realignment of forces within the leadership was essential. In the end, this had to mean conflict with Stalin.

Such a conflict was not, however, easy for Lenin. Lenin was isolated within his own faction. Zinoviev and Kamenev were co-operating with Stalin. They were, of course, still dependent on Lenin, but at the same time they could not but recognise that Lenin had returned for only a brief period, and they did not want to split with Stalin. Contrary to the stories spread in recent years, Lenin also was not close to Bukharin politically. Bukharin was one of the strongest advocates of concessions on the issue of the foreign trade monopoly. Yet the struggle against such concessions had been, in reality, the last part of Lenin's political activity before he suffered his second stroke. Therefore at this point Lenin was hardly likely to change his opinion that 'Bukharin is devilishly inconsistent in his policies'.[23]

In reality, Lenin must have understood that his only influential partner in the current situation was Trotsky, who also had many reasons for wanting to change the balance of forces in the leadership, although for different reasons than Lenin. It was this, not any common views on issues in dispute within the Party, which lay behind the projected alliance between Lenin and Trotsky.

The alliance being set up between Lenin and Trotsky requires careful analysis from another point of view, however. A *rapprochement* between Lenin and Trotsky could not be easy. In December 1922 they reached agreement on a joint statement on the issue of the foreign trade monopoly. When Lenin spoke to Trotsky about the struggle with bureaucratism, Trotsky alluded to bureaucratism within the Party. Lenin understood that Trotsky was referring to the Party Secretariat – that is, to Stalin – and therefore was not against accepting an alliance. This, in any case, is Trotsky's version of events.[24]

Nevertheless, the alliance between Lenin and Trotsky was never more than a plan. Immediately after his projected agreement with Trotsky, Lenin suffered his second stroke. It must have been clear to him that he would scarcely be able to resume leadership of the Party. For him, the aims of the intra-party struggle therefore changed. At the same time, he had no clear idea of how the leadership should be organised in such conditions. Lenin's proposals, expressed in his 'Testament', reflect his state of mind. He describes the six leading Party politicians, stressing their weak points, but does not put forward any solution for the leadership problem. This aspect of his 'Testament' was exacerbated by his additional proposal to remove Stalin from the post of General Secretary. Yet Lenin did not, of course, make any concrete proposals for the new occupant of the post.

In his 'Testament', Lenin described Stalin and Trotsky as the two most outstanding members of the Central Committee. Stressing the conflicts in their political and personal relationship with each other, he foresaw the danger of a Party split, and advocated broadening the Central Committee by including more workers, thus turning it into a sort of permanent Party conference. This, in his opinion, would prevent a split.[25]

All this creates the impression of a certain parity between Stalin and Trotsky in the Central Committee. In reality, however, there was no such parity. In the central Party institutions, the balance of forces was firmly on the side of the Troika, and thus of Stalin. The proposals to enlarge the Central Committee not only failed to offer any advantage in the sense of preventing a split, but actually played into Stalin's hands. The expanded Central Committee could not be an effective working organisation. Inevitably, therefore, there was a growth in the role of more restricted Party bodies, in which Stalin could more easily defend himself not only against Trotsky, but also against other members of the ruling collective.

In reality, Lenin's proposals provided no solution to the situation which had developed. While planning an attack on Stalin, Lenin provided no real support to Trotsky. Stalin and Zinoviev were well aware of this when, beginning in January 1923, they made a number of attacks on Trotsky and depicted him as a dissenter and opponent of Lenin's proposals.[26] Trotsky was driven into a defensive position, from which he could extricate himself only with Lenin's active support. However, such support was not forthcoming, and not only as a result of Lenin's illness. This was typical of Lenin. In March 1923 Lenin requested Trotsky's support for his position on the nationalities question. For this reason he sent Trotsky his notes on the nationalities issue, which were, of course, sharply critical of Stalin. He did not, however, give Trotsky the right to publish these notes. At the same time Lenin, after some hesitation, made Kamenev aware of his position, although he could not but realise that Kamenev would inform Stalin, who would be given the opportunity to take 'his own measures'.[27]

I have dwelt on these aspects of the matter in some detail because they give an accurate impression of Trotsky's real potential in 1923, not only in the struggle for the leadership of the Party but also in carrying out any of Lenin's requests to defend their joint positions within the Central Committee. Such a course of action would have brought Trotsky into open conflict with the Troika. In the spring of 1923, however, the time was not yet ripe for such a conflict, and it was a long time before it was clear what resources Lenin could contribute to the struggle. Lenin's third stroke occurred a few weeks before the opening of the 12th Party Congress. Therefore Trotsky delayed his open attack on the Troika until later, in autumn 1923, when there was no other course open to him. Given the current balance of forces, he was inevitably defeated. Whatever his personal aims and intentions, Trotsky never had any real chance of leading the RKP or the Soviet government – this also applies to the period of the trade union dispute outlined here.

Some words in conclusion

Nowadays, any discussion of the role of Trotsky in the Soviet leadership requires a reconsideration of the various viewpoints formed in the past. These viewpoints were formulated on the basis of research on the Soviet past which had been greatly deformed by political and ideological considerations.

Trotsky's role in the history of Russia and the USSR can, of course, be criticised. Such criticism must not, however, be governed by the extent to which Trotsky's views and policies diverged from those of Lenin or the Party, just as it must not proceed from the assumption that in conflicts between Lenin and Trotsky all right and truth lay on one side, and all evil and falsehood on the other.

Bolshevik policies, including Trotsky's policies, can be criticised as a whole. At the time, the criteria for such criticism were not only advanced by the enemies of the Bolsheviks; they can also be found in one of Trotsky's most perspicacious works of the post-revolutionary period – his series of articles in *Pravda* entitled 'Towards capitalism or towards socialism' (1925). Trotsky states here that, if capitalism recovered its equilibrium and started to develop rapidly, then this would mean that the Bolsheviks had incorrectly assessed the basic premises of their policy: the capitalist epoch had not come to an end, and the Bolsheviks could not realise the goals they had set themselves in the October Revolution.

Such criticism is, however, very general and does not provide an adequate means of evaluating the course of events and the role of individuals. Trotsky, of course, can and must be brought to account on the basis of an assessment of his opinions and actions. In this sense, his policy during the period of War Communism which has been discussed here has scarcely been justified by history.

Nevertheless, the decisive question in assessing Trotsky's role in history is the extent to which he actually determined the path of post-revolutionary development. And in this context, great significance should be attached to the question of Trotsky's place in the Bolshevik leadership, as addressed here: the fundamental charge which history must direct towards him is that, in October 1917, it was Trotsky who to a great extent ensured that victory in the revolution belonged to a party which was not his own party and which he did not control. Apart from the initial period of the revolution and Civil War, the only role open to him was as a critic of this party.

Notes

1. See, for example, I. Deutscher, *Trotzki*, Stuttgart, 1962, vol. 2, p. 135.
2. L. Trockij, *Stalin*, Berlin, 1985, vol. 2, p. 198.
3. *Voprosy istorii KPSS*, no. 5, 1990, pp. 36–7.
4. M. Reiman, *Lenin, Stalin, Gorbacev: Kontinuität und Brüche in der sowjetischen Geschichte*, Hamburg, 1987, Ch. 3; M. Reiman, 'Stalin pered zakhvatom vlasti', *Vremia i my*, vol. 83, 1985.
5. For more details, see M. Reiman, 'Trockij 1917: die Geburt einer historischen Personlichkeit', in *Pensiero e azione politica di Lev Trockij*, ed. Francesca Gori, Florence, 1982, pp. 187–97.
6. *ibid.*
7. Disagreements on military questions have been quite well researched. Stalin played a leading role in them. The tension in relations between Trotsky and Zinoviev broke through to the surface at the time of Yudenich's attack on Petrograd in the autumn of 1919. Trotsky spent the greater part of his time in journeys at the front, and did not participate directly in the work of the Moscow centre. On a number of occasions, this gave his political enemies full scope.
8. V. I. Lenin, *Polnoe sobranie sochinenii* (henceforth *PSS*), Moscow, vol. 42, pp. 459ff.; *Desiaty sezd RKP, mart 1921g: stenograficheskii otchet*, Moscow, 1963, pp. 800–3, 845ff.
9. Decisions on questions of the militarisation of labour were taken according to the report of Trotsky at the 9th Congress of the Russian Communist Party and received the support of the Party leadership. Decisions on the militarisation of transport trade unions were taken in the absence of Trotsky, but with the support of Lenin, Stalin and Zinoviev at the meeting of the Party Central Committee on 26 September 1920. Tomsky was opposed. See *Desiaty sezd*, pp. 357, 391 and 886, n. 161.
10. On the trade union discussion, see *Desiaty sezd*, especially pp. 337–401; *Vladimir Ilich Lenin: biograficheskaya khronika*, Moscow, 1978 and 1979, vols. 9 and 10; V. I. Lenin, *PSS*, vol. 42; *Pravda*, December 1920 and January–February 1921.
11. The ban on discussion was directed against both sides. Having lost on the question of a trade union commission, Trotsky attempted to gain the support of the Central Committee for the broadening of the discussion beyond the limits of the Central Committee. Having failed to achieve this, he gave up the struggle.
12. A compromise resolution was accepted by a majority of 8 to 7. In a full meeting of the Central Committee, i.e. 19 not including candidate members, the situation did not change.

13. *Desiaty sezd*, p. 98.
14. *ibid.*, p. 393.
15. See also L. M. Chizhova and N. I. Rodionova, 'Kak vybiralis delegaty na VIII–XI sezdy RKP/b', *Voprosy istorii KPSS*, no. 4, 1990, p. 61.
16. *ibid.*, p. 62.
17. *Desiaty sezd*, pp. 340–9. Zinoviev defended this thesis more fully at the Petrograd Party Conference in February. See *Pravda*, 3 February 1921.
18. *Desiaty sezd*, p. 27.
19. *ibid.*, Trotsky's speech, pp. 389–94.
20. *ibid.*, Lenin's speech, pp. 518–24, and the following discussion.
21. The changes in the Party organs bear best witness to this. If Trotsky had the support of up to half the members of the old Central Committee, he now possessed with his adherents just 3 votes in the Central Committee of 25 members. See M. Reiman, *Lenin, Stalin, Gorbacev*, p. 52.
22. V. I. Lenin, *PSS*, vol. 45, p. 345.
23., Trotsky often cited this characterisation of Bukharin made by Lenin. Trotsky also often made use of the comments of Lenin on Bukharin's malleability, which often made him the tool of demagogues.
24. Trotsky, 'Stalinskaya shkola falsifikatsii', *Voprosy istorii*, no. 9, 1989, pp. 120ff.
25. V. I. Lenin, *PSS*, vol. 45, p. 343.
26. See M. Reiman, *Lenin, Stalin, Gorbacev*, pp. 84–90.
27. *ibid.*, pp. 84–90. See also Trotsky, 'Stalinskaya shkola', p. 119.

6

On the verge of the break: Trotsky and the Comintern in 1928[1]

A. VATLIN

This essay concentrates on the events of a single year, but it was a year which saw an historic turn in the development of the Left Opposition in the international communist movement. Following the defeat of Trotsky and his supporters in the struggle within the All-Union Communist Party (CPSU), the conflict was transferred to the arena of the Communist International (Comintern). Little has been written on this period due mainly to the tendency of historians to concentrate on the administrative measures by which the Stalinist majority routed the opposition. Yet what happened during this year is vital for an understanding of the future course of the opposition, which led eventually to the formation of the Fourth International.

For Trotsky the year 1928 in effect began in December 1927 at the 15th Congress of the CPSU which, having being expelled, he did not attend. Considerable time was given to Comintern representatives of the Party, notably Clara Zetkin, to endorse vigorously the expulsion of the opposition. The oppositionists were accused of trying to forge links with co-thinkers in other parties. In contrast to their opponents, they put Party unity first, and were determined to avoid providing the slightest justification for accusations that they were trying to form a second party. Although accused essentially of 'being in the service of world capital', they refused to make an appeal outside the Party. They insisted that they would make no capitulation to 'bourgeois democracy', harking back rather to the discipline of Lenin's Party when faced with hostile circumstances.

Trotsky was exiled to Alma-Ata on 17 January 1928. At first he saw this as a temporary banishment. Complaints at his treatment from leaders of the Second International only fuelled Stalinist accusations that the opposition was playing the game of the class enemy. The opposition was weakened in part because it accepted the logic of this argument, if not its applicability to itself. In a directive issued early in 1928 it blamed the internal difficulties of the USSR on 'the insufficient activity of the European proletariat and the insufficient combativity of the European Communist Parties,' but concluded that 'European Social-Democracy (Menshevism), which gloatingly plays up all information about the internal difficulties of the USSR, bears the main part of the responsibility for these difficulties'.[2]

The reality was that the 'Bolshevisation' of the European sections of the Comintern did not benefit Trotsky's supporters internationally, but led to their suffering the same fate as the Soviet oppositionists. The Comintern leadership, headed by Bukharin, feared that Trotsky's supporters might gain a basis abroad. Their weapon against this was the 'left turn', begun in the autumn of 1927, which identified the Social-Democrats as the last barrier between the Communists and the worker masses, and jettisoned the last traces of the 'united front' policy pursued since the early 1920s. In appearance this new line actually seemed to correspond to some of the formulations of the opposition – for example, in a letter to the 7th Plenum of the ECCI on 14 December 1926, where they said: 'We consider the Social-Democratic leaders to be the greatest enemies of the labour movement.'

The 'left turn' was not brought about by any major change in the world situation (in contrast to the turn to the 'popular front' in the 1930s), but corresponded to the first signs of the grain-procurement crisis of the winter of 1927–8 within the Soviet Union itself. Bukharin denied – as he had to – that the new policy had taken over the theoretical ground of the opposition, and it is not clear whether the similarities between the new policies and previous opposition statements were coincidences or deliberate copying. But what is clear is that relations between the CPSU, the Comintern and the expelled oppositionists were redefined by the 'left turn': the definition of Trotskyism as a counter-revolutionary deviation now became policy rather than polemical rhetoric.[3]

Even before the opening of the 9th Plenum of the ECCI, which had the task of consolidating the 'left turn', a course towards sharpening the fight against the Trotskyists was proclaimed in the journal *Kommunistichesky Internatsional*. The reasons given for this decision present extraordinary interest. Expecting 'an increased flow of Social-Democratic workers to the Comintern', the leaders of the Comintern put forward a parallel with the revolutionary upsurge after the war, when such an onrush was checked by 'the centrists, who with their left-wing phrases restrained the masses from breaking with the Second International'. In the new conditions 'the counter-revolutionary mission ... now falls to the lot of the ultra-left and ultra-right Oppositionists, who partially remain inside and are partially already thrown out of the Comintern, and whom the Trotskyists are now endeavouring to unite'.[4]

The purpose of Bukharin's opening address to the 9th Plenum of the ECCI, on 9 February 1928, was to demonstrate the unity between Trotskyism and left-wing social-democracy, in the fight against the Comintern:

> From the stand-point of the problem of winning the masses, the Trotskyist opposition has to be seen not otherwise than as a barrier in the road to winning the masses for Communism. In the German Party, as in the parties of other countries, there was a debate about the role of the 'Left' Social-Democratic leaders. In one of the resolutions of the Essen Congress it was said that the leaders of the 'Left' wing of the Social-Democrats must be seen as the main enemy. And that was absolutely correct.[5]

Later, Bukharin made the point that criticism of the USSR by Left Social-Democrats and Trotsky was more dangerous than such criticism coming from other quarters, because the worker masses listened to these people.

In Bukharin's address in his debate at a distance with the already exiled Trotsky, considerable space was given to that question which was so much to the advantage of the victors, the question of the 'second party'. The opposition had repeated, in its statement issued on the eve of the Plenum, its devotion to the dictatorship of the Party, counterpoising thereto 'Thermidor', meaning a slide down into bourgeois democracy.[6] At the same time (let us recall once more the 'amalgam') an endeavour to form a 'second party' was attributed to the Stalinist Party apparatus. This inconsistency in the opposition's platform did not escape Bukharin's attention:

> Good. Suppose we have two parties. But that presupposes the existence of a first party, and if we have a first and second party, then, consequently, we have two parties. But we have always maintained the view that, if two parties can exist here in the USSR, only one of them will rule, while the other is in prison ...[7]

It cannot be denied that Trotsky shared this view; indeed, that he had himself played an active part in the process which the court historians were later to call 'the establishment of the one-party system in our country'. A simplified class approach had brought the Bolsheviks to the thesis 'one class, one party', which, however, life itself called into question, and which could not become a reality without the help of an apparatus of repression.

Rejection of the democratic mechanism of political struggle brought the Trotskyists to agree even with Bukharin's thesis that, 'in our country criticism such as the Trotskyist criticism leads inevitably to armed struggle for power'.[8] The opposition platform 'At a new stage' said practically the same thing – that a course towards a second party would lead the USSR to civil war. However, 'the goal of the opposition is not a second party or civil war but rectification of the line of the Party and the state by the methods of deep-going reform'.[9] Metaphysically counterpoising Party democracy and proletarian dictatorship and following the illusory choice 'Party reform or second party' resulted both from the closed, élitist character of Trotsky's opposition and from the limited, inconsistent character of its programme. Bukharin's calls for merciless struggle against Trotskyism in all the sections of the Comintern, his declaration that without smashing it there could be 'no real struggle against social-democracy',[10] obviously exaggerated the danger. That danger threatened from a different quarter – and it was precisely Bukharin who, on the eve of his conflict with the Stalinist majority in the Central Committee, failed to draw with sufficient sobriety the lessons of the anti-Trotskyist campaign.

The resolution of the 9th Plenum of the ECCI, which repeated the basic propositions of the 15th Congress resolution on the subject of the opposition, scarcely attracted as much attention among the exiled Trotskyists as the Plenum's decisions on sharpening the fight against the Social-Democrats, within the framework of the new 'class against class' tactic. The 'left turn' by the Comintern, along with the repressive measures taken in the course of the grain-procurement operation in the spring of 1928, evoked among the Trotskyists, as Trotsky's biographer Deutscher writes, feelings of literal exultation.[11] Indeed, despite the expulsion of the oppositionists, the Party and the Comintern seemed to have taken their stand on the opposition's ideological-theoretical platform. (Trotsky drew a parallel between his supporters and the Paris Communards, whose defeat nevertheless saved France forever from the danger of a monarchist restoration.)

Contrary to the pressure by the 'rights' on the Stalinist apparatus which Trotsky had prophesied, what actually happened was the opposite, if one takes into account the new disposition of forces. In his letter of 9 May to his supporters, Trotsky advocated critical support for the left course, even asserting that it 'facilitates the struggle for proletarian democracy'.[12] It is interesting that, immediately after the 9th Plenum of the ECCI, the campaign against Trotskyism in the Comintern press died down (contrary to what had been advocated in the Plenum's resolution on the opposition). The emphasis on 'ideological exposure' was shifted to different targets: namely, social-democracy and the warmongers. All the less firm were the grounds for the oppositionists to yield to capitulationist moods. After the repentance of Kamenev, Zinoviev and Piatakov followed a period which saw a certain consolidation of the opposition. Trotsky himself began active preparations for the 6th Congress of the Comintern, announced for the summer, and when he received a copy of the draft programme he at once set about making a critical analysis of this document.[13]

Remoteness from the day-to-day hurly-burly of political struggle unquestionably favoured Trotsky as a theoretician. In his *Critique of the Fundamental Positions of the Draft Programme of the Comintern*, which he had sent to Moscow by June, and which was a solid work superior in every way to the draft itself, Trotsky summarised all his theoretical innovations and political arguments from the period of the United Opposition, concentrating his fire on the theory of 'socialism in one country'. He could hardly have seriously supposed that his political opponents established in Moscow would allow this document to be discussed, or even that they would distribute it among the foreign delegates present at the Congress. The purpose of the *Critique* was different – to consolidate the forces of the opposition by creating a principled theoretical platform. Consequently, the overwhelming majority of the copies of the document were sent from Alma-Ata not to Moscow, but to the places where Trotsky's supporters were exiled.

Naturally, the draft programme as a whole was rejected as the product of slipshod work and because it had not been discussed in the Communist Parties. Its compromising character, due to Bukharin's attempts to combine in one document a sober economic analysis of the situation in the world with the old ideological postulates about 'world revolutions', did not escape Trotsky's notice. For him, however, what was of predominant importance was the ideological element in the document, which helped him find arguments to sustain the charge of opportunism and 'national reformism' against Stalin and Bukharin. This approach, though, prevented him from seeing the changes which had really taken place in the disposition of several political forces in Europe in the period of capitalist stabilisation.

Trotsky avows again and again his loyalty to a global, worldwide approach to the evaluation of the epoch – and forgets the other side of the coin, the national upsurge of the European states after the world war. The absence of a dialectical understanding of the national and the international endowed Trotsky's critique of the draft programme with some strikingly apocalyptic features. It proclaimed that:

> On August 4, 1914, the death-knell sounded for national programmes for all time. The revolutionary party of the proletariat can base itself only upon an international programme corresponding to the character of the present epoch, the epoch of the highest development and collapse of capitalism.[14]

In conformity with his vision of 'the itinerary of the world revolution' set forth as early as 1925 in his book *Where is Britain Going?*, Trotsky concentrates his attention on the Anglo-American antagonism, to which he gives a class colouring: 'The resolution of the European chaos through the Soviet United States of Europe is one of the first tasks of the proletarian revolution. The latter ... will ... most likely have to defend itself from the North American bourgeoisie.'[15] Let us give Trotsky his due for political perspicacity: his forecast of 'the world hegemony of the USA' did become a reality, though only after the Second World War. Interesting also is his specific vision (through 'revolutionary spectacles') of the inevitability of the process of European integration. In his *Critique*, Trotsky alleged that the Comintern had already abandoned the slogan of the 'United States of Europe' in the mid-1920s, and he evidently linked that with the hated theory of socialism in one country. However, this was not true. In the draft programme of the Comintern prepared by Bukharin in April 1928, the following thesis appeared:

> The fragmentation of Europe, its relative decline in comparison with mighty American imperialism, armed to the teeth, and the maturing of the proletarian crisis precisely in Europe – all render necessary the slogan of the Socialist Soviet United States of Europe, as a transition to the *European-Asian* and then the world union of proletarian states.[16]

Only after discussion in the Politburo of the Central Committee of the CPSU did this formulation disappear from the draft programme as it was presented to the ECCI.

It was the mutual dependence of the states of Europe, the traditions common to that continent, which led Trotsky to insist on the conception of the revolutionary process, characteristic of the first congresses of the Comintern, as a 'world-wide conflagration' which leapt easily over national frontiers. From this he drew the following conclusion, which ran counter to the realities of the time:

> For the proletariat of every European country, even to a larger measure than for the USSR – the difference, however, is one of degree only – it will be most vitally necessary to spread the revolution to the neighbouring countries and to support insurrections there with arms in hand, not out of any

abstract considerations of international solidarity, which in themselves cannot set the classes in motion, but because of these vital considerations which Lenin formulated hundreds of times – namely, that without *timely* aid from the international revolution we will be unable to hold out.[17]

The fatalism of such statements, in the eleventh year of the October Revolution, is evident. It was not so much 'socialism in one country' that alarmed Trotsky as the insufficiently thought-out character of its theoretical model, which threatened to doom the USSR to self-isolation from the surrounding world and arbitrary conduct by its ruling élite. But instead of constructive co-operation in the working-out of a new model, the logic of intra-party struggle led Trotsky into merely seeking for the weak points in his opponents' conceptions, misusing his polemical skill at the expense of Marxist theoretical analysis.

The question of the weaknesses of the Stalin-Bukharin conception of the building of socialism in one country goes beyond the limits of the present work. Let us turn our attention to the weak spot in its chief critic: namely, his thesis on the increasing contradiction between the growth of the productive forces and the national state form of their distribution. The first factor is treated as absolute (here Trotsky is close to orthodox social-democracy, in the spirit of Karl Kautsky), and the possibility of superstructural regulation of economic growth (which, as a rule, was carried out by the national state) was clearly underestimated. What we see, in fact, is a forcing of the terms of the problem to accommodate a ready-made solution: namely, 'world revolution'.

Here too, though, Trotsky puts forward some extraordinarily fruitful ideas, one of which is an elaboration of the question of the influence of technical progress (or, as we should say today, the scientific and technological revolution) on the competition between the two systems. Permit me to introduce a lengthy quotation:

> The new theory has made a point of honour of the freakish idea that the USSR can perish from military intervention but never from its own economic backwardness. But inasmuch as in a socialist society the readiness of the toiling masses to defend their country must be much greater than the readiness of the slaves of capitalism to attack that country, the question arises: why should military intervention threaten us with disaster? Because the enemy is infinitely stronger *in his technology*. Bukharin concedes the preponderance of the productive forces only in their military-technical aspect. He does not want to understand that a Ford tractor is just as dangerous as a Creusot gun, with the sole difference that while the gun can function only from time to time, the tractor brings its pressure to bear upon us constantly.[18]

All of Trotsky is in these words: brilliant polemical wit, ability to clothe Marxist categories in the vivid form of graphic formulations, and at the same time exaggeration in his own ideas, unquestioning faith in his initial axioms.

Descending from theoretical generalisations to questions of practical politics, he depicts the unenviable fate of the Comintern in the event that it should adopt the theory of socialism in one country:

> The task of the parties in the Comintern assumes, therefore, an auxiliary
> character; their mission is to protect the USSR from intervention and not
> to fight for the conquest of power. It is, of course, not a question of the
> subjective intentions but of the objective logic of political thought.[19]

These would seem to be prophetic words, spoken on the eve of the complete
Stalinisation of the Comintern, which really did, in a number of instances,
transform it into an instrument of the USSR's foreign policy, but in them there
was only a reflection of the truth. The 'logic of political thought' in Trotsky's case
led to his counterpoising of two component parts of the Comintern ideology,
reducing everything to 'the false comparative evaluation of the two levers of world
socialism – the lever of our economic achievements and the lever of the worldwide proletarian revolution. Without a victorious proletarian revolution we will
not be able to build socialism.'[20] However, the Achilles heel here is not in the
counterpoising of the 'levers', but in the reduction to them of all the wealth of
forms that social progress assumes.

The opposition's reaction to the left course adopted by the CPSU and the
Comintern was set out in Trotsky's declaration to the 6th Congress of the
Comintern dated 12 July 1928. The document is dominated exclusively by the
'Russian question'. Trotsky sees in this a certain contradiction with his oaths of
loyalty to the ideal of world revolution, and offers an explanation which is not
very convincing:

> A correct domestic policy in the USSR is inconceivable without a correct
> policy for the Comintern. Therefore, for us, the question of the Comintern's
> line, that is, the strategic line of the international revolution, stands above
> all other questions. However, a situation has developed historically in
> which the key to the Comintern's policy is the policy of the All-Union
> Communist Party.[21]

Following attentively events in the country, Trotsky stresses his view that
'whoever thinks that the present shift by the Party apparatus has cancelled out the
right danger is radically wrong'. That danger was never so great as now. Consequently, 'the opposition supports every step, even a hesitant one, towards the
proletarian line, every attempt, even an indecisive one, to resist the Thermidorian elements ... The opposition cannot have anything in common with ...
combinationist adventurism, counting on the aid of the right to overthrow the
centre.'[22]

So, then, the choice of strategy had been made: with Stalin against Bukharin,
maybe, but with Bukharin against Stalin, never. Let us remember these words.
Very soon, in September, all would change places: but in that hot summer of 1928
'tempos decided everything'. And the tempo of the political struggle was determined by Stalin. One can only guess what collisions would have awaited the Party
leadership had Trotsky been in Moscow in those days.

But he was in exile at Alma-Ata, writing and sending out his declaration to the
Congress, and not suspecting that at that very time the bloc between Stalin and

Bukharin was suffering an irreparable split. At the July Plenum of the Party's Central Committee they had managed to settle their conflict (which related, in the first place, to the taking of emergency measures for grain procurement). Stalin gave ground. However, the 6th Congress of the Comintern was approaching, and with it the threat of a fresh conflict. Already, at the beginning of June, Bukharin had written to Stalin:

> I told you that I am not going to fight and don't want to. I know too well what a fight could mean, especially in the conditions in which our country and our Party find themselves today. I now ask you to think over one thing: let the congress take place, don't cause any splits here, don't create an atmosphere of gossip (this isn't helped by such things as the impatient sending away of Slepkov).[23]

During the July Plenum it became clear to Bukharin that his requests had remained a voice crying in the wilderness, and he decided upon a step which he had denounced a thousand times in previous years. He began to seek allies among the oppositionists. On 11 July he met Kamenev and put his cards on the table:

> We consider Stalin's line disastrous for the revolution as a whole. This line could bring our downfall. The differences between us and Stalin are many times more serious than all the differences we had with you ... And for several weeks I have not spoken with Stalin. He is an unprincipled intriguer who subordinates everything to the preservation of his own power. He changes his theories depending on whom he wants to get rid of at the moment.[24]

Although Bukharin did not openly offer to form a bloc with Trotsky (only Zinoviev and Kamenev were involved), it was a question of a possible combination of all against Stalin. This demanded lightning decisions, of which Kamenev was incapable: he had not recovered from the wounds he had suffered as one of the leaders of the United Opposition, and, at the same time, his repentance had been regarded by Trotsky as amounting to capitulation. Nevertheless, Kamenev kept up contact with Trotsky, as is proved by the following passage in his note of the conversation on 11 July:

> I gave him your (personal) letter. He read it and said he is afraid of having things on paper. He is afraid a written article would bring trouble. It would be better to talk about the programme in person.[25] Bukharin: 'Stalin spoiled the programme[26] for me in many places. He himself wanted to give the report on the programme at the plenum (!!!) I had great difficulty fighting him off. He is driven by a desire for recognition as a theorist. He thinks that is the only thing he doesn't yet have.'

In the circumstances and the allusions of this conversation there are still too many secrets that historians will have to reveal. Clearly, in the summer of 1928 there was an opportunity to change the balance of forces in the leadership of the CPSU. However, the ditches dug by the representatives of the Bolshevik 'old guard' in their intensive conflict of 1926–7 proved to be too deep, and their ideological convictions too weak as compared with the discipline of the Stalinist

Party apparatus. We do not know how Trotsky would have reacted if he had known of the conversation which had taken place between Bukharin and Kamenev on 11 July. However, in his postscript to his declaration to the 6th Congress of the Comintern ('The July Plenum and the right danger'), dated 22 July, a simply hysterical view of the situation is given: Rykov has openly triumphed over Stalin, the leftward shift was just an episode, and a turn to the right is about to happen again:

> We say to our Party and to the Communist International: Rykov is openly beginning to surrender the October Revolution to the enemy classes. Stalin is standing now on one foot, now on the other. Bukharin is clouding the mind of the Party with the cobwebs of reactionary scholasticism.[27]

Trotsky turned out to be a poor chess-player: concentrating his attention on the right flank, he failed to notice the pawn that was breaking through towards his queen.

However, the Left Opposition itself, having been expelled from the Party, was by the summer not at all an ideological monolith. After the 'capitulation' of Kamenev and Piatakov, the principal figures on the opposition's chessboard were Trotsky and Radek, two Party leaders who had been well known in the first years after October, two important theoreticians of the Comintern, enjoying great popularity in the Communist Parties abroad. Their talents as polemicists and publicists ensured for them the role of ideological leaders even after the exiling of the most active oppositionists. Immediately after his arrival at Alma-Ata, Trotsky despatched telegrams to all the places where he thought Radek might be, asking after his health and requesting regular contact. Radek replied extremely curtly, without revealing his own cards.

So long as they were united in defining the 'Rights' as the main driving force in the Thermidorian degeneration of the CPSU and the Soviet state, matters did not come to a split between them. However, the differences on questions of strategy and tactics for the Comintern which had existed between Trotsky and Radek in the period of the United Opposition prepared the way, on the eve of the 6th Congress, for a serious breach between the two men. At the same time as Trotsky sent his declaration to the Congress presidium a letter was also sent to it, signed by Radek (and also by I. T. Smilga), which claimed unambiguously to be an official document of the opposition (it concluded with these words: 'We are sure that we are speaking on behalf of all the Bolshevik-Leninists who have been expelled from the CPSU and are in exile.' Radek's letter contained the fundamental propositions of the opposition's platform presented to the 15th Congress, singling out in the international section those opportunities missed by the Comintern which were connected with inattention to Radek's own theoretical innovations (especially the programme he worked out for transitional demands to be advanced by the Communist Parties before beginning the immediate struggle for power).

The document presented by Radek also rejected the draft programme of the Comintern as 'reflecting the mechanisation of its intellectual life', and hailed the 'left turn' projected by the 9th Plenum of the ECI. The approach seemed to be substantially the same as Trotsky's. But what Trotsky might permit in the case of his political allies he could not permit to a rival for influence in his 'own' circle. In general, the entire subsequent fate of Trotsky and the movement he headed was a succession of splits and capitulations which deprived first the 'Bolshevik-Leninist opposition' and then the Fourth International not so much of mass influence and social base (they lacked those from the start) as of sincere supporters. Contrary to its leader's proclamations of a world-historical mission, the Trotskyist movement degenerated further and further into a sect of left intellectuals, and the main responsibility for that degeneration lay not so much with Trotsky's authoritarian characteristics as with the organisational principles for building the Party which he advocated, and which did not depart from the framework of pre-revolutionary Bolshevism.

Having received from third persons the letter of Radek and Smilga to the 6th Congress, Trotsky sent to his supporters on 17 July (the day the Congress opened) some sharp comments upon it. Unlike Radek, who had hailed the leftward shift in the Comintern and the CPSU, Trotsky's feeling about that was more sceptical. While waging a campaign against the kulak, the Stalinists had not abandoned their bloc with the 'Rights':

> Matters are even worse when we come to the question of the Comintern. Radek's assessment of the February plenum as a great, in a way decisive, turn on to the road of Marxist policy, is fundamentally incorrect. The symptomatic significance of the February plenum is very great: it shows that the right–centrist policy has landed completely in a blind alley, and that the leadership is trying to find a way out not to the right but to the left. But that is all. There is no unifying idea in the leftism of the February plenum. This leftism reminds one a great deal of the leftism of the Fifth Congress.[28]

Trotsky charged Radek with conciliatory attitudes, though he refrained from speaking plainly about this: 'The general appraisal of the draft programme in Radek's theses is incorrect, that is, it is excessively good-natured. Contradictory, eclectic, scholastic, full of patches, the draft programme is no good at all.' Later, in the arrogantly witty style typical of him, Trotsky remarked regarding Radek's cautious criticism of the mistakes in the draft: 'It is as if Marxist man has already emerged full-grown out of the centrist monkey, but with one superfluous organ: "the tail".' His greatest objections were to Radek's new estimate of the prospects of the Chinese Revolution. In defiance of all the facts, Trotsky continued to insist on its socialist character, writing about the 'Chinese October' and regarding the summer of 1928 as merely a temporary ebbing of the revolutionary wave.

The situation in the opposition on the eve of the 6th congress bore witness to the fact that the attainment of critical mass on the eve of the 15th Party Congress entailed an irrepressible process of nuclear fission, artificially stimulated by Stalin, whose emissaries regularly visited the Oppositionists, promising them return to high positions in Party and state if they would repudiate Trotsky. In his letter Radek declared without ambiguity that he was ready for reconciliation: 'If history proves that a number of Party leaders with whom we crossed swords yesterday are better than the theories which they defended, then no-one will be more pleased than we!'[29] For Trotsky, of course, there was no such road: he could agree to anything *except* repentance before the Stalinist apparatus.

The documents addressed by Trotsky to the Comintern Congress which opened on 17 July 1928 became known to the delegates and were even discussed in the corridors, but in the actual Congress serious references to them were made only in order to discredit political opponents in various parties.[30] Yet Trotsky's name and his theory of 'permanent revolution' were very freely referred to by opponents: it is enough to read the discussion between W. Ulbricht and A. Evert on the 'right danger' in the German Communist Party, and the differences between V. Lominadze and J. Pepper on the significance of the Canton uprising.[31] 'Trotskyism', as understood by the participants in the Congress (in their official speeches, at any rate), had long lost any definite features and had become transformed into a sort of bogy which was actively utilised in struggles for personal influence in particular sections of the Comintern.

The absence of open supporters of Trotsky from the Congress did not help at all to clear its atmosphere of pre-storm moods. The results of the previous (July) Plenum of the Central Committee of the CPSU, which Trotsky had seen as a victory of the Rights over the Centrists, were perceived by many of the delegates as being, rather, the prelude to a turn in the struggle inside the Party. The 'corridor Congress', the latent clashes between Stalinists and Bukharinists in various parties, had grown heated even without this far from simple situation, so that, in order to counter the spreading of rumours, the Soviet delegation to the Comintern issued on 30 July a statement to the council of senior delegates in which they denied the truth of speculations about differences in the Party leadership.[32] The Dutch delegate De Visser alone subjected to criticism, at a plenary session, the isolated position of the CPSU and the way information about events in the USSR was kept from the brother-parties:

> Often, where important political questions were concerned, for example, in connection with the fight against the Trotskyist opposition, or with Ioffe's well-known letter, our party and our papers were left without news. Was the report that Trotsky had been exiled true or not? ... It is absolutely necessary that the International improve its service of information regarding the most important facts, especially where the USSR is concerned.[33]

Trotsky not only followed closely the reports of the Congress proceedings printed in *Pravda*; he also received information from his comrades-in-arms about the actual sentiments prevailing among the delegates. His archives contain letters from Moscow in which are quoted statements by prominent delegates testifying to their discontent and scepticism regarding the official line of the Comintern. One of these letters quotes these words spoken by Ercoli (P. Togliatti): 'Our tragedy has been that it was impossible to speak the truth about the most important, most decisive problems of the day. We didn't dare to speak. In this atmosphere the voice of truth would have had the effect of a bomb exploding.'[34] The Stalinist sappers did their work faultlessly: the speech of the Indonesian delegate Alfonso, who in the discussion on the programme supported a number of the opposition's proposals, was reduced in the official Congress report to one paragraph.[35]

Trotsky's hopes of a rapid break-up of the bloc of Rights and Centrists in the CPSU and the Comintern looked as though they would be confirmed as the Congress proceeded. However, a similar process was going on among the Oppositionists themselves, evidence of which was given by the declarations that Preobrazhensky and Radek sent to the Congress. In return it was mentioned that many of the differences had disappeared since the Comintern and the CPSU had adopted the 'left course', which had long been advocated by the opposition.[36] Trotsky had to make great efforts in order to ensure unity among his supporters. But he was unable to counterpoise anything to the tendency whereby the 'leftward shift' of Stalin's course (and still more his open conflict with the 'Rights') was stimulating a 'capitulationist' mood among the Oppositionists.

At the 6th Congress of the Comintern the question of the opposition in the CPSU was considered near the end of proceedings (22 August, Manuilsky's report). In the political report of the ECCI, which was given by Bukharin, this matter had been touched on only in passing. Bukharin remained faithful to the political 'distortion' according to which Trotskyism was a social-democratic deviation in the communist movement, but he added that, after the defeat of the opposition in the CPSU, the attempts of the 'ultra-Lefts' to form an international organisation of their own had been smashed, and what now came to the forefront was the danger of a 'right deviation'.[37] This belated manifestation of political realism, this return to an actual evaluation of the different tendencies in the Comintern did not save Bukharin from being charged, less than a year later, with 'right deviation in the Comintern', a construct which proved no less useful to Stalin than the 'social-democratic deviation' ascribed to Trotsky.

In Manuilsky's report, along with some of the worst examples of intra-Party polemic (on the position of the Trotskyists after the 15th Congress: 'the laughable statements made by persons who had lost their sense of the comic, about their willingness to help in implementing the "left zigzag" '), there were included some interesting ideas about the enthusiasm of Trotsky's supporters for the proletarian dictatorship, functions of administrative coercion and their exclusive orientation on the Western Communist Parties as instruments of world revolution.[38] These accusations were very soon to change their address and enter into the ideological arsenal of the Bulletin of the Opposition, when it criticised the 'great change' and the flowering of Stalinism. But, all in all, was much altered by this rearrangement of items?

The Comintern Congress ended its work on 1 September. The autumn of 1928 was the time when Stalin actively prepared for the decisive, final battle for exclusive leadership of the Party, the arena for which would also include the Comintern. The Rights replied by boycotting political activity: after the Congress, Bukharin did not even attend the meetings of the presidium of the ECCI. Like Trotsky in his time, Bukharin and his comrades hoped that, without them, the machinery of the state, the Party and the Comintern would grind to a halt –

and they were mistaken. In his turn, Trotsky continued to calculate which of the contending groups he would make an agreement with (that he would certainly be called upon, he had no doubt, even on the eve of his banishment from the USSR). However, in September, Trotsky withdrew the slogan 'with Bukharin, never', and put in the forefront the problem of the suppression of Party democracy and the omnipotence of the bureaucratised apparatus (including that of the Comintern).[39]

Trotsky's biographer Deutscher describes accurately enough the situation when Trotsky found himself equidistant from both groups in the leadership of the CPSU:

> If Stalin was taking one leaf out of Trotsky's book, the left course, Bukharin took another: he appealed to the Left Opposition in the name of proletarian democracy. Trotsky was in a quandary: he could not turn a deaf ear to Bukharin's appeal without denying one of his own principles; and he could not respond to it without acting, or appearing to act, against another principle of his by which he was committed to support the left course.[40]

As a result, he took up a waiting attitude, although in a number of letters (the first of them dated 12 September) he also spoke of a possible conditional bloc – with the Rights in defence of the principles of Party democracy. This produced a negative reaction among most of the Trotskyists, and Trotsky had to settle another crisis in his own ranks.[41]

Nevertheless, he did manage to perceive, in the autumn of 1928, that the danger threatening from Stalin's despotism was very much greater than that from all the Rights put together. Unlike Radek, who continued to affirm that 'if we strike a blow at the centre we shall become manure for the Rights', Trotsky tried to clarify the social roots of centrism, and even came to the conclusion that Stalin personified the interests of the middle peasant! But this did not last long: already in his first letters from abroad he sees a different content in Stalinism, as the accomplished bureaucratic degeneration of the proletarian state, and uses for the first time the actual term 'Stalinism'.[42]

But the beginning of a new stage in his theoretical work was made in a letter of 21 October 1928, in which Trotsky came out sharply against a bloc with the centre, and called the situation in the country 'a Kerensky period in reverse'.[43] The moderate Trotskyists, headed by Radek, saw this as a slide down into the position of the Democratic-Centralist faction, which demanded not reform of the Party, but a revolution in it. It was not accidental that the 'shift to the left' in Trotsky's views coincided with a harshening of the regime under which he was held in exile. Later, he was to recall:

> During the first ten months of exile our letters, though censored, nevertheless reached their destinations roughly fifty per cent of the time ... Toward the end of October last year a sudden change occurred. Our communications with co-thinkers, friends, even relatives, were suddenly stopped short; letters and telegrams ceased to reach us at all.[44]

In the autumn of 1928 there took place, or rather continued, the process of mutual recognition between Lenin's two 'heirs'. While Stalin understood that

Trotsky's views were parrying more and more his own intentions, and were therefore becoming increasingly dangerous, Trotsky understood the fate that awaited him on that account. In one of his first articles written in Constantinople, he noted that:

> As early as the first weeks of the campaign against the right wing, in a letter to my co-thinkers from Alma-Ata on November 10 of last year, I wrote that Stalin's tactical objective was, when the moment was right, 'when the right wing had been sufficiently terrified, to turn his fire abruptly against the left ... The campaign against the right is only to build up momentum for a new onslaught against the left. Whoever fails to understand this has understood nothing.'[45]

And yet an exaggerated estimation of his own movement (in one of his letters to Radek he wrote: 'we are the vanguard of the vanguard') prevented Trotsky from perceiving the true relation of forces in the leadership of the CPSU. In Moscow what was happening was more serious than a mere campaign to 'frighten' the Bukharinists. Stalin actually deprived Bukharin's supporters of potential allies from the Left Opposition not only by means of repressive measures (the mass exiling of Trotsky's supporters, which went on all through 1928), but also by his playing at leftism, with the uprooting in the autumn of 1928 of the 'right deviation' in the Comintern sections, particularly the German Party. On the eve of his open clash with 'Ivanovich's opposition', however, Stalin decided to cover his left flank firmly, and so he brought before the Politburo the question of banishing Trotsky from the USSR.

According to Trotsky himself, Bukharin, Rykov and Tomsky voted against this but were in a minority.[46] The decision to banish Trotsky already failed to fit in with the resolutions about not allowing 'international consolidation of the forces of the Trotskyist opposition' that had been passed by plenums of the ECCI since 1926. Stalin showed by this move that he looked on the interests of the Comintern as merely derivative of his own political ambitions; Trotsky, however, was during another four years to call for the emancipation of the Comintern from Stalin's dictatorship – so strong was his prejudice against a 'second party' and, consequently, a Fourth International.

On 16 December 1928, after the GPU had presented him with their ultimatums, Trotsky addressed a message to the leadership of the CPSU and the Comintern, realising that this letter too would remain unanswered. For him what mattered most was political self-justification: 'The demand that I abstain from political activity is equivalent to demanding that I renounce the struggle for the interests of the international proletariat, a struggle which I have waged uninterruptedly for thirty-two years, that is, throughout my conscious life.' Listing in his letter the mistakes made by the Comintern, beginning with the defeat of the German October in 1923, Trotsky explains them all by the circumstance that the wrong leaders were at the helm, since the CPSU was seen as the legitimate leadership of the Comintern:

> If this blind, cowardly, incompetent policy of adaptation of the bureaucracy

and the petty-bourgeoisie had not been followed, the situation of the working masses in the twelfth year of the dictatorship would be far more favourable; our military defence would be far stronger and more reliable; the Comintern would be in quite a different position, and would not have to retreat step by step before the treacherous and venal Social-Democracy.[47]

The decision to banish Trotsky from the USSR, which was conveyed to him on 18 January 1929, provoked not only a lively echo in the international labour movement, but also much diplomatic activity. Stalin did all he could to prevent Trotsky from finding a place of asylum in Europe (Trotsky himself had chosen Germany). When he learnt of the pressure being brought to bear on the German government in this connection, one of the leaders of the German Social-Democratic Party, F. Stampfer, wrote to the Reich Chancellor H. Müller, who was also a Social-Democrat:

> I have learnt with horror that objections have been put up against the admission of Trotsky. I quite fail to understand this. We have stood, as a matter of principle, for the German Republic to offer the right of political asylum to everyone who is obliged to leave his country owing to lack of freedom there. I do not see any practical grounds for departing from this principle. We cannot, after all, refuse to Trotsky what we grant to countless ultra-reactionary Russians. Trotsky cannot do us any harm. He will not damage Russo-German relations, since Russia herself has asked if we will accept him: If he can harm anyone it can only be the Communists.[48]

The refusal of the German government to grant asylum to Trotsky (in which not the least important factor was fear of strengthening the radical tendencies in the labour movement) evoked official condemnation by the Labour and Socialist International.[49]

The leader of the Russian Social-Democrats in emigration, F. Dan, called the banishment of Trotsky an example of mediaeval barbarism:

> And although, in the times when the 'new method' was first tried out on Russia's Social-Democrats, Trotsky stood along with Lenin at the summit of power and therefore bears responsibility for all that, we, Russian Social-Democrats, have no feeling of *Schadenfreude*. This is because the moral and psychological attitude of the Social-Democrats to the Communists is determined by their political attitudes, which, in contrast to the Bolshevist attitude, is not orientated on deepening and perpetuating the split, but on drawing closer and re-uniting the Communist and Social Democratic wings of the labour movement.[50]

Trotsky, who had to withdraw to one of the Prince's Islands belonging to Turkey, drew his own conclusions from what had happened. The refusal of a government headed by a Social-Democrat to grant his political asylum he perceived as yet another sign of the rottenness of bourgeois democracy in the West, and even more as a sign of the reactionary nature of hopes for a democratic transition to socialism.[51] Deprived of the possibility of exercising direct political influence in the labour movement in the European countries, Trotsky at once set about consolidating the forces of the supporters of world revolution and the worldwide dictatorship of the proletariat, to which theoretical propositions he was to remain faithful to the end of his life.

Notes

1. In the interests of the balance and overall length of the volume, Dr Vatlin's introductory section has been summarised by Terry Brotherstone.
2. *Pravda*, 15 January 1928. [*The Challenge of the Left Opposition 1928–1929*, p. 39].
3. Dr Vatlin's text takes over from here.
4. *Kommunistichesky Internatsional*, no. 4, 1928, pp 10–11.[*The Communist International*, vol. 5, no. 5, 1 March 1928, p. 111].
5. *Tsentralinyi partinyi arkhiv Instituta marksisma-leninizma* [*Central Party Archive of the Institute of Marxism-Leninism*] (*TsPAIML*), f. 495, op. 167, d. 31, 1. 19.
6. See the extracts from the Trokskyist platform 'At A New Stage' published in *Kommunistichesky Internatsional*, no. 6–7, 1928, pp. 14–18. [The full text is given in *The Challenge ... 1926–1927*, pp. 488–509].
7. *TsPAIML*, f. 495, op. 167, d. 31, 1. 24.
8. *ibid.*, 1. 28.
9. *Kommunistichesky Internatsional*, no. 6–7, 1928, p. 15. [*The Challenge ... 1926–1927*, p. 508].
10. *TsPAIML*, f. 495, op. 167, d. 31, 1. 38.
11. I. Deutscher, *Trotzki, Der unbewafferete Prophet 1921–1929*, Stuttgart, 1972, p. 388. [*The Prophet Unarmed 1921–1929* p. 405].
12. *ibid.*, p. 390. [*The Prophet Unarmed*, p. 407].
13. Even before the draft of a new programme had appeared, he sought, in a directive to the Oppositionists, to discredit it: 'Bukharin's programme is a bad programme of a national section of the Comintern, but not the programme of a world party' (*Pravda*, 15 January 1928). [*The Challenge ... 1928–1929* p. 45].
14. *TsPAIML*, f. 493, d. 93, 1. 4. [*The Third International After Lenin*, New York, 1957, p. 4].
15. *ibid.*, 1. 8. [*The Third International ...*, pp. 7–8].
16. *ibid.*, d. 42, 1. 48.
17. *TsPAIML*, f. 493, d. 93, 1. 16. [*The Third International ...*, p. 16].
18. *TsPAIML*, f. 493, d. 93, 1. 45. [*The Third International ...*,p. 48].
19. *ibid.*, 1. 53. [*The Third International ...*, p.60].
20. *ibid.*, 1. 54. [*The Third International ...*, p. 63].
21. *TsPAIML*, f. 493, d. 665, 1. 3. [*The Challenge ...* p. 135].
22. *ibid*, 1. 12. [*The Challenge ...* pp. 139, 142].
23. N. I. Bukharin, *Problemy teorii i praktiki sotsializma*, Moscow, 1989, p. 299.
24. A note of this conversation made by Kamenev is in the Trotsky Archives at Harvard University, USA (T. 1897). The writer thanks S. Cohen for enabling him to use it in this work. [*The Challenge ...* pp. 379–80, 382–3].
25. Kamenev had probably handed to Bukharin Trotsky's critique of the draft programme of the Comintern.
26. This refers to the draft programme which was submitted by Bukharin in April for discussion by the Politburo.
27. *TsPAIML*, f. 493, d. 665, 1. 82. Trotsky was analysing Rykov's report to

the Moscow Party activists on 13 July 1928. [*The Challenge* ... p. 175].

28. Trotsky, 'On Comrade Radek's theses', in *Byulleten oppozitsii*, no. 1, 1929, p. 12. [*The Challenge* ... p. 161].

29. *ibid.*, p. 13. [*The Challenge* ... pp. 162–3]. This story of the two parallel declarations by the opposition has a sequel. Radek was obliged to with- draw his letter, but, as the conflict within the opposition intensified, he attacked Trotsky's *Critique* (in his article, 'One must think it through to the end', written in September 1928). He said that he could not regard this as an official document of the opposition, and the suppression of his letters must be seen as 'an attempt to introduce Stalinist methods into our ranks'.

30. *Stenographic Report of the Sixth Congress of the Comintern* [in Russian], Moscow and Leningrad, 1929, instalment 1, p. 282.

31. *ibid.*, pp. 459, 571, 573.

32. *N. I. Bukharin i Komintern*, Moscow, 1989, p. 20.

33. *Stenographic Report* ..., instalment 1, p. 114.

34. P. Frank, *Geschichte der Kommunistischen Internatsionale, 1919–1943*, Frankfurt-am-Main, 1981, vol. 2, p. 531.

35. See the newspaper report (*Pravda*, no. 191) and instalment 3 of the *Stenographic Report*, pp. 57–8.

36. Deutscher, *The Prophet Unarmed*, pp. 407 ff.

37. *Stenographic Report* ..., instalment 1, pp. 58–9.

38. *ibid.*, instalment 5, pp. 85, 60–1.

39. See Trotsky's declaration to the 6th Congress (*TsPAIML*, f. 493, d 665, 11. 4–6).

40. Deutscher, *The Prophet Unarmed*, p. 446.

41. *ibid.*, pp. 428–9. Deutscher certainly overestimates Trotsky's readiness for this collaboration. In July a bloc with the Rights signified for him 'combinationist adventurism'.

42. 'Stalin's polemics are only the belated echo of his organisational tech- nique. What Stalinism is, above all, is the automatic working of the apparatus'. (Trotsky, *Chto i kak proizoshlo?*, Paris, 1929, p. 25). [*Writings*, 1929, p. 38].

43. *Pravda*, 24 January 1929. I have not been able to find the actual letter. [*The Challenge* ... 1928–1929, p. 274].

44. Trotsky, *Chto i kak proizoshlo?*, p. 13. [*Writings*, 1929, pp. 24–5].

45. *ibid.*, pp. 42–3. [*Writings*, p. 49].

46. *Byulleten oppozitsii*, no. 1, 1929, p. 3.

47. See the appendix to Trotsky's *Chto i kak proizoshlo?*, pp. 58, 61. [*The Challenge* ... 1928–1929, pp. 362, 363–4].

48. *Archiven der Sozialen Demokratie*, Bonn, H. Müller Collection, document 105. On Stampfer's letter Müller wrote this minute: 'Had a talk with Stampfer and told him that I found his letter no grounds for such a position.'

49. *Internationale Information*, 1929, p. 69.

50. *ibid.*, p. 163.

51. *Byulleten oppozitsii*, no. 1, 1929, p. 6.

7

Trotsky and Ryutin: from the history of the anti-Stalin resistance in the 1930s

BORIS STARKOV

The split in the ruling stratum of the Bolshevik Party, followed by the severance from political leadership of a large group of important leaders, led eventually to the establishment in Soviet society and the Communist Party, at the turn of the 1920s into the 1930s, of the authoritarian regime of Stalin's personal rule. L. D. Trotsky's group had suffered defeat in the political struggle of the 1920s. He himself had been first exiled to Alma-Ata and then banished from the USSR, and his supporters were either in exile or in political isolation-prisons. The organs of state security (OGPU and NKVD), the Party's Central Control Commission organs and the local control bodies were largely focused on struggle against dissidence. A rigorous dictatorial regime was increasingly established in the country.

However, there still remained some members of that stratum of the Party's old guard which had determined the policy of the Party and the state at the beginning of the 1920s. They held leading positions in local Party and Soviet organisations. Thus, at the 16th Party Congress, held in the summer of 1930, out of 1,329 leading Party workers, representing 165 districts, 1,178 (88.7 per cent) had joined the Party before 1920. It was they who organised resistance to Stalin's regime. Stalinism, the cult of Stalin's personality, simply could not triumph without overcoming this resistance.

During 1929 and 1930 letters were sent to the Party's Central Committee and to the Central Executive Committee of the USSR, the writers of which demanded that the Stalin clique be removed from their leading position in the Party and the state. S. I. Syrtsov, a Party worker of authority and a candidate for membership of the Politburo, became the spokesman for these views. Documents have been preserved in Soviet and Party archives which show that by the end of the 1920s Syrtsov was already beginning to express resistance to Stalin's line. Thus, although he had supported Stalin during his trip to Siberia, in the idea of applying 'extraordinary measures' to the kulaks, on the spot he directed that no haste should be shown in the introduction of harsh measures, and this led to conflict between Syrtsov and the Irkutsk regional organisation, the leaders of which strove to carry out the leader's instructions at any cost. In a conversation with G. K. Ordzhonikidze in 1930, K. Radek asserted that, before leaving for the June (1928) Plenum of the Central Committee and Central Control Commission, Syrtsov said, talking with his supporters, that he intended to raise the question of replacing Stalin in the post of General Secretary.

Having become, in May 1929, Chairman of the Council of People's Commissions of the RSFSR, Syrtsov carried on a struggle against Stalin and his circle principally on economic questions. Did the group of Syrtsov and Lominadze, who formed a bloc with him, have a programme of their own? Until recently it was thought that they did not. Further research, however, has had the following result. Such a platform-programme might have been set out in a letter which was sent to the Party's Central Committee in September 1930 by I. O. Nusimov and G. A. Kavraisky, who had joined the leadership of the Syrtsov–Lominadze group. The group suffered failure and defeat mainly through being penetrated by agents of the GPU, who were acting on Stalin's orders.

The year 1932 occupies a special place in the history of the organised resistance to Stalin's regime. It was in that year that the Central Executive Committee took its decision to deprive Trotsky and his close relatives of their Soviet citizenship, about which more will be said later. It was in 1932 that Trotsky sent his letter to the Politburo in which he said that the salvation of the revolution depended now on one thing alone – 'removing Stalin'. And the year 1932 is connected in the history of the anti-Stalin resistance with the name of M. N. Ryutin. For a long time his name was erased from Soviet history. There were many myths and legends about him. Now, when his name has been restored to the Soviet people, the truth about the man must be told.

In his *Portraits of Revolutionaries* Trotsky called Uglanov and Ryutin the most authoritative and competent members of the Central Committee after Zinoviev and Kamenev. A member of the Bolshevik Party from 1914, Ryutin took an active part in the fight for Soviet power in Siberia and engaged in Party work in Daghestan. In 1923 he was working in the Moscow Party organisation. In the fight against the Left Opposition in the 1920s, Ryutin, as Secretary of the Krasnaya Presnya district committee of the Party, was one of the main figures. In those days he was spoken of as the leader of 'Uglanov's hooligans'. He took on the hardest tasks in the fight against the opposition, and so it was no accident that the Moscow Party Committee assigned him to speak at Ioffe's funeral. He had to compete with the oratorical skill of Trotsky in convincing the people. It was with the name of Ryutin that the most important organised action against Stalin in the 1930s was connected.

He did not arrive at once at the idea of combating Stalin and his circle. In the spring of 1928 he still considered that the chief danger to Party and state lay in Trotsky's ambitions. Three years later, in his work 'Stalin and the crisis of the proletarian dictatorship', he wrote this:

> Trotsky's prognosis has been confirmed. The Party is degenerating so fast that only bold, resolute and energetic measures can save the situation … Trotsky's passionate struggle to return the Party to the path of intra-Party democracy and healthy democratic centralism constitutes an immense service to history and the revolution, which neither calumny nor any

previous mistakes of his can take from him.

Ryutin gave in this work a detailed characterisation of Trotsky. Here it is:

> Not genius, only very great talent. A comprehensive European education, brilliant wit, but not a profound intellect. No profound theoretician, only a publicist in Marxist writing without a peer in the whole world, inclined to favour beautiful schemes and brilliant revolutionary phrases instead, at times, of concrete analysis. An iron will which sometimes degenerates into obstinacy. A colourful, big personality, an outstanding orator, a world-scale tribune, sincerely and deeply devoted to the cause of Communism – that is Trotsky as a leader.

He evaluated Trotsky's role in the socialist revolution as objectively beyond compare: 'The victory of the proletarian revolution and its highest ascent will always be linked with the name of Trotsky.' Later, Ryutin comments on Stalin's insinuations against Trotsky:

> Stalin's statement that Trotskyism is the vanguard of the international counter-revolutionary bourgeoisie is simply stupid. Today it is the Fascist organisations that are that vanguard ... Stalin calls any opposition to his policy counter-revolutionary. However, it is the duty of every honest Communist and proletarian who is loyal to the Party to oppose Stalin's anti-proletarian and anti-Leninist policy.

Recognition that Trotsky was right was very probably not easy for Ryutin. It meant, first and foremost, recognising his own delusions and errors in the past, in the period of the most acute struggle within the Party. Evidently, all who in their time had fought actively against the Left Opposition were coming to that opinion.

> The moment has now arrived when a fresh open stand is called for, from all former leaders, all honest Bolsheviks, with a bold, open programme of their own for getting out of the impasse and returning to Leninist principles in the way the country of the proletarian dictatorship is led. Otherwise, history will nail them forever to the pillory of shame.

Thus wrote Ryutin.

The group formed by Ryutin, with V. N. Kayurov and M. S. Ivanov, for resistance to Stalin was at first entitled the Union for the Defence of Leninism, but later it took the name Union of Marxist–Leninists, and it entered into history under that name. At two meetings of this organisation, held illegally in Golovino village, near Moscow, and in Ivanov's flat, they discussed their basic documents – a theoretical platform, 'Stalin and the crisis of the proletarian dictatorship', and a manifesto, an appeal 'To all Party members'. The leading organs of this organisation were elected. They chose as their main method of struggle against the Stalin regime appeals against Stalin's actions, addressed to the broad masses of the Party and the proletariat. Removing Stalin from the leadership meant, essentially, dismantling a system which had already to a considerable extent come into being and which was taking the next steps to consolidate itself.

Soviet society was at that time not at all as monolithic as our official historiography asserted until recently. Anti-Stalin sentiments were characteristic of part of the proletariat, and especially of the peasants and the intelligentsia. This is proved, in particular, by the summaries of political sentiments which were prepared for the country's leaders by the Information Department of the OGPU. In October 1932 such a summary was compiled by the Secretariat of the Central Executive Committee for a massed circle of the Party and Soviet leadership, on the basis of 408 letters which had been received by the Central Executive Committee (CEC). One of these letters said:

> You do not know the real sentiments of the working masses. You have based your line not on the working class masses but on the technicians and bureaucrats, who carry out unquestioningly all ideas from above even when they know that this means dooming the masses to ruin and death [for example famine in the Ukraine and in North Caucasia]. All this is done in the name of the general line, to please Stalin. They fear to show the leaders the actual situation of the masses, lest they lose their briefcases and their titles as secretary of some Party organ or chairman of some executive committee. Your staking on the leading personnel is obvious to us. This is no accident, but rather the policy of the 'chief', Stalin, who has driven the best forces out of the leading apparatus, those staunch Bolshevik-Leninists who could have stoutly upheld their views and attended to the needs of the worker masses.

Such sentiments were typical of the working masses. Among the Moscow workers in particular there was a saying: 'After the Five Year Plan all that will be left will be a Party card, a portrait of Stalin and the skeleton of a worker.' This period saw a considerable resumption of activity by those supporters of Trotsky who had survived the break-up of their group. This happened in Kharkov and Belorussia, where the survivors of these groups tried to make contact with the members of the Union of Marxist-Leninists. Copies of the 'Appeal Manifesto' and the platform were circulated for discussion. According to the information of the Secret Political Department of the GPU and the Central Control Commission, in Moscow, Leningrad, Kharkov, Minsk, Novosibirsk, Tomsk and other towns, leaflets with Trotskyist content began to appear more frequently, and, at the same time, such groups became consolidated. This was especially observable among the youth. It was therefore no accident that, in all the trials of 'enemies of the people', the year 1932 was to figure as 'the period of actual unification of all the counter-revolutionary forces drawn from the oppositional groups, from the Trotskyists to the Bukharinists'. (This quotation comes from a letter of Stalin's to Molotov in connection with the appointment of N. I. Yezhov as People's Commissar for Internal Affairs.)

It must be said, however, that in none of the programmatic statements or other documents have we found evidence of any calls for armed uprising or terror directed against Stalin and his clique. Many documents contain the demand 'to remove Stalin', which for many Party members was associated with Lenin's call for his transference and removal from posts of Party-political leadership. It was this demand, though, that the workers of the administrative organs and the Central Control Commission treated as meaning a move towards a campaign of terror against the Stalin circle. In particular, such stupid charges were levelled against a group of old Party members headed by N. V. Eismont, A. P. Smirnov and V. N. Tolmachev in November 1932.

As already mentioned, very effective methods were applied against oppositionally-minded groups, through the punitive organs of the Soviet state and the Party's central organs. The activity of Trotsky and his supporters had been kept under close surveillance by the GPU's secret political department since the mid-1920s. Abroad, his activity was the object of no less careful observation by members of OGPU's foreign department. The materials assembled by the Central Executive Committee in connection with the stripping of Soviet citizenship from Trotsky and his close relatives include information about his 'anti-Soviet and counter-revolutionary' activity after he went abroad. This information was compiled by S. A. Messing, the head of the foreign department, and the report was signed by the deputy-chairman of the OGPU, V. A. Balitsky. The information collected shows that Trotsky's activity was observed and thoroughly examined by able state security organs operating abroad.

Special attention was given to the channels by which Trotsky maintained contact with his supporters in the USSR; and the activity of his daughter Zinaida Volkova and his son L. L. Sedov-Trotsky, who had both been deprived of Soviet citizenship along with their parents. Typically, Trotsky's case was dealt with together with the cases of well-known Russian Social-Democrats such as Garvi. For Stalin and his circle at that time, Menshevism and social-democracy were synonymous with counter-revolution and fascism. Consequently, linking Trotsky with Social-Democrats and his ideas with Menshevism automatically meant accusing him of anti-Soviet, counter-revolutionary activity. 'Counter-revolutionary Trotskyist activity' began from this time to figure, and in the second half of the 1930s, to predominate in trials.

At the same time, the GPU's secret political department launched an operation called 'Opponents', to expose through the work of agents those right-wing elements which were hostile to the Party's general line. As has now been established, its starting point was a statement made by two old Party members (one of whom was Maximilian Saveliev) to the Central Committee, which was passed to the GPU. This statement reported that they had been approached by a group of Party members who talked, in a way that was incompatible with their continuance in the Party, about Stalin's leadership and the policy he was pursuing in all spheres of the country's economic and political life. All the persons mentioned in the statement were subsequently arrested. The targets of the operation were originally the supporters of N. I. Bukharin from his 'school', and later extended to Party activists in regional, city and district committees, and responsible Soviet officials. Also arrested were non-Party people who were known, through observation by agents of materials produced in the course of investigations, to be discontented with the Party's policy.

Primarily, the investigators of the secret-political department aimed to uncover organised illegal work against the Party and its leaders, and to discover who was involved in this. Later, after they found one platform, the basic document entitled 'Stalin and the crisis of the proletarian dictatorship', their work took a new direction, trying to discover terrorist tendencies in the work of the 'Opponents' which was aimed at Stalin. The formula 'remove Stalin' appears in the reports, and is more and more often made to refer to a terrorist act. It should also be mentioned that most instructions in this sense were given personally to each investigator by the head of the GPU's secret political department, G. A. Molchanov or by the departmental chiefs, A. F. Rutkovsky and others. The work of the GPU's secret political department was directed by the deputy chairman of the OGPU, V. A. Balitsky, and later by Ya.S. Agranov.

Similar lines were followed also in the work of the Party's Central Control Commission. Some interesting documents have been preserved which set out rules for the work of investigators within the Party. It is clear from these documents that the main enemy to be tracked down was identified as the Trotskyists and their co-thinkers. Special attention was to be given to discovering possible links between the 'Right deviators' and the Trotskyist opposition, as we learn from an instruction dated November 1932. The leaders of the Party's Central Control Commission, Ya.Z. Rudzutak, E. M. Yaroslavsky and M. F. Shkiriatov, were given their orders by Stalin himself. We know that Stalin personally wrote the resolution of the October 1932 Plenum of the Party's Central Committee 'On the counter-revolutionary group of Ryutin and Slepkov'.

When they spoke on the matter at this Plenum, Stalin, P. P. Postyshev, E. M. Yaroslavsky and V. A. Balitsky emphasised:

> This is a platform which directly calls for terror against the Central Committee, and in particular against its leading members. This document counts on civil war under the conditions of the proletarian dictatorship. It calls for that to happen. It is a programme for the restoration of individual farming, dissolution of the collective farms, bringing back the kulak and the private trader – altogether, a programme for the restoration of capitalism, covered up with phrases about Marxism–Leninism. It is, through and through, a slanderous, foul, counter-revolutionary document. Also, the document counts on unification of all who are discontented with the Party's policy – Trotskyists, Rights, the Workers' Opposition – for joint action against the Party line, and in particular against Comrade Stalin.

The basis for repressive measures to be taken against Communists was, as already mentioned, the resolution of the Plenum which had been prepared by Stalin in person. This served as a fully specific directive to the Party organisations. The essence of it was immediate expulsion from the Party of all who knew about the existence of this counter-revolutionary group, especially those who read its counter-revolutionary documents and did not report them to the Central Control Commission and the Central Committee of the Party – as harbourers of 'enemies of the Party and the working class'.

As can be seen, the step from 'enemies of the Party' to 'enemies of the people' was quite short.

This resolution provided the basis for preparations for the session of the Presidium of the Central Control Commission held on 9 October 1932. The shorthand report of this meeting shows that the main blow was struck at former leading Party members, primarily Zinoviev and Kamenev, since they were available, and also, especially, at Trotsky. It was a further step towards the latter's political discreditation. Accordingly, most of the speakers gave great attention, quite groundlessly, to the fact that the Ryutin group's documents had been circulated among members of the Left Opposition in Kharkov and Moscow. The basic proof of an attempt to form a united front against Stalin and his circle consisted of additional depositions obtained on 5 October 1932 from G. E. Rokkhin. According to his statement, it was to take the form of a joint attack on the Party's Central Committee by all the leaders of former oppositions.

A ready-prepared draft of a resolution was sent on that same day by Yaroslavsky to the Central Committee, with a covering note that read as follows:

> I am sending you a draft prepared by the Presidium of the Central Committee. Don't you agree that another point should be added at the end: a call to all Party members to strengthen class vigilance in relation to the activity of such double-dealers and to fight against the slightest sign of a conciliatory attitude towards opportunist views and opportunist activity on the part of any Party members?

This note and draft were addressed to Rudzutak and Stalin.

Stalin read the draft resolution and made some important alterations to it. In particular, he deleted the whole introductory section, in which the Union of Marxist-Leninists and its ideas were described. In the draft which had been prepared, Yaroslavsky proposed to divide all the persons involved in the affair into three categories: first, the direct organisers and inspirers; second, those who circulated the documents; and third, Zinoviev and Kamenev alone, on the grounds that they had merely known that these documents existed. Kamenev asserted that he had done no more than glance for a few minutes at a document 150 pages long.

Stalin, however, considered it possible to have only two categories, and he arbitrarily assigned Kamenev and Zinoviev to the first of these. In this way they were artificially included among the organisers and inspirers of the Union of Marxist-Leninists. Stalin also strengthened the point, calling on the OGPU to take punitive measures against the organisers and harbourers of the Union and its documents. According to eye witnesses, when, on 11 October 1932, Yaroslavsky announced this decision to Zinoviev, he collapsed into an armchair and began to sob, after which he became ill and was carried away on a stretcher. Kamenev walked up and down the room looking so gloomy as to be unrecognisable. 'Nothing can be done about it: it's signed by Iosif Vissarionovich himself', said Yaroslavsky, 'comforting' him.

That same day the collegium of the OGPU, consisting of V. R. Menzhinsky, G. G. Yagoda, V. A. Balitsky and the procurator Pruss decided on the penalties to be imposed on the persons accused in the case of the Union of Marxist-Leninists. M. N. Ryutin received the longest prison sentence – ten years.

The case of Ryutin and his supporters had far-reaching consequences. First and foremost it entailed a harshening of the regime, a gradual transition to a policy of annihilating the Party and Soviet élite in the ruling stratum. By Stalin's order the OGPU organs, and primarily the secret-political department, began to get to work on all who in any way spoke critically of Stalin. At a gathering of heads of territorial, regional and republic organs of the OGPU, orders for guidance were issued by Rudzutak, the chairman of the Central Control Commission, and L. M. Kaganovich, the secretary of the Central Committee. They required the state security organs to concentrate their efforts on uncovering illegal, underground organisations and organisations of the Ryutin type. Special attention was given to the need to make more severe the custodial regime for persons convicted of counter-revolutionary Trotskyist activity. This was a sort of prelude to the Moscow trials in the years of the 'Great Terror'.

How did public opinion react to what had happened? Above all, Stalin and his circle did everything to ensure that as little information as possible got out. The article in *Pravda* accompanying partial publication of the resolution of the Central Control Commission failed to present the true picture. Furthermore, everyone connected with the Union of Marxist-Leninists was denounced as accomplices of the White Guards and counter-revolutionaries. Stalin gave orders on how matters were to be explained in the press. Ryutin and his supporters were called Trotskyists. Obscure information on this point was conveyed at plenums of Party committees in Moscow, Leningrad, Yaroslavl, Rostov, Novosibirsk and other places.

Nevertheless, they did not succeed in deceiving the Party masses. This is proved by the letters from Communists (mostly anonymous, for easily understandable reasons) which were sent to the Central Committee, to *Pravda* and to the central Soviet organs:

> The masses want Lenin's Party, not Stalin's. Distrust of Stalin's leadership has increased among the masses. Ninety-nine per cent of the working people are in solidarity with the expelled members, who are true Leninists, while the Stalinist leadership is following a policy that leads to the crushing and impoverishing of the working people. We must openly acknowledge that Lenin's Party is no more. The peasants are experiencing military feudalism. Long live Lenin's Party, not Stalin's.

So reads one of these letters.

Here is a very typical excerpt from another letter:

> Uglanov, Ryutin, Zinoviev are counter-revolutionaries. Who says so? It is not they but the Stalinists who are counter-revolutionaries. You have terrorised the country. You have driven the Party underground. The country is ruled by Stalin's dictatorship, a savage and bloody regime such as it has never known before.

This, be it noted, was written in 1932–3.

In our opinion it was precisely then that there took place the transition to Soviet totalitarianism as a system of all-round terror and oppression in the harshest forms. November 1932 saw the arrest, to be followed by repression, of Party members N.V. Eismont, A. P. Smirnov and V. N. Tolmachev, whose chief crime consisted in their having talked at evening parties about the need to remove Stalin from the post of General Secretary of the Party. On 23 January 1933 it was decided to remove A. P. Smirnov from membership of the Presidium of the Central Executive Committee of the USSR. A. S. Yenukidze called him 'the actual leader of this counter-revolutionary group'.

In December groups of the Ryutin type were discovered in Irkutsk and Novosibirsk and in the Belorussian town of Mozyr. In what was called 'the Mozyr case' fourteen former leaders of Soviet and Party organs were brought to trial and condemned. The OGPU's plenipotentiary in Belorussia, A. M. Zakovsky, tried to present this case as one of a counter-revolutionary conspiracy. The scenario of the charge, the focus of the investigation and the course of the examination by the central commission of the Belorussian Communist Party had much in common with the 'Ryutin case'.

The hunt for Trotskyists and Ryutinists also affected the Central Asian region. On 3 January 1934 the chairman of the Central Executive Committee of Tadzhikistan, Maksum, and the chairman of that republic's Council of People's Commissions, Khodzhibaev, were removed from the Central Executive Committee of the USSR, dismissed from their posts and expelled from the Party. Previously, Abdurakhmanov, the chairman of the Council of People's Commissions of Kirghizia, had been expelled from the Party and dismissed from his post. The reason for this harsh treatment was given as their having 'displayed mistrust of the correctness of the Party's policy, distorted the party line, sown mistrust among the leaders regarding the possibility of high tempos of procurement of grain and meat, and displayed mistrust in the victory of the collective-farm system'. In their case the practice was tried out of having them give public testimony at a meeting of the Party Faction at the third session of the 6th Central Executive Committee of the USSR. This took place on the eve of the 17th Party Congress, which played a vital role in consolidating Stalin's despotism.

One sometimes hears of a 'Kirovist alternative to Stalin', of socialism with Kirov's face. This idea seems to us to lack adequate foundation. S. M. Kirov, the leader of the Leningrad Communists, was indeed distinguished by a certain degree of democratism, as compared with Stalin. He had succeeded in winning definite authority in one of the largest Party organisations. But he was just as much a Stalinist as the rest. A purge of Trotskyists and Zinovievists from the Leningrad Party organisation was carried out with his direct participation, and he encouraged excesses in the establishment of collectivisation. The special position of Leningrad as 'the second capital' and centre of the Soviet defence industry to a large extent guaranteed him a special position in the Party Central Committee's Politburo.

It was evidently for that reason that a group of delegates, led by Varekis, went to him with a complaint about Stalin's rudeness. Later, at a meeting with Ordzhonikidze, they proposed that Kirov stand against Stalin as the Central

Committee's secretary. (Stalin was to be transferred to the post then held by V. M. Molotov.) Kirov told Stalin frankly about this, saying that he had caused dissatisfaction by his conduct. Kirov's action had no result except to arouse hostility and suspicion towards himself and the whole Congress on Stalin's part. The 'Congress of Victors' took place in accordance with a scenario well prepared by the apparatus. This included public declarations of repentance by the former oppositionists, Bukharin, Kamenev, Zinoviev and Lominadze. There were no supporters of Ryutin or Trotsky among them, for *they* directed their appeal to the broad masses of the people, to the proletariat.

An active role in supervising the work of the Congress was played by the special and secret-operations departments of the OGPU, whose responsibilities included not only watching over former oppositionists, but also checking on the procedures for elections to the Party's central organs. In spite, however, of all the measures taken, about a quarter of all the delegates voted against Stalin. According to information published in the Soviet press, only 169 votes were not cast for Stalin; of these, 3 were against and 166 were abstentions. This remains controversial since O. G. Shatunovskaya, who headed the Central Committee's Commission appointed in the 1960s to investigate the circumstances of the murder of Kirov, has recently given different figures, suggesting that those above were Stalinist falsifications. In any case, this shows that opposition to Stalin did exist and was actually able to reveal itself. At the Congress and afterwards there took place a further strengthening of Stalin's despotism. The Party's organs were given a new structure, the control organs were made accountable to the Central Committee, and in the summer of 1934 the OGPU was abolished, its functions being transferred to the People's Commissariat for Internal Affairs (NKVD). In practice this consolidated Stalin's personal control over the state security organs and the entire apparatus for imposing penalties by administrative means. The post of General Secretary of the Party's Central Committee was actually abolished at the 17th Congress because of his commanding role in the Party and State apparatus.

Every opposition was crushed. This was to a large extent facilitated by the last Party purge. All the same, members of the Party's old guard might always form a potential nucleus for opposition. From time to time Trotskyist leaflets were distributed among the youth. In Moscow, Leningrad and Kiev the *Bulletin of the Opposition*, edited by L. L. Sedov-Trotsky, was passed from hand to hand. Stalin and his circle continued to spread the idea of a special danger from world Trotskyism as a variety of fascism, as the advanced detachment of the world counter-revolutionary bourgeoisie. After the murder of Kirov, Stalin went over to the physical extermination of the Party's old guard.

Under these conditions of terror and lawlessness attempts were still made to resist repression. We know that, during the June 1937 Plenum of the Central Committee, G. N. Kaminsky and I. A. Piatnitsky spoke out against it. After both had been politically discredited and arrested by the Party's control commission, a statement was sent to M. F. Shkiryatov by the secretary of the Krasnogvardeisk

district committee of the Party, Mikhailov, about the anti-Party counter-revolutionary conduct of Piatnitsky and Kaminsky. Yet neither of them was expelled
from the Party, though their Party membership was automatically cancelled in
1940. Piatnitsky was accused of having connections with Trotsky, through Radek,
who was alleged to have formed a Trotskyist organisation in the Comintern. At
his interrogation, replying to the stupid charges of connections between Trotsky
and Piatnitsky and the Gestapo, Piatnitsky said that General Hammerstein's
daughter actually was a Communist and at the same time sided with Trotsky's
supporters in Germany. G. N Kaminsky was accused of forming a terrorist Right-
Trotskyist organisation in the People's Commissariat for Health. Both men were
shot. The expression 'terrorist Right-Trotskyist counter-revolutionary activity'
was now firmly established in the formula for accusations. Stalin and Yezhov
succeeded in achieving the impossible, uniting the Rights and Lefts in a single
bloc and making the latter counter-revolutionaries instead of champions of world
socialist revolution. It was nonsense indeed, a grimace of history to treat as
counter-revolutionaries people who had devoted their whole lives to the victory
of the revolution. The speeches made by Kaminsky and Piatnitsky were a way of
trying, through words rather than action, to put a stop to the terror. By this time
any initiative undertaken within the country was doomed to inevitable defeat. To
combat any such attempts Stalin's circle launched accusations of imaginary acts of
diversion and attempts at assassination, not shrinking from actual forgery and
falsification of documents.

In this dreadful period some voices still rang out against the Stalin regime.
Members of the Bolshevik Party holding responsible positions abroad appealed to
world opinion, to the international working-class movement. These were the
Soviet intelligence agents N. M. Poretsky (I. Reiss) and V. G. Krivitsky (Walter)
(Samuel Ginzberg), and also the diplomats A. Barmine and F. F. Raskolnikov.
The first of them to announce his break with Stalinism was Reiss. In the summer
of 1937 he sent a letter to the Party's Central Committee in which he said he was
going over to the representatives of the Fourth International, meaning Trotsky.
'Back to Lenin' was, in short, the leitmotiv of his declaration. Krivitsky issued to
the international working-class press a call against Stalin's actions.

Barmine addressed himself to the committee which was investigating the
Moscow trials. The loudest echo was obtained at the time by Raskolnikov, who
wrote an open letter to Stalin. It was stated officially that these men were all
Trotskyists, although none except Reiss spoke of joining Trotsky's supporters. The
attempt was made to brand them as traitors and betrayers of socialism, just as had
been done with Ryutin and Trotsky in their time. Reiss and Krivitsky were
murdered abroad, like Trotsky. Raskolnikov killed himself. What happened to
Barmine we do not know.

Why did the anti-Stalin resistance suffer defeat? Obviously one has to speak of
a complex of causes which ultimately led to the defeat of the fighters against the
Stalin regime.

In the first place, after the ending of elements of NEP, the removal of

Bukharin's group from political leadership and the banishment abroad of Trotsky, no one was left in the Party's Central Committee who was capable of developing and putting forward a programme of socialist construction which could compete with Stalin's. Declarations against Stalin usually spoke only of his removal from the post of General Secretary. Secondly, all who came out against Stalin's regime of personal power had been Stalinists, more or less, in the 1920s. They had all been active proponents of Stalin's policy of industrialisation and collectivisation based on 'extraordinary measures'. Active fighters against all signs of dissidence in the Party and the state, they had to a considerable extent facilitated the establishment of the authoritarian administrative command system. Most of them were against Stalin, but not against the system he had created.

Thirdly, practically all the moves made against Stalin were of the 'palace coup' type. They were confined within the limits of the Politburo or the Central Committee plenums. The exception, and therefore the most dangerous for Stalin, was the Ryutin group, which appealed against Stalin's actions to the Party members as a whole. However, they had no success among the broad masses of the Party and the proletariat. The rapid growth of the working class told negatively upon its qualities as a political vanguard.

When they stood up for the ideals of the socialist revolution and the best traditions of democratism, the representatives of the Bolshevik old guard found themselves without support among wide factions of the Party and the people as a whole. The chronic disease of the Russian liberation movement made itself felt, the syndrome of the Decembrists: 'For the people, but without support from the people.' This isolation was, in its turn, due to a considerable degree to the gap in levels of political culture between the broad masses and the proletarian vanguard embodied in the Party's old guard.

Fourthly, the contending forces were unequal. Stalin was able to use in his service the best traditions and the worst prejudices inherited from the periods of underground struggle and civil war. On Stalin's side was the power not only of the Party machine, but also of the entire state-administration machine. The artificial merging of the functions of Party and state, the existence of the 'Party, state' political organism, enabled Stalin to manipulate such concepts as 'anti-Soviet', 'anti-Party' and 'counter-revolutionary activity'. Those who were closest to Stalin saw in him the definite guarantor of their own positions, so that while expressing discontent in words, they always were at his side when it came to action.

Fifthly, we must not leave out of account the gigantic propaganda apparatus which was part of Stalin's armament: the media of mass information which imposed Stalin's propaganda on public opinion, using its power to discredit the oppositionists by bringing up past mistakes and facts concerning social origin, or simply accusing them of having degenerated. Participants in the Trotskyist opposition were, they said, at bottom so many 'spies and diversionists', enemies of the Soviet people and the Communist Party.

The processes of democratisation of Soviet society have created the possibility of restoring truth and justice. So far only the first steps have been taken in carrying out this great and important task. I think that further steps need to be taken. I am an optimist and I want to believe that, among the fighters for the victory of the socialist revolution, our literature will find a worthy place for the name of L. D. Trotsky.

Notes and commentary

The documentary basis of this work consisted of materials held under the 'special depository' regime, in the state and departmental public records of the Soviet Union. Some of these came to light recently in connection with the publication of materials concerned with work of the commission for the further study of materials connected with the baseless repressions of the 1930s, 1940s and the early 1950s. Another secton of these archives continued to be subject to the 'special depository' regime, and consequently provision of references according to the normal rules is somewhat difficult.

The Soviet journal *Izvestiia TsK KPSS* (*Transactions of the Central Committee of the Communist Party of the Soviet Union*) has recently published materials for a political portrait of M. N. Ryutin (in no. 3, 1990), together with his basic book *Stalin and the Crisis of the Proletarian Dictatorship*, under the title 'The platform of Ryutin's group' (in nos. 6–12, 1990); and Ryutin's prison letters (in no. 3, 1990). There has been partial publication of materials concerning the crushing in November–December 1932 of the group of A. P. Smirnov, N. B. Eismont and N. V. Tolmachev (in no. 11, 1990). These publications confirm the correctness of the propositions I put forward in this paper. At the same time, I think I should provide some notes and comments.

1. The anti-Stalin resistance at the end of the 1920s and in the first half of the 1930s arose on a wave of widespread discontent among the workers, peasants and intelligentsia regarding the practice of socialist construction and, especially, of industrialisation and collectivisation. Documents at my disposal – in particular summaries of information about political moods, compiled by various information services of the Party and Soviet apparatus – enable us to conclude that in 1929–30 the country was on the brink of another civil war.

Materials kept in the archives of the Central Executive Committee, the All-Union Central Executive Committee, the Central Committee of the CPSU(B), the Central Control Commission and the People's Commissariat of Internal Affairs, show that the manifestations of discontent were headed by Soviet and Party officials. Consequently, what was of particular danger to Stalin and his circle was the presence of oppositional sentiments among a certain section of authoritative Party officials, which might include the leaders of resistance. There were also some waverings on this question in the army.

2. Given these conditions, Trotsky and his supporters, Zinoviev, Kamenev and others, could hardly claim the role of leaders of the new movement. On the one hand they had been thoroughly discredited by the Stalinist leadership during the political struggle of the 1920s. An absolute majority of the Oppositionists were in prison or exile, while those still at liberty were under constant surveillance by the OGPU. There were also OGPU agents in Trotsky's immediate entourage. This is proved by materials held by the Central Executive Committee of the USSR relating to the cancellation of Trotsky's Soviet citizenship.

3. The struggle against the political opposition in the USSR was carried on under the leadership of the Central Control Commisson and the OGPU. In the Central Control Commission this work was concentrated in the Party Collegium and the Presidium of that body headed by M. F. Shkiriatov and E. M. Yaroslavsky. In the OGPU the work was undertaken by the secret-political department, headed by G. A. Molchanov. The activity of other departments in this sphere was supervised and co-ordinated by Ya. S. Agranov.

4. In the course of the implementation of the operation code-named 'opponents', which I mention in my article, persons belonging to the 'right deviation' were discredited and later destroyed. This fate was later suffered by all who had a negative attitude to Stalin. Another operation, code-named 'Brothers-in-law', effected the discrediting and subsequent destruction of G. E. Zinoviev, L. B. Kamenev and Trotsky's former supporters.

5. In the mid-1930s, after the murder of S. M. Kirov, the struggle against political opposition assumed the form of mass terror against everyone whose attitude to Stalin was negative. Soviet and Party institutions were subjected to a total purge, along with public bodies and associations. Those who had formerly belonged to opposition groups were now, in the new circumstances, subjected to physical destruction.

6. As regards this period one can speak of resistance only in the sense of opposition to repressive measures. This was shown by some Party officials, by some NKVD officials, by military prosecutors, and others. All of them fell victim to baseless repressive measures themselves. Any disagreement with the policy of the Stalinist leadership was equated with counter-revolutionary activity, and Trotskyism was treated as equivalent to fascism. Evidence of this is to be found in the guidance documents of the NKVD issued at the time. There can be no talk of organised resistance to these processes under such conditions.

This article appears without scholarly apparatus, owing to the nature of the sources on which it is based.

8

L. D. Trotsky and the Second World War

SERGEI KUDRIASHOV

The question of 'Trotsky and the Second World War' has not been much studied. There exist only a few works in which certain aspects of this subject have been dealt with, yet it is of particularly acute importance where events in the Soviet Union are concerned, since Trotsky was one of the few politicians – and, on the eve of the war, perhaps the only one – who publicly criticised Stalin and his foreign policy from Marxist positions.[1]

This article will focus especially on the following questions: Trotsky's views on the causes and character of the Second World War; his analysis of the policies of the Western powers, of fascist Germany and of the USSR, and, in particular, his evaluation of Stalin's actions in the sphere of foreign policy in 1939 and 1940; Trotsky's attitude to the war as a whole, his prognoses and programme of action for the working-class movement; and Trotsky's political and moral position and his influence in 1939–40.

Trotsky on the causes and character of the Second World War

Trotsky saw the outbreak of another world war as a natural and inevitable process. He saw the sources of the war as lying in inter-imperialist contradictions, singling out particularly the striving by Germany and Japan for a re-partition of the world. In Trotsky's view, these countries, together with Italy, had come late, for reasons both internal and external, to the distribution of spheres of influence, and their further development was hindered by their territorial limitations. In one of the interviews he gave in March 1939 he declared: 'The inevitability of the war flows first from the incurable crisis of the capitalist system; second from the fact that the present partition of our planet, that is to say, above all, of the colonies, no longer corresponds to the economic specific weight of the imperialist states.'[2]

Trotsky connected the origin of the war also with the crisis of democracy, of pacifism and even fascism. The war was one way of resolving the contradictions, but at the same time it would prepare a fresh revolutionary explosion which, as Trotsky saw it, would result in the triumph of Marxist ideas. Trotsky also considered the war inevitable because, in his opinion, there were no forces present in the world that were capable of preventing it. The working-class movement, thanks to the Stalinist leadership of the Comintern, was practically paralysed and encountered the war in just as fragmented a condition as in 1914. Noting that the policies of the countries participating in the war were based on imperialist interests, Trotsky defined its character from the start as a predatory, imperialist conflict. At the same time, Trotsky saw as the main danger to peace fascist Germany and fascism generally, and called for active struggle against this.[3]

Trotsky on the foreign policy and actions of the Stalinist leadership on the eve and at the beginning of the war

From the beginning of the 1930s, even before the Fascists came to power in Germany, Trotsky frequently said that for Stalin there would be nothing better than co-operation with Hitler. He noted that on 4 March 1933, when Hitler was already firmly in the saddle, *Izvestiya* wrote with pride that the USSR was the only country that bore no hostility towards Germany, and this 'regardless of the form and composition of the government of the Reich'.[4] It is interesting that, although he lacked complete information, Trotsky, possessing as he did a subtle psychological understanding of Stalin, was able to perceive with precision the tendency in which relations between Stalin and Hitler would develop, their spiritual closeness, and he proved correct in forecasting a future alliance between them. In April 1938, long before the signing of the Pact, Trotsky wrote openly that fascism was gaining victory after victory, and its chief helper in all parts of the world was Stalinism.[5]

The bacchanalia of Stalinist repressions caused the question of the nature of the Soviet state to assume special acuteness in the revolutionary circles in the West: was it a socialist, workers' state, whose interests Stalin was expressing, and what, on the social plane, was the Soviet bureaucracy? A number of activists in the working-class movement, including some of Trotsky's supporters, put forward the view that the Soviet Party–state bureaucracy was nothing other than a 'new class', performing the function of exploiter. From this conclusion there inevitably followed the question of whether it would be expedient to defend such a state in the event of war. Those who held the 'new class' doctrine were inclined to take up a position of revolutionary defeatism – that is to say, that, if war should come, this might facilitate the downfall of the bureaucracy, and so there was no need to call for defence of the USSR. Intervening actively in the discussion, Trotsky sharply opposed that view. With good grounds he observed that the fact that the USSR did not come within the generally-accepted definitions of Marxist sociology did not at all signify that the Soviet Union had, in its essence, ceased to be a proletarian state. Real life very often diverges from theory. In Trotsky's opinion what was needed was to make use of the Marxist dialectical method to try and explain how the Soviet state had evolved, and to define its nature. Trotsky was convinced that Stalinism had not succeeded in destroying the fundamental achievement of the October Revolution – the expropriation of private property – and therefore the Soviet state in the 1930s was, for him, still basically a workers' state. But this state was gradually decaying and disintegrating. The main reason for this process of degradation was Stalinism, which, Trotsky wrote, was not an abstraction of 'dictatorship' but an immense bureaucratic reaction against the proletarian dictatorship in a backward and isolated country: 'Stalinism re-established the most offensive forms of privilege, imbued inequality with a provocative character, strangled mass self-activity under police absolutism, transformed administration into a monopoly of the Kremlin oligarchy and regenerated the fetishism of power in forms that absolute monarchy dared not dream of.'[6]

Trotsky considered that the proletariat, ruling in a single, backward country, nevertheless continued to be an oppressed class. The source of the oppression was world imperialism, and the Soviet bureaucracy served as the transmission-mechanism for this oppression. In Trotsky's thinking the bureaucracy was not an independent class but an instrument of classes. Accordingly, the bureaucracy in the USSR objectively served the interests of the imperialist bourgeoisie.[7] Trotsky considered that there were in the USSR between 12 and 15 million privileged persons, concentrating in their hands about a half of the national income and calling this state of affairs 'socialism'.[8] Trotsky's view deserves attention, but, evidently through insufficient information, he exaggerated the degree of alienation of the bureaucracy and Stalinism from the social order existing in the USSR. For Trotsky, Stalinism was a disease, an anomaly in development, and on that level it is difficult not to agree with him. At the same time, however, he viewed Stalinism too much as a political, superstructural phenomenon. Consequently, Trotsky supposed that it would be enough to remove Stalin and break up the bureaucracy for the healthy principle engendered by the October Revolution, meaning property in the hands of the people as a whole, to make itself felt. One might blame Trotsky for approaching the problem in a simplistic way, but that would be unjust. Trotsky's service was, precisely, that he was one of the first in the world to study Stalinism as an historical phenomenon, and the extent to which Stalinism had damaged the structure of Soviet society (its politics, economics, culture, science, etc) became clear only in the period of *perestroika*.

Trotsky drew a distinction of principle between Stalinism on the one hand and Bolshevism and socialism on the other: 'Stalinism originated not as an organic outgrowth of Bolshevism but as a negation of Bolshevism consummated in blood.'[9] He constantly defended Lenin and Leninism from Stalinist distortions, and actively opposed attempts to put the sign of equality between Lenin and Stalin. Trotsky's line of argument acquired topical importance in the period of *perestroika*.[10]

Discussing the nature of the Soviet state, Trotsky remarked, with reason, that Stalin performed a dual function. He served the bureaucracy, and thereby the world bourgeoisie, but he could not serve the bureaucracy unless he preserved the social foundation which the bureaucracy exploited in its own interests. In defending the USSR, Stalin and the bureaucracy were defending, first and foremost, themselves within the USSR, but this defence was being effected by methods which prepared the way for an all-round collapse of Soviet society. It was just for this reason, Trotsky thought, that the Stalin clique and the hated bureaucracy had to be overthrown, but overthrown by the peoples of the USSR themselves: this was a task they could not entrust to anyone else.[11] Trotsky resolutely rejected the charge brought against him by some bourgeois newspapers that he wanted to help Hitler beat Stalin. He wrote:

> The USSR and Stalin are not the same thing. I am an adversary of Stalin but not of the USSR ... Hitler's victory would signify frightful economic, political and national slavery for all the peoples of the USSR and above all the restoration of the rights of private capital ... To defend the nationalisation of the means of production realised by the October Revolution – against Hitler as against all other imperialists – I consider this the elementary duty of every socialist, beginning with myself.[12]

At the same time Trotsky stressed that defence of the USSR did not in the least mean *rapprochement* with the Kremlin bureaucracy, adopting its policy or reconciling oneself to the policies of its allies.[13]

Trotsky's slogan of 'unconditional defence of the USSR' gave rise to many disputes among his supporters. He patiently explained that this was a vital necessity, since facilitating the overthrow of the Stalin clique by supporting an external enemy would in practice mean helping to destroy the state which was objectively the stronghold of socialism. Trotsky said that the slogan 'unconditional defence of the USSR' did not put any conditions to the Stalinist bureaucracy. This meant that, regardless of the occasion or cause of war, the social foundations of the USSR were to be defended, if and when they were threatened with attack by imperialism.[14]

In connection with events taking place in the Soviet Union, and especially in connection with Stalin's foreign policy after the signing of the pact with Germany, there was much discussion in the West concerning the similarity between fascist Germany and the USSR. Thus a new word, 'Communazi', made its appearance, and an editorial in the New York Times of 18 September 1939 affirmed that 'Hitlerism is brown communism, Stalinism is red fascism'.[15] Trotsky opposed the identification of fascism with socialism. For him these were fundamentally opposite social systems. In the Manifesto of the Fourth International, written by Trotsky, it was expressly emphasised that 'Fascism is a chemically pure distillation of the culture of imperialism.'[16] Fascism was engendered by a society based on private property, whereas socialism was based on public ownership of the means of production. This difference Trotsky considered to be one of principle.[17] Fascism and Stalinism were a different matter. Stalinism had transformed the Soviet Union into a new prison of peoples, and under its influence the political regime in the socialist country, in Trotsky's opinion, had finally come to resemble that of a penal battalion.[18] Trotsky agreed with Mussolini when he said that nobody in the whole world had struck such blows at the idea of communism (the proletarian revolution) and exterminated communists with such ferocity as Stalin.[19] Stressing the fact that the political methods of Stalin and Hitler differed little from each other, and turning attention to the possible development of Stalinism in the direction of fascism, Trotsky nevertheless did not identify fascism with Stalinism. Being parasitic upon socialism and exploiting the results of the revolution, Stalinism was obliged, for the sake of self-preservation, to do something also for socialism. Consequently, Stalinism was not a mirror image of fascism.[20] So, while pointing to the similarity between fascism and Stalinism, Trotsky resolutely opposed attempts to place the sign of equality between fascism and socialism.

Trotsky was, in fact, the first to criticise one of the basic postulates of the doctrine of totalitarianism, which acquired wide popularity in the West a little later. Although he did indeed often use the term 'totalitarian', he never gave it any scientific significance. For him the term was merely a graphic adjective indicating something cruel, oppresssive and dictatorial, but in no way a sociological concept containing the notion that fascism and socialism were the same. With hindsight we can confidently assert that those Western scholars who tried to make sense of Soviet history by means of the doctrine of totalitarianism failed to arrive at solid results. If one starts from the basic positions of the doctrine as put forward in the works of Arendt, Friedrich and Brzezinski,[21] one cannot understand why the Soviet state has developed and achieved certain successes, and why such a phenomenon as *perestroika* is possible. It is all the more surprising that the doctrine of totalitarianism has acquired 'new' life in the Soviet Union. Some writers, intoxicated by *glasnost*, are uncritically borrowing many propositions from out-of-date Western publications and passing off their reflections as a new stage in knowledge.[22]

The non-aggression treaty of 23 August 1939 between the USSR and fascist Germany did not take Trotsky and his supporters by surprise. After Munich, and especially after the 18th Congress of the CPSU(B), Trotsky regarded the outcome of events as most likely. He observed, sarcastically, that, for the Stalinists, it was a lot harder to fight fascism than to shoot and poison old Bolsheviks.[23] In an article with the eloquent title 'Stalin's capitulation', Trotsky described the General Secretary's speech at the 18th Congress as a feeler put out to Hitler. He wrote:

> During the last three years Stalin called all the companions of Lenin agents of Hitler. He exterminated the flower of the armed forces' commanders. He shot, discharged and deported about 300,000 officers – all under the same charge of being agents of Hitler or his allies. After having dismembered the Party and decapitated the army, now Stalin is openly posting his own candidacy for the role of ... principal agent of Hitler.[24]

Nearly half a year before the pact was signed, Trotsky firmly emphasised that an agreement between Stalin and Hitler would change nothing essential in the counter-revolutionary function of the Kremlin oligarchy. In his view it would merely expose this function, make it more brazen and hasten the collapse of illusions and falsifications.[25] Observing the course of events in the autumn of 1939, Trotsky was able to convince himself that he had been right. On the one hand, he saw the Soviet–German pact as a sign of the degree to which the Soviet bureaucracy had degenerated, of its contempt for the international working-class movement, the Communists included; while, on the other, he saw in it a manifestation of the weakness of the USSR, the Kremlin's panic in the face of Germany – a capitulation of Stalin before fascist imperialism with the end of preserving the

Soviet oligarchy.[26] While pointing out that by means of the pact Stalin had bought himself the possibility of staying out of the war in the immediate future, Trotsky very correctly described the pact of non-aggression as an agreement to maintain 'a passive attitude toward German aggression'.[27] At the same time, Trotsky considered the alliance between Stalin and Hitler as offensive in character, with the partners' roles strictly defined: Hitler carried on military operations, while Stalin functioned as his quartermaster.[28]

Fascist Germany received supplies, of course, not only from the Soviet Union, but the Nazi government regarded the supplies from the USSR as of very great importance. Stalin, however, did not hurry, showed unwillingness to compromise and insisted on reciprocal supplies of equal value. The negotiations aimed at concluding an economic agreement between Germany and the USSR had produced no tangible result by February 1940, and it was only then that Stalin, having received a personal message from Ribbentrop, agreed to meet the Germans' demands. The German Foreign Minister had pointed out to Stalin that the question of the speed and amount of the supplies required could not be looked at from the economic standpoint alone, but must be linked with the general political understanding which had been arrived at between the two countries. Ribbentrop resentfully reminded Stalin that 'this understanding has meanwhile made it possible … for the Soviet Government to realise its desires regarding the former Polish Territory and to develop and protect its interests in the Baltic' and that 'this was possible not least of all because of the German victory in Poland'. All of which, according to Ribbentrop, provided serious justification for Germany's desire to obtain support from the USSR now, as it continued the war against France and Britain, by means of as rapid and extensive deliveries of raw materials as possible.[29] With Stalin's intervention the situation changed abruptly, and on 8 February the parties reached agreement. According to the German documents, Stalin personally proposed that the Soviet Union provide supplies to the value of 650–60 million Reichsmarks over a period of eighteen months (i.e. until August 1941), while Germany's reciprocal supplies to the USSR should be spread over a period of two years and three months. The Nazi officials did not conceal their profound satisfaction.[30] On 11 February 1940 there was also signed a secret protocol by which the USSR undertook to purchase metals and other commodities in third countries and sell them to Germany.[31]

The head of the German economic mission in the Soviet Union, K. Schnurre, fittingly evaluated in a memorandum of 26 February 1940 'the desire of the Soviet Government to help Germany' and to supply even more than was needed. Schnurre noted sympathetically that the USSR had to deliver these supplies to some extent at the expense of its own supply situation. In his view, the agreement opened for Germany a wide door to the East, as a result of which the effects of the British blockade were greatly weakened.[32] Thus, even though Trotsky did not have all the information at his disposal, he was not far from the truth when he called Stalin Hitler's quartermaster.

With regard to the pact, Trotsky drew attention particularly to a question of political principle: namely, the possibility of agreements between a socialist state and capitalist states. On this question Trotsky fully shared Lenin's position. In his work *Left-Wing Communism: an infantile disorder*, Lenin argued that, in the practical political questions confronting a specific historical movement, it is important to identify compromises which are intolerable because they involve opportunist treachery fatal to the revolutionary class, and to exert all efforts to expose and combat them. But he also wrote that 'one must learn to distinguish between a man who has given up his money and firearms to bandits so as to lessen the evil they can do and to facilitate their capture and execution, and a man who gives his money and firearms to bandits so as to share the loot'.[33] Applying Lenin's attitude to compromises to the case of Stalin's pact with Hitler, we can conclude that Stalin was one of those who became, in Lenin's words, '*accomplices* in imperialist banditry'.[34]

Agreeing with Lenin, Trotsky showed on the eve of the Second World War that, given the isolated situation of the socialist state, it was compelled, to one extent or another, to enter into agreements with the imperialists. But he pointed plainly to the criterion to which the Soviet Republic had adhered in its policy after 1917: namely, that the workers in the capitalist countries were not to be bound by any of these empirical agreements made by the workers' states where their class struggle against their own bourgeoisie was concerned. Stalin's compromise transgressed the limits of the permissible and, in Molotov's words, ensured for Germany 'calm confidence in the East'.[35] Trotsky acutely notices that it was characteristic of Stalin to proclaim ideological solidarity with whatever state he allied himself with. One has to agree that Trotsky was right when he wrote openly in 1939 that 'the fundamental trait of Stalin's international policy in recent years has been this: that he *trades* in the working-class movement just as he trades in oil, manganese and other goods'.[36]

Trotsky emphasised that Germany's goodwill could be bought only by co-operating in Germany's plans. He forecast prophetically that one of Stalin's main concessions would be the cessation of anti-fascist propaganda.[37] Stalin went even further than that and ratified his 'friendship' with Hitler with the blood of convinced anti-fascists. In September 1939 intensive contacts began between the NKVD and the Gestapo. A large group of German anti-fascists and Jews who had escaped into the USSR from Nazi persecution were handed over to the Gestapo. Anti-fascists from other countries, and also Soviet citizens who did not adjust themselves to 'friendship' with Germany were subjected to repressive measures.[38] All of which gave Hitler grounds for saying, on 4 January 1941, that 'as long as Stalin was alive, it was absolutely impossible that Russia would start anything against Germany'.[39]

It seems that Trotsky was right when he noted that personal motives played a part in Stalin's policy towards Poland. He had in view the defeat suffered by the Red Army's forces before Warsaw in 1920, which happened not without some 'help' from Stalin. Now, in the autumn of 1939, Stalin took his peculiar revenge.[40] Stalin's personal motives showed themselves also during the war between the

USSR and Germany: especially striking was Stalin's demonstrative unwillingness to give substantial help to the Warsaw rising in 1944.

In my view Trotsky was right in objecting to any comparison of the non-aggression pact to the Brest-Litovsk peace treaty, calling such comparison 'forgery'. Trotsky's argument retains its importance today, since apologists for the pact are trying, as before, to present the matter as though the situation in 1939 was like that in 1918. Trotsky emphatically declared that there was nothing in common between the two treaties. In 1918 the Bolsheviks were forced to accept conditions for a peace treaty imposed on them in an ultimatum, since what was at stake was a matter of life or death for the young Soviet republic, which lacked sufficient forces and means to resist external aggression. The Bolsheviks well appreciated the full gravity of their compromise with Germany and carried out extensive explanatory work among the masses, and no one dared even to think of 'friendship' with Kaiser Wilhelm. Any such idea would have been taken as a betrayal of the revolution's ideals. The Bolsheviks' conscience was clear when they signed the Brest treaty. Moreover, the Brest treaty, unlike the pact, was not accompanied by any secret protocol by which the fate of third countries was decided. Trotsky did not know about the secret protocol and the subsequent secret agreements between Stalin and Hitler, but, as an experienced politician who followed the course of events, he realised that there was some sort of understanding between them. (Today it is already clear, not only from the German but also from the published Soviet documents, that the initiative for the secret protocol came from the Soviet side.)[41] Defining the Kremlin's policy as the policy of 'the Bonapartist bureaucracy of a degenerated workers' state under conditions of imperialist encirclement', Trotsky noted that an inevitable consequence of the alliance with Germany was Stalin's invasion of Poland and the Baltic states. Trotsky frequently pointed out that, behind all the rhetoric of Soviet propaganda, the basic motive of Stalin's policy was his fear of Hitler, fear of war with him. In Trotsky's opinion the circumstances on the western frontier of the USSR were developing in such a way that Stalin could escape war only by fleeing forward: not through giving up old positions, but through taking new ones. 'In his alliance with Hitler and on Hitler's initiative Stalin decided to take "guarantees against Hitler".'[42] Thus, according to Trotsky, the pact with Germany was not so much the result of accidental circumstances as the natural outcome of Stalin's cynical policy. Having created inside the country an atmosphere of terror and universal suspicion, and having annihilated millions of people, Stalin and his circle had themselves created the situation in which, in order to stay out of war, it was necessary to indulge Hitler. Unlike the Bolsheviks in 1918, Stalin soiled himself with his pact and discredited many Communist Parties. Trotsky rightly emphasised that the first victim of the pact of 23 August 1939 was the Comintern.[43]

Stalin actually compelled the Communist Parties of Europe to collaborate with the fascists. During the German onslaught on France, the French Communists directly helped the Germans by their activities. Ribbentrop wrote about that to Ciano with some satisfaction. The Communists even appealed to the occupying authorities for permission to publish *l'Humanité*. On 1 July 1940 an issue of the paper appeared in which De Gaulle was branded as a British 'agent'.[44] In this period Trotsky wrote, with sarcasm, that Stalin and his Communists were undoubtedly the most valuable agents of imperialism.[45]

Trotsky's moral positions, his programme and prognoses

Trotsky's morality was a class morality. Throughout his conscious life in politics he saw defence of the interests of the proletariat as the sacred duty of a revolutionary. The morality of the proletarian revolution was for Trotsky the highest stage of human morality, because it was based on loyalty to the cause of emancipating the oppressed.

On the eve of the war, especially after the Stalinist show trials, the question of the Bolsheviks' morality became topical, or, more precisely, many media of mass information in the West, including so-called specialist newspapers, identified Bolshevism with Stalinism and Lenin with Stalin, developing a campaign in which the Bolsheviks were accused of 'amoralism'. To this Trotsky sharply replied with a polemical pamphlet, *Their morals and ours*. It is noteworthy that Trotsky, in exile, rarely failed to reply to attacks on Lenin and Bolshevism, and in my opinion his arguments are still valid today. Under conditions of *perestroika* in the Soviet Union some writers have made it fashionable to compare Lenin to Stalin and also to compare Stalin to Trotsky, presenting them as uterine brothers born of the October Revolution who committed equivalent crimes.[46] Trotsky's retort would hardly be to the liking of today's 'intellectuals', liberated by *glasnost*. He wrote: 'Verily, boundless intellectual and moral obtuseness is required to identify the reactionary police morality of Stalinism with the revolutionary morality of the Bolsheviks.'[47] Trotsky pointed out that the state created by the Bolsheviks reflected not only the mind and will of Bolshevism, but also the cultural level of the country, the social composition of the population, the pressure of a barbarous past and of no less barbarous world imperialism. Consequently, to depict the process of degeneration of the Soviet state as the evolution of pure Bolshevism meant ignoring social reality in the name of one of its elements logically isolated from the rest. In Trotsky's view, by taking state power the Party obtained the means to influence the development of society with power that had been unavailable to it previously, but, as against that, the Party was itself subjected to a tenfold greater influence from all the other elements in society. It could be ejected from power by direct blows from hostile forces. In the longer term, it could, after taking power, undergo degeneration from within. Trotsky considered that this dialectic of history was what was not grasped by those who 'try to find in the decay of the Stalinist bureaucracy an annihilating argument against Bolshevism'.[48]

Trotsky wrote that the morality of any party is derived from the interests which this party represents. The morality of Bolshevism, which included self-sacrifice, disinterestedness, audacity, and contempt for every kind of tinsel and falsehood, was derived from revolutionary intransigence in the service of the oppressed. The Stalinist bureaucracy imitated in this domain the words and gestures of Bolshe-

vism. But when 'intransigence' and 'inflexibility' were applied by a police apparatus in the service of a privileged minority they became a source of demoralisation
and gangsterism. Consequently, Trotsky decisively counterpoised the revolutionary heroism of the Bolsheviks to the cynicism of the Stalinists.[49]

Trotsky reacted no less sharply to attempts to ascribe to the Bolsheviks the so-
called 'Jesuit' principle, that 'the end justifies the means'. He said that dialectical
materialism knows no duality between means and ends. The end flows naturally
from the movement of history. The means are organically subordinated to the
end. The immediate end becomes the means to a further end. But the end itself,
Trotsky declared, must be justified. In his view, from the standpoint of Marxism
an end is justified if it leads to increasing the power of man over nature and to the
abolition of the power of man over man. At the same time, this does not signify
that all and every means are permissible for the attainment of that end. Trotsky
stressed that a great revolutionary end spurns those base means and methods
which set one section of the working class against others, or which attempt to
make the masses happy without their participation, or lower the faith of the
masses in themselves and their organisation, replacing it by worship of 'leaders'.
Above all and irreconcilably, revolutionary morality rejects servility in relation to
the bourgeoisie and haughtiness in relation to the working people – that is to say,
those characteristics in which petty-bourgeois pedants and moralists are thoroughly steeped.[50]

In this same connection, Trotsky waxed sarcastic at the attempt to counterpoise to proletarian morality, the morality of 'common sense' – or 'generally
recognised' rules of morality. There are indeed certain elementary moral precepts
developed in the course of human history, but in Trotsky's view these are
indeterminate in character and the extent of their action is extremely limited and
unstable, since morality itself is a product of social development, serves definite
social interests and has nothing immutable about it.[51] Common sense proves
adequate for bargaining, healing, writing articles, leading trade unions, voting in
Parliament, marrying and producing children. But when this same common sense
tries to go beyond its valid limits into the arena of more complex generalisations,
it exposes itself, according to Trotsky, as a mere clot of the prejudices of a
particular class and a particular epoch.[52]

Trotsky did not like it when his activity was presented as a particular tendency
called 'Trotskyism' and when his followers were called 'Trotskyists'. If he happened to use these terms, he often preferred to put them between quotation marks.
Trotsky saw himself as the continuer of Lenin's work, and the *Bulletin of the
Opposition* was published as the organ of the 'Bolshevik-Leninists'. In my view, the
differences between Lenin and Trotsky on the question of world revolutions,
which have been artificially stirred up by Soviet propaganda and official
historiography, provide no adequate basis for counterposing Leninism to
'Trotskyism'. Analysis of Trotsky's writings when in exile makes it possible to
conclude that he was one of the few who publicly defended Leninism against
Stalinism and against bourgeois criticism. And at the beginning of the Second

World War, Trotsky seems to have remained the only Marxist who criticised Stalin's policy from Leninist positions.

Trotsky always expressed his views frankly. His position at the beginning of the war was consistent: against imperialism, against fascism and against Stalinism; for socialism and for unconditional defence of the USSR.[53] This was the strategic principle underlying the Manifesto of the Fourth International on the Imperialist War and the Proletarian Revolution, which was adopted on 26 May 1940 by an extraordinary conference of the Fourth International.[54] After fascist Germany's attack on the Soviet Union, the executive committee of the Fourth International issued a call to 'Defend the USSR'.[55]

One can say without exaggerating that the Fourth International created by Trotsky was one of the few political organisations in the world which had a fairly clear programme under the conditions of the Second World War. The activity of the Fourth International after Trotsky's assassination calls for serious scientific study.

On the eve of the war and during it, Trotsky frequently made prognoses. And what is interesting is that in his prognoses for the future he proved to be amazingly correct. Trotsky forecast the pact, the Soviet-German economic agreement, the changes in the policy of the Comintern and the European Communist Parties, and Stalin's policy towards Western Ukraine and Western Belorussia, Finland and the Baltic states. Trotsky was sure that war between Germany and the USSR was only a question of time, however Stalin might strive to avoid it. Trotsky supposed that the war would inevitably lead to a revolutionary explosion in many countries, and in that he also proved to be right, but the war did not lead, as Trotsky hoped, to the downfall of capitalism and the triumph of socialist revolution – not in most countries of the world at least.[56] Trotsky warned Western statesmen not to underestimate the defensive strength of the Red Army. The former People's Commissar for Military and Naval Affairs and Chairman of the Revolutionary War Council of the Republic prophesied that in the event of an attack by Hitler on the USSR the Red Army would put up a stubborn defence of its territory.[57]

Trotsky underestimated the strength of Stalinism, its ability to adapt to changed conditions. He thought that the Stalinist bureaucracy would not survive the war, that Stalin's apogee was behind him and the fall of his dictatorship near. Trotsky wanted very much to believe that this would happen, but, even so, voiced the supposition that 'defence against foreign intervention would undoubtedly strengthen the position of the bureaucracy'.[58]

Alas, the war did not lead to the fall of Stalinism. On the contrary, victory over fascist Germany enhanced the prestige both of the system and of Stalin personally. Using its powerful apparatus of propaganda and repression, Stalinism succeeded in identifying its interests with those of the country in the consciousness of the Soviet people. When Trotsky asserted that 'the popular masses of the Soviet Union hate the greedy and cruel ruling caste' he obviously overestimated the level of consciousness of the working people.[59] Nevertheless, at the beginning of the war the Stalinist leadership did encounter organised protest by workers and peasants against the bureaucracy. There are documents in the Central Party Archive, in the section for the department of propaganda and agitation in the Central Committee of the CPSU(B), which give evidence of frequent strikes by workers and collective farmers. These strikes did not assume any clearly expressed political character as protests against the prevailing regime. As a rule they were directed against local Party and Soviet officials. Thus, as a result of conduct by Party bureaucrats who were trying above all to ensure their own safety, the autumn of 1942 saw disturbances in Saratov region, which went so far as people leaving the Party. Owing to the unreadiness of the administration to take account of the needs of the working people there were frequent refusals to work on the part of working women employed in the Ivanovo textile mill named after Molotov: they resorted to a concealed form of strike, what was called 'dawdling'.

Although mistaken as regards the concrete timing of the fall of the Stalinist dictatorship, Trotsky was certainly right on the main point – that Stalinism would inevitably be overthrown by the working people of the Soviet Union, and that Stalin's name 'would become a byword for the uttermost limits of human baseness'.[60] This is precisely the process that we now see unfolding in the USSR.

Despite the hounding of Trotsky over many years by Stalinist and post-Stalinist propaganda, and the deliberate distortion of his views by official historiography, Trotsky's name is returning to Soviet history. Many falsifications concerning Trotsky survive only because his works are inaccessible to the ordinary Soviet reader. With the publication of Trotsky's writings which has begun in the USSR these falsifications will fade away by themselves.

Trotsky was never an enemy of socialism and the USSR. He was an irreconcilable opponent of Stalinism, and in struggle against it he died. The attempt by some writers to put the sign of equality between Trotsky and Stalin shows their incompetence and the tenacity of 'anti-Trotskyist' stereotypes in social consciousness, implanted by Stalinist propaganda itself.

In descriptions of Trotsky reference is often made to Lenin's statement about his 'non-Bolshevism'.[61] But Lenin did not explain in his 'Testament' what meaning he was giving to the concept 'Bolshevism'. To judge by the characterisations of the top Party leaders which Lenin provides in his 'Letter to the Congress', none of them understood Bolshevism in the way that Lenin understood it. Besides, Trotsky then still had time to become a Bolshevik. And if by Bolshevism we understand profession of the ideas of historical and dialectical materialism, struggle for the interests of the oppressed, devotion to the idea of proletarian revolution and dictatorship of the proletariat, and honesty in struggle against ideological opponents,[62] then, at the end of the 1930s, Trotsky was a greater Bolshevik than the whole of the CPSU(B).

Notes

1. See I. Deutscher, *The Prophet Outcast: Trotsky, 1924–1940*, London, 1963, pp. 458–73; M. Dreyfus, 'Sur l'histoire du mouvement trotskiste en

Europe de 1930 à 1952', in *Le Mouvement social*, no. 96, 1976, pp. 111–24; *Les Congrès de la IVème Internationale*, vol. 1, p. 1978; J. Pluet-Despatin, *Les Trotskistes et la Guerre 1940–1944*, Paris 1980; P. Broué, *Trotsky*, Paris, 1988, ch. 59, pp. 909–22.

2. *Byulleten oppozitsii* [*Bulletin of the Opposition* – hereafter *BO* – trans.], no. 75–6, Mar.–Apr. 1939, p. 5. [*Writings 1939–40*, p. 231].

3. Pluet-Despatin, *Les Trotskistes*, p. 30; *BO*, no. 70, Oct. 1938, pp. 6–7; no. 71, Nov. 1938, pp. 2–3; no. 72, Dec 1938, p. 4; no. 84, Apr.–Sept.–Oct. 1940, pp. 11–15.

4. *Izvestiya*, 4 Mar. 1933; *BO*, no. 65, Apr. 1938, p. 6. [*Writings 1937–38*, p. 239].

5. *BO*, no. 65, p. 1.

6. *ibid.*, no. 68–9, Aug.–Sept. 1938, p. 13. [*Their Morals and Ours*, New York, p. 28].

7. *ibid.*, no. 62–3, Feb. 1938, pp. 17–19.

8. *ibid.*, no. 81, Jan. 1940, p. 2.

9. *ibid.*, no. 77–8, May–June–July 1939, p. 22. [*Writings 1938–39*, p. 337].

10. *ibid.*, no. 68–9, pp. 6–19.

11. *ibid.*, no. 62–63, p. 17; no. 82–3, Feb.–Mar.–Apr. 1940, pp. 4–7.

12. *ibid.*, no. 74, Feb. 1939, p. 14. [*Writings 1938–39*, pp. 163–4].

13. *ibid.*, no. 79–80, Aug.–Sept.–Oct. 1939, p. 7.

14. *ibid.*, no. 81, p. 11; no. 82–3, p. 12.

15. T. Paterson, *Meeting the Communist Threat*, New York, 1988, pp. 5–7; R. Douglas, *From War to Cold War*, New York, 1981, p. 2.

16. *BO*, no. 84, p. 15. [*Writings 1939–40*, p. 193].

17. *ibid.*, no. 75–6, Mar.–Apr. 1939, p. 3.

18. *ibid.*, no. 66–7, May–June 1938, p. 17; no. 68–9, Aug.–Sept. 1938, p. 3.

19. *ibid.*, no. 65, Apr. 1938, p. 7.

20. *ibid.*, no. 62–3, Feb. 1938, pp. 17–19; no. 66–7, May–June 1938, p. 20; no. 75–76, Mar.–Apr. 1939, p. 3.

21. See H. Arendt, *The Origins of Totalitarianism*, New York, 1951; C. J. Friedrich and Z. K. Brzezinski, *Totalitarian Dictatorship and Autocracy*, Cambridge, Mass., 1956.

22. See *Totalitarizm kak istoricheskiy fenomen*, Moscow, 1989.

23. *BO*, no. 71, Nov. 1938, pp. 6–7; Pluet-Despatin, *Les Trotskistes*, p. 31; Broué, *Trotsky*, pp. 914–15.

24. *BO*, no. 75–6, p. 4. [*Writings 1938–39*, p. 218].

25. *ibid.*, p. 3.

26. *ibid.*, no. 79–80, pp. 2–9; no. 84, Aug.–Sept.–Oct. 1940, p. 17. [*Writings 1939–40*, p. 82].

27. *ibid.*, no 79–80, p. 15; no. 82–3, p. 5. [*Writings 1939–40*, p. 78].

28. *ibid.*, no. 79–80, pp. 15, 17–18.

29. *Akten zur deutschen auswärtigen Politik 1918–1945*, Ser. D, Bd. VIII, pp. 581–3. [*Documents on German Foreign Policy, 1918–45*, Series D, vol. 8 (HMSO), pp. 740–1].

30. *ibid.*, pp. 594–5. [*Documents …*, pp. 752–4].

31. *ibid.*, p. 605. [*Documents …*, pp. 768–9].

32. *ibid.*, p. 643. [*Documents …*, pp. 814–17].

33. See V. I. Lenin, *Poln. Sobr. Soch.*, vol. 41, p. 53. [*Collected Works*, vol. 31, p. 69].

34. *ibid.*, pp. 20, 22. [*Collected Works*, vol. 31, pp. 38, 39].

35. *Izvestiya*, 2 August 1940.

36. BO, no. 75–6, pp. 1–2. [Writings 1938–39, p. 202].
37. ibid., no. 81, Jan. 1940, p. 2.
38. See Komsomolskaya Pravda, 24 August 1988; Khrushchev Remembers, London, 1971, p. 124.
39. Documents on German Foreign Policy, Series D. vol. 11, p. 1019.
40. Leon Trotsky, Oeuvres, vol. 22, Paris 1985, p. 38. [The reference is to an unpublished document, entitled 'Joseph Stalin, Hitler's New Friend', dated 22 September 1939 – T. 4631 in the Trotsky Archives].
41. See Mezhdunarodnaya zhizn, no. 9, 1989, pp. 102–4.
42. See BO, no. 82–3, p. 5; no 81, pp. 2–3; no. 79–80, p. 15; Trotsky, Oeuvres, vol 22, pp. 37–8. [Writings 1939–40, p. 141. The Oeuvres reference is to the same document as in note 40.]
43. BO no. 79–80, p. 16; no. 81, p. 10.
44. A. Rossi, Les Communistes français pendant la drôle de guerre, Paris, 1951, pp. 74–5, 123–4, 380.
45. BO, no. 81, p. 10.
46. K. Khachatov, 'Oba Khuzhe. Razmyshleniya v godovschiny ubiistva Trotskogo', Literaturnya gazeta, 22 August 1990, p. 13.
47. BO, no. 68–9, p. 13. [Their Morals ..., p. 29].
48. Trotsky, Stalinizm i Bolshevizm, London, 1988, p. 9. [Writings 1936–37, p. 420].
49. ibid., p. 13.
50. BO, no. 68–9, pp. 7–8, 18.
51. ibid., p. 9.
52. ibid., p. 10.
53. ibid., no. 82–3, p. 12; Trotsky, Oeuvres, vol. 23, Paris, 1986, p. 251. [The Oeuvres reference is to an unpublished writing, 'Notes on the USSR', tentatively dated March 1940, which is in the New York Library of Social History.]
54. BO, no. 84, pp. 11–18.
55. ibid., no. 87, August 1941, pp. 2–4.
56. ibid., no. 70, pp. 6–7; no. 74, p. 11; no. 75–6, p. 5; no. 82–3, p. 10.
57. ibid., no. 82–3, p. 7; no. 87, p. 15.
58. ibid., no. 82–3, p. 3. [Writings 1939–40, p. 164]; Trotsky, Oeuvres, vol. 22, p. 39. [The reference is to the unpublished article mentioned in note 40.]
59. BO, no. 81, p. 7. [Writings 1939–40, p. 124]. See also no. 84, p. 17.
60. ibid., no. 74, p. 13. [Writings 1938–39, p. 181].
61. Lenin, Poln. Sobr. Soch, vol. 45, p. 345. [Collected Works, vol. 36, p. 595].
62. Sovetskaya istoricheskaya entsiklopediya , Moscow, 1962, Vol. 2, pp. 599–600.

Part III

Approaches to Trotsky

9

Trotsky: October and its perspective[1]

V. P. BULDAKOV

Trotsky's well-known testament, written about six months before his assassination, concludes thus: 'whatever the circumstances of my death I shall die with unshaken faith in the communist future. This faith in man and in his future gives me even now such power of resistance as cannot be given by any religion'.[2] These words clarify much about Trotsky's personality and about the revolution he represented. They ring out like a condemnation of that epoch which reduced the humanistic ideal to deadly class intolerance, and readiness, in the name of 'love' for an abstract future humanity, to crush everything that actually exists. Trotsky was not at all a fanatic in the traditional, historical sense of the word. His *faith* was in those days called *science*. The contradiction between humanity and worship of progress is basic to Trotsky's personal drama, which expresses, in a way, the tragedy of the Russian Revolution as a whole. Few, alas, in present-day Soviet historiography, appreciate this.

More than five years of *perestroika* did not bring the public rehabilitation of Trotsky. This was not understood in the West. Robin Blackburn, for one, misrepresented the situation when, in the *Independent Magazine* (19 August 1990), he implied that Trotsky's works were being published uninterruptedly and interest in him was at a high level. Interest in Trotsky was actively hostile: the Lefts (the 'Democrats') proclaimed him Stalin's precursor, while the Rights (the 'Patriots') were disposed to see him as the central figure in a 'Zionist conspiracy' against Russia. Such were the grimaces of *perestroika* which, though intended to strengthen the socialist ideal, turned out to be hostile to that ideal. Under these conditions Trotsky still remained incomprehensible to the masses who, disappointed in their expectations of a trough filled with plenty called 'communism', had sunk into senseless defamation of the October Revolution.

The situation was made worse by the fact that in the forefront of the work undertaken to explain Trotsky stood persons thoroughly unqualified for the task. N. A. Vasetsky transformed himself from an 'exposer' of Trotskyism into an 'expert' on it, and colonel-general of philosophy D. A. Volkogonov revealed a unique capacity for writing about Stalin with his right hand and about Trotsky with his left. This general even publicly stated that, if Trotsky had come to power, he would have made the whole world a gulag.

It would not be an exaggeration to say that Soviet 'anti-Trotskyism' at the beginning of the 1990s was a complex product of the Stalin era. Against that background the few objective essays on Trotsky[2] that appeared were marked by extreme caution and reticence.

One can say that in the West, too, Trotsky had not been entirely fortunate. In the works written by Trotskyists[3] his personality was, as a rule, detached from its historical context, while in academic researches his views were presented as though identical with present-day Trotskyism.[4] Yet Trotsky expresses most completely, perhaps, the contradictoriness of the October phenomenon.

Trotsky was more than a natural product of the revolution. He was, in a way, a typical representative of that special marginal milieu known as Russia's radical intelligentsia 'outside of the order of estates' which by the beginning of the twentieth century included not only persons with the psychology of 'penitent noblemen' but also elements of bourgeois origin.[5] Trotsky severed early on his links with his own family. He was a 'marginal personality' also in the specifically ethno-psychological sense: a scion of the Jewish community, he openly despised this community for its small-town limitedness and petty-bourgeois way of life (in this respect he resembled Karl Marx).

The Russian intelligentsia strove to create for itself, on the basis of the most radical doctrines it could borrow, a special sub-culture of its own, a sort of antidote to what P. A. Kropotkin called 'a whole world of habits, customs, ways of thinking and moral cowardice'. In principle, given the conditions of an evolutionary development of society, this process might have culminated in the establishment of the complex of ideas typical of a law-governed society. But the intelligentsia milieu found itself in a socially stressed situation which was made worse, as V. I. Vernadsky noted, by its isolation from the directly productive forces of the country. Hence the intelligentsia's peculiar emotional state, as observed by M. Gorky, which led to 'the preaching of social fanaticism' and 'an extreme instability of democratic sentiments'.

Against this background Trotsky could be called a case of 'marginality squared'. He sometimes openly despised the mass of the intelligentsia for its extreme ambivalence, quoting N. K. Mikhailovsky's idea that the Russian *intelligent* was 'split in two' – 'humanism in thought, idleness in action'.[6] Social contempt, of course, gives force only to all-embracing negativism, and not to the creation of positive doctrines. The usual means whereby a revolutionary thinker is preserved from a destructive dose of scepticism is a primordial Protestant-religious sense of purpose. (Soviet philosophers have recently distinguished this in the early Marx and Engels.)[7] It was no accident that in Russia so many revolutionaries came from priestly families: when they 'repented' they usually returned to religion and a devout nationalism. Trotsky's position was more difficult, and it cannot be accidental that in 1938, in his article 'Their morals and ours', he spoke of himself as one 'who does not care to return to Moses, Christ or Mohammed'.

In principle, a 'marginal personality' is in every epoch destined for a tragic fate, as we see with Byron's Cain, William Faulkner's Joe Christmas, or Ivan

Karamazov. For the time being, the Russian revolutionary *intelligenty* were saved by faith. Trotsky, like the *raznochintsy* of the 1860s to 1890s, believed in the people. Subsequently, he had occasion more than once to change his social orientation.

Trotsky's first change of views was connected with his turn from the Narodniks to the Marxists. For the late 1890s in Russia this was altogether a very significant move, and Trotsky made it with particular passion. (His bitter attacks on the 'apostate' P. B. Struve are well known.) It seems that his conversion to Marxism did not rid Trotsky of his populistic ways (which marked him off from many spineless *intelligenty*), and these came to be combined with faith in the immutability of the laws of history. Hence his sense that he, personally, was at the cutting edge of social progress. Hence, too, his special fervour as a neophyte calling to the 'uninitiated'. But then, this is rather typical. There is an opinion that all revolutionary leaders have combined 'radical voluntarism and anthropological pessimism'[8] – they strive to do a favour by force to the 'undeveloped' mass of the people. Russia's history shows more than enough examples of that. Trotsky felt himself to be a 'citizen of the world' who was training 'provincials' to follow the road to universal progress.

Reference is made rather often to a mechanistic quality in Trotsky's thinking, but that is hardly correct. One has to remember that this was a characteristic of every determinist mentality in that period. And in the *intelligentsia* milieu, any nuances of personal opinion were considered an impermissible luxury. Trotsky, of course, took that into account.

Unquestionably, Trotsky remained within the framework of the political culture of the Second International. But that was true, until October, of the overwhelming majority of the Bolsheviks as well. Trotsky, however, was distinguished by a special sort of leftism. This is usually associated with the theory of 'permanent revolution', the source of which was belief that in the twentieth century a bourgeois revolution had become impossible, because the 'internationalisation' of capital endowed every revolutionary explosion with an international-proletarian character. There is, though, another point of view: namely, that what was distinctive of Trotsky was a Jacobin dichotomism in his thought, a conception of social consciousness as bipolar, counterpoising the proletariat to all the other classes.[9] Trotsky really did surrender himself to belief in the 'saving mission' of the international proletariat.

Can we make out, in this connection, a basic world-outlook to which Trotsky's thinking always returned after recurrent confusions? It would appear that we can, if we define his attitude to the ideas of freedom and culture, taking into account the fact that the erosion of these principles is fraught with great danger for the revolutionary and for the revolution as a whole.

Characteristic of Russian social thought, beginning in the nineteenth century, was a certain interpretation of the idea of the unity of all mankind. In Trotsky's opinion this tendency served no practical purpose. Following Chaadaev, he considered that Russian society did not produce ideas itself but merely borrowed them. As he saw it, even V. Solovev was, for this reason, unable to create a school of his own in Russia.[10] The achievements of Russian social thought might be admired, but it was impossible to be guided by them. Hence the revolutionary 'globalism' which Trotsky deliberately (and probably not without inner resistance) counterpoised to socio-cultural tradition.

At the same time, Trotsky was not at all a nihilist of the Bazarov type (a phenomenon he liked to recall). His intense attention to the culture of the past was due to a clear awareness that if the revolution was not made fast by a new socio-cultural stereotype it would be doomed to moral degeneration. Lenin solved this question simply. He divided the cultural heritage into 'democratic' and 'reactionary' elements and regarded it as necessary to take possession of the former alone. Bukharin showed himself to be a light-minded 'Proletkultist'. Trotsky was a different case. The problem of world revolution was for him a question of the globalising of culture.

Trotsky was, of course, against total destruction of the old 'bourgeois' culture, despite the fact that its 'maddened power' bore the guilt of unleashing the world war.[11] 'I don't believe the whole of our European culture is doomed to perdition, that Capital will destroy it with impunity,' he said, even after October.[12] It was from this standpoint that Trotsky also sought to evaluate literary life in Russia after the Civil War.

The outcome was original. It turned out that, while the revolution had overthrown the bourgeoisie, it definitely had not ousted that class from the cultural sphere. In the creative writing of his time, Trotsky distinguished an old 'non-October literature', a Soviet 'peasant-singing' literature and also 'bohemian – revolutionary' Futurism, which was a peculiar offshoot of the previous artistic heritage. 'Proletarian art' was going through a period of apprenticeship. It is likely that Trotsky made this evaluation according to the 'class' principle not without inner resistance. He undertook no apologia for 'proletarian art'. 'It is fundamentally incorrect to contrast bourgeois culture and bourgeois art with proletarian culture and proletarian art,' he declared firmly:

> The latter will never exist, because the proletarian regime is temporary and transient. The historic significance and the moral grandeur of the proletarian revolution consist in the fact that it is laying the foundations of a culture which is above classes and which will be the first culture that is truly human.[13]

At the same time, Trotsky resolutely refused to put the sign of equality between the 'class' content of literature and its aesthetic value. He considered that, where culture was concerned, the proletariat has to stand on the shoulders of its predecessors. Consequently, he called on the proletariat to show tolerance to its many 'fellow-travellers'.

Thus, with all his revolutionary impatience, his desire to urge progress forward, Trotsky recognised that the revolution was conceivable only as a protracted socio-cultural process of transformation. To what extent could the proletarian state intervene in this process? 'We must … take possession, politically, of the most important elements of the old culture, to such an extent, at least, as to be able to pave the way for a new culture', but this must be done with the greatest caution.[14] The task to be given priority was that of raising the people's cultural level. Hence his appeal to the youth and his hopes for 'mass culture'.[15]

There is a view that post-October writing about the revolution was wholly permeated with the theme of 'death-birth', consonant with Christian eschatology.[16] Trotsky realized this. 'In spite of occasional cruelty and the sanguinary relentlessness of its methods, the revolution is, before and above all, the awakening of humanity, its onward work, and is marked with a growing respect for the personal dignity of every individual, with an ever-increasing concern for those who are weak', he wrote in *Pravda*, 15 May 1923.

Thus, Trotsky's world-view, despite his ostentatious apologia for revolutionary coercion, was determined, nevertheless, by a general-humanist constant. His attitude to democracy confirms this.

In principle, Trotsky unquestionably gave preference to civil society over dictatorship. He thought highly of the 'innovatory experiments' made by those emigrants from Europe who were the first in the world to proclaim, on the soil of America, the inalienability of the rights of man and the citizen.[17] The revolutionary epoch itself made him a convinced anti-parliamentarian. As he saw it, representative democracy had become the principal brake on progress.[18] 'The most dangerous of the aberrations of the revolution arises when the mechanical accountant of democracy balances in one column yesterday, today and tomorrow and thereby impels the formal democrats to look for the head of the revolution where in reality is to be found its very heavy tail', he wrote later.[19]

In 1917, not accidentally, he changed from being the would-be writer of social-democracy into a thunderer against social-democratic conciliation with the bourgeoisie. It would have been hard to give a greater shock to the democrats of that time than the one Trotsky gave them. For example, in analysing his speech at the Democratic Conference, the right-wing socialist *Kievskaya Mysl*, the very paper in which Trotsky had regularly published his articles on literature and art for several years before the war, commented:

> Trotsky is not merely a talented orator. He is a great politician. Not a dilettante and not a politician by trade, but a politician from passion. Trotsky has a great deal of intelligence and of knowledge. He has travelled all over the world ... [He] understands everything but does not love much. To the people of today, with their dark, gloomy souls and real blood Trotsky is profoundly indifferent. The world with all its horrors and great tragedies appears in his imagination as a striking spectacle composed of absolutely antagonistic forces, in which he, Citizen Trotsky, has been chosen and prepared for the role of Lassalle.
>
> Trotsky has a cold intellect and a still colder heart, but he is endowed with iron pertinacity. All his thoughts and all his works are steeped in that pertinacity. It gives his thrusts enormous striking force.[20]

This description does not lack shrewdness. At the same time it shows how furious 'class' passion antagonised the Democrats.

It is appropriate to point out also that the elemental force of revolution itself tended to oppose parliamentarism. This was Trotsky's real source of inspiration.[21] To a considerable extent it was what caused him to take up his 'special position' at the time of Brest-Litovsk. It impelled him afterwards to talk like a Narodnik: 'We shall create one brotherly state on the land which nature gave us. This land we shall plough and cultivate on associative principles, turn into one blossoming garden, where our children, grandchildren and great-grandchildren will live as in a paradise', he said in April 1918.[22] One may suppose that this was not just a revolutionary prophecy intended to correspond with the chiliastic hopes of the masses, but Trotsky's own conception, at that time, of what was to be Russia's future. Trotsky was, in those days, manifestly against statism.

A revolutionary upsurge grips its leaders but also engenders the illusion that they are omnipotent. Time went by and People's Commissar for Military Affairs Trotsky, who had formerly been a very civilian sort of person, began to assert that the militarisation of social life provided the best road for educating the man of 'the new culture'.[23] This idea corresponded to the whole psycho-mentality of War Communism.

However, Trotsky himself became drawn into the process which eventually established the 'command' style in the economy. On 11 February 1920 he telegraphed from Samara to Lenin and Rykov:

> The Economic Council [Sovnarkhoz] must be given, as a special task, the duty to increase, at any cost, the production of paper. In the absence of a gigantic expansion in agitational work we cannot talk seriously about labour armies and labour service. The reduction in the amount of agitational literature which has taken place, the closing down of local newspapers and so on are radically subverting the work of economic recovery. I propose that a meeting be held to draft emergency measures for dealing with this problem.[24]

Such a statement, analysed in the context of 'war communism', is quite understandable. But it shows how the 'war communist' mentality departed from 'normal' common sense and strengthened the tendency towards 'Partocracy' at the expense of purely intellectual considerations.

To Trotsky's credit it must be said that he realised the need to return to common sense. Evidence of this is given by his famous letter of February 1920 to the Central Committee about replacing the requisitioning of grain by a tax in kind.[25] This was not yet, of course, the New Economic Policy, but Trotsky was more prepared for its introduction than were other Bolshevik leaders.

In analysing the movement of Trotsky's doctrinal aims we have to note that during the Civil War years he made a final break with the usual linear conception of the development of the revolutionary process. The idea of permanent revolution was transformed into his revolutionary-geopolitical vision of the contemporary world. As early as 1 May 1919 Trotsky wrote in *Pravda* about a possible transfer of the centre of the Third International to Berlin, Paris or London. In

August 1919 there followed a fresh proposal – Trotsky's famous note about a plan to strike at world imperialism through the East.[26] This is sometimes seen as part of the utopian notion of world revolution. If, however, we consider that during the Civil War Great Britain was, above all, worried about retaining its colonial rule over India, and that, technically, it was quite realistic to organise a cavalry breakthrough into India, Trotsky's proposal appears reasonable enough. In this connection it should be mentioned that in 1923 the outstanding Tatar revolutionary M. Sultan-Galiev[27] proposed, in the event of a weakening of the European impulse of the world revolution, the adoption of a multiform plan for activating the revolutionary process in the East.[28] The idea of revolutionary geopolitics (active utilisation of the Chinese and Indian factors if Soviet Russia found itself isolated) was put forward by Lenin, too, towards the end of his life.[29] Trotsky's idea thus amounted to what can be called a systematic analysis of revolutionary developments on the world scale. This was what to a considerable degree defined the distinctiveness of his position in the 1920s.

With historical hindsight it is clear that the introduction of the New Economic Policy (NEP), had to be accompanied by the creation of a two-bloc system of representation. Once the market mechanism of economic collaboration had been stabilised, the workers and peasants might be able to come to an agreement between them. What actually happened was the opposite. The Bolshevik Party consolidated itself after staging a trial of its most dangerous opponents, the Socialist Revolutionaries (SRs), banishing unwelcome representatives of Russia's 'bourgeois' science and culture, and waging a campaign without precedent against the Orthodox clergy. A great variety of factors brought about this turn into a dead-end: the extreme situation caused by the famine of 1921, the psychological inability of the victors to surrender even part of their power, and their desperate hopes for world revolution, which grew especially strong in 1923. The New Economic Policy was doomed, for it proceeded under the sign of the strengthening Party bureaucracy. Trotsky found himself placed in a rather difficult position.

By a cruel irony of fate, Trotsky had, on the one hand, to restrain those very War Communist moods which had developed not without help from him, and, on the other, to keep to the generally accepted rhetoric, as this was now a ritual element in the functioning of Partocratic rule. In these circumstances, any revolutionary thinker would have suffered a feeling of disorientation, and, undoubtedly, Trotsky did not escape such a crisis.

What determined the development of Trotsky's thinking during the transition to NEP? What doctrinal imperative predominated with him?

There is a view that Trotsky, having mastered well the lessons of the great French Revolution, directed his efforts mainly to preventing a 'Thermidor'.[30] Trotsky himself mentioned that, before the introduction of NEP and in its first phase, he had conversations about this subject with Lenin.[31] But at that time the danger of a Thermidor was traditionally linked with the numerical preponderance of the peasantry. More sustainable appears the view that Trotsky concerned himself seriously with the problem of Thermidor only after 1926, in connection with the struggle against Stalin and his circle.[32] (It was no accident that Trotsky distinguished between the 'Kronstadt' Thermidor and the 'Stalinist' Thermidor, even while indicating that there was a certain continuity between them.[33]) It would appear that the fight against bureaucratism was of secondary importance for Trotsky during the initial phase of NEP. He treated economic questions as the matter of first importance at this time.

He continued, of course, to see himself principally as the theoretician of world revolution. But here he lagged behind the real process of history. After the First World War, with the establishment of universal suffrage in the European countries, the introduction of the eight-hour day and a series of social programmes, evolutionary tendencies necessarily prevailed. Trotsky clearly underestimated this factor, being influenced, apparently, by his memories of the failure of the reforming efforts of Russia's Provisional Government.[34]

But now the integrity of his outlook, so necessary for overcoming psychological crisis, was determined by something different – by statism and technocratism. Documents recently published enable us to conclude that Trotsky was at variance in principle with Stalin and his circle of apparatus men.[35] In particular, Trotsky's letter of 23 October 1923 to the Central Committee and the Central Control Commission of the Party, and his polemic with Stalin at the joint plenum of these bodies on 26 October, leave no doubt that Trotsky, in promoting his idea of transferring the centre of gravity of state activity to the Supreme Economic Council and Gosplan, was essentially proposing to 'depoliticise' the work of administration. Stalin saw in this a threat to domination by the Party apparatus, and defended its existence with doctrinal demagogy.

Trotsky unquestionably tried, from the very beginning of NEP, to construct an optimal model for the administration of the economy which took account of Russia's place in the world economy. His starting point was the idea of retaining the state sector of the economy, identified as the basic element of socialism. It might seem that this fully conformed to the general Party conceptions of that time. But Trotsky's approach to economic questions was much broader. At the basis of his views lay the idea of the international division of labour, which was something new against the background of War Communist autarky. Trotsky demanded, in this regard, that 'the flower of the young generation' be given the task of undertaking 'independent theoretical work on questions of the revolution, in close connection with all our internal and international activity'.[36] Did this mean that he had been transformed from the ideologist of world revolution into a Russian economic theorist?

R. B. Day, who on the whole supports that view, at the same time directs attention to the point that in 1924–6 Trotsky, unlike Zinoview and Kamenev, did not object to Stalin's idea of building socialism 'in one country taken separately', and only later worked out his own original view of socialism in one country which would not be isolated from the world economy, a notion which lay midway between the lines of Bukharin and Stalin.[37] Day overestimates, of course, Stalin's capacity for independent thinking in general and fails to allow for the immanent instability and scholasticism of Bukharin, but at the same time he evaluates correctly the well-thought-out and original views of Trotsky on economic questions. It is necessary, though, to take more fully into account the factor of ideological reflection to which he was undoubtedly susceptible in 1924–6. Also, being willy-nilly an 'oppositionist', Trotsky was placed in a false position. He had, in any case, to act within the framework of the established mentality – to uphold the unity of the Party's leadership, while knowing that it had fallen into flagrantly unworthy hands; to reject the accusation of faction forming, while knowing that, in fact, his views were incompatible with the attitudes prevailing in the Party; and to insist on command methods of administration in both inner political life and the Comintern, while knowing that these ought to be not perfected but restricted. Contrary to the habit of a revolutionary tribune, Trotsky was obliged to put forward his views with extreme caution, appearing as merely an 'interpreter' of the heritage of Lenin. In short, Trotsky expressed his views in the 1920s in consciously inadequate form.

In analysing the nature of 'Trotskyism' it is appropriate to begin with Marx himself. From the outset Marxism was not free from ambivalence. As a politician, Marx stressed the class dividedness of social being under capitalism. As a theoretician, he certainly appreciated the interconnectedness of the socio-economic organism created by the bourgeoisie. During most of his life Lenin treated as absolute the first-mentioned factor in Marx's teaching rather than the other, and when he came to power he did not succeed fully in looking in a new way at the working of the economic mechanism.

Trotsky, unlike Lenin, adopted from the outset Lassalle's conception of the organic connection between all economic phenomena: his hatred for whatever was 'bourgeois' had more of an emotional basis. When abroad he revealed the essence of his conception of Marxism. 'Marxism takes its point of departure from world economy, not as a sum of national parts', he wrote, 'but as a mighty and independent reality which had been created by the international division of labour and the world market and which in our epoch imperiously dominates the national markets.'[38] Beyond question, such an approach differs markedly from Lenin's views regarding the 'insolubility' of the contradictions of imperialism.

The foundation of Trotsky's view was his conviction that 'the USSR's economy can develop only as a part of world economy', which presupposes strengthening its links with the world market and its dependence thereon.[39] He considered that to take account of this objective factor could be useful in the interests both of economic rebirth and of building socialism. Let us recall that at this time Stalin was publicly declaring that dependence made the country 'more vulnerable … to the blows of our enemies'.[40]

Nowadays, Trotsky's proposition seems an elementary truth for the practitioners of 'catching-up-with' and 'surpassing' development. In the 1920s, however, quite different attitudes prevailed among the Bolsheviks. Trotsky's proposition could be regarded by them as a case of ideological disarmament in the face of 'world imperialism'. And, in that connection, it seems almost incredible that Trotsky, whose name was associated with the idea of world revolution propagated by force, nevertheless had the courage to put forward such an idea. The development of the worldwide revolutionary process was now seen by him not only in the context of the collapse of capitalism, but also as a guarantee of peaceful socialist construction in the USSR.[41] Did this signify recognition of the prospect of 'peaceful coexistence'? Hardly. But it *was* a repudiation of revolutionary adventurism.

Trotsky's idea, which he formulated most clearly at the end of 1926, was based on the assumption that there would be temporary periods of stabilisation in the world economy.[42] Given that it was difficult to establish the rhythm of a capitalist economy, he proposed that three possible variants be taken into consideration: '(a) a new upsurge of Europe on capitalist foundations, (b) economic decline of Europe, and (c) continuation of the present situation, with some vacillations'. In so far as NEP allowed for a priority growth of agricultural production as compared with industrial, there would, in the first case, be the possibility of increased exports of agricultural produce, which would be favourable for economic development generally. But, in his view, the advantages of such a path would be more than dubious for proletarian power. A quickening of the capitalist elements would inevitably ensue, and that would gradually stifle the state sector of industry. 'We should have fallen from our work of socialist construction into a hopeless situation',[43] Trotsky concluded. This was a completely logical conclusion, if one starts from the identification of socialist development with industrialism, which in those days was regarded as axiomatic. In the event of a downturn in Europe's economic development, Trotsky considered, a different situation would arise: exporting to Europe would become more difficult, and then it would be necessary to reduce imports of equipment. The tempo for building socialism would inevitably slow down. Even if the USSR strengthened its positions in Europe, it would find itself in an extremely unfavourable situation in relation to American capitalism. In any case, it would be ridiculous to think of building socialism rapidly in circumstances of a general 'decay' of the world economy. Trotsky categorically rejected the idea that Russia could obtain temporary advantages by taking a line of indifference to the fate of socialism on the world scale.

There remained the variant of 'an unstable equilibrium of forces': 'capitalist Europe neither declines nor advances; the proletariat is strong enough to prevent the bourgeoisie from crushing the Soviet republic, but not strong enough to take power'. This, the actually existing situation, Trotsky considered, was also the most favourable. There was a chance for the USSR to strengthen its position in the economy, and, at the same time, the European proletariat might become more active.

In any case, Trotsky placed his hopes on the revolution, saying that 'the capitalist regime has exhausted itself on the world scale, because there is no way out of its contradictions'.[44] However, we should note some of the characteristic reservations he made. Thus, in 1924 he frankly acknowledged that the Bolsheviks miscalculated the tempo of the world revolution,[45] and still earlier, in 1922, he expressed ideas about the Left Bloc.[46] (Later he was to show, on this basis, the stupidity of Stalin's attitude to European social-democracy as a variety of fascism.)[47] We see, then, that fully realistic surmises about the possibility of combining democracy with socialism in Europe occurred to Trotsky quite early. But he made no attempt at all to develop them with his characteristic vigour. Apparently, it was difficult enough to work out the optimum relation between the introduction of the NEP in Russia and support for an independent communist movement throughout the world. However that may be, it is important to try and answer this question: were Trotsky's views formed into a system of coherent ideas about the new stage in the revolutionary process, or was he, in the main, subject to that condition of general ambivalence which was then corroding Bolshevism?

On this matter, let us turn our attention to the weakest elements in Trotsky's thinking. What seem shakiest are his statements to the effect that the revolution had not succeeded in Western Europe owing to the subjective mistakes and weaknesses of the Communist Parties. Thus, in 1924 he said that in Italy in 1919 there had been a 'sabotaged' revolution, and in Germany in 1923 the Communists had 'permitted it to slip by'.[48] These views cannot be called innovatory, given that individual Bolsheviks had already recognised that the 'commanding' style of the Comintern leadership had brought about a narrowing of the mass basis of the proletarian movement.[49]

It was only in 1926 that Trotsky's position on questions of the international communist movement became sufficiently precise. But this was not a personal contribution on his part. At that time an anti-Stalin bloc was formed, which included some influential Bolsheviks. This opposition declared, as against Stalin's line of building socialism 'in one country taken separately', that 'socialism will be victorious in our country in inseparable connection with the revolutions of the European and world proletariat and with the struggle of the East against the imperialist yoke'.[50] Thereafter, Trotsky too was to emphasise this point. He, however, emphasised mostly that 'the principal reason for the survival of the capitalist regime is the incongruity between the objectively revolutionary situation and the insufficient strength of the Communist Parties'.[51]

In making such statements Trotsky was, of course, carrying out the purely tactical task of discrediting the Stalinist leadership. In any case, in September 1926, in his theses for the 14th Conference of the Party he ventured to take a very crucial step. He proposed a change in the tactical line of the international working-class movement which greatly resembled his earlier efforts to unite the forces of the RSDLP. This was, though, no mere reproduction of an old schema. He urged that the entire communist movement be reconstructed so as to take account of the peculiarities of the movement in particular countries and the position of the USSR amid capitalist encirclement. The Communist Parties of Europe were, in fact, recommended to turn themselves into independent factors in the internal political life of their respective countries.

It is important to note that Trotsky proposed to deal with internal economic difficulties in a way that took account of the world conjuncture. Understanding that the root of Russia's economic disorders was conditioned by the unbalanced development of the industrial and agricultural sectors of the country's economy, he raised the question of not only restoring the 'bond' between the proletariat and the peasantry, but also achieving a balanced relation between town and country, on a market basis, which would allow for price formation in international economic relations.[52] Day considers that he even gave an original description of socialism in terms of international trade. Trotsky's view was that the proletariat's victory on the world scale would have to bring about a rearrangement of the actual foundations of the economy, in accordance with a more productive international division of labour, which would also provide the true basis for socialism.[53]

Like Lenin, Trotsky originally hoped that foreigners would take up concessions and grant credits.[54] After the 'concessions' policy had failed, he laid stress on technological rearmament of the USSR's economy, using internal reserves. He thought that priority should be given to the growth of heavy industry, though he was certainly not a 'super-industrialiser', as Stalin and Bukharin later tried to make out. In fact, his position was highly flexible. Trotsky proceeded from the notion that 'the overall material base of industrialisation gives a correct policy and could be considerably increased, but on the *given* material base, industrialisation should not be pushed ahead with the help of unreal credits'.[55] He distinguished sharply between growth on the old technical basis, which was fraught with danger of crisis, and a salutary acceleration of the economy on the basis of a renewal of fundamental resources. At the same time he appreciated that this approach required rejection of administrative methods and development of producers' democracy,[56] an increase in the productivity of labour, electrification and standardisation of production. He raised the question of the connection between quality in production and the general cultural level and well-being of the working class.[57]

Trotsky also advocated the achievement of a balance between wholesale and retail prices for industrial and agricultural products, and the development of an infrastructure for the economy. At the same time he warned against the danger of unleashing market spontaneity and called for a well-thought-out strategy of commercial balance.[58] The declarations of Bukharin and Stalin concerning the 'adequacy' of the tempo of industrial development met with sharp criticism from him.[59] All his proposals and warnings were absolutely reasonable. Some recent researches[60] enable one to affirm that, on each occasion, Trotsky advocated the most rational decisions.

In evaluating Trotsky's views on the organisation of the economy we must mention that they fully conformed to the general development of administrative thought in the USSR in the 1920s. We have, however, to remember that, despite recognition by leading specialists, particularly A. A. Bogdanov, of the historical limitedness of the authoritarian type of administration,[61] in those days everyone still idealised the military principles of organisation.[62] The prevailing idea was that 'the twentieth century will be the century of rational organisation',[63] while even some Party leaders were inclined to believe that it would assume an increasingly machine-like, faceless character.[64] In any case, the principle of state planning was treated as absolute, and the importance of natural market relations was underestimated. In practice all writers most likely took as their point of departure the experience of War Communism, as if they had decided that their aim was to construct and introduce an ideal administrative model, without giving any special thought to human individuality. Even such outstanding specialists as A. V. Chayanov and N. D. Kondratev were statists, and everyone saw leadership by the Party as the force which could best embody their ideas. In an atmosphere like that, War Communism was able to get its second wind.

Trotsky stood out against this background not only by the breadth of his views. Unlike the specialists in administrative theory, as early as 1926 he perceived that the Partocracy might turn their ideas into something absolutely opposite, that the mobilisation model of economic development might in their hands become an instrument for ruining the economy.

In the past, Trotsky had believed in the possibility that the idea of world revolution might be realised during his lifetime. That belief determined the social code of his conduct. In the course of his political journey, the symbols of that belief changed – the people, the proletariat, technocratic administration, the man of the new culture – but what stayed unchanged was his conviction that his personal aim could be translated into attainable ideals for the future.

Trotsky's powerful instinct for life enabled him to escape for almost a decade from the Comintern terrorists. Only, it would seem, the incredible exaltation of Stalin, the failure of the revolution in Spain and the approach of a new world war which held no promise of world revolution brought about a weakening of that instinct. Reality fitted less and less into the all-embracing formula: 'history means the class struggle'. In the last years of his life Trotsky appears as a man oppressed by the general lassitude of democracy, which was incapable of resisting fascism. He probably felt even more keenly that he was a general without an army. It was under the influence of such moods that he wrote his 'Testament'. It would seem that it was not illness but the intransigence of a revolutionary that made him write those words about suicide. His former heightened sense of danger now began, from a sense of futility, to weaken, and this eventually eased the task of Ramón Mercader. Trotsky's departure into physical non-existence expressed the fading of the spirit of the Russian Revolution, for the words 'Great October' had already become no more than an incantation by the 'priests of the Marxist parish' and an object for purely ritual worship by the masses.

Today, however, it is clear that Trotsky's basic ideas were merely ahead of his time. 'We considered and we still consider', he wrote in March 1927, 'that the United States of Europe and our Soviet Union will join together in one economic whole. We said ... the Soviet Union was a gigantic bridge between a socialist federation of Europe and a federation of Asia ... An interchange of values ... is a necessary condition of economic progress.'[65] These words epitomise the humanistic spirit of October and its true perspectives.

Notes

1. A few minor editorial cuts have been made, mainly through reducing the length of some quotations. In Buldakov's typescript Trotsky's 'Testament' is more fully quoted in his first few paragraphs. It can be read in full in Sarah Lovell, ed., *Leon Trotsky Speaks*, New York, 1972, pp. 311–13, and elsewhere. The passage quoted below was added to the main document (dated 27 February 1940) on 3 March.

2. V. I. Startsev, *L. D. Trotskii (stranitsy politicheskoi biografii)*, Moscow, 1989; S. V. Tyutyukin, *Lev Trotskii: put k Oktyabryu, Istoriki otvechayut na voprosy*, vol. 2, Moscow, 1990. For a bibliography of Soviet writings on Trotsky, see *Sovetskaya bibliografiya*, no. 1, 1990, pp. 78–92.

3. It appears that the best of them are the three volumes by I. Deutscher – *The Prophet Armed*, 1954; *The Prophet Unarmed*, 1959; and *The Prophet Outcast*, 1963 (London and New York) – and the recent book by P. Broué, *Trotsky*, Paris, 1988.

4. This is the case, in particular, with one of the recent monographs: P. Beilharz, *Trotsky, Trotskyism and the Transition to Socialism*, London and Sydney, 1987.

5. Trotsky has left an extremely acute description of this phenomenon. See his *Sochineniya*, vol. 20, Moscow and Leningrad, 1926, pp. 332–41. ['Concerning the intelligentsia', *Partisan Review*, fall 1968].

6. Trotsky, *Sochineniya*, vol. 20, p. 59. [Trotsky's 1902 essay on G. I. Uspensky]. One of his early pseudonyms is significant: 'Antid Oto', i.e. the antidote.

7. See K. M. Kantor, 'Dva proekta vsemirnoi istorii', *Voprosy filosofii*, no. 2, 1990, pp. 76–86.

8. F. Fehér, 'The Dictatorship over needs', in *Telos*, spring 1978, no. 35, p. 34.

9. See Beillary, *Trotsky*, pp. 11–12, 31.

10. Trotsky, *Sochineniya*, vol. 20, pp. 336–7.

11. Trotsky, *Literatur i revolyutsiya*, Moscow, 1924, p. 144. [*Literature and Revolution*, Ann Arbor, 1960 p. 190].

12. Trotsky, *Sochineniya*, vol. 17, part I, Moscow and Leningrad, 1926, p. 197. [*A Paradise in this World*, Colombo, 1957, p. 29].

13. Trotsky, *Literatura i revolyutsiya*, pp. 7, 10, 11. [*Literature and Revolution*, p. 14].

14. *ibid.*, pp. 145, 167. [*Literature and Revolution*, pp. 191, 219].

15. Trotsky, *Pokolenie Oktyabrya*, Petrograd and Moscow, 1924, pp. 133–7, 161.

16. R. Freeborn, *The Russian Revolutionary Novel*, Cambridge, 1982, pp. 70, 257.

17. Trotsky, *Sochineniya*, vol. 20, p. 371. [An article entitled 'Tempting parallels', for *Kievskaya Mysl*, 1913].

18. *Kommunisticheskaya Oppositsiya v SSR 1923–1927* [hereafter *KO*], vol. 1, p. 131. 'Our differences', Nov. 1924, section 'The combined type of state', in *The Challenge of the Left Opposition, 1923–1925*, pp. 284–92].

19. Trotsky, *Fevralskaya revolyutsiya*, Berlin, 1931, p. 478. [*History of the Russian Revolution*, vol. 1, 1932, p. 445].

20. *Kievskaya Mysl*, 27 September 1917.

21. When analysing revolutions one must never underestimate the influence exercised on the leaders by the masses. Antonio Gramsci noted that 'the gigantic strength of the masses ... exerts an almost unbearable pressure

on the isolated individual, demanding from him the greatest possible output of volitional energy' (Gramsci, *Izb. proizv* [*Selected Works*], in 3 volumes, Moscow, 1957, vol. 2, p. 200).

22. Trotsky, *Sochineniya*, vol. 17, part I, p. 187. [*A Paradise in This World*, p. 19].

23. Trotsky, *Kak vooruzhalas revolyutsiya*, vol. 2, part 1, Moscow 1923, p. 127. The actual expression does not appear at the reference given. What Trotsky says is: 'What does militarising mean? It means inculcating the sense of responsibility and, therefore, forming the best type of cultured person.' *How the Revolution Armed*, vol. 2, 1979, p. 182.

24. Trotsky, *Sochineniya*, vol. 15, p. 518.

25. Trotsky, *Moya Zhizn: Opyt avtobiografii*, Berlin, 1930, vol. 2, pp. 198–9. [*My Life*, New York, 1930, pp. 463–4. However, see on this matter John Channon's article 'Trotsky, the peasants and economic policy', in *Economy and Society*, vol. 14, no. 4, Nov. 1985].

26. *The Trotsky Papers*, vol. 2, pp. 620–6.

27. See A. Bennigsen, and Ch. Lemercier-Quelquejay *Sultan-Galiev le père de la révolution tiers-mondiste*, Paris, 1986.

28. See *Izvestiya TsKKPSS*, no. 10, 1990, pp. 79–82.

29. Lenin, *PSS*, [Collected Works] vol. 45, p. 404.

30. See I. Deutscher, *Marxism, Wars and Revolution: Essays from four decades*, London, 1984, pp. 34–45, 233–4.

31. *KO*, vol. 4, p. 14. ['Thermidor', summer 1927, in *The Challenge ...1926–1927*, pp. 258–9].

32. B. Knei-Paz, *The Social and Political Thought of Leon Trotsky*, Oxford, 1979, p. 394.

33. *KO*, vol. 4, p. 46. ['Reply to Maniusky' and 'Kronstadt', both dated 3 August 1927. Neither of these is in *The Challenge ...*].

34. He made a typical statement to this effect in 1922. See Trotsky, *Osnovnye voprosy revolyutsii*, Moscow and Petrograd, 1923, p. 386.

35. See *Izvestiya TsKKPSS*, No. 10, 1990, pp. 167–87.

36. Trotsky, *Osnovnye voprosy revolyutsii*, p. 9.

37. R. Day, *Leon Trotsky and the Politics of Economic Isolation*, Cambridge, 1973, pp. 3, 6, 150.

38. *Byulleten oppozitsii*, no. 12–13, 1930, p. 31. [Introduction to the German edition of *The Permanent Revolution*, London, 1962, p. 22].

39. *KO*, vol. 2, pp. 124, 204, 239. [Draft resolution on economic questions for the 15th Party Conference, November 1926: 'Can we achieve economic independence?', 19–27 March 1927; 'About our independence of the world market', 15 April 1927].

40. *XIV sezd Kommunisticheskoi Partii (bolshevikov). Stenograficheskii otchet*, Moscow and Leningrad, 1926, p. 29. [Stalin, *Works*, vol 7, 1954, p. 308].

41. *KO*, vol. 2, p. 18. [*The Challenge ...*, p. 84].

42. See *Planovoe Khozyastvo*, no. 6, 1925, p. 176, and no. 1, 1926, pp. 194–6.

43. *KO*, vol. 2, p. 143. ['The theory of socialism in one country on its own', 12 December 1926].

44. *ibid.*, p. 146.

45. Trotsky, *Zapad i Vostok. Voprosy mirovoy politiki i mirovoy revolyutsii*, Moscow, 1924, p. 25. ['On the paths of the European revolution'. He says that they erred in expecting 'a rapid and victorious development of the European revolution' because they 'understimated the importance of the revolutionary party'].

46. *ibid.* pp. 78, 142–4. [Introduction to *The First Five Years of the Communist International*, 1973 edition, p. 12: article of 2 March 1922 on the united front; speech to the 8 June 1922 Plenum of the ECCI; speech to activists of the Moscow Party organisation, 20 October 1922; excerpt from 'On the "contradictions" of Soviet policy', 3 November 1922. The last-named article appeared in English in the *Communist Review*, December 1922].

47. *Byulleten opozitsii*, no. 10, 1930, p. 4; no. 11, pp. 14–15; no. 17–18, p. 5 [*Writings*, 1930, p. 140].

48. Trotsky, *Zapad i Vostok*, pp. 12, 67, 128–9, 133. ['On the paths of the European revolution': Introduction to *The First Five Years ...*, p. 2; 'Through what stage are we passing?' *Fourth International*, vol. 1, no. 2, summer 1964, p. 74].

49. *KO*, vol. 1, pp. 95–6, 143–8. [Letter of S. Medvedev to a Baku comrade, January 1924; Radek, 'Draft theses on Comintern policy', August 1925].

50. *KO*, vol. 2, p. 19. [*The Challenge ...*, p. 86].

51. *ibid.*, p. 54. [Replies to questions from B. Nikitin, 5 September 1926].

52. Day, *Leon Trotsky*, p. 147.

53. *ibid.*, p. 170.

54. *Pravda*, 29 May 1925.

55. *Byulleten oppozitsii*, no. 10, 1930, p. 16. [*Writings 1929*, pp. 401–2].

56. *Izvestiya*, 2 June 1925.

57. Trotsky, *Kachestvo produktsii i sotsialisticheskoe khozyaistvo*, Moscow and Leningrad, 1925.

58. *KO*, vol. 1, pp. 24, 38, 43, 159, 218, 226; vol. 2, pp. 14, 72–3, 113 ['On the question of credits for fixed capital', 12 February 1923; theses on industry, section 3, 6 March 1923; ditto, section 6; theses, December 1925; correction to Rykov's resolution on the economic situation in the USSR, 12 April 1926; the law of socialist accumulation, 2 May 1926].

59. *KO*, vol. 2, p. 60. [The development of industry, 7 September 1926]. See also *Byulleten oppozitsii* no. 7, 1929, p. 3; no. 10, 1930, p. 3. [*Writings 1929*, p. 362; *Writings 1930*, p. 138].

60. Yu. P. Bokarev, *Sotsialisticheskaya promyshlennost i melkoe krestyanskoe khozyaistvo v SSSR v 20-e gody*, Moscow, 1989; A. G. Dongarov, *Inostrannyi kapital v Rossii i SSSR*, Moscow, 1990.

61. A. A. Bogdanov, *Ocherki vseobshchey organizatsionnoi nauki*, Samara, 1921, pp. 94–5.

62. L. Zhdanov, *Pyat printsipov upravleniya*, Taganrog, 1992, p. 31; V. V. Dobrynin, *Osnovy nauchnogo upravleniya predpriyatiyami i uchrezhdeniyami*, Leningrad, 1926, p. 167; I. N. Butakov, *Organizatsiya promyshlennykh predpriyatii kak nauka i iskusstvo*, Tomsk, 1926, p. 2.

63. R. S. Maizels, *Upravlenie i organizatsiya uchrezhdenii*, Moscow and Leningrad, 1926, p. 7.

64. E. F. Rozmirovich, *NOT, RKI i Partiya*, Moscow, 1926, pp. 204–7.

65. *KO*, vol. 2, pp. 204–5. ['Can we attain economic independence?', 19–27 March 1927].

10

Between Hegel and Habermas: the political theory of Leon Trotsky

RICHARD DAY

Fifty years after the death of Leon Trotsky is an appropriate time to suggest general conclusions concerning his place in history. Judgements of this kind can be facilitated by situating a thinker within the tradition of which he is a part. I shall attempt to do this by relating Trotsky to his predecessors (Hegel, Marx and Engels), to his most important contemporaries (Lenin, Bukharin and Stalin), and also to a modern social theorist (Jürgen Habermas), whose work may help to clarify Trotsky's accomplishments as well as some of his limitations. My approach will be to begin with Hegel and Marx, concentrating upon themes to which I shall return in my discussion of Trotsky. These include (1) the role of consciousness in making history; (2) the institutional relations between political and economic life; and (3) the tension between Hegel and Marx concerning the claims of practical and technical reason. By selecting these three themes, I hope to demonstrate what I take to be Trotsky's most unique contribution as a theorist of socialist transition: namely, his attempt to reconcile Hegel and Marx by emphasising the political dimension of economic planning. In my conclusion, I shall consider why Habermas believes such a reconciliation cannot be fully accomplished.

Hegel, Marx and Engels

Hegelian philosophy is committed to the view that human beings are destined to create their own destiny. In his *Phenomenology of Spirit*, Hegel interpreted the history of culture as the coming-to-be of conscious self-determination. The *Phenomenology* treated consciousness as subjective spirit; the *Philosophy of Right* turned to objective spirit, or consciousness going out of itself to create its own world in laws and social institutions. Hegel began with property as the initial determination of the will. By embodying his will in property, a person exists as reason and at the same time becomes his own object.[1] But this initial identity of subject and object also implies being for another. Thus property issues in contract and mediation into a common will through mutual recognition between property owners.[2] When the right to property is subsequently exposed to wrong, Hegel contends that the abstract rights of property owners presuppose a higher universal in the state and the laws. Our most fundamental claims upon the material world turn out to be subjective claims upon other people. Property is a social relation and is inconceivable without a state. Because of its logical priority, it is the idea of the state which determines itself in the production and exchange relations of civil society.

Hegel regarded civil society as the system of needs, which is mediated unconsciously through division of labour and the market. But the division of labour also creates corporate bodies, which consciously seek recognition of particular needs and interests. The contradictory claims of corporations presuppose determination of their rights. If the laws of the state are to uphold subjective freedom, corporate bodies must regard the laws as their own self-determination. Freedom is self-determination of necessity. The universality of the laws requires mutual interpenetration of the state and civil society. The presence of the political state in the corporations is signified through selection of their officers by a combination of election and appointment; conversely, the corporations establish themselves in the state through appointing deputies to the legislature. The role of deputies is to ensure that 'the state enters into the subjective consciousness of the people and … the people begins to participate in the state'.[3] As determinations of thought, the laws are universal: the ethical purpose which they articulate can enter simultaneously into the consciousness of all the particulars of civil society.[4]

The Hegelian state was the concrete universal of ethical life. The agency responsible for mediating between particulars and the universal was the civil service, or the universal class. Should the universal class attempt to set its own interests before the needs of the community, Hegel believed the rightful authority vested in corporations would constitute an institutional barrier to 'subjective caprice'.[5] Corporations completed 'from below' the system of state control from above; they would prevent the civil service from assuming the 'isolated position of an aristocracy and using its education and skill as a means to arbitrary tyranny'.[6] Hegel claimed that individuals and corporate bodies 'have duties to the state in proportion as they have rights against it'.[7] The highest labour of citizens was to create laws and institutions, which, as expressions of social consciousness, also determined the consciousness of citizens. The dialectical movement was a circle of necessity, wherein universal truth became practical truth in the rightful consciousness of the people. Theory and practice were reconciled in the identity of subject and object. In subjectively authoring the laws, the people had their own consciousness as their object.

Karl Marx's earliest response to Hegel's *Philosophy of Right* enunciated a theme that would prevail in all of his subsequent writings: 'the political constitution is the constitution of private property'.[8] Hegel argued that the idea of the state creates civil society; Marx replied that civil society creates the state. Because both are grounded in private property, the state loses its claim to universality by excluding the propertyless from political life. Marx considered the Hegelian state to be a false universal, in which the civil service was one particular interest among many. It represented a 'hierarchy of knowledge'; but rather than expressing the spirit of the community, bureaucrats demanded deference and 'dumb obedience'. The truth of the political state was that every bureaucrat used it for purposes of self-promotion.[9]

In *The German Ideology*, Marx and Engels translated Hegel's philosophy of consciousness into an objective history of human coming-to-be. What men are at any particular time, they declared, is historically determined not by what they think but by '*what* they produce and ... *how* they produce'.[10] German philosophy's 'empty talk about consciousness', as the Spirit of the world and author of history, was now replaced by the real life-process of satisfying physical needs.[11] Consciousness did not produce the world; rather economic life produced consciousness as an expression in thought of objective class divisions over property. To transcend class divisions required the 'natural premises' of production to be collectively appropriated. The organisation of communist society would be 'essentially economic, the material production of the conditions of this unity.'[12]

In the *1844 Manuscripts*, Marx had spoken of the human species-character as 'free conscious activity'. But to realise this potential, man had first to make 'his life-activity itself the object of his will and consciousness'.[13] Self-determination of labour became the analogue of the *Phenomenology's* self-determination of Spirit. In the *Grundrisse*, Marx saw material realisation of this potential in modern technology as the mediating link between thinking and being. Following Hegel's emphasis upon the activity of reason, Marx found in civilised means of production the objectification both of physical labour and of human thought. Modern technologies represented actual reason; they were 'organs of the human brain, created by the human hand; the power of knowledge objectified'. Knowledge was becoming 'a direct force of production'; and scientific labour, as the labour of thought, had the same potential for universalisation as Hegel saw in the laws.[14] Modern reason, as the science of production, portended the rational organisation of labour in an actual unity of subject and object.

To realise this unity, however, presupposed universal appropriation of social knowledge and transcendence of the division between mental and physical labour. Communal ownership of property would give universality its objective dimension; communal appropriation of objectified knowledge would represent the subjective universalisation of reason. Marx believed conscious self-determination of social labour was already implicit in capitalism. Its actualisation in scientific planning required the universal worker as the counterpart of universal means of production. Modern industry had eliminated particular skills of handicraft workers and converted labour into a pure abstraction; but in order to work with sophisticated instruments of embodied knowledge, the workers themselves must acquire universal skills. Capitalism had already posited the need for production of man himself as 'the most total and universal social product'.[15] Technologically cultured workers would become the self-conscious regulators of their own social life-process. The 'human being who has become', wrote Marx, would be the one 'in whose head exists the accumulated knowledge of society'.[16] The Absolute Reason of Hegelian philosophy must be made concrete through social self-enlightenment.

In *The Philosophy of Right*, Hegel had written that 'the abstraction of one man's production from another's makes work more and more mechanical until finally man is able to step aside and install machines in his place'.[17] In the *Grundrisse*, Marx elaborated this same theme: 'Labour no longer appears so much to be included within the production process; rather, the human being comes to relate more as watchman and regulator to the production process itself .... He steps to the side of the production process instead of being its chief actor'.[18] Modern technology would allow a revolutionary expansion of free time for the self-development of individuals, whose knowledge and productive skills would be mediated into a concrete universal through the conscious plan.[19] The plan would permit mutual recognition by the associated producers of each individual's contribution to socially necessary labour. Marx believed he had brought Hegel's dialectic to a positive (rather than merely speculative) conclusion by demonstrating that the laws of communal life must become transparent in the plan. The laws of economic planning would replace the Hegelian laws of ethical life, for each worker would acquire the knowledge to participate directly in planning rather than relying upon Hegelian institutions of corporate mediation.

Marx circumvented Hegel's political theory by adopting Hegel's own emphasis upon the universalising activity of reason. The crucial difference was that Hegel took science to mean philosophical knowledge of the Absolute, whereas Marx understood science as the activity of technical reason. For Hegel's exaltation of right, Marx substituted a system of economic claims, measured in terms of each individual's contribution of labour time to the social product. By revolutionising productivity, however, communist society would both *elevate* and *eliminate* (or transcend) the claims (or 'rights') of all. Characterised by economic abundance, the higher stage of communism would enable each individual to draw upon the social product in accordance with his needs.[20] There would be no need for particular rights, for as scarcity receded, each could spontaneously recognise the needs and rights of all. There would be no need for politics, for there would no longer be any particular claim to right which needed to be enforced by an apparatus of compulsion. There would be no need for a state, for the end of economic contingency would remove the need Hegel had seen to secure the personality through embodiment of the will in property.

Marx completed his transformation of Hegelian dialectic in the sections of the *Grundrisse* dealing with technology and scientific production. As the notebooks for *Capital*, which Marx never completed, the *Grundrisse* remained unpublished and was unknown to Trotsky's generation. Most Marxists learned what they did of Hegel and dialectics from Engels. In *The Dialectics of Nature*, Engels promised that illustrations from the natural science would make Hegel's *Logic* 'simple and clear as noonday'.[21] In reality, Engels obscured the relation between *determinism* and *self-determination*, a matter which Marx thought he had finally resolved. Engels argued that the Hegelian dialectic of consciousness, which Marx understood as an *active* relation of man to nature, was in fact a reflection of dialectical movement in the material world itself. In *Anti-Dühring*, Engels portrayed reason as nature's own evolutionary product. The 'products of the human brain' were simply 'products of nature'.[22] The laws of thought did not contradict the laws of nature, but were in 'correspondence' with them. The correspondence theory of consciousness was what Engels called 'pure materialism'.[23] Mind was brain, and brain was 'the highest product of matter'.[24] Whereas Hegel regarded nature as mind asleep, Engels regarded mind as nature awake. Engels helped to create confusion for an entire generation of Marxists. If the material world evolved of its own accord and produced thought as a reflection of matter, how could thinking beings undertake to *make* the social world rational?

Trotsky and his contemporaries

Regarding social change as the central question of history, Leon Trotsky agreed with Engels to a point: 'the dialectical view of nature and humanity coincides with the so-called "evolutionary" view of nature'.[25] But Trotsky also thought it was a mistake to confuse the science of social production with the science of nature. He commented that it would be 'completely naive and unscientific … to carry over the conclusions of biology to society'.[26] It was true that materialism took being to be the premise of thought; and thought certainly could not 'liberate matter from its materiality'.[27] However, the real question was whether materiality exercised dominion over consciousness. Here Trotsky differed from Engels by insisting that the laws of thought, or logic, expressed the laws of consciousness 'in its active relationship to the external world'.[28] The prevalent theme of Trotsky's notebooks on dialectics was that 'dialectic cognition is not *identical* with the dialectic of nature'; instead, it is 'a *result* of the lively interaction between consciousness and nature'.[29] In Trotsky's view, the development of being compelled thought to adjust its conceptual grasp and thus confirmed Hegel's exposure of the 'failure of static thinking'.[30]

Trotsky considered evolutionary theory to be one-sided and 'less concrete'[31] than dialectics because it failed to incorporate consciousness as a 'specialised part of the objective world'.[32] History could only be comprehended by recognising humanity's imprint. As Trotsky declared, 'the psyche, arising from matter, is "freed" from the determination of matter, so that it can independently – by its laws – influence matter'. Human consciousness always played 'an autonomous, that is, within certain limits, an independent role in the life of the individual and the species'.[33] If consciousness did not play such a role, then, said Trotsky, 'it is unnecessary, useless; it is harmful because it is a superfluous complication – and what a complication!'[34]

For Trotsky, the distinguishing role of thought in history was its pursuit of 'certain practical outcomes'.[35] It was impossible to speak of historical causality without acknowledging teleology, or purpose, as 'a partial aspect of the cause'.[36] Determinism, as a theory of objective causality, denied the salience of human intervention. Pure materialism and objective determinism suggested the impossibility of political practice, whereas Trotsky believed it was precisely through political life that quantitative social change becomes qualitative. Human history did not happen; it was made. And politics grew out of economics for the purpose of reconstituting economic relations. 'Living people' used political institutions as superstructural 'levers' to impose their own subjective ends upon the objective world.[37] Trotsky's philosophical differences with the tradition stemming from Engels distinguished him clearly from the mainstream of Bolshevik thought.

Those Bolsheviks who did not absorb Engels' views directly picked them up indirectly through Lenin's early writings. In *Materialism and Empirio-Criticism*, Lenin declared that 'the mastery of nature, manifested in human practice, is a result of an objectively correct reflection within the human head of the phenomena and processes of nature'.[38] Lenin followed Engels in the view that practice referred to experimental science and successful utilisation of natural laws, which operate 'independently of our will and mind'. Scientific knowledge required a strictly 'objective criterion of truth'.[39] Only in his later *Philosophical Notebooks* did Lenin turn to Hegel directly, and here his conclusions were strikingly similar to Trotsky's. 'Man's consciousness', he wrote, 'not only reflects the objective world but creates it.' When the world does not satisfy man, he 'decides to change it by his activity'.[40] Lenin's notes on Hegel, which were published only posthumously, treated 'cognition' and 'will' as the two sides of 'practical activity', which abolishes the 'one-sidedness' both of subjectivity and of objectivity'.[41] Following his rediscovery of Hegel, Lenin became convinced that 'it is impossible to understand Marx's *Capital* ... without having thoroughly understood the *whole* of Hegel's *Logic*. Consequently, ... none of the Marxists understood Marx!!'[42]

Nikolai Bukharin was one of those who, according to Lenin, had neither studied nor fully understood dialectics.[43] Bukharin's most comprehensive treatment of dialectics came in *Historical Materialism: A system of sociology*. Nature and society alike were said to be governed by 'natural law' and objective causality.[44] There was 'no difference at all ... between the social sciences and the sciences concerned with nature', for man was merely 'a portion of nature'. Matter was the 'mother of mind',[45] human society was 'a product of nature';[46] the phenomena of consciousness were 'a property of matter organised in a certain manner, a "function" of such matter'.[47] The final degeneration of Marxism came with Stalin, who plumbed the depths of silliness and cynicism simultaneously. Stalin too thought 'mind is secondary, derivative, since it is a reflection of matter, a reflection of being'.[48] In *Economic Problems of Socialism in the USSR*, Stalin turned directly to the question of how consciousness might transform the world if, at the same time, it is merely a reflection of what is. He argued that the laws of political economy, like those of nature, 'operate independently of the will of man'.[49] But Stalin also declared that 'man can discover laws [and] get to know and master them'.[50] What he meant was that economic laws operate independently of the will of *workers*, as *objects* of the plan, but are discovered and mastered by bureaucrats, who fancy themselves to be the universal *subjects* of history.

From Hegel's *Philosophy of Right* and Marx's critique of universal bureaucracy, we have now journeyed to Stalin's metaphysics of bureaucratic planning. The remaining task is to clarify how Trotsky's philosophical differences with Stalinism shaped his reflections on the possibility of restoring socialist democracy. During the years of War Communism and Civil War, neither Trotsky nor any other

Bolshevik leader attached high priority to democracy. In 1920 the Bolshevik revolution hung by a thread, and Trotsky's preliminary thoughts on economic planning emphasised 'unity of will, unity of direction, unity of action', achieved through the mobilisation and militarisation of labour.[51] Beginning in 1923, however, with his articles on the 'new course', Trotsky increasingly spoke of 'democracy' and 'centralism' as two aspects of Party leadership which had to be reconciled through 'organisational self-determination' at all levels.[52] In 1926 he referred to 'vigilant control' by workers and the 'collective control' of public opinion as necessary safeguards against bureaucratic arbitrariness.[53] Socialism could not be built by administrative orders from above, but only through 'the greatest initiative, individual activity, persistence and resilience of the opinion and will of the many-millioned masses, who sense and know the affair to be their own business, who never hope that someone will do the job for them'.[54]

Trotsky anticipated the revolution's bureaucratic degeneration in the 1920s, but he only addressed the problem comprehensively in *The Revolution Betrayed*, which was written in 1936 and appeared at the height of Stalin's purge trials. By this time the bureaucracy had emerged and consolidated itself as 'an uncontrolled caste alien to socialism'.[55] In his *Critique of Hegel's 'Philosophy of Right'*, Marx had criticised Hegel's alleged 'separation of the political state from civil society'.[56] Trotsky likewise claimed that the Stalinist bureaucracy protected its monopoly of power through 'separation between the state and society'.[57] The bureaucracy controlled society, but society had no presence in political life. Stalinist planners claimed to be the 'universal mind' of society;[58] in fact they had transformed the state from Hegel's ethical universal into a 'universal merchant, creditor and industrialist'.[59] The means of production supposedly belonged to the state; but the state, Trotsky charged, '"belongs" … to the bureaucracy'.[60] Marx's philosophical commitment to the totality of reason had been distorted and manipulated to rationalise a regime which was, in fact, 'totalitarian'.[61]

Trotsky saw the principal cause of degeneration in economic backwardness. Forced industrialisation had universalised the social division of labour and stratified society into workers and commanders. The need to overcome backwardness resulted in privilege for those groups 'whose existence was necessary for defence, for industry, for technique and science'.[62] The need for incentives had developed into a 'cult of bureaucracy, of officialdom, an aristocracy of technique'.[63] These hierarchical inequalities found their horizontal counterpart in what Trotsky termed the 'struggle of each against all'.[64] Emphasising heavy industry at the expense of consumer goods, the planners had caused social solidarity to collapse into a universal 'struggle for individual existence'.[65] Expanded reproduction of economic scarcity drove peasants and workers alike to display complete indifference to nominally socialist property. Destruction of the rouble through inflation meant that 'graft and speculation' became universal and social mediation occurred through criminality, favouritism and parasitism.[66] Through its own miscalculations, the plan simultaneously reproduced its opposite in the black market, without which it could not function. *Ex ante* planning errors required *ex post* mediation through anarchic market forces. The secret of bureaucratic rule was 'the poverty of society in objects of consumption', the result of which was to shatter social solidarity and disorganise any resistance to exploitation.[67]

As a Marxist dialectician, however, Trotsky believed that a higher universal would result from the sundering of an original unity into its parts. The traditional society of Russia had been fragmented by the five-year plans, with millions of raw recruits being drafted from the once self-sufficient villages into new industries. The central issue was how these atomised social relations might be politically reconstituted, how the people might actively reorganise social relations of production through use of political 'levers'. The social antagonisms of Stalinism convinced Trotsky that 'a stifled but passionate political struggle is being waged throughout the country'.[68] Believing that politics grows out of economics, he regarded the economic struggle as implicitly political, with economic necessity providing an objective basis for self-conscious organisation of the workers.

Trotsky saw the link between economic struggle and political action in the rouble: a technically coherent plan was inconceivable without a stable currency for accounting. The labour market similarly required currency stabilisation in order to provide real incentives. The bureaucracy would be compelled to recognise that its own fate was tied to that of the rouble. To restore the rouble, however, was also to create an instrument of control from below. The contradictions of planning necessarily reproduced the market, in which the rouble had the capacity to serve as 'an instrument for the influence of the population upon economic plans'.[69] In a socialist market, with a real currency, the movement of prices might replace administrative determination of needs with popular self-expression. In a country that had been politically strangled, everyday relations of production and exchange could become 'an important lever for the mobilisation of opposition forces'.[70]

Marx had seen the transparent reason of communal life articulated in the plan; Trotsky expected that economic struggle would render transparent the social contradictions of Stalinist exploitation. 'Money accounting', he wrote, 'cannot fail to give a more open character to the struggle of the different strata for the distribution of national income. The question of the wage scale ... is now decisive for the workers, and with it the question of the trade unions.'[71] Confident that the struggle over income shares 'necessarily becomes a political struggle',[72] Trotsky predicted that Soviet workers would inevitably raise the demand for greater trade union autonomy: 'The designation of trade union officials from above is destined to meet more and more resistance'.[73] Stalinism could not sustain itself without a 'politically atomised society'.[74] But if workers succeeded in imposing their economic demands, they would mitigate the immediacy of needs and free their thought for 'general problems of politics'.[75] The dialectical re-emergence of socialist democracy would begin with control from below, from the shop floor and the objective contradictions of bureaucratic administration.

Addressing problems which Marx had never anticipated, Trotsky intuitively found his way, through Marx's dialectic, back to Hegelian concerns. Like Hegel, he believed that freedom would be no more than a hollow abstraction until concretely institutionalised. This meant that Soviet trade unions could not remain apart from political processes. In a manner similar to Hegel's treatment of corporations, Trotsky concluded that workers' organisations must become 'an important corrective *in the Soviet state system*'.[76] The state and the unions represented a unity of opposites, wherein the state apparatus would wither away, or undergo 'destatification', in the same measure as society raised its own institutions to universality through 'statification' of the unions.[77]

In the *Philosophy of Right*, Hegel had spoken of a coalescence of rights and duties: 'right and duty coalesce, and by being in an ethical order a man has rights in so far as he has duties, and duties in so far as he has rights'.[78] Trotsky took a similar view when he spoke of the 'coalescence' of trade unions and the state.[79] Unions had duties to the state in so far as they had the right to participate in its deliberations. The Stalinist separation of state and society would have to be transcended by having workers' representatives, like Hegel's corporate deputies, participating in authoring the plan. At the same time the state, being socialised from below, must appoint its own representatives to responsible trade union bodies. In this mutual interpenetration of state and society, Trotsky saw the hope of making socialist democracy into a concrete universal.

Where Trotsky differed from Marx was in his unique awareness of the political needs of a transitional society. The division of labour, its social implications aggravated by economic backwardness, inescapably dictated the struggle for recognition of particular needs, or what Hegel had called 'rights'. Like Marx, Trotsky hoped that introduction of new technologies, of 'delicate mechanisms which demand both technical and general culture', would help to extend the conscious horizons of Soviet citizens.[80] But determination of new goals and social values was also an inherently political process. Marxism had always promised 'to subordinate nature to technique and technique to plan'.[81] However, the practical dimension of socialist freedom also demanded 'a free conflict of ideas'.[82] A plurality of political parties was needed in order that political self-education might replace 'humiliating control'[83] from above with self-imposed 'cultural discipline'[84] growing out of 'education, habit and social opinion'.[85] Trotsky's critique of Stalinism sought to preserve the emancipatory promise of Marxism by reinstating an Hegelian respect for the dignity of political life. He believed that socialist political life, arising from the system of needs, would promote the awakening of personality in 'the realm of spiritual culture'.[86] Political self-determination was necessary for the emergence of a higher consciousness, for 'critical views, the development of one's own opinion, the cultivation of personal dignity'.[87]

Jürgen Habermas

Jürgen Habermas would certainly endorse Trotsky's call for a free and responsible discussion of public affairs. His work begins, however, with a conviction that both the Hegelian philosophy of consciousness and its Marxist reinterpretations have exhausted their capacity to explain the contradictions of modernity. The philosophy of consciousness is conceptually oriented upon a single world, within which human subjects can knowingly appropriate their own creations. Habermas believes that we live conceptually in three worlds: the objective world of nature, the social world of relations with others, and the world of personal subjectivity to which each of us alone has direct access. The question then becomes: how can these three worlds be linked in meaning? Habermas believes they are linked neither by Hegelian reason nor by Marx's labour process, but primarily through the dialogue of everyday life. He argues that 'Reaching understanding is the inherent telos of human speech'.[88] When a speaker orients himself to reaching understanding with another, his speech act necessarily raises three validity claims: he asserts that his statement is true, that he had the normative right to make it, and that he is sincerely expressing his personal intentions.[89] The three validity claims refer to the objective, social and subjective worlds. Speech acts acquire binding (and bonding) force when participants in a dialogue mutually expect that their validity claims can, if necessary, be discursively redeemed.

Whereas Hegel and Marx spoke of the universality of reason, Habermas believes that rationality refers to the behaviour of speaking and acting subjects who are capable of giving 'good reasons'.[90] People co-ordinate their actions when they relate them to reasons that are mutually acceptable. When a validity claim is contested, the only court of rational appeal is argumentation, which ideally excludes 'all force ... except the force of the better argument'.[91] The dialogue of everyday life can clarify problematic situations, but Habermas does not believe it can ever yield the kind of transparency associated with the thought of Hegel or Marx. Language and culture are symbolic interpretations rather than a transparent revelation of truth. They define a group's horizon, or what Habermas calls the lifeworld of communicatively shared understanding. The lifeworld is a cultural inventory of pre-reflective patterns of interpretation in the form of 'taken-for-granted background assumptions and naively mastered skills'.[92] Unless we share such 'unshaken convictions', it is impossible to give each other good reasons or to recognise each other as reasonable beings.[93]

Habermas finds the closest empirical reference for the lifeworld, as a total concept, in archaic communities. Unlike Hegel and Marx, he associates the ideal of universality with a state of cultural backwardness, in which the 'nearly total' institution of kinship 'reproduces itself as a whole in every single interaction'.[94] The 'totalising power of the "savage" mind' generates an equally total world-view, weaving nature and culture into 'a single network of correspondences'.[95] This abstract universality is overcome when the process of modernisation rationalises the lifeworld through internal differentiation. Culture becomes distinguished from the magical and ritualised control of contingency; the social domain of interaction is differentiated from relations contingent upon birth; and individuated personalities emerge that are capable of maintaining their integrity in the face of a proliferation of social roles.

Habermas' account of the rationalisation of lifeworlds is reminiscent of Hegel's

Phenomenology of Spirit. Structural differentiation of the lifeworld causes some relaxation of its prejudgemental powers, allowing individual actors increasingly to negotiate mutual understanding through their own interpretive accomplishments.[96] In this way, Habermas provides an internal perspective on the emergence of institutionalised discourses on science, law and art (linked respectively to the objective, social and subjective worlds). But as in Hegel's *Philosophy of Right*, where the idea went out of itself to create a world of social institutions, Habermas also sees an historical process of externalisation. The community expands its power to act upon the world instrumentally by separating out from the lifeworld the systems of state and economy. In a world of increasingly complex social relations, it is impossible to share every intention discursively.[97] Instead, the political and economic systems mediate individual actions through power and money. At the same time, however, there is a danger that state and economy will congeal into 'the "second nature" of a norm-free sociality that can appear ... as an *objectified* context of life'.[98]

The lifeworld becomes rationalised, enabling speakers to co-ordinate their actions through rational consensus; but they are now also situated within systems that are functionally rather than consensually integrated. The systemic organisations of modernity tend to become self-steering mechanisms, detached from normative constraints. The result is that systemically steered interactions are deprived of meaning. The fundamental contradiction of modernity is between lifeworld and system, and between communicative competence and the objectivating effects of systems. The 'dialectical concept of totality' therefore collapses into its '*disjecta membra*'.[99] Human consciousness is split, and the moments of reason disintegrate. Hegel's political community and Marx's consensual plan were intended to bring the autonomous process of economic growth back into the lifeworld of mutual understanding. Habermas replies that system differentiation is a necessary response to the complex interactions of modernity. At the same time, he shares Marx's fear of systemic dehumanisation. Social systems tend to become domains of action detached from 'good reasons'. The philosophical ideal of transparency and universal freedom gives way to the threat of opacity and systemic bondage.

Developing in accordance with functional imperatives, systems undertake 'colonisation' of the lifeworld.[100] Sytemic co-ordination economises time and reduces the risk of misunderstanding in dialogue; it also reduces human beings to objects. Problematic situations in the lifeworld are transformed, through 'violent abstraction', into legal 'situation-definitions', whereby people are objectivated as 'cases' and dealt with by technicians and bureaucrats.[101] Formal law is produced through a technical discourse of jurisprudence, in the same way as science and the arts become the cultures and discourses of experts. Separation of these expert cultures reinforces cultural impoverishment of the lifeworld.[102] The more everyday life is technically administered rather than communicatively co-ordinated, the more meaningless it becomes. The domain of intersubjectivity contracts: '*Everyday consciousness* is robbed of its power to synthesise; it becomes

fragmented.'[103] Thus modernity confronts us with exactly the concerns that motivated Hegel and Marx: '(i) whether a reason that has been objectively split up
into its moments can still preserve its unity, and (ii) how expert cultures can be
mediated with everyday practice'. The most urgent challenge continues to be
'mediation of the moments of reason'.[104]

Habermas believes that the link between theory and norm-based practice, as
Hegel argued, lies in the law, for it inescapably joins systems and the lifeworld.[105]
The law is both a de-moralised means for organising media-controlled systems and
an expression of the normative convictions of human subjects. The dual character
of the law means that functional organisation is ultimately dependent upon
practical justification of the legal order as a whole. Otherwise political and
economic systems will 'appear in the end as wanting legitimation'.[106] The laws are
similar to speech acts: they make validity claims which must be discursively
redeemed. The 'violent abstraction' of modernity results from failure to achieve
balanced institutionalisation of discourses. Practical discourse has been suppressed in a state system that replaces communication with diffuse propaganda.
To the extent that it restricts public dialogue in the name of technical expediency, the modern state inevitably provokes either resistance or anomic indifference. The pathologies induced by abstract power can be remedied only by the
broadest opportunities for discursive formation of political will.

Habermas believes, however, that universal discourse will remain an unattain-
able ideal. When he speaks of the 'perspective of reconciliation and freedom', he
clearly describes it as 'utopian'.[107] The universality which Hegel and Marx had in
mind is impossible to realise: modern societies can no more fully internalise
media-steered systems than they can return to kinship organisation and the
'totalising power of the "savage" mind'. At the same time, the struggle for shared
meanings can never end: it is 'built into the linguistic mechanism of the reproduction of the species'.[108] Culture, society and personality are reproduced through
communicative action; they cannot be manufactured according to a plan.

Conclusion

If the debates of Soviet Marxists are now reinterpreted retrospectively, through
the Habermasian theory of communicative action, much of what has been said in
this chapter can be stated rather differently. The debate over objective determinism can now be regarded not simply as philosophical degeneration, but also as an
insight into the contradictions of modern life. From this perspective, reduction of
human consciousness to nature by Bukharin and Stalin becomes an ideological
reflection of reality in so far as modern systems *do* act with the impersonality of
natural forces and *do* demand adaptation of consciousness to their own functional
imperatives. Stalinist bureaucratic socialism can be reinterpreted as the planned
imposition of administrative mechanisms of systemic co-ordination. The planning system, in Habermasian terms, was 'draped out as the lifeworld', a domain of
mutual recognition and understanding, whereas in reality public life became
meaningless. Stalinism attempted to mass produce meaning, but this 'shamming

of communicative relations' did nothing to repair the fragmentation of public consciousness upon which bureaucratic administration depended.[109]

Leon Trotsky saw this fragmentation of public consciousness for what it was: a Hobbesian 'struggle of each against all' in a politically atomised society. What Trotsky referred to as 'separation between the state and society' can now be reinterpreted as the uncoupling of a modern industrial and administrative system from the lifeworld of the Russian village. Trotsky's hope that economic needs might lead to reconstitution of political life can likewise be understood as an intuitive grasp of lifeworld resistance to systemic integration. For Habermas, normative claims relate to 'alternative orderings for the satisfaction of interests'.[110] A normative consensus regulates 'legitimate chances for the satisfaction of needs', conceived in both material and ideal terms.[111] A basic problem of the 1930s was that village norms of equality contradicted the functional need for highly differentiated incomes. It is from this contradiction that the internal tension in Trotsky's own thought arose. Opposed both to primitive egalitarianism and to the exaggerated privileges of the Stalinist bureaucracy, Trotsky hoped that the struggle over incomes and corresponding opportunities for self-expression might be communicatively resolved. Mutual recognition of legitimate needs would come through an institutionalised discourse concerning planning priorities.

The problem was that Trotsky's philosophical commitment to enlightenment was impossible to reconcile with the darkness of village culture. Trotsky was perfectly aware of the cultural as well as the economic obstacles to socialist democracy. In *The Revolution Betrayed*, he commented that 'The Russian people never knew in the past either a great religious reformation like the Germans, or a great bourgeois revolution like the French. Out of these … came bourgeois individuality, a very important step in the development of human personality in general.'[112] Trapped in material want and cultural backwardness, the Soviet peasant-proletarians of the 1930s could not have been more remote from Marx's ideal of the universal worker. Recently torn from the countryside, the majority of Soviet workers did not possess the strength of personality, the stability of social bonds, or the communicative competence to resist the Stalinist administrative machine. As Habermas might say, the pre-industrial lifeworld did not provide the inventory of interpretive patterns needed to impart meaning to the new conditions of life. Or as Trotsky commented, 'The very necessity of acquainting tens of millions of grown-up people with the alphabet and the newspaper … shows what a long road must be travelled before you can really speak of a new socialist culture.'[113]

The pathos of Trotsky's hope for socialist democracy in the 1930s was evident in his own recognition that one of the first tasks of cultural modernisation was to provide soap and a toothbrush to 'millions who up to yesterday never heard of the simplest requirements of neatness'.[114] When peasants had to be educated to stop beating their wives and spitting on the floor, how could Trotsky expect them to emancipate themselves from tyranny? How could there develop institutional mediation between the system and the lifeworld when the lifeworld was collapsing? How could socialist democracy be possible for millions of industrial recruits to whom industrialisation was meaningless?

The Habermasian reconstruction of social modernisation helps to clarify Trotsky's theoretical accomplishments as well as his limitations. Stalinism industrialised the Soviet Union within a system of totalitarian controls designed explicitly to prevent any awakening of social self-understanding. Today this same process of modernisation has set in motion the cultural and systemic differentiation described by Habermas. The complexity of social interaction has eluded the grasp of bureaucrats at the same time as lifeworld rationalisation has generated the communicative competence of citizens who demand 'good reasons' for the regime's continued existence. Recent developments confirm Habermas' thesis that discursive formation of political will presupposes cultural modernisation, enabling citizens to negotiate for themselves a shared understanding of problematic situations and to co-ordinate their own action intentions. Trotsky was mistaken in thinking that political democracy would arise out of economic needs. He and Habermas would agree, however, that political freedom requires institutionalisation in order that citizens might hold the laws and those who author them accountable for reasoned explanations. 'Mediation of the moments of reason', to whatever extent it remains possible, is unthinkable without a free and responsible discourse in the practical dialogue of political life. Fifty years after his death, Leon Trotsky's political theory continues to direct our attention to fundamental issues on the modern agenda.

Notes

1. *Hegel's Philosophy of Right*, trans. T. M. Knox, London, 1967, p. 236.
2. *ibid.*, p. 57.
3. *ibid.*, p. 192.
4. *ibid.*, p. 156.
5. *ibid.*, p. 192
6. *ibid.*, p. 193.
7. *ibid.*, p. 261.
8. Karl Marx, *Critique of Hegel's 'Philosophy of Right'*, ed. Joseph O'Malley, London, 1970, p. 99.
9. *ibid.*, p. 47.
10. Robert C. Tucker, ed., *The Marx–Engels Reader*, 2nd edn., New York, 1978, p. 150.
11. *ibid.*, p. 156.
12. *ibid.*, p. 193.
13. *ibid.*, p. 76.
14. Marx, *Grundrisse: Foundations of the critique of political economy*, trans. Martin Nicolaus, New York, 1973, p. 706.
15. *ibid.*, p. 409.
16. *ibid.*, p. 712.
17. *Philosophy of Right*, p. 198.
18. Marx, *Grundrisse*, p. 705.
19. *ibid.*, p. 706; cf. pp. 711, 171.
20. Tucker, *Marx–Engels Reader*, p. 531.
21. Frederick Engels, *Dialectics of Nature*, trans. C. P. Dutt, New York, 1940,

p. 27.
22. Engels, *Herr Eugen Dühring's Revolution in Science (Anti-Dühring)*, trans. Emile Burns, London, 1954, p. 45.
23. Marx and Engels, *Selected Works*. Moscow, 1962, vol. 2, p. 373.
24. *ibid.*; cf. *Anti-Dühring*, p. 131. Hegel's philosophy of nature also saw a logical dialectic in the evolution of existent things, but this approach presupposed the ontology of the *Logic*.
25. *Trotsky's Notebooks, 1933–1935*, ed. and trans. Philip Pomper, New York, 1986, p. 96.
26. *ibid.*, p. 51.
27. *ibid.*, p. 77.
28. *ibid.*, p. 87.
29. *ibid.*, pp. 101–2.
30. *ibid.*, p. 103.
31. *ibid.*, p. 96.
32. *ibid.*, p. 98.
33. *ibid.*, p. 106.
34. *ibid.*, p. 104.
35. *ibid.*, p. 106.
36. *ibid.*, p. 114.
37. *ibid.*, p. 107.
38. V. I. Lenin, *Materialism and Empirio-Criticism*, New York, 1927, p. 192.
39. *ibid.*.
40. Lenin, *Collected Works*, London, 1972, vol. 38, pp. 212–13.
41. *ibid.*, p. 208.
42. *ibid.*, p. 180.
43. *Leon Trotsky on the Suppressed Testament of Lenin*, New York, 1946, p. 7.
44. Nikolai Bukharin, *Historical Materialism: A system of sociology*, Ann Arbor, 1969, pp. 20–1.
45. *ibid.*, p. 54.
46. *ibid.*, p. 60.
47. *ibid.*, p. 54.
48. Joseph Stalin, *Dialectical and Historical Materialism*, New York, 1940, pp. 15–16.
49. Stalin, *Economic Problems of Socialism in the USSR*, New York, 1952, p. 7.
50. *ibid.*, p. 11.
51. Leon Trotsky, *Terrorism and Communism: A reply to Karl Kautsky*, Ann Arbor, 1961, p. 108.
52. Trotsky, *The New Course*, Ann Arbor, 1965, p. 93.
53. *Trotsky Archives*, no. T. 895.
54. *Izvestiya*, 2 June 1926.
55. Trotsky, *The Revolution Betrayed*, New York, 1945, p. 255.
56. Marx, *Critique of Hegel's 'Philosophy of Right'*, p. 123.
57. Trotsky, *Revolution Betrayed*, p. 286.
58. Trotsky, *Byulleten oppozitsii*, no. 31, 1932, p. 8.
59. Trotsky, *Revolution Betrayed*, p. 66; cf. p. 43.
60. *ibid.*, p. 249.
61. *ibid.*, p. 279.
62. *ibid.*, p. 59.
63. *ibid.*, p. 238.
64. *ibid.*, p. 112.
65. *ibid.*, p. 53.

66. *ibid.*, p. 113.
67. *ibid.*, p. 112.
68. *ibid.*, p. 3.
69. *ibid.*, p. 76.
70. *ibid.*, p. 175.
71. *ibid.*, p. 274.
72. *ibid.*, p. 122.
73. *ibid.*, p. 274.
74. Trotsky, *Byulleten oppozitsii*, no. 36–7, 1933, p. 9; cf. *Revolution Betrayed*, p. 278.
75. Trotsky, *Revolution Betrayed*, p. 285; cf. *Byulleten oppozitsii*, no. 36–7, 1933, p. 8.
76. Trotsky, *Byulleten oppozitsii*, no. 34, 1933, p. 3.
77. *Trotsky Archives*, no. T. 3542; cf. *Byulleten oppozitsii*, no. 34, 1933, p. 3.
78. *Philosophy of Right*, p. 109.
79. Trotsky first used the term 'coalescence' (*srashchivanie*) in the trade union debate of 1920. See Trotsky, *Rol' i zadachi professional' nykh soyuzov*, Moscow, 1920, p. 10. The two aspects of 'coalescence' were 'statifiction'; (*ogosudarstvlenie*) of the unions and 'workerisation' (*orabochenie*) of the state. See *Rol' i zadachi*, p. 23. In 1933 the terms *ogosudarstvlenie* and *razgosudarstvlenie* were used to refer to the same process: appointment of union personnel to planning bodies and state personnel to union bodies.
80. Trotsky, *Revolution Betrayed*, p. 12.
81. *ibid.*, p. 180.
82. *ibid.*, p. 276.
83. *ibid.*, p. 258.
84. *ibid.*, p. 262.
85. *ibid.*, p. 46.
86. *ibid.*, p. 176.
87. *ibid.*
88. Jürgen Habermas, *The Theory of Communicative Action*, Boston, Mass., 1984, vol.1, p. 287.
89. *ibid.*, p. 99.
90. *ibid.*, p. 22.
91. *ibid.*, p. 25.
92. *ibid.*, p. 335.
93. Habermas, *Communicative Action*, Boston, Mass., 1987, vol. 2, p. 124.
94. *ibid.*, p. 157.
95. *ibid.*, vol. 1, pp. 45–6.
96. *ibid.* vol. 2, p. 133.
97. *ibid.*, pp. 183 and 263; cf. vol. 1, p. 341.
98. *ibid.*, vol. 2, p. 173.
99. *ibid.*, vol. 1, p. 343.
100. *ibid.*, vol. 2, p. 196.
101. *ibid.*, pp. 362–3.
102. *ibid.*, pp. 326–7.
103. *ibid.*, p. 355.
104. *ibid.*, pp. 397–8.
105. *ibid.*, vol. 1, p. 342.
106. *ibid.*, vol. 2, p. 324.
107. *ibid.*, vol. 1, p. 398.
108. *ibid.*

109. *ibid.*, vol. 2, p. 386.
110. Quoted in Stephen K. White, *The Recent Work of Jürgen Habermas*, Cambridge, 1988, p. 57.
111. Quoted in White, p. 69.
112. Trotsky, *Revolution Betrayed*, p. 176.
113. *ibid.*, p. 172.
114. *ibid.*, p. 175.

11

Trotsky and the Russian Social-Democratic controversy over comparative revolutionary history

UDO GEHRMANN

The revolutionary outlook of the Russian Social-Democrats was forged in the events of 1905 and 1917, but also contained a 'Russian' interpretation of the history of modern revolutions. The historical parallels and analogies which were used served not only as tailor-made arguments for the credibility of new ideological systems, but also, even more, as an indicator of the changing conceptions of modernisation amongst the Russian Social-Democrats at the beginning of the twentieth century.

In international research into the life and work of Lev Davidovich Trotsky,[1] contributions on individual aspects of the general subject matter are relatively few. This is doubtless partly because Trotsky represented a taboo subject for research amongst Soviet historians concerned with problems relating to how Russian social-democracy incorporated previous experiences of revolution,[2] such as V. S. Alexeyev-Popov, V. M. Dalin, B. S. Itenberg, M. S. Persov, V. G. Revunenko and others.[3]

The first attempts at working over these 'blank spots' in Russian intellectual history were produced in the West by – amongst others – A. von Borcke, R. Jahn and W. Scharlau.[4] The fact, however, is unavoidable. Whereas in the East the criminalisation of Trotsky initiated by Stalin resulted in a significant taboo area in historical studies, in the West the highlighting of Trotsky as leader of the anti-Stalinist opposition clearly resulted in a one-sided emphasis on the 1920s and 1930s. This is most evident in the work of O. Answeiler, J. Bergman, I. Deutscher, D. Law and others.[5] Thus, the contributions under discussion only touch on, and leave otherwise outside of their scope, the question of the revolutionary conceptions of the young Trotsky, and his position in the turmoil in the Russian Social-Democratic Labour Party (RSDLP) on the eve of, during and in the years after the revolution of 1905–7.

This controversy was given a strong impetus at the London Congress of the RSDLP in 1903.[6] From the point of view of the history of ideas, the programme which was agreed at this Congress established the framework both for the assessment of modern revolutions within a unified theoretical outlook, and also for the overdue democratic revolution (expressed in the minimum programme) and for the proletarian revolution in Russia (maximum programme) which was already under discussion. But this led in the RSDLP to a sharp dispute on the basic question of whether this outlook was based in any sense on historical experiences, or whether these experiences had been wrongly evaluated and interpreted. Around two decades later, Martinov (Alexander Samoylovich Piker), whom Trotsky considered to be a 'main critic of the theory of permanent revolution' in the years 1905 to 1923,[7] recalled the beginning of this controversy in these words:

> It seemed to me that in London ... I had suddenly been transported into the French Convention of 1793 – to such a degree did the contributions of the Party delegates remind me of the behaviour of the Montagnards. Here, at the Party Congress, I asked myself the question: can the history of the French Convention at the end of the eighteenth century be repeated in Russia at the beginning of the twentieth century?[8]

The question had not been formulated in those words at the 1903 Congress; however, particularly after 1904 – as Trotsky also noted – two opposed views were developing in the debate on the question. The representatives of the 'Jacobin' wing of the RSDLP, such as Lenin and Anatoly Lunacharsky argued that Russia required not simply a repeat of 1789, but rather a 'bourgeois-democratic' revolution without the bourgeoisie, under the leadership and in the interests of the proletariat. From this it followed that the task for the Russian Social-Democrats, as Lunacharsky stressed in 1905, was to take from the great bourgeois revolutionaries not 'what had made them bourgeois revolutionaries, but what had made them *great* revolutionaries'.[9]

The Social-Democratic 'Girondists', on the other hand, who either, like Alexander Martinov, operated in the 'co-ordinates' of 1789, or, like Irakly Tseretelli, strove for an eclectic synthesis of the experiences of 1789 and 1848, expected a revolution under the hegemony of the bourgeoisie. For this reason, the workers had simply to play the role of an 'extreme opposition',[10] as Pavel Axelrod, Ilya Tsederbaum (Martov) and Georgy Plekhanov also agreed. This kind of understanding of revolution was characterised, as Trotsky said, 'by extraordinary superficiality and in the final analysis boiled down to crude historical analogies'.[11]

The young Trotsky himself adopted a stance on this controversy which was little known at the Congress of 1903, but was original for all that. His understanding of revolutionary history meant that he could transform the polemic between the 'Jacobins' and the 'Girondists' of Russian social-democracy into a principled debate. Later, in 1906, he maintained that history did not repeat itself: 'However often the Russian Revolution is compared with the great French Revolution, the former is far from being a simple repeat of the latter!' Thus it was a crude mistake to 'simply equate [the Russian Revolution] with the events of 1789–1793', since the general sociological definition of 'a bourgeois revolution' could not replace the social analysis of a concrete historical situation.[12]

It was by no means an accident that a similar premise was also defended by Lenin; but – as Trotsky considered in 1928 – this was an expression of the latter's approach towards the positions adopted by the radical wing of the RSDLP in the years 1905–7.[13] However, considerable differences arose between the two thinkers even in the years of the first Russian Revolution, and not only in the year in which Trotsky's *Our Political Tasks*[14] appeared, when 'the revolution for him was still largely a "theoretical abstraction", while Lenin had already and completely recognised its reality'.[15] Thus, Lenin had clearly preferred to proceed deductively and had formulated his hypothetical axioms, as Trotsky said, 'largely to a deliberately algebraic character'.[16] Trotsky, on the other hand, drew his prognoses from an essentially inductive method of thought, in which the empirical historical analysis of the concrete Russian conditions took on primary significance. This sharply focused his view of the peculiarities of the events in Russia, but also involved a danger of laying too much stress on the particular rather than the general in explaining the individual components of historical events.

An almost perfect example of this was to be found in their attempts to characterise the major upheavals of the modern age. Lenin, who tried to deduce the specifics of 1789 and 1848 from the general tendencies of the revolutionary cycles in France (1789–1871) and in Germany (1848–71), believed that he had thereby found for Russia alternative routes to bourgeois revolution, an '1848 type' or a '1789 type'.[17] Trotsky, on the other hand, strove by induction from the particular features of the events of 1789 and 1848 to abstract more precisely a typology of revolution of significance for Russia. So he too suggested 'two opposed types' of revolution. But in his case there was, on the one hand, a type of revolution in which, 'as shown between 1789 and 1793', 'accounts were settled consistently with despotism by the powerful *unity of the whole nation*', while on the other hand there was a revolutionary model, which had not yet been put to the test of history, in which the necessary energy for a radical overthrow of the *ancien regime* was tapped by 'a mighty development of the *class struggle* within this self-liberating nation'.[18] Trotsky considered the '1848 type', which Lenin had thought relevant to Russia, to be the 'worst possible compromise'.[19]

The raising of a single component in the revolutionary process to the level of a general criterion for a revolutionary typology, in the form of the mutual relationship between 'national' and 'social', resulted in large part from an inductive way of thinking. And this also influenced the ideas of the young Trotsky on the character of Russian events. Whereas Lenin expected that the '1789 type of revolution' would be more advantageous than '1848' for Russia, Trotsky accepted that Russian society would neither take the 1848 route nor experience a revolution of the 1789 type.[20] For, as he said, as early as the middle of the nineteenth century 'the national task of political emancipation could not be resolved by the unanimous and homogeneous pressure of the whole nation.'[21] Such a stance also bore witness to the deep division between Trotsky and the 'Girondists', although the idea of 'national revolution' was common to both. Thus Martinov, referring to his 'Two Dictatorships' of 1907, stressed that the Russian Revolution could only be successful if, as in 1789, the social conflicts were not settled 'at the cost and expense of the unified national character of the revolution'.[22] Trotsky, on the contrary, allowed the possibility of a revolution in Russia which would admittedly begin as a bourgeois revolution, but whose victory would only be achieved by social tensions reaching breaking point and the proletariat gaining dominance: that is, by overcoming the unified national character of the revolution.[23]

Amongst the advantages in Trotsky's thinking about the history of revolutions must be counted his attempt to deduce the peculiar character of events in Russia from an analysis of the interconnectedness of industrial and social modernisation in the country.[24] He thereby arrived at the real theoretical nub of the controversy. This consisted in the concrete historical analysis of the relationship between the social forces involved at particular times and the tasks of the bourgeois revolution. In contrast to the 'Girondists', who thought they recognised the indicator for bourgeois dominance in the democratic task of the Russian Revolution, Trotsky was not satisfied with such 'formal logic'. Rather, he tried to grasp the changes in the constellation of forces against the background of industrial development, not only between the social layers and classes, but also – like Karl Kautsky[25] – within them. Trotsky considered the most important elements as follows:

1. The irrelevance of the urban craftsmen in Russia as a result of there being four million village 'kustar' craftsmen, when compared to the craftsmen in the revolutionary districts of Paris during the great French Revolution, who constituted a majority.

2. The 'clearly separate class of wage-labourers' had replaced the urban craftsmen in twentieth-century Russia, as a result of the industrial factory-system. These represented the 'core of the population of a modern town', and this undermined the democracy which had found 'the support of the urban petty-bourgeoisie in earlier revolutions'.[26]

3. The Russian bourgeoisie, 'small in numbers, isolated from "the people", partly of foreign origin, without any historical tradition and only driven by the lust for profit', in Trotsky's view only resembled a caricature of the enlightened, active bourgeoisie of heroic France, who had known how to 'make their revolution great'. But in 1848 there was already the need for 'a class which was capable of mastering the events without the bourgeoisie and indeed in opposition to them'.[27] However, since neither the urban petty-bourgeoisie nor the peasantry were in a position to achieve this, in Trotsky's opinion it could only have been achieved by the proletariat.[28] 'Precisely this class which was largely unknown at the time of the great French Revolution, was to play the decisive role' in the Russian Revolution.[29] However, it should be noted that Trotsky, in contrast to Lenin and his deductive method of thought, did not deduce the dominance of the proletarian elements in the democratic revolution in Russia *a priori* from his analysis of tendencies in European modernisation and the assumption that a new revolutionary-historical epoch had arrived. Rather he considered the latter – probably quite justifiably – as the product of a specifically Russian constellation of forces. And this did not only involve the extremely limited social basis for democracy, as a result of the insignificance of the urban petty-bourgeoisie. In particular, the dimensions and tempo of foreign investment and the 'importance' of foreign entrepreneurs for Russian absolutism had led, as the young Trotsky suggested (quoting the authority of Kautsky, a man of international reputation), to extra-

ordinary disproportions in the growth in size, power and influence of the working class and of the bourgeoisie. 'The proletariat', wrote Trotsky in 1906, 'suddenly found itself concentrated in enormous masses, and between it and absolutism stood only a numerically weak capitalist bourgeoisie.'[30]

For Russia, one of the important questions in understanding the driving forces of the revolution concerns the role of the peasantry. Trotsky's differences with the 'Girondists'[31] in this connection were less significant in the history of the development of theory than his difference of opinion with Lenin, although Trotsky later declared himself to be 'a pupil of Lenin … since the autumn of 1902'[32] on the question of the agrarian revolution. Thus Trotsky, 'deviating' from his 'teacher' in his investigation of the emancipation of the Russian peasantry, did not proceed from Lenin's analogies with the revolutions of the sixteenth and seventeenth centuries, but rather from the study of revolutions since 1789. Accordingly, the peasantry could indeed represent 'a rich seam of chaotic revolutionary power at a certain moment', but nonetheless it still handed over the revolutions of 1789–93 and 1848 'to the Imperial or Arch-Absolutist reaction'.[33] The differences between the Russian Revolution and those of recent times was to be found less in the changed character of the peasantry than in the constellation of forces for the liberation of the peasantry and the forces emerging from this liberation. In 1789 and 1848, the 'emancipation of the peasantry' had been succeeded immediately by the coming to power of the moderate bourgeoisie. The liberated peasants therefore had lost their interest in the continuation of revolution in the towns. In Russia, however, the fate of 'the whole class of the peasantry' would be bound up 'with the fate of the proletariat'. 'On finding itself in power', wrote Trotsky in 1906, 'the proletariat will appear to the peasantry as the liberating class.'[34]

This interpretation, debatable when judged against strict historical fact, also contained direct parallels between a 'bourgeois' and a 'proletarian' dictatorship over the peasantry. In contrast to the revolutions since 1789, which had been 'a history of the subjection of the country to the town', in Russia all the positions of the bourgeoisie, including their 'revolutionary hegemony over the peasantry', would pass to the proletariat. Thus, there would be nothing left for the peasantry 'except to adhere to the regime of workers' democracy'. By thus recognising the changed relationship on the land:

> during the first and most difficult period of the revolution the Russian peasantry would have just as much interest in supporting the proletarian regime (of 'workers' democracy') as the French peasantry had in supporting the military regime of Napoleon Bonaparte, which, with its bayonets, guaranteed to the new landowners the inviolability of their lands.[35]

From the logic of these historical parallels, which were to find confirmation particularly after the October events of 1917, it was not possible, as the young Trotsky had prophesied, to form a political coalition in the shape of an alliance of equal status between workers and peasants, for which Lenin hoped.

Therefore it seemed to Trotsky in 1905–7 that it was impossible to follow the Social-Democratic 'Jacobins', who regarded the peasants as potential partners of the proletariat in the democratic revolution and who designated it a 'peasant' or 'agrarian revolution'.[36] Although Lenin considered that the tendency known since 1793 as the 'Vendée' would also apply to Russia, he believed that the historical precedent for the emancipation of the Russian peasantry was to be found in the bourgeois revolutions of the sixteenth and seventeenth centuries. But in these, 'the peasantry had played an outstanding revolutionary role'.[37] Trotsky, on the other hand, held fast to the quintessence of his comparisons to modern revolutions: the peasantry 'despite its enormous social and revolutionary weight' was incapable at any time 'of playing an independent political role'.[38] Therefore the bourgeois revolution in Russia would necessitate the establishment of proletarian dictatorship in the form of a 'revolutionary workers' government'. This idea met with incomprehension, both among the 'Girondists', who, like Martov and Plekhanov, had demanded even in 1906 the institution of a bourgeois republic, and among the 'Jacobins', who, like Lenin and Stalin, believed in the goal of a 'democratic dictatorship of the proletariat and peasantry'.[39]

These contradictory formulations of the question of power, which in Trotsky's view represented the 'main task of the revolution',[40] formed the focal point for differences of opinion. And these culminated in the interpretation of Jacobinism, especially in the diverging positions on the French Convention. The 'Girondists', such as Martinov, regarded the Convention of the Jacobins 'as the revolutionary dictatorship of the most radical elements of the bourgeoisie at the birth of bourgeois society' in the eighteenth century. After this revolutionary form of rule, there only remained the 'dictatorship of the proletariat'.[41] But since Russia was not yet ripe for that, as the Caucasian Social-Democrats stressed in 1905 or as Plekhanov suggested in Stockholm in 1906, then the workers should not repeat the Jacobin mistake by seizing power themselves or taking part.in a revolutionary government.[42]

Georgy Plekhanov, the 'Nestor of Russian social-democracy', who as author of the Draft Programme at the 1903 London Congress had managed to defend the 'dictatorship of the proletariat' against all the reservations of Axelrod, Martov and others, moved decisively away from this radical position two years later.[43] Thus, at the 4th Party Congress of the RSDLP in Stockholm in 1906, he put forward the view that it was a question of seizing power by conspiracy – following on from the idea developed by Lenin – but not of 'seizing power in the way that the Convention did in the French Revolution'. Lenin argued against this: 'If you recognise the Convention but rage against the revolutionary-democratic dictatorship of the proletariat and peasantry, then you are simply contradicting yourself.'[44] The spokesmen for the Jacobin wing of the RSDLP understood the Convention of the year 1793 to be a 'dictatorship of the lower classes of the populace'. According to them, there was an analogy between the historical precedent 'of a seizure of power of the Convention type' and the 'dictatorship of the workers and peasants' in the idea of the 'conquest of power by the mass of the people'. For them, however, the basic historical difference between the two lay in the fact that in Russia the leading role in the democratic revolution would be played not by the bourgeoisie but by the proletariat. They understood the Jacobin Convention of 1793 as a necessary substitute for the direct leadership of the bourgeoisie, but fulfilling its historic interests.[45]

Trotsky had made a similar, though essentially different, point in 1905–6 regarding the interpretation of the Jacobins, although even in 1903 the 'young neophyte of the New Iskra-ites' had comforted Akimov (Makhnovets) with the words: 'He [Akimov] is afraid of the dictatorship of the proletariat since it is a Jacobin action. He forgets that this dictatorship would only become possible if the Social-Democratic Party and the working class … were to become virtually congruent.' Accordingly, the proletarian dictatorship was not to be seen as a conspiratorial 'seizure of power', but rather as the form of rule of the workers who formed the majority of the nation.[46] This Jacobin conception, coloured by historical distance, scarcely provides evidence of David Ryazanov's version of an incarnation of Trotsky as 'Lenin's cudgel' at the 2nd Party Congress of 1903. Rather, it anticipated the text *Our Political Tasks* of the following year, in which Trotsky warned against superficial analogies and distanced himself from 'Jacobinism' as well as from the general outlook of 'Maximilian Lenin'.[47]

But it appears that, by 1905–6, Trotsky had already forgotten these thoughts, although the Social-Democrats and the workers had not got anywhere close to congruence, nor had the latter formed the majority of the 'nation'. Unlike Plekhanov's change of stance, the direct participation of Trotsky as chairman of the Council of Workers' Deputies in the revolutionary events in St Petersburg in 1905 had apparently contributed to a radicalisation of his position. Thus, he evaluated the 'Girondist' plea for the non-participation of the Social-Democrats in a provisional government as 'a betrayal of the cause of the revolution'. His apology for proletarian dictatorship now determined more than ever his interpretation of the French Convention. Trotsky saw in this the historical example 'of political rule by the Russian working-class', unlike the Social-Democratic 'Jacobins', who perceived 'a government of the working masses'. For the Convention was certainly '*formally* a national representative body, composed of Jacobins, Girondists and a massive swamp, but *basically* was a Jacobin dictatorship'. Accordingly, there was no possible question of 'some special form of proletarian dictatorship within the framework of the bourgeois revolution', nor even, as Lenin proposed, 'the democratic dictatorship of the proletariat and peasantry'.[48]

It remains to be noted on the history of the interpretation of the French Revolution that Trotsky certainly did not expect a revolution 'of this type' in Russia, but proposed historical parallels between the Convention and his concept of a 'workers' government'. This raises the question of whether there was here one interpretation for 1789 and another for 1793: that is, a nascent 'de-Jacobinisation' of the French Revolution. Since 'the Jacobin, sans-culotte, terrorist democracy of Robespierre in the year 1793' was assessed as a phenomenon of developing bourgeois democracy,[49] there can be no talk of a 'de-Jacobinisation'. Rather, Trotsky's concepts were coloured both by the analogy between Jacobin dominance and revolutionary 'workers' democracy' to the left of the liberal bourgeoisie, and by considerations of historical distance. On the one hand, Trotsky, in his youthful optimism, proceeded from the belief that the workers' movement had 'long ago put its historical reckoning with Jacobinism behind it' – that is, it had 'subjected [Jacobinism] to a theoretial criticism', recognised its utopian phraseology and broken with its traditions. But, on the other hand, the proletariat had undertaken to protect 'Jacobinism' against 'all attacks, slanders and crude insults'. The heart of the workers, believed Trotsky, beat in 'full sympathy for the words and deeds of the Jacobin Convention'.[50]

Within this framework, Trotsky surmised that the historical parallels between Jacobin rule and revolutionary 'workers' democracy' consisted in the substitution of bourgeois hegemony. But he saw the crucial difference as the fact that in 1793 this substitution was carried forward by the 'terrorist dictatorship of the victorious sans-culottes', i.e. principally by the urban petty-bourgeoisie, whereas in Russia the industrial proletariat formed the main mass of the urban population. 'Just this analogy alone', wrote Trotsky in 1908, 'points to the possibility of such a historical situation in which the victory of the "bourgeois" revolution would only be achieved by the proletariat'. Nevertheless, at least for the initial period of the Russian Revolution, it would be a question of a substitution and not of a historically determined removal of bourgeois hegemony by the workers. Trotsky adduced as a reason for this the fact that, even under proletarian guidance, there would at first be problems of a democratic nature to be resolved, and there would be the danger 'that the proletariat would be toppled by a coalition of the bourgeois classes, including the very peasantry which had been liberated by the proletariat', and thus 'the revolution would be halted at its limited bourgeois phase'.[51]

This excursion into the history of the social thought of Russian social-democracy shows that the young Lev Davidovich Trotsky in the first decade of the twentieth century adopted an independent stance in the decisive controversy between the 'Jacobins' and 'Girondists' on the questions of modern revolutions as they affected Russia. His position was different both from Lenin's and from that of the Mensheviks. We can see three broad phases in the genesis of his understanding of revolutions:

1. On the eve of the Russian events of 1905, Trotsky still understood the revolution generally as a 'theoretical abstraction'. He turned decisively against superficial analogies, since these distorted historical truth. In 'Jacobinism', a central subject in the argument, he perceived a limited bourgeois 'utopia condemned to failure', which permitted no parallels with Russia. Characteristic here also were the reservations he expressed on the proletarian dictatorship proclaimed by the Jacobin wing of the RSDLP.

2. In the revolutionary years 1905–7 there was a clear *rapprochement* with the radical positions of the Social-Democratic 'Jacobins'. At the centre of his increased preoccupation with historical experiences stood the analysis of the function of the driving forces and forms of rule in the period of the smashing of the *ancien régime*. The axioms formulated at this time culminated in the polemic against the conceptions of the 'Girondists'. Unlike Lenin, however, Trotsky

preferred induction as the instrument of an attempted revolutionary typology. This sharpened his vision of the peculiarities of Russian events, but involved a danger of overemphasising particular factors. Characteristic of this could also have been the conception of permanent revolution. This led, amongst other determining social factors, to the expectation of a rising curve in the course of the revolution, similar to that of 1789. In this respect, the premises of Trotsky and Lenin diverged markedly: with one, it was the 'proletarian 1789'; with the other, the 'proletarian-peasant 1793'.

    3. After the events of 1905 Trotsky's analysis of revolutions again took in the year 1794. But, in contrast to his pre-1905 studies, Trotsky now considered 'Thermidor' as a conceivable 'bourgeois counter-revolution' for Russia as well. The 'revolution in permanence' now included not only, *mutatis mutandis*, the years 1789 to 1793, but also the year 1794. So we see here the beginnings of the ideas on Thermidor which later appeared more pronounced in Trotsky's opposition to Stalin.[52] It was this historical analysis of revolutions which explains why Trotsky, after the defeat of the revolution of 1905, wanted an end to the polemic between 'Jacobins' and 'Girondists', and sought a compromise. The Social-Democratic Girondists, who warned against a 'Russian 1793' precisely because of the possibility of a '1794', remained in the historical 'co-ordinates' of 1789 to 1792, while Lenin and his supporters certainly preferred the Jacobin year 1793 for Russia, but closed their eyes to a 1794. Nevertheless, it was precisely 'Thermidor' which became the fateful question of the Russian Revolution.[53]

Notes

1. See, for example, W. Lubitz, *Trotsky Bibliography: A classified list of published items about Leon Trotsky and Trotskyism*, Munich and New York, 1988.

2. On this question of Soviet historiography, see M. Reiman, 'Perestroika i izuchenie sovietski istorii', *Voprosy istorii*, No. 12, 1989, pp. 156–8; A. V. Pantsov, 'Lev Davidovich Trotsky', *Voprosy istorii*, No. 5, 1990, pp. 65–7; R. Binner, 'Alte und neue Trotzki-Editionen', *Jahrbucher für die Geschichte Osteuropas*, vol. 37, no. 3, 1989, pp. 393–5.

3. See V. S. Alekseyev-Popov, 'L'expérience de la Révolution française et la classe ouvrière de Russie à la veille et pendant la Révolution de 1905 à 1907', *Studien über die Revolution*, Berlin, 1969, pp. 139–56; V. M. Dalin, 'Lenine et le jacobinisme', *Annales historiques de la Révolution française*, vol. 203, 1971; B. S. Itenberg, *Rossiya i velikaya frantsuzskaya revolutsiya*, Moscow, 1988, pp. 220–30; M. S. Persov, *Obobshchenie i ispolzovanie istoricheskogo opyta v rabotakh V. I. Lenina*, Saratov, 1970; V. G. Revunenko, *Marksism i problema yakobinskoy diktatury (istoriografichesky ocherk)*, Leningrad, 1965.

4. See A. von Borcke, *Die Ursprünge des Bolschewismus. Die jakobinische Tradition in Russland und die Theorie der revolutionären Diktatur*, Munich, 1977; R. Jahn, *Lenins Verhältnis zur Geschichte – dargestellt vornehmlich am Beispiel der Französischen Revolution*, Erlangen-Nürnberg, 1973; W. Scharlau, 'Parvus und Trotzki, 1904–1914', *Jahrbücher für die Geschichte Osteuropas*, vol. 2, no. 12, pp. 349–88.

5. See O. Answeiler, 'Der Thermidor der russischen Revolution',

Wissenschaft und Unterricht, vol. 11, 1960, pp. 390–401; J. Bergman, 'The perils of historical analogy: Leon Trotsky on the French Revolution', *Journal of the History of Ideas*, vol. 48, no. 1, 1987, pp. 73–98; I. Deutscher, 'The French Revolution and the Russian Revolution: some suggestive analogies', *World Politics*, no. 4, 1951–2, pp. 369–75; D. Law, 'Trotsky and Thermidor', *Pensiero e azione politica di Lev Trockij: Atti del Convergo Internazionale per il quarantesimo anniversario della morte*, ed. Francesca Gori, Florence, 1982, vol. 2, pp. 433–49.

6. See I. Deutscher, *The Prophet Armed: Trotsky, 1879–1921*, New York and London, 1963, pp. 76, 84, 91–6; Jahn, *Lenins Verhältnis*, pp. 64–71; Bergman, 'The perils', pp. 79–82.

7. L. Trotsky, *Ergebnisse und Perspektiven. Die Permanente Revolution*, ed. H. Dahmer and R. Lorenz, Frankfurt-am-Main, 1971, p. 37.

8. A. Martinov, *Velikaya istoricheskaya proverka*, chast *II, Nashi raznoglasiya v epokhu pervoy russkoy revolutsi (1901–1910)*, glava III; 'Rossiiskie korni nashego dolgoletnego partiinogo raskola', *Krasnaya Nov*, vol. 2, no. 12, 1923, p. 244.

9. See *Trety sezd RSDRP, aprel-mai 1905 goda, Protokoly*, Moscow, 1959, p. 106; V. I. Lenin, 'Die Selbstherrschaft und das Proletariat', *Werke*, vol. 8, Berlin, 1950, p. 8; 'Zwei Taktiken der Sozialdemokratie in der demokratischen Revolution', *Werke*, vol. 9, Berlin, 1960, pp. 74f.; 'Bericht über den Vereinigungsparteitag der SDAPR', *Werke*, vol. 10, Berlin, 1959, p. 280; I. Deutscher, *Marxismus und die UdSSR*, Frankfurt-am-Main, 1974, p. 29.

10. See *Protokoly V sezda RSDRP*, Moscow, 1935, pp. 201–10; A. Martinov, *Dve diktatury*, Geneva, 1905, p. 49.

11. Trotsky, *Ergebnisse und Perspektiven*, p. 121.

12. *ibid*, p. 53.

13. *ibid.*, p. 101; V. I. Lenin, 'Prinzipielle Fragen der Wahlkampagne', *Werke*, vol. 17, Berlin, 1962, p. 402.

14. See Jahn, *Lenins Verhältnis*, pp. 71–3; Bergman, 'The perils', pp. 80–1.

15. I. Deutscher, *Trotzki*, Stuttgart, 1963, vol. 3, p. 240.

16. L. Trotsky, *Die permanente Revolution*, p. 23.

17. See Lenin, 'Zwei Taktiken', p. 47; 'Eine Revolution vom Typus 1789 oder vom Typus 1848?', *Werke*, vol. 8, Berlin, 1958, pp. 248ff.; *Studien zur vergleichenden Revolutionsgeschichte, 1500–1917*, ed. H. Kossock, Berlin, 1974, pp. 124–30, 184–6.

18. Trotsky, *Ergebnisse und Perspektiven*, pp. 53–6.

19. *ibid.*, p. 54.

20. See Lenin, 'Zwei Taktiken', p. 35; 'Brief an I. I. Skortsov-Stepanov' in V. I. Lenin, *Briefe*, Berlin, 1967, vol. 2, no. 172, p. 222.

21. Trotsky, *Ergebnisse und Perspektiven*, p. 61.

22. *Protokoly V sezda RSDRP*, Moscow, 1935, p. 393.

23. See Trotsky, *Ergebnisse und Perspektiven*, p. 53.

24. *ibid.*, p. 43.

25. See K. Kautsky, *Die Klassengegensätze im Zeitalter der Französischen Revolution*, Stuttgart, 1920, 'Vorwort zur Ausgabe von 1909', pp. 4f.

26. Trotsky, *Ergebnisse und Perspektiven*, pp. 48f.; *Protokoly V sezda RSDRP*, pp. 420f.

27. See Trotsky, *Ergebnisse und Perspektiven*, pp. 52–7.

28. See L. Trotsky, 'Der Arbeiterdeputiertenrat und die Revolution', *Die Neue Zeit, Wochenschrift der Deutschen Sozialdemokratie*, vol. 2, 1907, pp. 78f.

29. Trotsky, *Ergebnisse und Perspektiven*, p. 49.
30. *ibid.*, p. 52.
31. See *Protokoly V sezda RSDRP*, pp. 393, 397–9; L. Trotsky, 'Die Duma und die Revolution', *Die Neue Zeit*, vol. 2, 1907, pp. 383–5, 419–22.
32. Trotsky, *Die permanente Revolution*, p. 23.
33. Trotsky, *Ergebnisse und Perspektiven*, pp. 58–9, 73.
34. *ibid.*, pp. 73–5.
35. *ibid.*, pp. 74f.
36. See *Protokoly II sezda RSDRP*, Moscow, 1932, p. 214; *Bauern und bäuerliche Revolution*, ed. M. Kossok and W. Loch, Berlin, 1985, pp. 276–305.
37. V. I. Lenin 'Zur Einschatzung der russischen Revolution', *Werke*, vol. 15, Berlin, 1962, p. 45; 'Referat über die teilnahme der Sozialdemokratie an einer provisorischen revolutionären Regierung', *Werke*, Berlin, 1958, vol. 8. p. 389.
38. Trotsky, *Ergebnisse und Perspektiven*, p. 74.
39. See *IV Obedinitelnyi sezd RSDRP, Protokoly*, Moscow, 1959, pp. 141, 216–18; *Protokoly V sezda RSDRP*, p. 348; V. I. Lenin, *Werke*, Vol. 9, Berlin, 1960, p. 126; J. V. Stalin, *Werke*, vol. 1, Berlin, 1950, pp. 119ff., 196, 210ff.
40. Trotsky, 'Der Arbeiterdeputiertenrat', p. 85.
41. A. Martinov *Dve diktatury*, Geneva, 1905, p. 49.
42. See *IV Obedinitelnyi sezd RSDRP*, pp. 141, 216–21.
43. See *II sezd RSDRP*, Moscow, 1959, p. 182; M. Jowtschuk and I. Kurbatova, *Georgi Plechanow, eine Biographie*, Berlin, 1983, pp. 159ff., 210f., 216ff.
44. V. I. Lenin, 'Bericht über den Vereiningungsparteitag der SDAPR', *Werke*, vol. 10, p. 372.
45. On A. V. Lunacharsky's views, see *'Vpered' i 'Proletarii' pervye bolshevistskie gazety 1905 goda*, vyp. 1, Moscow and Leningrad, 1925, pp. 24–30, 125; vol. 2, Moscow, 1924, pp. 52, 161; on this question, see also *Vergleichende Revolutionsgeschichte – Probleme der Theorie und Methode*, ed. M. Kossok, Berlin, 1988, pp. 54–60.
46. *Protokoly II sezda RSDRP*, pp. 122–4.
47. See L. Trotsky, 'Unsere politischen Aufgaben', *Schritten zur revolutionären Organisation*, ed. H. Mehringer, Reinbek nr Hamburg, 1970, pp. 113–16; Trotsky, *Stalin: Eine Biographie*, Herrsching, 1980, p. 96; I. Deutscher, *Stalin*, Berlin, 1990, pp. 86–90.
48. Trotsky, *Ergebnisse und Perspektiven*, pp. 72, 82–3, 123; *Lenin über Trotzki*, Frankfurt-am-Main, 1970, p. 7.
49. Trotsky, *Ergebnisse und Perspektiven*, p. 55.
50. *ibid.*, p. 55.
51. Trotsky, *Die permanente Revolution*, p. 65.
52. See Trotsky, *Stalin*, p. 510.
53. See R. Payne, *Stalin – Aufstieg und Fall: Eine Biographie*, Stuttgart, 1967, pp. 429–30.

12

Trotsky's conception of the revolutionary process

ROBERT V. DANIELS

Half a century after the death of Trotsky, with the idea of communism in full retreat everywhere, it is difficult to consider revolutionary leaders as anything but misguided fanatics. Yet Trotsky stands out uniquely among major revolutionaries in articulating a broad theory of the nature of revolution *pari passu* with his own political career. Obviously much of what he had to say, especially after the Soviet regime was established, was for purposes of polemics or self-justification. Nevertheless Trotsky was making a serious effort to understand the events in which he was involved and by which he was ultimately destroyed.

The aim of this chapter is to weigh the merit of that effort, and to assess the validity of the insights Trotsky had into the course of the Russian Revolution, measured against the nature of the revolutionary process as it is more broadly known to history. My contention is that in endeavouring to come to terms with the peculiarities of revolution in Russia, Trotsky transcended the limitations of his Marxist faith and approached, step by step, the conception of revolution as a long but interconnected process of political and social change.

The theory of revolution as such a process was widely developed by numerous Western writers during the first two decades following the Russian Revolution, after the upheaval in Russia impressed upon them its parallels with the French Revolution. Robert Lansing, American Secretary of State under President Woodrow Wilson, foresaw for Russia 'first, moderation; second, terrorism; third, revolt against the new tyranny and restoration of order by arbitrary military power.'[1] The notion of revolution as a natural sequence of distinct stages, punctuated by violence, was given academic form by the American church historian Lyford P. Edwards.[2] Following Edwards, the well-known historian Crane Brinton proposed a medical image of the phenomenon:

> We shall regard revolutions ... as a kind of fever ... This works up, not regularly but with advances and retreats, to a crisis, frequently accompanied by delirium ... Finally the fever is over, and the patient is himself again, perhaps in some respects actually strengthened by the experience, immunized at least for a while from a similar attack, but certainly not wholly made over into a new man.[3]

In the perspective of the process theory, revolution is not an event but a complex chain of causes and effects, as one state of affairs leads to another over a period of years.[4] In contrast to a mere coup, a true revolution involves a general political breakdown and a progression of violent action through discernible stages, from the moderate to the extreme, followed by retreat and consolidation. A revolution of this sort is a profound structural crisis in the development of a country, typically brought on by a tempo of social change – that is, modernisation – that a rigid traditionalist government cannot accommodate. Contrary to what all revolutionaries have assumed, revolution is not a plannable, elective political tactic available whenever they choose to resort to it, nor do its ultimate results necessarily or even usually conform to the intentions of those who endorse it. As Napoleon said, 'A revolution can be neither made nor stopped.'[5]

By the test of the process model, the Marxist theory of revolution, which the Russian Social-Democrats including Trotsky took as their starting point, is entirely inadequate. Marxism makes much of revolution as the transfer of power from one class to another, but devotes little theoretical attention to the way revolutions actually unfold.[6] Revolution as the simple displacement of classes is belied by the mix of social elements, interests and ideas in every actual revolution. More importantly, classical Marxism misses the essential nature of revolution as a complex and extensive process. It offers no conception of the natural sequence of stages in the revolution. Further, Marxism misstates the causal conditions for revolution, seeing them as the full development of the old social system. In Marx's famous words, 'No social order ever disappears before all the productive forces for which there is room in it have been developed.'[7] Thus the flowering of capitalism is believed to be the precondition for the next revolution (which is assumed without proof to be 'proletarian'). Actually, history shows revolution to be most likely at an intermediate point in the modernisation process as it affects a given country, when the tempo of change is at its maximum and expectations have risen beyond the particular country's capacity to satisfy them. It is not true, as Marx believed, that 'Mankind always takes up only such problems as it can solve.'[8] Revolutions invariably overreach, beyond what the material conditions and psychological development of the given society will support, and hence must inevitably, sooner or later, go into retreat.

It is a familiar paradox that Russian radicals were attracted to Marxism at the turn of the century by its quasi-scientific laws of progress towards utopia, despite the difficulty in applying the doctrine to a country deemed unready for proletarian revolution and socialism. The attraction was not logical but psychological, and psychology governed as well the ways in which different Russian Marxists addressed the problem of the waiting period between the still unachieved bourgeois revolution and the ultimate proletarian revolution. The Mensheviks, including most of the older leaders of the Social-Democratic movement, were prepared to play the loyal opposition while Russia accomplished the requisite capitalist development – a position of correct Marxism but of fatal politics, as matters turned out. Lenin and his Bolsheviks, determined to lead the workers to power without delay, bent their Marxism to fit their own psychic requirements, by asserting that the proletariat would have an immediate role in taking over the bourgeois revolution from its weak middle-class sponsors and then presiding over the country while economic development caught up with political. Lenin was never one to acknowledge his revisions of Marx. But in his 1905 vision of the workers taking over the bourgeois-democratic revolution, 'when the bourgeoisie recoils from it and when the masses of the peasantry come out as active revolutionaries side by side with the proletariat' to create the 'revolutionary-democratic dictatorship of the proletariat and the peasantry',[9] he was in fact beginning to recognise revolution as a complex, multi-stage process, a process, moreover, which could carry the political regime to a point beyond that which the socio-economic stage of the country would normally sustain.

It fell to Trotsky to carry this modification of the Marxian concept of revolution to a bold new statement of the complex revolutionary process in Russia. This was his famous 'theory of permanent revolution', or 'uninterrupted revolution' as Trotsky himself originally styled it, which he worked out, first as a participant-observer in the events of 1905, and then during the leisure of imprisonment following the revolution of 1905.[10] Prompted by his friend of those years, the German Social-Democrat Alexander Helphand, alias 'Parvus', Trotsky undertook to assess the social forces which had manifested themselves in Russia in that abortive upheaval and to justify an immediate radical role for the workers.[11]

The terms of the theory are familiar to all students of Russian history. In brief, 'permanent revolution' held that in Russia, because of the 'law of uneven development' or 'combined development', the workers had become a revolutionary force while the middle class vacillated and the peasant mass waited for leadership. Consequently, a bourgeois revolution would lead in an uninterrupted development to intervention by the workers to impose their socialist demands:

> Within the limits of a revolution at the beginning of the twentieth century, which is also a bourgeois revolution in its immediate objective aims, there looms up a prospect of an inevitable, or at least possible, supremacy of the working class in the near future.[12]

Inadvertently, in a compound class theory designed for Russia alone, Trotsky had grasped the nature of revolution as an unfolding process leading through various stages. His bourgeois revolution corresponded to the moderate phase in the Brintonian model of revolution, and the proletarian takeover corresponded to the extremist phase. 'Above all' writes the commentator John Molyneux, 'he [Trotsky] perceived that the revolution was an historical process which, once unleashed, could not be stopped half way.'[13]

Trotsky furthermore sensed, in the Russian case at least, that the process would temporarily carry extremist politics to a point more advanced than the nation would indefinitely sustain. Therefore, barring external factors, the revolution would inevitably be set back in a step he was later to equate with the Thermidorean reaction. However, he hoped that defeat for the workers would be averted by a *deus ex machina*, the international proletarian revolution that he believed would be triggered in the mature industrial countries by the Russian example. This prognosis gave the uninterrupted or permanent revolution an international dimension as well. 'The political emancipation of Russia led by the working class will raise that class to a height as yet unknown in history ..., will make it the initiator of the liquidation of world capitalism'.[14] Such an argument was not Marxism but Russian messianism, but it eventually gave the Bolsheviks of 1917 their theoretical rationale for seizing power. When this particular forecast proved wrong, the Communists were left extremely sensitive about the depend-ence of their political virtue on revolutionary events abroad. According to Trotsky's theory, the failure to win revolutionary support abroad portended the inevitable decay of the workers' regime in Russia. Coming to terms with this implication was the central problem in Trotsky's later thinking about revolution.

Trotsky's theory of permanent or uninterrupted revolution in its internal, Russian sense was borne out to an amazing degree by the sequence of revolutionary events in 1917. This was one of the rare historical instances where reality validated theory and was in turn steered by the adherents of the theory. The moderate revolution installed a 'bourgeois' leadership but also initiated a revolutionary mobilisation of the worker and peasant masses and ended in an extremist take-over, which its beneficiaries chose to style a proletarian revolution. In line with his theory, Trotsky was able to predict in March 1917, 'The Russian Revolution will not stop ... the Revolution will make a clean sweep of the bourgeois liberals blocking its way, as it is now making a clean sweep of the Tsarist reaction'.[15]

The October Revolution was accomplished by a party explicitly or implicitly sharing the premises of 'permanent revolution'. Lenin's embrace of this viewpoint was what shocked his followers when he returned to Russia in April 1917: 'The present situation in Russia ... represents a *transition* from the first stage of the revolution – which ... placed the power in the hands of the bourgeoisie – *to the second* stage, which must place the power in the hands of the proletariat and the poorest strata of the peasantry'.[16] Nikolai Bukharin told the clandestine Party Congress in August 1917: 'We are going to have a great new upsurge of the revolutionary wave ..., the declaration of a revolutionary war ... By such a revolutionary war we will light the fire of world socialist revolution'.[17] Disbelief in the effect of such Russian messianism was what lay behind the opposition of Zinoviev and Kamenev to the armed seizure of power in the October Revolution.[18]

No modesty inhibited Trotsky from proclaiming his prescience when he wrote shortly afterwards.

> The standpoint he [the author, Trotsky in 1906] then supported can be outlined as follows: The Revolution, having begun as a bourgeois revolution as regards its first tasks, will soon call forth powerful class conflicts and will gain final victory only by transferring power to the only class capable of standing at the head of the oppressed masses, namely, to the proletariat.[19]

The mechanism of this shift he saw as a suddenly accelerated process of social psychology, going beyond the classic Marxist framework:

The significance of the revolution lies in the rapid changing of the judgement of the masses, in the fact that new and ever new strata of population
acquire experience, verify [test] their views of the day before, sweep them
aside, work out new ones, desert old leaders and follow new ones in the
forward march.[20]

He now recognised the same process of a grand 'sweep' or 'ascending line' at work
in the French Revolution, worked out through the politics of 'dual power': 'By the
steps of the dual power the French Revolution rises in the course of four years to its
culmination'.[21] In the Russian case, Trotsky affirmed the crucial role of the
Bolshevik Party and its leadership (including himself) in consummating the
extremist victory, but he conceded later on: 'The most favourable conditions for
an insurrection exist, obviously, when the maximum shift in our favour has
occurred in the relation of forces … in the domain of consciousness'. The party
had to grab the crucial moment because 'during revolution all these processes take
place with lightning speed'.[22]

Throughout the violent period of civil war, terror and utopian experiment
from 1918 to 1921, known appropriately as War Communism, Trotsky continued
to view the struggle as a validation of his theory, and the theory as a justification
of the revolutionary dictatorship. 'The events in which we are now participating'
he wrote in 1919, 'and even our methods of participating in them, were foreseen
in their fundamental lines some fifteen years ago.'[23] Critics of Bolshevik extremism – notably the Mensheviks and Western Social-Democrats like Karl Kautsky –
were, as far as Trotsky was concerned, traitors to the working class. In his
theoretical scheme of revolution no distinction could be made between the
sequence of class stages, from bourgeois to proletarian, and the sequence of
revolutionary methods, from moderate to extremist: 'The question as to who is to
rule the country, i.e. of the life or death of the bourgeoisie, will be decided on
either side, not by references to the paragraphs of the constitution, but by the
employment of all forms of violence'.[24] Trotsky was convinced that everything the
Bolshevik regime did was necessitated by the circumstance of a workers' government in Russia struggling to hold against all the forces of bourgeois reaction until
the world revolution would itself be triggered by that struggle.

With the failure of world revolution to materialise after the high hopes of 1919,
and the crystallisation of powerful opposition – especially peasant – to the regime
of War Communism, the Bolshevik leadership was faced with the necessity of a
fundamental reconsideration not only of the tactics of their regime, but of its
fundamental theoretical rationale. Up to this point messianic notions about the
international impact of their revolutionary example had spared them from hard
thoughts about the later course of the revolution. But Trotsky had given a clear
warning back in 1906 of what would happen to the workers' government if the
world revolution should somehow fail them. As he recognised in retrospect: 'War
Communism had exhausted itself. Agriculture and with it everything else had
arrived in a blind alley … It was a crisis of the whole system of War Communism'.[25] The outcome, of course, was the New Economic Policy, which Lenin

introduced in 1921 with the concurrence of the entire Party leadership, including Trotsky.

The transition to the NEP made immediate the question of where the revolutionary process would lead after the period of Jacobin-Bolshevik extremism. To certain outside observers the trend was clear: 'With the New Economic Policy of 1921 began Russia's Thermidor', Brinton wrote.[26] The main anomaly was that this 'strategic retreat' (as Lenin called it) from the pinnacle of revolutionary zeal was self-executed, not imposed by a *coup d'état*. The Mensheviks, including Martov, immediately recognised the Thermidorean parallel.[27] Kautsky, whose writings as a publicist seem more insightful than his theorising, even predicted such a self-initiated shift, writing as early as 1919:

> Lenin's government is threatened by another 9th Thermidor ... in some other way ... It is not impossible that the collapse of the communist experiment in Russia may not equally transform the Bolsheviks, and save them as a governing party ... The Bolsheviks have developed the art of adaptation to circumstances in the course of their rule to a remarkable degree'.[28]

The most particular thing about the Soviet Thermidor was the inability of the Soviet leadership to recognise their own move for what it was, despite – or perhaps because of – their own identification with the Jacobins. At that point they could still see Thermidor only in terms of the violent overthrow of the radical party by outright counter-revolutionaries. Only when he found himself slipping out of the inner circle as the succession struggle began in 1923 did Trotsky awaken, and then not to a Thermidor already accomplished, but only to the possibility of 'Thermidorean influences'.[29] In his slashing attack on the Party leadership in late 1923, particularly in his 'New Course' articles, Trotsky called for a campaign to preserve the revolutionary spirit against the encroachment of 'bureaucratism', and warned: 'The internal social contradictions of the revolution which were automatically compressed under War Communism ... under the NEP unfold unfailingly and seek to find political expression'. Replying to Menshevik predictions of an anti-Bolshevik coup comparable to the overthrow of Robespierre, Trotsky insisted that the Russian Revolution still had its strong proletarian base with peasant support, and would be sustained by an 'inevitable extension of the revolution' throughout Europe. Nevertheless, he warned that a recrudescence of capitalistic elements under the NEP could lead to 'either the direct overthrowal of the workers' party or its progressive degeneration'.[30]

Trotsky's hints of a possible Thermidorean tendency within the Communist regime were particularly galling to the leadership, who sought some way of countering him in the arena of theory as well as by direct political pressure. One result was Stalin's celebrated 'theory of socialism in one country', designed to argue with appropriately culled quotations from Lenin that the Soviet regime was in no danger of losing its proletarian purity because it did not after all need the world revolution in order to hold out in Russia as a genuine workers' state.[31] Another tactic was to turn French revolutionary analogy against Trotsky by accusing him, as Commissar of War, of representing a threat of Bonapartism. This charge served to justify his removal from that strategic post in 1925.

In 1926 and 1927, after he had allied himself with Zinoviev and Kamenev for the last-ditch fight against Stalin and Bukharin, Trotsky responded to the growing repression of opposition with more and more shrill charges against the Party leadership. At the same time, he expressed a new pessimism about the revolutionary process. In a diary entry of November 1926 he noted: 'Revolutions have always in history been followed by counter-revolutions. Counter-revolutions have always thrown society back, but never as far back as the starting point of the revolution.' Accordingly:

> In a sense the hopes engendered by the revolution are always exaggerated. This is due to the mechanics of class society ... The conquests gained in the struggle do not correspond, and in the nature of things cannot *directly* correspond, with the expectations of the broad backward masses.

Here was the extraordinary admission by Trotsky that all revolutions are naturally premature in relation to the availability of resources to carry out their promises. Revolution could outrun its base thanks to temporary political momentum: 'the awakening of the broad backward masses upsets the ruling classes from their accustomed equilibrium, deprives them of direct support as well as confidence, and thus enables the revolution to seize a great deal more than it is later able to hold'. But the backswing was sooner or later hard to escape: 'The disillusionment of these masses, their return to routine and futility is ... an integral part of the post-revolutionary period'.[32]

This new fatalistic sense of the revolutionary process Trotsky tried to throw in the teeth of the Party leadership during his last stand before expulsion and exile. Defending himself before the pro-Stalin Central Control Commission in the summer of 1927, he invoked the full cycle of the French revolutionary model:

> In the Great French Revolution there were two great chapters, of which one went like this [points upward] and the other like that [points downward] ... When the chapter headed like this – upwards – the French Jacobins, the Bolsheviks of that time, guillotined the Royalists and the Girondists. We, too, have had a similar great chapter when we ... shot the White Guards and exiled the Girondists. And then there began another chapter in France, when the French Ustrialovs[33] and semi-Ustrialovs – the Thermidorians and Bonapartists from among the Right-wing Jacobins – began exiling and shooting the Left Jacobins – the Bolsheviks of the time.

Reshaping his notion of Thermidor as a mere retreat, not a rout, Trotsky observed: 'It is thought that the Thermidoreans were arrant counter-revolutionaries, conscious supporters of the monarchic rule, and so on. Nothing of the kind: The Thermidoreans were Jacobins, with this difference, that they had moved to the right.'[34] In Marxist terms, for Trotsky, the situation in Russia was simple: 'Thermidor ... is a departure from the rails of the proletarian revolution to the petty-bourgeois rails', opportunistically condoned by the revolutionary leadership themselves.[35]

Trotsky was a theorist who did his most creative work under the immediate impact of events around him. When he first formulated permanent revolution, and on through his initial perception of the revolution in decline, he made no effort to extend his theory to countries other than Russia. It was the abortive Communist bid for power in China in 1927, first in alliance with Chiang Kai-shek's Nationalists and then against them, that prompted him to universalise his process concept. He wrote in April 1927, just before Chiang turned against the Chinese Communists, of 'an alliance of workers and peasants, under the leadership of the proletariat', and foresaw a 'possibility of the democratic revolution growing over into the socialist revolution', while the Soviet Union would play the role of outside ally envisaged for the Western proletariat in the original, Russian version of permanent revolution.[36] By extension, this situation made permanent revolution the general model for underdeveloped and colonial countries.[37] The Italian scholar Pier Paolo Poggio comments: 'For Trotsky in Russia and in general in backward countries, the seizure of power by the consciously organised proletariat ... will be easier and quicker than in the advanced capitalist countries'.[38] Incorporating this perspective into his polemical reformulation of permanent revolution in 1928, Trotsky presented what Les Evans and Russell Block term 'the theory of permanent revolution as we know it today – as a general theory of the necessity of socialist revolution in the colonial world'.[39]

The radical new departures undertaken by Stalin after Trotsky's defeat, including his break with the Communist right wing and the initiation of intensive industrialisation and collectivisation, threw his critics into a new theoretical quandary. At first Trotsky was inclined to describe the Stalin revolution as a 'prolonged zigzag to the left', compelled somehow by pressure from the workers and the Left Opposition, but still under the pull of the 'Thermidorean' bureaucracy.[40] 'Stalinism is inverted Kerenskyism', he suggested, 'on the road to Thermidor, the *last* form of the rule of the proletariat.'[41] By now the trend of the NEP years was clear to him: 'A period of reaction can occur not only after a bourgeois revolution but after a proletarian one as well. For six years we have been living in the USSR under conditions of mounting reaction against October, paving the way for Thermidor.'[42] To his supporters in Italy he wrote: 'When we speak of Thermidor, we have in mind the creeping counter-revolution which is being prepared in a masked way and which is being accomplished in several stages'.[43]

With the perspective of an additional half-decade Trotsky was more uncertain about the retrograde course of the Russian Revolution: 'Stalin ... is the living embodiment of a bureaucratic Thermidor'.[44] Looking back from the year 1935, he concluded:

> Today it is impossible to overlook [the fact] that in the Soviet revolution also a shift to the right took place a long time ago, a shift entirely analogous to Thermidor, although much slower in tempo, and more masked in form ... The year 1924 – that was the beginning of the Soviet Thermidor.[45]

Thus Trotsky finally recognised that a Thermidor had in fact occurred, not as an overt bourgeois coup, but as a more subtle political shift within the ruling party. His only trouble was that he persisted, for reasons of his own self-justification, in placing the shift three years beyond the real turning point of 1921.

Simultaneously with his recognition of the Russian Thermidor, Trotsky was compelled to admit the possibility of a further post-revolutionary phase, distinct from Thermidor, which was still not clearly a counter-revolution. In the French model this was the era of Bonapartism. Thermidor, in this context, was 'a transitory phase between Jacobinism and Bonapartism'.[46] Stalin naturally became the embodiment of this last stage of the revolutionary process. Russia was thereby observing the laws demonstrated in 'the consecutive stages of the great French Revolution, during its rise and fall alike', though Trotsky still endeavoured to describe these stages as a sequence of distinct class elements. 'In the successive supremacy of Mirabeau, Brissot, Robespierre, Barras, and Bonaparte, there is an obedience to objective law incomparably more effective than the special traits of the historic protagonists themselves.'[47]

For a Marxist, Trotsky had an unusually supple understanding of history in general and of revolution in particular. While wedded to the usual class categories of political explanation, he was able to grasp the complexities of a phenomenon such as revolution that in fact transcended the Marxian mode of analysis. He attempted a running explanation of unfolding developments in Russia by applying a process conception and extending it as new stages appeared. This was more than a mere analogy, though it was expressed in French revolutionary terminology. Constantly attempting to use his understanding of the revolutionary process as a political weapon, Trotsky did not always react at once to a new stage, notably Thermidor and the rise of post-revolutionary dictatorship. In time, however, he was able to set the realities of these phenomena in Russia into the framework of his model. 'Revolution itself is neither a single nor a harmonious process', he wrote in 1931. 'Revolution is full of contradictions. It unfolds only by taking one step back after taking two steps forward. Revolution in its own turn sweeps into power a new ruling stratum which strives to secure its privileged position.' Here was a hint of the 'new class' theory. Finally, Trotsky called the whole Marxian logic into question: 'The epochs of ideological reaction which, more than once in history, have run parallel with economic successes, engender the need for revising revolutionary ideas and methods; and create their own conventional lie.'[48]

Notes

1. Robert F. Lansing, *War Memoirs*, Indianapolis, 1935, pp. 337–8.
2. Lyford P. Edwards, *The Natural History of Revolution*, Chicago, 1927.
3. Crane Brinton, *The Anatomy of Revolution*, New York, 1938, 1952, pp. 16–17.
4. I have developed this approach more fully elsewhere. See Robert V. Daniels, 'Whatever happened to the Russian Revolution?', *Commentary*, November 1978.

5. J. Christopher Herold, ed., *The Mind of Napoleon: a selection from his written and spoken words*, New York, 1956, p. 64.

6. A good negative example is Karl Kautsky, *The Materialist Conception of History*, abridged edn, New Haven, 1988, where revolution is mentioned often, but only in passing.

7. Karl Marx, *A Contribution to the Critique of Political Economy*, New York, 1904, p. 13.

8. *ibid.*

9. Lenin, 'Two tactics of social democracy in the democratic revolution', July 1905, *Selected Works*, Moscow, 1950–2, vol. I, book 2, pp. 87, 107.

10. Published as 'Itogi i perspektivy' [Results and prospects] in *Nasha revoliutsiya* [*Our Revolution*], St Petersburg, 1906; English translation in *Our Revolution*, New York, 1918. The more confusing term 'permanent' revolution was applied to the theory by later commentators, but it stuck and Trotsky accepted it. See Baruch Knei-Paz, *The Social and Political Thought of Leon Trotsky*, Oxford, 1978, pp. 152–3. On Trotsky's earlier steps in formulating the theory, see Michael Lowy, 'The theory of permanent revolution', in *Pensiero e azione di Lev Trockij*, ed. Francesca Gori, Florence, 1982, pp. 149–54.

11. See Z. A. B. Zeman and W. B. Scharlau, *The Merchant of Revolution: The life of Alexander Helphand (Parvus), 1867–1924*, London, 1965, pp. 66–8, 110–11.

12. Trotsky, *Our Revolution*, p. 92.

13. John Molyneux, *Leon Trotsky's Theory of Revolution*, New York, 1981, p. 59.

14. Trotsky, Foreword to Ferdinand Lassalle's *Address to the Jury*, June 1905, quoted in 'Results and prospects', in Trotsky, *The Permanent Revolution and Results and Prospects*, London, 1962, p. 240. Cf. Lowy in *Lev Trockij*, p. 154.

15. Trotsky, 'Dva litsa: vnutrennie sily russkoi revoliutsii' ['Two faces: the inner forces of the Russian Revolution'], *Novyi Mir* [*The New World*], New York, 17 March 1917, quoted in Knei-Paz, p. 240. See also Trotsky, *The History of the Russian Revolution*, Ann Arbor, Mich., 1932, 1957, vol. 1, appendix 2.

16. Lenin, 'On the tasks of the proletariat in the present revolution' [The 'April theses', 7 [20] April 1917], *Selected Works*, vol. 2, book 2, p. 14.

17. *Shestoi sezd RSDRP (Bolshevikov), avgust 1917 goda, Protokoly*, Moscow, 1934, p. 101.

18. See Zinoviev and Kamenev, 'Statement to the principal Bolshevik Party organisations', 11 [24] October 1917, in Lenin, *Collected Works*, New York, 1929, vol. 21, book 2, appendix, pp. 328–31.

19. Trotsky, 1919 Preface to 'Results and prospects', in *The Permanent Revolution and Results and Prospects*, pp. 162–3.

20. Trotsky, *From October to Brest-Litovsk*, New York, 1919, p. 28.

21. Trotsky, 1919 Introduction to *Results and Prospects*, New York, 1919, pp. 185–7; *The History of the Russian Revolution*, vol. 1, p. 211.

22. Trotsky, *Uroki oktiabria*, Moscow, 1924; translated as *Lessons of October*, New York, 1937, pp. 70–1.

23. Trotsky, Introduction to *Results and Prospects*, pp. 163–4.

24. Trotsky, *Terrorizm i kommunizm*, 1920; English edn, *Dictatorship vs Democracy: A reply to Karl Kautsky*, New York, 1922, p. 54.

25. Trotsky, 'Letter to the Bureau of Party History concerning the falsification of the history of the October Revolution, the history of the Revolu-

tion and the history of the Party', 21 October 1927, in *The Stalin School of Falsification*, New York, 1937, p. 29.

26. Brinton, *Anatomy of Revolution*, p. 228.
27. See Simon Wolin, 'The Mensheviks under the NEP and in emigration' in *The Mensheviks: From the revolution of 1917 to the Second World War*, ed. Leopold Haimson, Chicago, 1974, p. 248; Jay Bergman, 'The perils of historical analogy: Leon Trotsky on the French Revolution', *Journal of the History of Ideas*, Jan–Mar. 1987, p. 82 and n. 40.
28. Karl Kautsky, *Terrorism and Communism: A contribution to the natural history of revolution*, London, 1920, pp. 214–15.
29. First expressed by him, as far as can be determined, in a pamphlet of early 1923: 'Mysli o partii' ['Thoughts on the Party'], in Trotsky, *Zadachi XII sezda RKP* [*The Tasks of the Twelfth Congress of the Russian Communist Party*], Moscow, 1923, appendix, pp. 54–5.
30. Trotsky *The New Course*, New York, 1943, pp. 39–41.
31. See Robert V. Daniels, *The Conscience of the Revolution*, Cambridge, Mass., 1960, pp. 248–52.
32. Trotsky, 'Theses on revolution and counter-revolution', first published in *The Fourth International*, October, 1941; reprinted in Isaac Deutscher, *The Age of Permanent Revolution: A Trotsky anthology*, New York, 1964, p. 142.
33. A reference to N. V. Ustrialov, an *emigré* Russian economist who had hailed the NEP as a return to capitalism.
34. Trotsky, *The Stalin School of Falsification*, p. 143 (speech to the Central Control Commission, 1927).
35. 'The real situation in Russia and the tasks of the Communist Party' (opposition platform of September, 1927), in Trotsky, *The Real Situation in Russia*, New York, 1928, p. 187.
36. Trotsky, 'Class relations in the Chinese Revolution' (3 April 1927), *The New International*, March 1938, p. 89.
37. See Curtis Stokes, *The Evolution of Trotsky's Theory of Revolution*, Washington, DC, 1982, pp. 133 ff.
38. Pier Paolo Poggio, 'Le peculiarità storiche della Russia nell'analisi e nella prospettiva di Trockij', in *Pensiero e azione di Lev Trockij*, p. 108.
39. Trotsky, *Permanentnaya revoliutsiya*, Berlin, 1930; Les Evans and Russell Block, eds, *Leon Trotsky on China*, New York, 1976, editors' preface, p. 19.
40. Trotsky, 'The defense of the Soviet Republic and the opposition' (7 September 1929; *The Militant*, 21 December 1929 and 25 January 1930), *Writings of Leon Trotsky*, New York, 1978, vol. 1, pp. 280–4.
41. *ibid.*, p. 287.
42. Trotsky, *Chto i kak proizoshlo*, Paris, 1929, *Writings of Leon Trotsky*, vol. 1, p. 26.
43. Trotsky, letter to the Italian Left Communists, (25 September 1929), *Writings of Leon Trotsky*, vol. 1, p. 323.
44. Trotsky, 'The terror of bureaucratic self-preservation' (2 November 1935), *Writings of Leon Trotsky*, vol. 8, p. 119.
45. Trotsky, 'The workers' state and the question of Thermidor and Bonapartism' (1 February 1935; *The New International*, July 1935), in Trotsky, *The Class Nature of the Soviet State*, London, 1968, p. 49.
46. Trotsky, 'On the question of Thermidor and Bonapartism' (November 1930), *Writings of Leon Trotsky, 1930*, p. 71.
47. Trotsky, *The Revolution Betrayed*, New York, 1936, pp. 86 ff.
48. Trotsky, *The Stalin School of Falsification*, foreword to the 1931 Russian edition, p. xxxviii.

13

The defence of terrorism: Trotsky and his major critics

GEORGE L. KLINE

This chapter explores the ideological and philosophical presuppositions of Trotsky's defence of terrorism as a necessary (present) means for achieving the desired (future) end of socialism/communism: namely, his quite Marxist-Leninist hatred and contempt for the historical *present* and his powerful orientation toward the historical *future*. Of the two major critics of Trotsky's position considered here, only Dewey, a non-Marxist, sensed, if without full clarity or self-consciousness, the connection between Trotsky's future-orientation and his readiness to devalue and instrumentalise present human lives.

I have had a good deal to say in other places[1] about the obsessive future-orientation of Marx and the Marxist-Leninists (including Trotsky), a position which involves both what I have called the (ontological) 'fallacy of the actual future' and the related (axiological) 'fallacy of historically deferred value'. These philosophical errors result in a moral monstrosity, the devaluing and instrumentalising of present existents – communities, cultures, practices, and, especially, *persons* – for the sake of a 'world-historical future' treated as *actual* in the sense of being both definite and valuable. No present existent is held to have intrinsic, non-instrumentalisable value; consequently, *every* present existent – living persons, in particular – may justifiably be treated as a means, as something having only instrumental value (positive if it facilitates, negative if it obstructs) for the producing of the existents of the remote historical future. Those future existents – whether communities, cultures, practices or persons – are treated in the present as *ends*, entities which *will* in the remote future have, or acquire, the intrinsic value that is denied to *present* existents. The groups, classes and individuals against whom Trotsky is ready, indeed eager, to direct the sword of revolutionary terror are held to be particularly, and unacceptably, obstructive of the future-oriented process of the 'building [*stroitelstvo* or *postroenie*] of communism'.

In his magisterial study of Trotsky's social and political thought, Baruch Knei-Paz declares:

> Marxism was the most future-oriented of doctrines, a fact so obvious as to require little elaboration. Rejecting the whole of existing reality, it enthusi-astically contemplated the necessary advent of a novel [future] society ...

The promise of a [future] millennium was inherent in Marxism and the chiliastic dream was certainly a part of its appeal.[2]

In his 'Testament' of 1940 Trotsky ringingly asserted: 'I shall die with unshaken faith in the communist future. This faith in man and his [communist] future gives me even now such power of resistance as cannot be given by any religion'.[3] As we shall see, this powerful commitment to and faith in the communist future also gave Trotsky – as it has given countless other Marxist-Leninists – an unshakeable conviction that their devaluing and instrumentalising of the lives of present persons for the sake of that radiant communist future was unquestionably and unqualifiedly justified.

The view defended in detail by Trotsky was shared by other Bolsheviks, including both Lenin and Lunacharsky. Lenin's statements, though characteristically brief and programmatic, bluntly proclaimed the instrumentalising view of morality, and of the present, which Trotsky was to defend. Perhaps Lenin's most famous statement was made in 1920: 'At the foundation of communist morality lies the [present] struggle for the strengthening and [future] completion of communism [and] our morality is wholly subordinated to the interests of the class struggle of the proletariat.'[4]

The problem of ends and means, terrorism and the dictatorship of the proletariat was posed sharply, not only at the level of theory, but even more urgently at the level of policy and practice, in the early years of the Soviet regime. During this period, Lenin continued to put his instrumentalising theory into practice, but he wrote relatively little on the subject. He did sketch the position, elaborated by Trotsky in 1920 and 1938, that violence used by the exploiters is directed against the historical development of mankind and thus is historically doomed, but violence used against the exploiting minority who are blocking historical progress is effective and those who use it can be confident of success.

> In general [Lenin declared] socialism is opposed to violence against human beings. However, except for Christian anarchists and Tolstoyans, no one has ever concluded from this that socialism is against *revolutionary* violence. Thus, to speak of 'violence' in general, without an analysis of the conditions which distinguish reactionary violence from revolutionary violence, is to be a Philistine who renounces the revolution, or else simply to deceive oneself and others with sophistry.[5]

The chief theoretical statement of the Lenin–Trotsky position was evoked by grave charges brought in 1919 by Karl Kautsky, leading spokesman of European democratic socialism. Kautsky sharply attacked what he called the Bolsheviks' 'immoral and anti-democratic' methods, making specific reference to the 'Red Terror'.[6] Trotsky answered these charges the following year in a slim volume entitled *Terrorism and Communism*.[7] Kautsky published a reply in 1921[8] and a final word in 1930.[9] After Kautsky's death in 1938, Trotsky, then in exile in Mexico, returned to the subject in the article 'Their morals and ours'.[10]

Trotsky's 'theoretical' justification of recourse to terrorism, violence and deception on the part of revolutionary governments may be reduced to four 'theses', of which the first two are in his own eyes most important and impressive, and less historically conditioned or contingent – in other words, more theoretical, more clearly a matter of 'principle':

1. Ends and means are separable, dissociable, and a good (future) end justifies any (present) means; furthermore, different socio-economic classes may use the same means (e.g. terrorism) to achieve very different, even opposed, ends.

2. Socialism cannot be achieved, at least under present (1920) conditions of capitalist encirclement and intervention, without revolutionary violence and repression. Whoever desires the end of socialism must accept the means of terrorism.

3. All governments use violence to stay in power, and all historical revolutions have used violence to break that power.

4. The reign of terror in Russia was started not by the Bolsheviks, but by the counter-revolutionary (White Guard) forces. In other words, the White Terror came first; the Red Terror was only a response to it.

During this polemical exchange Kautsky attacked, and the Bolsheviks (prominently including Trotsky) defended, Lenin's position. Trotsky refused to recognise any moral limitation upon the choice of means, concluding that terrorism, violence and deceit were all antecedently justified by their serving to bring about the good end of communism. Kautsky, in contrast, insisted that Bolshevik terrorism represented not only a reversal of the historical trend toward an increasingly humane morality, but also a violation of the sanctity of human life, a refusal to recognise the human individual as a *Selbstzweck* ('end in himself'). 'The end', Kautsky wrote, 'does not sanctify every means, but only those which are in harmony with it' (TuK 139). In other words, Kautsky held that there are certain moral principles or values which set absolute and inviolable limits to the choice of means for realising given socio-political ends. He thus came very close to Kant, and Trotsky – who derisively repudiated Kautsky's 'Kantian-clerical, vegetarian-Quaker chatter about the sanctity of human life' (TiK 61) – could justly charge that Kautsky had taken up a position inconsistent with Marxian ethical relativism.

It is clear that Kautsky's advocacy of a constitutional winning of power by socialists through free elections, accompanied by education in the aims of socialism, and his insistence that only thus could the end be kept uncorrupted, are much closer to the democratic and humanistic traditions of the West than is Trotsky's future-oriented revolutionary instrumentalism. But who was closer to Marx?

Kautsky did not deny that Marx had favoured revolutionary violence and terrorism in 1848,[11] but he insisted that by 1871 Marx had come to the conclusion that bloodshed and terror were not necessary to revolutionary success. And Kautsky implies that this doctrinal shift was a result of wider experience and maturity. 'Marx', he wrote, 'was completely right when he pointed out with satisfaction that the second Paris Commune was free of all the acts of violence of which the first had seen so many' (TuK 40). Kautsky adds that, as early as 1872, 'Marx expressed his expectation that in such countries as America, England and Holland the proletarian revolution could take on peaceful forms' (TuK 101).

Trotsky can hardly restrain his impatience with such views. Kautsky, he declares acidly, is not a (revolutionary) Marxist; his theory of history is a vulgar eighteenth-century doctrine of peaceful progress. For Kautsky, Trotsky says sarcastically, the 'whole of history reduces to a continuous ribbon of printed paper, and Kautsky's venerable writing desk stands at the [very] centre of this "humane" process' (TiK 26).

I shall try to state the essence of Trotsky's four 'theses' as systematically and concisely as possible, formalising his argument somewhat, but leaving its substance unchanged.

1. Trotsky insists that different socio-economic classes may use analogous means (e.g. terrorism) for totally distinct and opposed ends. This follows, he suggests, from the essential separability and independence of ends and means.[12] What is moral and justified when directed towards one end is immoral and unjustified when directed towards a different end. Trotsky in 1938 put this in a graphic image: 'Only contemptible eunuchs', he wrote, 'maintain that the slave-owner who, by deceit and violence, places a slave in chains is the equal before morality of the slave who, by deceit and violence, casts off his chains' (IMN 15a).

The same point had been made, more solemnly, by an official of the Soviet Secret Police (Cheka) in 1918: 'Murder, lies and treachery are amoral [i e. immoral] and shameful if they are harmful to the cause of the proletarian revolution; these same lies, treachery and murder are moral and laudable if they serve this [future-oriented] revolution'.[13] And in 1921 A. V. Lunacharsky declared: 'Although it is abominable in the hands of a ... [past-oriented] reactionary government, violence is sacred [!] and necessary in the hands of a [future-oriented] revolutionary.'[14]

Further questions remain, however. Assume for the moment that one could agree with Trotsky (as Kautsky did during their polemical exchange) that socialism is a 'good' end, where the criterion of 'goodness' – in Trotsky's own words – is the extent to which the given socio-economic order 'leads to the increase of man's power over nature and the abolition of the power of man over man' (IMN 18a). The difficulty arises when it is proposed to use terrorism, violence and deception as a means for attaining this 'good' end.

There are at least two possibilities. (a) One who accepts socialism as the ultimate end may disagree with others, and with the 'leaders' of the revolutionary party, about the *effectiveness* of terrorism as a means. Such a disagreement would be a theoretical one, and it could presumably be settled, as Trotsky tries to settle it, by appeals to evidence and logic, the final argument being: but it *is* working, and it *has* worked. (b) But even one who agreed with Trotsky about the effectiveness or expediency of terrorism as a means for achieving socialism might (with Kautsky) conclude that such means conflict radically with some other norm or principle (e.g. respect for human life or individual rights).

In other words, one might find the means *theoretically* effective, but *morally* unacceptable. Then, one could either (i) have recourse to a less effective, but nevertheless not totally ineffective, means of realising the given end (socialism) –

this is precisely what Kautsky did in his appeal to constitutional, parliamentary reform – or else (ii), if it can be shown (as Trotsky tried to do) that terrorism, violence and deceit are the *only* possible means of establishing socialism, one must accept them, recognising their immorality (but asserting that these immoral means are justified by the good end) – or else give up the end altogether.

Trotsky does not recognise any *moral* limitation upon the use of terrorism; he insists that the degree and nature of repressive measures are purely a matter of expediency, not a matter of principle. And he explicitly repudiates any Kantian 'metaphysical-bourgeois' dictum that the dignity and worth of the individual person should be respected, asserting that, where necessary, individuals are, and should be, treated merely as means.

Kautsky had charged that the architects of the Red Terror, unlike the initiators of the *White* Terror (who, after all – on his view – were mostly representatives of the exploiting classes), violated their own principles, in particular the principle of the 'sanctity of human life, which they themselves have proclaimed' (TuK 139). Trotsky, of course, is emphatic in his denial that he or any other Bolshevik leader ever subscribed to such a principle. Indeed, he calls it the most hypocritical and stupid 'principle' imaginable. So long, Trotsky insists, as society is exploitative and predatory, the 'principle of the "sanctity of human life" remains the basest lie, intended to keep oppressed slaves in their chains' (TiK 61). In other words, it applies primarily to the life of the exploiter and oppressor, and is invoked to protect him from the righteous indignation of his victims. 'In order to make the individual person sacred [in the future], one must [in the present] destroy the social order which crucifies the individual. And this task can be carried out only with iron and blood' (TiK 61).

2. Trotsky's reference to 'iron and blood' leads us directly to his second main 'thesis': without terrorism it is impossible to achieve socialism.

> Anyone who renounces terrorism in principle [Trotsky declares] ... must [also] renounce the political rule[15] of the working class, its revolutionary dictatorship. Anyone who renounces the dictatorship of the proletariat [also] renounces the social revolution and writes 'finis' to socialism. (TiK 23)

Socialism, he adds, means a society without class divisions, without exploitation, wholly 'without deceit and violence. But it is not possible to throw a bridge toward that [future] society except by the methods of ... violence' (IMN 14a).

'Violent revolution was necessary [in Russia] ... ', according to Trotsky, 'because the undeferrable demands of history [*sic*!] proved incapable of clearing a road [to the future] through the [present] apparatus of parliamentary democracy' (TiK 35). Under pressure from Kautsky, Trotsky goes as far as to admit that, in the historical struggle against feudalism, 'formal' democratic principles (the individual as an end in himself, universal suffrage, freedom of expression) had played a progressive role. But at present, he insists (in 1920), they exhibit their reactionary aspect: 'the setting up of the control of an ideal norm above the real demands of the working masses and the revolutionary parties' (TiK 38). In other words, such principles – and above all the principle which specifies that individual persons have intrinsic, non-instrumental value – introduce an unacceptable constraint upon the otherwise unrestricted recourse to violence, terrorism and deceit.

The essential theoretical differences between Trotsky and Kautsky should now be clear: the former holds that socialism can be achieved only by the violent means of proletarian dictatorship and terrorism. The latter insists (although earlier [in 1909] he was closer to Trotsky's position) that a constitutional winning of power through free elections, accompanied by propaganda and education in the aims of socialism, is the only way to keep the end uncorrupted.

3. Trotsky's third argument is, in essence, that Bolshevik violence, terror and deception are 'justified' because *all* governments have recourse to such measures. Trotsky cites a number of examples from contemporary (1920) events in Western Europe to support his thesis, and concludes: 'It would be vain, in our time, to seek anywhere in the world a regime which did not have recourse to measures of harsh mass repression in order to maintain itself' (TiK 15; cf. 53).

For Trotsky, the form and extent of repressive measures (e.g. imprisonment versus shooting) is a matter not of principle but of expediency. And imprisonment is not an effective means of intimidating the counter-revolutionaries, since the latter – as of 1919–20 – think that the Bolshevik government will soon be overthrown and that they will be released. 'The extensive recourse, in the Civil War, to execution by shooting', Trotsky adds, 'is to be explained by this one simple but decisive fact' (TiK 56). '*Intimidation* is a powerful instrument of both foreign and domestic policy .... The revolution ... kills individuals and [thus] intimidates thousands' (TiK 56–7).

4. Trotsky next turns briefly to his fourth argument: that the terror was started not by the Bolsheviks but by the counter-revolutionaries, 'who were supported by foreign money, men and supplies'. Historically, this is a dubious assertion, but I shall not pause to challenge it.

Apart from the question of means and ends, Kautsky says, we must recognise that 'even the end (purpose) of Bolshevik terrorism is not unobjectionable. Its immediate task is to maintain control of the military–bureaucratic apparatus of power which [the Bolsheviks] have created' (TuK 140). Kautsky goes even further: 'The holding down of a discontented proletariat', he retorts, with irony, 'such is the noble end which is supposed to sanctify the base means of mass-murder in Russia today' (TuK 141–2). This is not Marxism, Kautsky insists: the Bolsheviks have discarded Marx's theory and retain only the magic slogan 'dictatorship of the proletariat'. By using this expression, he writes, 'they thought they could gain absolution for all their sins against the spirit of Marxism' (TuK 110).

Trotsky predicted, with nonchalant self-assurance, that in the future the terror would be reduced: 'The further we go [into the future], the easier it will get, the freer each citizen will feel himself to be, the more imperceptible will the coercive force of the proletarian state become' (TiK 163). Trotsky's last point is crucially and, I suspect, deliberately ambiguous. Will the coercion be less perceptible because it will *actually* have lessened, or only because Soviet citizens will have become more thoroughly *habituated* to it?

Kautsky's comment, a decade later, is worth noting. 'Terror in the Bolshevik system', he declared, 'is not a mere wartime measure [i.e. one confined to the period of civil war]. Rather it has become more deep-rooted in the ten years of peace since 1920.'[16] And he adds that 'there are two kinds of counter-revolution [in Russia], the primitive or "White-Guard" counter-revolution, and the Bonapartist or fascist–Bolshevik counter-revolution'.[17]

On this anti-Stalinist point, at least, despite their bitter differences on other matters, Kautsky and Trotsky (author of such fiercely anti-Stalinist tracts as *The Revolution Betrayed*, 1937) were in substantial agreement.

After an interval of eighteen years Trotsky returned in 1938 to the defence of terrorism. The occasion appears to have been the need to defend himself against mounting charges that in suppressing the 1921 Kronstadt uprising he had launched a truly Stalinist terror against members of the *working class*.[18] Dewey's reasons for joining the debate[19] seem to have been twofold: (a) on the one hand, he had just chaired the Commission which, in Mexico, had sifted the evidence presented in the Moscow show trial against Trotsky and found it unconvincing; and (b) on the other, Dewey did not wish to appear as a defender of Trotsky's Marxist-Leninist views – views of a kind that he had for decades criticised and rejected.[20] He feared that his defence of Trotsky from Stalinist injustice would be interpreted as a defence of Trotsky's views of terrorism and the dictatorship of the proletariat. As he put it: if Trotsky were cleared by the Dewey Commission, he would be cleared *only* of 'the specific charges upon which [he] was convicted in the Moscow trials'. His 'political ideas and policies' would in no way be vindicated.[21]

In contrast to Kautsky, Dewey made no effort to disassociate Trotsky's views on terrorism from those of Marx. But he introduced a fresh and important distinction between two different senses of the word 'end' in Trotsky's assertion that 'the end justifies the means': (a) 'end' in the sense of objective future consequence of present choice and action; and (b) end in the sense of 'end-in-view' or *telos*, the presently envisaged future goal to be brought about by present choice and action. Dewey notes that the end-in-view tends to be relegated to a hazy and *remote* historical future, whereas *volens nolens* the first of the many objective consequences of present action will tend to emerge in the relatively *short-term* future.

Dewey asserts forcefully that means and ends (in both senses) are interdependent and continuous. He charges Trotsky with subordinating the professed end, the end-in-view, to the instrumentality of violent class struggle – proclaimed as the only possible effective means.[22] Since, for Trotsky, Dewey writes:

> the view that [class struggle] is the only means is reached deductively and not by an inductive examination of the means-consequences in their interdependence, the means, the class struggle, does not need to be critically examined with respect to its actual objective consequences. It is automatically absolved from all need for critical examination.... [T]he *end-in-view* (as distinct from objective consequences) justifies the use of any

means in line with the class struggle and … justifies the neglect of all other means. (MAE 71)

Perhaps the following reformulation will make Dewey's point somewhat clearer. According to Dewey, Trotsky accepts an end-in-view, E, and asserts that to attain this end one must resort to certain means, M (class struggle, terrorism, etc.). But, Dewey maintains, when we use M, certain (perhaps unanticipated) objective consequences, C, ensue; and some or all of these consequences are incompatible with E. Yet they were generated by M, which was asserted to be essential to the attainment of E. The reason for this paradoxical situation, Dewey argues, is that M is arbitrarily declared to be the only possible means to E, and thus is exempted from critical examination, and in particular from an investigation as to its probable objective consequences, C. Such analysis and criticism, if undertaken, would have made it clear that M would (probably) generate objective consequences, C, that would be incompatible with, or would 'undermine', the original end-in-view, E.

> It is one thing [Dewey continues] to say that class struggle is a means of attaining the end of the liberation of mankind. It is a radically different thing to say that there is an absolute *law* of class struggle which determines the means to be used. For, if it determines the means, it also determines the end – the actual consequence. (MAE 71)

There are many ways, Dewey points out, of carrying on a class struggle. We should choose critically among them – assuming that we have adopted 'class struggle' in general as the appropriate means for achieving our *end-in-view* (which Dewey himself did not) – by examining their consequences, not by deduction from an alleged 'law of history'.

Dewey, who made a central place for the category of habit in his own ethical and social theory, is, I think, suggesting that the Trotskyite recourse to terror might become habitual, that the objective consequences of such a historical habit might be a kind of institutionalisation of terrorism, and that such a habit might prove extremely hard to break, might indeed last for generations. To put the point differently, Dewey is presciently suggesting that the Marxist-Leninist terrorism so passionately defended by Leon Trotsky would lead to the institutionalised terrorism of *Stalin's* fully fledged totalitarian system. The only point – and it is a central one – that Dewey did *not* clearly articulate is that Trotsky's defence of terrorism was underpinned by his Marxist-Leninist devaluing and instrumentalising of the historical present for the sake of the 'radiant future of communism'.

Notes

1. See my essay, '"Present", "past", and "future" as categoreal terms, and the "fallacy of the actual future"', *Review of Metaphysics*, vol. 40, 1986–7, esp. pp. 219–20, 223–5, 229–30; and 'The use and abuse of Hegel by Nietzsche and Marx', in *Hegel and His Critics: Philosophy in the aftermath of Hegel*, ed. William Desmond, Albany, NY, 1989, pp. 1–34.
2. Baruch Knei-Paz, *The Social and Political Thought of Leon Trotsky*, Oxford, 1978, pp. 568–9. See also Ernst Bloch, *Das Prinzip Hoffnung in Werke:*

Gesamtausgabe, Frankfurt-am-Main, 1959, vol. 5, pp. 724–5, cited by Steven Lukes, *Marxism and Morality*, Oxford, 1985, p. 37; and Joel Tabora, *The Future in the Writings of Karl Marx*, Frankfurt, 1983, esp. pp. 353, 354–5.

3. Trotsky, *Diary in Exile*, trans. Elena Zarudnaia, London, 1957, p. 141.

4. V. I. Lenin, *Sochineniya*, vol. 31, pp. 412–13, 410.

5. Lenin, *Sochineniya*, vol. 23, p. 379.

6. Karl Kautsky, *Terrorismus und Kommunismus: Ein Beitrag zur Naturgeschichte der Revolution* Berlin 1919, p. 55. (Hereafter references will be given in the text, using the siglum 'TuK' followed by page number.) There is an unsatisfactory English translation: *Terrorism and Communism: A contribution to the natural history of revolution*, London, 1921.

7. *Terrorizm i kommunizm*, Petrograd, 1920 (also republished in Trotsky *Sochineniya*, vol. 12). (Hereafter references will be given in the text, using the siglum 'TiK' followed by page number.) The British edition was entitled *In Defence of Terrorism*, the American edition *Dictatorship vs Democracy*; the 1961 American reprint is entitled *Terrorism and Communism*.

8. *Von der Demokratie zur Staatssklaverei: Eine Auseinandersetzung mit Trotzki*, Berlin, 1921.

9. *Der Bolschewismus in der Sackgasse*, Berlin, 1930. English translation, *Bolshevism at a Deadlock*, London, 1931.

10. 'Ikh moral i nasha', *Byulleten oppozitsii*, no. 68–9, Aug.–Sept. 1938, col. 6a–19b ('IMN'). English translation, 'Their morals and ours', *New International*, vol. 4, 1938, reprinted in *Their Morals and Ours*, ed. George Novack, New York, 1973, pp. 13–52.

11. In a passage referred to by both Kautsky and Trotsky, Marx declared: '[T]here is only *one means* by which the murderous death agonies of the old society and the bloody birth throes of the new [future] society can be shortened ... and concentrated – and that is by *revolutionary terror*' (*Neue Rheinische Zeitung* 7 Nov. 1848; in *Marx–Engels Collected Works*, London, 1970, vol. 7, pp. 505–6). This passage is regularly cited by Soviet commentators who are making the Leninist–Trotskyite distinction between future-oriented revolutionary terrorism and past-oriented reactionary terrorism, e.g. by N. A. Beliaev and M. D. Shargorodsky, *Kurs sovetskogo ugolovnogo prava: Chast obshchaia*, Leningrad, 1970, vol. 2, p. 250.

12. Trotsky's reference in 1938 to the 'dialectical interdependence (*vzaimozavisimost*) of means and ends' (IMN 18a) is only an apparent and superficial qualification of this basic position.

13. Martin Latsis, *Mech*, no. 1, 1918; quoted in V. S. Grechko, *Kommunisticheskoe vospitanie v SSSR*, Munich, 1951, p. 6.

14. A. V. Lunacharsky, 'Svoboda knigi i revoliutsiia', *Pechat i revoliutsiia*, no. 1, 1921, p. 4.

15. Trotsky even speaks of the proletariat's *edinovlastie*, literally, 'monarchy' or 'monopoly of power' (TiK 22).

16. *Der Bolschewismus in der Sackgasse*, pp. 93–4.

17. *ibid.*, p. 102.

18. See Knei-Paz, *Social and Political Thought* ... esp. p. 417 n. 134.

19. With the essay, 'Means and ends: their interdependence, and Leon Trotsky's essay on "Their morals and ours"', *New International*, vol. 4, 1938; reprinted in George Novack, ed., *Their Morals and Ours*, pp. 67–73.

I will refer to this essay by using the siglum 'MAE' followed by the page number of the Novack edition.

20. As early as 1922 Dewey had referred to the 'monstrous [Marxist] belief that class-struggle civil war is a means of social progress' (*Human Nature and Conduct*, New York, 1922; 2nd edn, 1930, p. 273). In 1939 he added perceptively: 'one may ... find evidence to support the view that the dictatorship of the proletariat became first that of a party over the proletariat and then the dictatorship of a small band of bureaucrats over the party', the latter having 'adopted, with greatly improved technical skill in execution, all the repressive measures of the overthrown Czarist despotism' (*Freedom and Culture*, 1939; New York, 1963, p. 89).

21. See *The Later Works of John Dewey*, ed. Boydston, Carbondale, Ill., 1981–, vol. 11, p. 318, cf. pp. 311, 312, 317, 598; vol. 13, p. 347. I am grateful to James Campbell for these references.

22. There are useful discussions of the Dewey–Trotsky polemic in Knei-Paz, *Social and Political Thought* ... pp. 561–3 and in Lukes, *Marxism and Morality*, pp. 118–22. However, neither commentator recognises the importance of Trotsky's powerful future-orientation or his instrumentalising of the lives of present persons.

14

Trotsky and Martov

PHILIP POMPER

Trotsky's writings about Martov and the Mensheviks during and after 1917 reveal a great deal about Trotsky himself. They tell us about Trotsky's own inner doubts, his efforts to overcome them, and his notions of revolutionary leadership. I present the following hypothesis: Trotsky's self-affirmation as a leader issued from his sense that he had successfully overcome in himself or outgrown those characteristics that consigned Martov to the dustbin of history. Yet his nagging doubts about his fitness as a leader continued to affect his political behaviour. Anyone attempting a psychological explanation should offer a general picture of Trotsky's personality and, however sketchily, I propose to do so.

Trotsky occupied a marginal place in Russian society as the son of a Jewish farmer. The young Trotsky's sense of not quite belonging in any given community no doubt strengthened the well-studied tendency for many Jews in the intelligentsia to seek a rational cosmopolitan identity. Trotsky made such an identity central to his life plan. He dedicated himself to internationalism and rejected all parochial identities. I need not dwell on this characteristic, which Isaac Deutscher, among others, has probed so well, but rather will sketch out the sources of some important aspects of Trotsky's personal and political style.

First of all, his parents sent him to school in Odessa when he was only nine. Early uprooting from a rural setting to an urban one and enrolment in St Paul's school had a number of traumatic aspects. The young boy had to learn city dress and manners. His aunt noted in her brief memoirs that he became so fastidious that he constantly picked lint from his clothing. Worse still, he discovered that he spoke some sort of jargon. He had to spend a year in a preparatory class. Trotsky's lifelong meticulousness, indeed compulsiveness, about dress and language probably were symptoms of overcompensation for these early deficiencies. More important, he acquired a nagging sense that he was an impostor, and that, too, created a strong tendency towards overcompensation.

In *My Life* Trotsky candidly recounts childhood experiences of weakness, of illness, of physical ineptness, and an adolescent episode of paralysing indecisiveness. He was exceedingly highly-strung. In adulthood, when Trotsky applied Marxian analysis to these and other traits, he associated them with a Jewish, petty-bourgeois and intelligentsia background. But even with the self-confidence conferred by Marxian analysis and his own psychological insight, Trotsky could not erase from his own psyche the consequences of his personal development. The somewhat quixotic cast of his later political career owes a great deal to Trotsky's overcompensations for his early weaknesses and reaction-formations to attitudes and emotions that threatened his positive identity. The defence mechanisms Trotsky used to protect his positive identity produced a certain grandiosity in his self-image and *machismo* in both his rhetoric and political behaviour. All of this became especially acute after he rejected the Mensheviks, who, collectively and sometimes individually, embodied precisely what he fought in himself, and joined the Bolsheviks, whose suspicion of him strengthened his sense of impostorship and increased his already strong tendency towards overcompensation.

The impostor theme runs through Trotsky's autobiography. The first revealing episode occurs when Lev Bronstein, aged nine, sets out for his first day of school in Odessa. All decked out in the regalia of St Paul's *realschule* and proudly parading to school, he encounters a street urchin, who:

> stopped, looked me up and down, hawked deeply and spat on my sleeve. It was as if a lightning bolt had struck from a clear sky and reduced me to ashes. It seemed especially unfathomable, that he could spit on this wonderful new uniform, which signified a profound change in my life.[1]

Trotsky is not yet punished for impostorship, only for his magnificent appearance and hubris. The story continues. When he arrives at St Paul's yard the school monitor strips him of his medallion, braid, buckle and buttons. (Preparatory students did not have the privilege of wearing the full regalia.) Now Trotsky is punished for his impostorship; his humiliation is complete. When a man of fifty tells a tale of this sort, he reveals not only the trauma inflicted more than forty years earlier, but perhaps offers clues to his personality. Trotsky signals that he is doomed to be humiliated in other contexts, that he will be resented and punished for later attempts to make 'profound changes' in his life and for putting on the trappings of power.

One wonders if Trotsky unconsciously sensed the connection of the above story with another one describing an outing to the opera in Paris in 1903, when he was still an ally of Lenin on *Iskra*:

> Once we decided to take Lenin to the opera ... An utterly unmusical reminiscence is always associated in my mind with this visit to the opera. In Paris Lenin had brought himself a pair of shoes that had turned out to be too tight. As fate would have it, I badly needed a pair of shoes just then. I was given Lenin's, and at first I thought they fitted me perfectly. The trip to the opera was all right. But in the theatre I began to have pains. On the way home I suffered agonies, while Lenin twitted me all the more mercilessly because he had gone through the same thing for several hours in those shoes.[2]

Perhaps this not only signifies identification with Lenin, but suggests that Trotsky should not have attempted to step into Lenin's shoes. Always ambivalent about his heirship to Lenin, Trotsky probably expressed his sense of impostorship as well. His anxieties about replacing Lenin surfaced in a number of ways. He did not want the other Bolsheviks to believe that he was 'casting dice for Lenin's chasuble', as he put it in his account of his behaviour in connection with Lenin's 'Testament'. It is important to recognise the fully conscious, rational and realistic components in Trotsky's assessment of his position in the Party during Lenin's last illness and after his death. However, I hypothesise that an unconscious sense of impostorship affected his actions as well.[3] Some aspects of Trotsky's political behaviour issued from the simultaneous working of conscious motives and lucid assessments of his position and distortions connected with unconscious defence mechanisms.

Trotsky knew very well that he remained an impostor in the eyes of the Bolshevik oligarchs after 1917. The Judas label, often applied to him by Lenin and the Bolsheviks before 1917, only reinforced Trotsky's anxiety about impostorship. The Judas theme is simply a variation on the theme of impostorship, for one species of impostor falsely professes loyalty. Trotsky felt constrained to be the best Bolshevik, the most loyal Leninist. The nagging anxiety that he might indeed be an impostor forced Trotsky to overcompensate by avoiding 'soft' positions. In political struggles that evoked his sense of impostorship he irrationally overcompensated in other ways. His famous 'my party, right or wrong' speech at the 13th Party Congress is a good illustration. But Trotsky also overcompensated by savagely attacking people who had some of the traits that he repudiated in himself. This is where Martov enters the picture.

Trotsky dedicated one of his typically lapidary 'political silhouettes' to Martov. It contains some telling remarks and serves well as a starting point. He pays homage to Martov's gifts as a writer, his political resourcefulness, his penetrating Marxian intellect, his tenacity, but in the end Trotsky assigns a 'minus' to Martov's contribution to revolutionary history. What traits so overwhelmingly negated Martov's virtues? According to Trotsky, a deficit of courage and will deprived Martov's thought and insight of driving force. Note that Trotsky does not accuse Martov of a lack of *personal* courage or will. Rather, he singles out Martov's *thought* as lacking courage and will. The Marxian commitment required a special sort of collaboration between thought and will in order to achieve its completion in revolutionary action. Martov lacked the requisite balance to give his thought 'physical force'. Slipping into a more ironic tone, despite the disclaimer, Trotsky wrote:

> One can hardly imagine either now or at some future time another socialist political actor exploiting Marxism with such talent to justify divergencies from it and outright betrayals. In this respect, without the slightest irony, perhaps Martov deserves to be called a virtuoso.[4]

With even greater irony Trotsky noted that alongside Martov, Hilferding, Bauer, Renner and even Kautsky looked like 'awkward apprentices' when it came to political distortion of Marxism – that is, 'interpreting it [Marxism] so that passivity, accommodation and capitulation are the highest forms of uncompromising class struggle ... [Martov's] dialectics became the subtlest casuistry'.[5]

Trotsky credits Martov with 'revolutionary instinct', but then adds that lack of will ruined it. Martov was 'stubbornly indecisive'.[6] But, as already noted, Trotsky did not have in mind precisely Martov, the person. Rather, Trotsky saw in Martov's style of thought and leadership features connecting him with broader political, social and cultural phenomena. This is in keeping with everything we know about Trotsky's Marxian approach to biography.[7] From other writings it is clear that Trotsky believed that biological factors also came into play during the struggles among revolutionary leaders. More will be said about this later. Here, it is important only to establish the key negative features that Trotsky identifies. In addition to lack of will and passivity, Trotsky added the vulgarity (*poshlost*) and cowardice of the petty-bourgeois intelligentsia.

At first glance, we find nothing striking here. Trotsky, after all, is describing an *intelligent* and Menshevik. Martov's traits combine the weaknesses of the intelligentsia with peculiarly Menshevik ones. The intelligentsia's weaknesses included: 'pliancy, receptivity, sensitivity, feminine features of the psyche' – all of which 'trimmed away the physical power of thought'.[8] Menshevik failings were identified by Trotsky in somewhat different terms: philistinism (*meshchanstvo*), the risk-averse mentality of the small shopkeeper, side by side with the hope of becoming 'a Rothschild'.[9]

The latter traits suggest the association (whether conscious or unconscious) of Menshevism's petty-bourgeois features with Jewishness. Trotsky decisively – and quite consciously – repudiated his own petty-bourgeois Jewish background, but this does not preclude an unconscious dimension underlying his attitude towards Jewish revolutionaries, particularly towards their weaknesses. Despite his brilliance and insight, Trotsky suffered the fate of most members of oppressed minorities. He had internalised stereotypes of Jews. Jews were money-grubbers and cowards. I think it safe to say that he deplored in the Mensheviks traits that he associated with his own past and violently rejected – the identity of Jews in general, and his own negative identity, in psychological terms.[10] All of this came to the fore when Trotsky passed into the Bolshevik camp. The 'Russianness' of the Bolsheviks compared to their Social-Democratic opponents is well established. The Bolsheviks, whether Russian or not, showed considerable sensitivity about their political base in the Great Russian heartland. Trotsky himself took this into account, particularly in a rather shameless attempt to show that Lenin combined the best traits of the Russian proletarian and *muzhik* in an essay appearing in *Pravda* on 23 April 1920 commemorating Lenin's fiftieth birthday.

It is not necessary to review Trotsky's writings and positions on Jewish nationalism, the Bund, Zionism, or on such matters as pogroms, the Beilis trial and other incidents involving either world Jewry or the Jews of the Russian Empire and Soviet Union. Trotsky showed considerable consistency in his Marxian approach. Like Marx, he believed that historically the socio-economic position of the Jews had created a special Jewish mentality, and his attacks on the Mensheviks faintly echo Marx's observations about the 'Jewish question'.[11] Trotsky would neither affirm his own Jewishness nor ignore injustices and atrocities committed against

Jews. As a member of a proletarian party in a multinational state and then as leader of an international movement, Trotsky knew the disadvantages of his background and did everything possible to avoid calling attention to it. He thus had to tread a narrow path. All of this was quite conscious and measured. But issues involving self-identity do not so easily yield to conscious control.

Trotsky's Marxian approach to the position and mentality of Jews on a socio-psychological map shows in a number of ways in his remarks about Mensheviks and petty-bourgeois socialists. It shows in repeated references: to *meshchanstvo*, to petty shopkeepers, to a 'combination of debilitating sobriety and sterile fantasising'.[12] Aspiring Rothschilds lurked behind the miserly hucksters, the penny-pinching *lavochniki*. In one inspired attack on the Mensheviks, Trotsky's agile mind leapt to the image of Sancho Panza, Don Quixote's companion who, in Trotsky's view, embodied the odd combination of vulgar practicality and romanticism found in Menshevism. To be sure, the use of Sancho Panza hardly suggests a narrow association of Jewishness with the petty-bourgeois mentality. But what do all of these associations taken together suggest? Is this merely effervescent rhetoric issuing from Trotsky's effort to sketch a generalised petty-bourgeois political style?

The calling up of Don Quixote's companion is quite suggestive. Perhaps Trotsky knew Turgenev's essay of 1860, 'Hamlet and Don Quixote', which contained a typology easily applicable to the Russian intelligentsia. In reality, as in fiction (Turgenev's *Rudin*, for example), intelligentsia Hamlets often turned into Don Quixotes after reacting to their own indecisiveness and lack of will, their passivity. Reaction-formation against passivity led to exaggerated, quixotic action. The Sancho Panza figure is like the petty-bourgeois Jewish *intelligent* who attaches himself to his equally inept Russian counterpart. Together they produce grandiose, quixotic visions and actions, but this cannot hide their Hamletic side, their lack of physical force – their impotence. But Trotsky himself had experienced paralysing indecisiveness during a phase of his adolescence. Between the spring of 1896 and the late autumn of the same year, his lack of will power led to self-doubt, depression and severe psychosomatic symptoms.[13] However, he overcame the symptoms precipitated by his struggle with his father over his career, successfully rebelled – and became Trotsky.[14]

Trotsky's pride in his achievement, expressed in striking images of self-affirmation in *My Life* and *The History of the Russian Revolution*, masked continuing anxieties. In these works he ranges himself alongside Martov, to the latter's disadvantage. He repudiates Martov's Hamletism and lack of will power. For example, in *My Life* when describing 1905 Trotsky wrote:

> In October, I plunged headlong into the gigantic whirlpool, which in a personal sense, was the greatest test of my powers. Decisions had to be made under fire. I can't help noting that those decisions came to me quite obviously … Later, I observed with astonishment and a sense of estrangement how every event caught the cleverest of the Mensheviks, Martov, unawares and threw him into confusion. Without thinking about it – there

was so little time for self-examination – I organically felt that my years of apprenticeship were over, although not in the sense that I'd stopped learning.[15]

There is a briefer passage echoing Trotsky's earlier note of self-affirmation alongside criticism of Martov in *The History of the Russian Revolution*. Trotsky brilliantly makes the point for anyone looking for psychological clues to his positive and negative identities. The following description of Martov comes shortly after Trotsky quotes his own speech at the 2nd Congress of Soviets in 1917 consigning Martov to the dustbin of history: 'The Hamlet of democratic socialism, Martov would make a step forward when the revolution fell back as in July; but now when the revolution was ready for a lion's leap, Martov would fall back.'[16] The image of a timid, indecisive Martov alongside a coiled, predatory Trotsky sufficiently makes the point. Trotsky's name, Lev, or Leon, of course means 'lion'.

More clues to the deeper attitudes underlying Trotsky's self-affirmation and his vehement rejection of Martov appear in Trotsky's notes for his unfinished biography of Lenin. A small section of one of the notebooks is entitled 'Lenin and Martov'. Here Trotsky repeats his admiration for Martov's virtuosity in dialectics, but contrasts Martov's mastery of dialectics with Lenin's:

> His [Martov's] dialectic was a dialectic of derivative processes and limited scale, episodic changes ... On the contrary, Lenin's dialectic had a massive character. His thought ... 'simplified' reality, indeed swept aside the   secondary and episodic in order to deal with the basic ... the Leninist dialectic was a dialectic for the large scale ... Martov's thought was the thought of a watchmaker in politics. Lenin's thought worked on the scale of Dneprostroi.[17]

The notion that Martov worked on a limited scale at the level of thought suggests more than a personal failing. Petty-bourgeois characteristics are called to mind, particularly by the image of the watchmaker. And, if the conjectures above are correct, the cluster of associations called up included physical weakness, reduced masculinity, or indeed effeminacy, and Jewishness.

Another clue can be found in Trotsky's essay 'Lenin and the old *Iskra*', included in the collection published shortly after Lenin's death. There Trotsky compared Lenin to Akselrod in terms similar to the Lenin–Martov comparison. Trotsky wrote:

> Akselrod analysed with the greatest skill the tendencies of the different groupings of the revolutionary *intelligentsia*. He was a homeopath of prerevolutionary politics ... The quantities with which he worked were always very small; the societies with which he had to do he would measure with the finest scales. Not without reason did Deutsch consider Akselrod like Spinoza, and not in vain was Spinoza a diamond-cutter – a work that requires a magnifying glass. Lenin, on the contrary, looked upon the events and conditions as a whole and understood how to grasp the social complex in his thought.[18]

Akselrod and Spinoza, both Jews, show the same penchant for small-scale, albeit painstaking work. The image of the petty-bourgeois apothecary or jeweller comes to mind. Mensheviks, Jews, thought at a petty level and could not rise to the occasion in revolutionary situations because they came from a petty milieu and worked on a petty scale. To be sure, Trotsky's own Jewish comrades in arms (not to speak of Trotsky himself) refuted this notion, but Trotsky always had to fight the stereotype that he had internalised himself.

Returning to Martov, once again we find in Trotsky's notebooks some striking passages reinforcing the above conjectures: 'Martov's delicate, fragile thought halted, powerless in the face of major events ... Martov's intellect, psychology [was] feminine. From this issued his letters – a magnificent stream – better than his articles, and his articles – are better than his books.'[19] Clearly, lack of physical force and small-scale activity had feminine associations in Trotsky's mind as well as petty-bourgeois and Jewish ones. Thus, the Jew, the petty-bourgeois, the Menshevik failed in their revolutionary undertaking because their thought lacked masculine force and will to power. According to Trotsky's sociology of knowledge, the small scale and impotence of their thought issued from their lack of ties to the broad working class. We thus find a Marxian analysis of dialectic styles and styles of leadership alongside stereotypes of Jews and women. But this also calls to mind some of Trotsky's comments about the Russian intelligentsia cited above.

In summary, Martov signified Trotsky's own weaknesses, his negative identity. Martov represented not only the weak Jew, the kind of Jew Trotsky did not want to be, but also the Hamletic personality, the overly scrupulous, paralysed, intelligentsia figure. Trying to put behind him the unmasculine reputation evoked by such terms as 'organisational Platonism', Trotsky had to prove that he, a Jew, former Menshevik and critic of Lenin, was worthy of the 'hard' Bolsheviks. He also had to show that he was not a Menshevik in disguise. Martov, the Menshevik and Jew, embodied characteristics that Trotsky had to reject. Trotsky's rejection of Martov and the Mensheviks preceded his conversion to Bolshevism, but surely his former association with them affected the vehemence of his attack upon Martov and his formulation of Martov's traits.

A few words should be said as well about Trotsky's positive identity. First of all, when Trotsky juxtaposed Lenin to Martov he unconsciously meant Lenin to stand for himself. The reference to Dneprostroi in the comparison of Lenin's and Martov's dialectical style, of course, evokes Trotsky, who had conceived the project. Trotsky's achievements in 1917–21 stood up well in comparison with Lenin's. He, too, commanded a dialectic of vast scope. Trotsky believed that some people were more suited by nature than others for such visions and for leadership in conditions of real struggle. References to Lenin's heredity and his special fitness appear in Trotsky's biography of Lenin and in notes for the biography. In notes under the heading 'Genius', Trotsky wrote: '[Is it] an individual anthropological phenomenon or a social one? [It is] a combination, the interaction of one with the other. "Selection" and "exercise" – the application of Darwinian terms to the formation of genius.'[20] A striking formulation of Trotsky's sense of his own organic fitness, if not genius, as a leader appears in My Life. Trotsky depicted revolutionary leaders as those who could descend into the revolutionary whirlpool (plunging into water often symbolises descent into the unconscious mind in Trotsky's writings) and through fusion with the masses liberate a vast reservoir of instinctual energy. Without a gift of intuition (one of the few intelligentsia traits prized by Trotsky) and instinctual energy leaders could not achieve such fusion:

> Marxism considers itself to be the conscious expression of an unconscious historical process ... a process that coincides with its conscious expression only at its very highest points, when the masses with elemental force smash down the doors of social routine and give victorious expression to the deepest needs of historical development. The highest theoretical consciousness of an epoch at such moments merges with the immediate action of the lowest oppressed masses who are the farthest away from theory. The creative union of consciousness with the unconscious is what we usually call inspiration. Revolution is the violent inspiration of history. Every real writer knows moments of creativity when someone else, stronger than he, guides his hand. Every genuine orator knows minutes, when something stronger than he speaks through his lips. This is 'inspiration'. It issues from the greatest creative tension of all one's powers. The unconscious climbs up from its deep lair and subjects the conscious effort of thought to itself, merging with it in some kind of higher unity. The latent powers of the organism, its deepest instincts, its flair, inherited from animal ancestors, all of this rose up, smashed down the doors of psychic routine and – together with the highest historico-philosophical generalisations – stood in the service of revolution. Both of these processes, individual and mass, were based on the combination of consciousness with the unconscious, of instinct, the mainspring of will, with the highest forms of generalising thought.[21]

Only leaders with the right kind of instinctual equipment were fit to lead in such moments. Lenin and Trotsky possessed the requisite gifts; Martov and the Mensheviks did not.

However, it would be dreadfully wrong to infer some sort of biological anti-Semitism at work here. Although not free of the self-hatred stimulated by anti-Semitism, in creating his own positive identity Trotsky found strong Jews with whom he could identify, not to speak of revolutionary comrades in arms. One hardly need mention Marx. Lassalle was another. Moreover, there is evidence, however slight, that Trotsky believed Lenin to have Jewish ancestry. This he could not say openly. However, in 1926 in the article he wrote on Lenin for the *Encyclopedia Britannica*, he mistakenly gave Lenin's mother's maiden name as 'Berg' instead of Blank.[22] Berg is a distinctly Jewish name. Trotsky later corrected his error. Another indirect clue can be found in a curious passage in *My Life*. Claiming that the Whites in the Civil War failed to make any headway with anti-Semitic propaganda, Trotsky quoted a White Guard writer to support his case:

> A Cossack who came to see us was hurt by someone's taunt that he not only served under, but actually fought under the command of a Jew – Trotsky –

and retorted with warm conviction: 'Nothing of the sort. Trotsky is not a Jew. Trotsky is a fighter. He's ours ... Russian! ... It is Lenin who is a communist, a Jew, but Trotsky is ours, ... a fighter ... Russian ... our own![23] The quotation shows that the Cossack was indeed anti-Semitic, but that he had failed to identify Trotsky as a Jew. Unconsciously, it appears, Trotsky wanted to show that he had acquired a reputation as a fighter so far surpassing Lenin's that not he, but Lenin was taken for a Jew!

The story, in a sense, also *unmasks* Lenin. Trotsky is the true fighter; Lenin is the impostor. The thought that Lenin might be partly Jewish even affected Trotsky's positive identification with him, but in an odd, convoluted way. In the end, Trotsky shows both profound self-ambivalence and ambivalence toward Lenin. It shows in the above story and in his own 'Testament', written a few months before his assassination, in which Lenin and Leninism are nowhere mentioned.

Brilliant, gifted, not without psychological insight himself, Trotsky nonetheless showed the psychic wounds of a member of a victim minority, as well as those issuing from his personal development. The defence mechanisms he deployed against his negative identity and sense of impostorship clearly affected his political behaviour. Trotsky's portrayals of Martov contain the negative identity associated with Menshevism, the Hamletic aspect of the intelligentsia, Jewishness and his own early weaknesses. The workings of defence mechanisms show not only in images associated with Martov, but in grandiose self-portrayals, even if in slightly masked form, such as the 'lion's leap' of the revolution, or in laudatory descriptions of Lenin, which apply equally well to Trotsky. Trotsky's profound self-ambivalence generated both self-repudiation and grandiose expressions of self-affirmation. Unconscious anxieties, as well as rational political calculation, show in his relative paralysis and psychosomatic illness during the succession struggle. Trotsky's flight from Hamletism and his sense of impostorship did not fully succeed. His vast achievements during the years of the revolution and Civil War were bracketed by a career that showed typical intelligentsia features. For the greater part of his tragically foreshortened life, Trotsky acted mainly as a brilliant critic of irrational power.

Finally, were Trotsky's self-ambivalence and sense of impostorship sources mainly of strength or weakness? They undoubtedly contributed to his vivid style of writing and political action. However, defence mechanisms alone obviously cannot account for human achievement. Without Trotsky's extraordinary gifts the exaggerated behaviour associated with a tendency to overcompensate and reaction-formations might have yielded only a blowhard, exhibitionist and Chaplinesque dictator. Together, his abundant talents and defence mechanisms produced a memorable corpus of revolutionary journalism, remarkable theoretical forays, brilliant oratory and a bold style of revolutionary leadership. But even a man as gifted as Trotsky could not escape the consequences of his personal history. He fell to the ruthless process of political selection taking place in the 1920s, and in 1940 to the revenge of another 'marginal' man, with his own complex psychology.

Notes

1. I have used both a manuscript in the Eastman collection in Lilly Library in Indiana University and Trotsky's later version in his autobiography to produce the version in the text. Trotsky Mss., 'Otvet na voprosy t. Istmena', 26 Feb. 1923, Lilly Library; Trotsky, *My Life*, New York, 1970, p. 47.
2. *ibid.*, p. 149. Trotsky places the incident in 1902. Other sources suggest it occurred in 1903.
3. The traditional Freudian Oedipal conflict has been used to analyse much of Trotsky's anti-authoritarian behaviour and his problems with his own authority and power. See, for example, E. Victor Wolfenstein, *The Revolutionary Personality*, Princeton, NJ, 1967, pp. 259–75.
4. L. Trotsky, *Sochineniya*, 21 vols, Moscow and Leningrad, 1924–7, seriia 2, vol. 8, p. 67.
5. *ibid.*
6. *ibid.*
7. For a good analysis, see Baruch Knei-Paz, *The Social and Political Thought of Leon Trotsky*, Oxford, 1978, pp. 513–32.
8. Trotsky, *Sochineniya*, vol. 20, p. 336.
9. Trotsky, *Sochineniya*, seriia 1, vol. 3, part 1, p. 225.
10. I believe the term 'negative identity' is Erik Erikson's invention.
11. Knei-Paz is, I think, correct when he writes: 'Marx's severe anti-Jewish language was not echoed in Trotsky's writings' (*op. cit.*, p. 537.) However, he is quick to dismiss the possibility that Trotsky suffered from a 'Jewish complex'. I assume here that Trotsky's language and the associations evoked by it reflect some sort of Jewish complex. It appeared as a tendency to associate certain negative features with Jewishness. Trotsky reacted against those allegedly Jewish traits irrationally. That is, he overcompensated. Such complexes are familiar enough. In Trotsky's case Jewishness was involved; in others, some other minority identification with negative associations.
12. Trotsky, *Sochineniya*, seriia 1, vol. 3, part 1, p. 225.
13. Max Eastman, *Leon Trotsky: The portrait of a youth*, New York, 1925, pp. 32, 34.
14. The best efforts to psychoanalyse Trotsky obviously focus on his struggle with his father. I have already cited E. Victor Wolfenstein, *The Revolutionary Personality*. Another study deserves mention. It is based upon Erik Erikson's stages of psycho-social development. Steven Englund and Larry Ceplair, 'Un essai de psycho-histoire: portrait d'un jeune révolutionnaire, Leon Trotsky', *Revue d'histoire moderne et contemporaine*, vol. 24, 1977, pp. 523–43. Although I believe both works contain insight into Trotsky's development, my own analysis is somewhat different.
15. Trotsky, *My Life*, New York, 1970, p. 184.
16. Trotsky, *The History of the Russian Revolution*, trans. Max Eastman, 3 vols., Ann Arbor, Mich., 1932, vol. 3, pp. 311–32. For some reason, Eastman translated 'lion's leap' as 'tiger's leap'. I have corrected this, but the rest of the translation is Eastman's.
17. Trotsky, *Trotsky's Notebooks, 1933–1935*, New York, 1986, pp. 94–5.
18. Trotsky, *Lenin*, London, 1925, p. 81. Trotsky's (or Deutsch's) information about Spinoza was incorrect. Spinoza did not cut diamonds, but ground lenses.
19. Trotsky, *Trotsky's Notebooks, 1933–1935*, p. 83.

20. *ibid.*, p. 84.
21. This is my translation from Trotsky, *Moia zhizn*, 2 vols., Berlin, 1930, vol. 2, p. 56.
22. The original can be found in Trotsky, *Portrety revoliutsnerov*, ed. Iu. Felshtinksy, Benson, Vt, 1988, p. 7. I have seen the same mistake made on notes in Trotsky's archives. Interestingly, 'Blank' too is a Jewish name, and rumours abound that Lenin was indeed Jewish on his mother's side. Currently, Russian nationalists like Valentin Rasputin make use of this rumour to discredit Lenin's revolution.
23. Trotsky, *My Life*, pp. 360–1.

15

Trotsky and Black nationalism

BARUCH HIRSON

Nationalism and the colonial question

There is no indication that Leon Trotsky participated in any of the discussions in the first four conferences of the Comintern (1919–22) at which the problems of the colonial societies were discussed. In all the debates between Lenin and M. N. Roy, and all the reports on the colonies, I have found no evidence that Trotsky spoke.

There might be missing records that show that Trotsky did contribute, in committee, or in private discussions, to the debates on the subject – but if he did, there are no references to such in his autobiography, or in any available histories. It is possible to suggest reasons for his absence from these debates. There were so many issues in which he was called upon to play a leading role, both organisationally and theoretically, that he might have been spared the need by his comrades to take part in yet another long wrangle. Yet, his apparent silence on so crucial an issue – and his own intervention in 1923 on the 'Negro question' – does call for comment.

There can be little doubt that Trotsky was the one socialist able to present an analysis of the problems confronting a nascent proletariat in the era of finance capital. In his analysis of Russia in 1905 (initially with Parvus) he had followed the method of Marx in providing a critique of the political economy of Russia. That was the only way to proceed. From such an analysis would follow an understanding of the nature of the ruling class (its strengths and weaknesses), the relative position of the proletariat, and even more important the nature of the contradictions in a society in transition. Given his understanding of the nature of uneven and combined development, developed to explain events in Russia, he was admirably placed to contribute afresh to the problems facing backward societies in the twentieth century.

When Trotsky published *Results and Prospects* in 1906 socialists believed that the key to the socialist revolution was to be found in western Europe, and the possibility of socialism in a backward state like Russia seemed remote. In fact, Trotsky and Parvus were almost alone in their assertion that the coming Russian Revolution would lead to the dictatorship of the proletariat. But they were careful to avoid any suggestion that socialism could be built in Russia alone. The workers of western Europe – or at least in Germany – would take up the challenge, and the revolution would become permanent in the sense that it had embraced the people of more than one state.

It is almost embarrassing to have to restate the case twenty-five years on. What should by now be accepted knowledge among socialists everywhere still remains the intellectual baggage of small scattered groups. Yet, it must be restated in the setting of the discussion that follows.

The Russian Revolution followed the path predicted by Trotsky, but the workers of Germany (and elsewhere) were unable to wrest state power from their ruling classes.

The Russian workers, weak initially, were weakened further by the Civil War in which the Western powers gave their support to the counter-revolution. In the circumstances the Bolsheviks were the first socialists who turned to the people of the colonial countries for support. Mick Cox provides an analysis of the discussions in the Comintern on this issue in *Searchlight South Africa*, no. 4 – and, although there have been previous analyses, his article is unique in setting the problem against the failure of the Bolsheviks to come to terms with the lessons of their own revolution.[1] That is, despite Lenin's 'April theses', which led to the jettisoning of the slogan of the democratic dictatorship, the Bolsheviks never absorbed the meaning of that change, either for their own country or for the rest of the world. Trotsky raised the question (for Russia) in 1923 in his *Lessons of October*, and Bukharin's attack on the book signalled the beginning of the onslaught on the Left Opposition. In effect, this also signalled the end of any move to apply Marxist ideas to the colonial countries.

But it was not only Bukharin (and the Party apparatus with him) who got it wrong. Lenin erred when he raised the question of the colonial peoples – not in attacking the imperialist powers, or in calling for support from the colonial people, but in failing to undertake a detailed analysis of the political economies (and with this the class structures) of specific colonial societies. If this had been undertaken, the muddled thinking over Turkey might have been avoided. Likewise the debates in the Comintern on the colonies might have provided more light and less rhetoric.

I argue with the benefit of hindsight. At the time the new socialist government was encircled and embattled. The government, and with it the Comintern, was in desperate need of allies. If Russia could hold out as a workers' state, and if some of the eastern states would join with it in opposition to the imperialist powers, the spent energy of the European workers might be revived. It could not succeed because, in the early 1920s, the colonial people were not yet ready to overthrow their ruling class, or the colonial powers. Over and above the immediate problem facing the Russian state, the debates in the Comintern, which concentrated on the political aspects of the problem, set a wrong tradition. Calls for social change, important as they are, are rendered ineffective or even counterproductive unless they proceed from a critique of the political economy of the given territory – using all the tools provided by Marx and extended so brilliantly by Trotsky. By failing to stress this, the precedent was set. Communists (and this included close allies of Trotsky) fell back into the very system that Marx and Engels had condemned. This was no longer 'scientific' socialism, but a retreat to the utopian socialism that had been opposed so bitterly in the 1840s.

There was also a further factor which, unseen at the time, was to act as a barrier to serious discussion of colonial problems in later years. The 'line' which had been laid down in the Comintern debates had Lenin's imprimatur. Consequently, discussions on the colonial question inside the Left Opposition were restricted to the period after 1924, where the blame for all the errors committed was ascribed to ascendant Stalinism. The earlier period – precisely because it was Leninist – is thereby denied the critical attention it deserves. Indeed, Trotsky himself hardly discusses the years before 1924. His new and limpet-like adherence to Leninism made him critically shy of analysing Lenin on the national and colonial question. The cult of Lenin affected everyone, and not only the official Soviet leadership in the 1920s.

The Black question was first raised in the Comintern in 1921 when David Ivon Jones, the South African communist, moved that the Executive Committee of the Communist International (ECCI) devote serious attention to the Blacks, and the workers' movement among the Blacks, as an important part of the Eastern (i.e. colonial) question.[2] This was accepted, although ECCI only acted on the issue when US Blacks arrived in 1922.

Jones said of the 1921 conference that 'The Indian and African movements do not count for much in the great struggle now pending, [but the Comintern] brings in all toiling humanity, and says to the white worker, not only of South Africa, but of all lands, solidarity with the black working masses is the first step to emancipation.' Discussing his contribution, he wrote:

> I was asked to speak, not so much for South Africa, but on the Negro question in general, the centre of which question, however, is South Africa. Most of my 'co-orientals' were dark or olive, and a murmur of surprise ran through the tables when they saw that the South African delegate was white! My remarks were directed to emphasising the importance of the whole question to the international movement, and to point out that in South Africa is being evolved a solution for the problem, the most aggravating form of which is found in America.[3]

Jones impressed many with his devotion and seriousness, and he was elected to the Executive Committee of the Communist International with a 'consultative voice'. In 1922 he wrote on 'American imperialism and the Negro', in the *Communist Review*[4] discussing American control of Haiti (to ensure the strategic control of Panama), and the domination of Liberia through indebtedness. He condemned Marcus Garvey, the messianic Black leader in New York, for condoning imperialism by welcoming the 'intrusion of Yankee money' in Africa, but commended the African Black Brotherhood in the USA which looked to Russia for 'guidance and inspiration in the struggle' and joined with class-conscious White workers in seeking proletarian emancipation.

In December 1922, when the Communist International met again in conference, Jones was ill. Warren K. Billings from the USA reported on the Negro
question (printed in *International*, 2 March 1923) and, although he started and
ended his report by speaking about the colonial question, he spoke mainly on the
position of Blacks in the USA. Billings ended by presenting a 'thesis' on the Negro
question. This was probably drawn up by a Comintern committee – and its
contents seem to have been based more on hopes than substantive facts. Billings
said that there had been a movement of revolt among the colonial people against
imperialism after the war, and it was recognised by the colonial powers (and by US
magnates) that the further accumulation of capital depended on more intensive
colonisation of regions inhabited by the Black races. He called on the Comintern
to support 'every form of Negro movement which tends to undermine or weaken
capitalism or imperialism'; to organise Negroes everywhere and form a united
front 'when Negro and White working masses coexist'. He also called for work
among Negroes to be carried out by Negroes, and asked that immediate steps be
taken to hold a Negro congress in Moscow.

Jones took up the latter issue and wrote his own 'thesis' into his article 'Africa's
awakening: for a World Negro Congress', which appeared in *International* on 13
July 1923. It called on 'Party organs in Britain, America, Belgium, etc. ... [to]
devote special attention to the Negro question and to the preliminary work
necessary for the calling of a World Negro Congress under the banner of the
Comintern'.

Jones had thought afresh on the problem since the general strike of 1922 in
South Africa, with its racist overtones, and this was reflected in his new writing.
Foreshadowing C. L. R. James and Eric Williams, he said:

> [The Negro] is the greatest living accuser of capitalist civilisation. The
> wealth of England and America is built upon his bones. The slave ships of
> Bristol and New York, with good Quaker prayers to speed them, founded the
> fortunes of many a Christian home. Every British capitalist in South Africa,
> the French in the Cameroons, Belgium in the Congo, and the German
> Empire in Damaraland – they all constitute the blackest record in human
> history of mass slaughters and human violation of every primitive human
> right continued up to the present day. Even the liberation of the American
> slave was only an incident of a civil war between two factions of property
> holders engaged in a quarrel over the forms of exploitation, and was not the
> aim of the war as it is commonly supposed. And as an aftermath of that war
> there was created a social attitude towards the Negro race which leaves the
> one time chattel slaves still degraded outcasts among the peoples of the
> earth.

Racial animosity, he said, was 'artificially generated'. It pervaded all Anglo-Saxon
society, and had also infected the working class.

> The African Negro is the hewer of wood and the drawer of water even for
> the White workers of Europe. The workers of England are trained from
> childhood to regard the Zulu and Matabele wars as heroic exploits, rather

than foul pages in English history. Hence the apathy and social prejudice towards the Negro race, for we hate most what we have injured most. But this period is passing, just as the days of the Second International are passing. The workers of Europe are no longer sharing the profits of their master. The Communist International has appeared, and calls into the one great proletarian family Negroes of Africa, as well as the peoples of the East, along with the revolutionary proletariat of the capitalist countries.

He condemned Black congresses 'composed of ... the thin layer of Negro intelligentsia, who placed vain hopes in professions of loyalty to their oppressors ... [and] greeted the recruitment of Negroes into the French army as a mark of citizenship'; and also those called by Garvey 'who has captured the imagination of the Negro masses in America, and whose slogans "Back to Africa" and "Africa for the Africans", are even spreading into Africa itself'. By way of contrast, he wrote, the Comintern offered the 'first ray of hope for the Negroes throughout the centuries of their oppression'. Jones continued.

The proletarian character of the Negro mass is not so distinct in America as, for instance, in South Africa ... [where] the Negroes form a race of labourers, without any shopkeeping or small tenant element. Probably the small property psychology of the tenant farmers and the small trader element in America reflecting on the purely labouring Negro masses, has a lot to do with what is now notoriously known as 'Garveyism', a charlatan exploitation of awakening race consciousness, which, in so far as it takes anti-White forms, is secretly encouraged by the capitalist class both in America and South Africa. The number of Negro farmers, mostly with very small holdings, according to the last American census was 949,889, which, with their families, represents a big proportion of the Negro population in America.

But awakening race consciousness in Africa tends to have a positive side among the large industrial masses, namely, the outliving of old tribal sectionalism. What the South African bourgeoisie calls a native hooligan is one who, having worked some time in the towns, no longer recognises the authority of his tribal chief. Race consciousness, in the case of the Negro in Africa, is a step towards class consciousness, because his race is a race of labourers. The coming World Congress will have to decide the question, how far the movement towards race consciousness can be directed into proletarian forms.

Jones praised Burghardt Du Bois, 'the foremost leader of the Negro intelligentsia in America', whose books contained 'a glimmering apprehension of the truth that Negro emancipation can only come through proletarian emancipation ... Undoubtedly, America will supply the leaders of Negro emancipation.' But Negro emancipation was not an American question.

it is a question of Africa, as our American comrades themselves have declared. Who is to get this great Africa, the capitalist class or the Comintern? And when is the European proletariat going to stretch out the hand of brotherhood to the masses of Africa, and wipe out centuries of capitalist wrong? The status of the American Negro cannot be raised without the awakening of Africa. But it is no less true that the European Proletariat cannot obtain a real link with Africa except through the more advanced Negroes of America.

In South Africa, he said, reversing his standpoint in the report on South Africa to the Comintern in 1921, Blacks saw every White as an oppressor, a master or boss.

Even the oppressed among the Whites appear to the Black the most violent curser of the Negro. And therefore it is no wonder that news of class emancipation in Europe must appear to him a purely domestic affair of the Whites. A few young industrial workers are beginning to hear news of the Communist Party and of its actions on behalf of the Blacks ... They see Communists gaoled for declaring the solidarity of Black and White workers. But a more imposing gesture is needed to convince the Negro masses that a new dawn is breaking, that 'White man' and 'oppression' are not one and the same thing, that there is an army of liberation coming to aid him, the revolutionary proletariat. Time is pressing, the Negro armies of imperialism are already on the Rhine. Only the Communist International can reconcile the Negro and the White races, and only through proletarian solidarity can this reconciliation be achieved.

Trotsky is not on record as having entered the discussions in the early 1920s. His only contribution seems to have been a letter to Claude McKay, the Black revolutionary poet, who asked him to answer questions on the position of US Negroes. It is not always clear what the questions were, but they seem to have included problems that arose from the use of Black troops in occupied Germany; the racism of the White workers; and the form of organisation most suitable for US Negroes.

Trotsky could offer no answer to the last question, claiming that he was 'insufficiently informed regarding the concrete conditions and possibilities' in the USA. On the other issues he repeated (albeit with greater sophistication) what Jones had been saying since 1921. The Negroes (and the colonial people) had to resist the moves to use them to police Europe – and had to fight against the 'caste presumptions of the privileged upper strata of the working class'. One approach, he said, 'consists in enlightening the proletarian consciousness by awakening the feeling of human dignity, and of revolutionary protest, among the American slaves of American capitalism'.[5]

The Comintern's 'Revolutionary' Turnabout

The 'Negro question' reappeared on the agenda of the Comintern in 1927–8. On this occasion it arose from two quite distinct problems. One was rooted in the difficulties stemming from attempts by the Comintern to forge an international anti-imperialist front. In the case of the USA there were genuine difficulties that arose from the racism found among sections of the White working class and the failure to win over appreciable numbers of Blacks to the CPUSA. This issue became a pawn in the inter-factional fights inside the CPUSA, with each grouping adapting to Comintern demands to prove they were the more 'militant'.

The second issue emerged inside the newly formed League Against Imperialism which met in Brussels in 1927. At that gathering a South African delegation was met with acclaim and the Black nationalist leader, Josiah Gumede (in a brief flirtation with the left), was cheered when he moved the resolution calling for 'the right of self-determination through the complete overthrow of capitalism and imperial oppression'.

Emerging from two totally different situations, blackness was treated as a single problem by the newly created Comintern body, the Permanent Commission on the Negro Question. This was an issue that needed airing, and the Commission might have earned a place for itself if it had contributed to a problem that was being poorly handled by the Communist Parties of the USA and (to a lesser extent) South Africa. But, like all Comintern bodies, it became a centre for removing dissident elements and for laying down the latest line. In 1928 it proved to be an ideal instrument for furthering the campaign against the Left Opposition.

The decisions that were taken at the 6th Comintern Congress were all prepared long before the sessions opened, and any opposition was pushed aside. Stalin had declared that the 'stabilisation' of capitalism had come to an end, giving way to a period in which imperialism was planning to attack the USSR. Socialism was being built in one country, and national Communist Parties should be so powerful that no capitalist country would dare attack the USSR. Accepting the analysis, the Comintern predicted a catastrophic economic crisis in capitalist countries followed by a chain of revolutions. Consequently, Communists had to prepare for the seizure of power through a general strike and armed insurrection. To prepare for this revolution Comintern rules were altered, obliging parties to obey all ECCI directives.

The US Party was instructed to demand 'national self-determination in the southern states where the Negro forms a majority' and the South Africans were instructed to advance the slogan of 'an independent native [i.e. Black] South African Republic as a stage towards a workers' and peasants' republic with full equal rights for all races, Black, Coloured and White'.

The new slogans were backed by sweeping generalisations in which all countries were fitted into one of four types, ranging from highly industrialised to backward peasant societies. From that followed their political tasks in preparation for the coming world revolution. The classification was crude, and some countries were found by these pundits to contain aspects of different economic systems. Where Blacks were concerned, the discussions were simplistic and crude. I quote the statements that emanated from the Comintern committee elsewhere and will refrain from restating them here.[6] But one description is of particular interest because of its re-emergence later. I quote:

> The Party [the CPSA] must show that the basic question in the agrarian situation in South Africa is the land hunger of the Blacks and that their interest is of prior importance in the solution of the agrarian question. Efforts should be made immediately to develop plans to organise the native peasants into peasant unions and the native agricultural workers into trade

unions, while attention to the poor agrarian Whites must in no way be minimised.

When the Negro question was discussed at the 6th Congress of the Comintern there was no obvious intervention from members of the Left Opposition. In fact it is not known whether they attended. Denied the right to circulate their documents openly, and straining to get a hearing for their views on the position in the USSR and in China, members of the Left Opposition had to conserve their strength.[7] If my supposition is correct, this would explain their failure to find their way to the South African leader, S. P. Bunting, who opposed the new diktat and rejected the crude characterisation of conditions in Africa.

Trotsky talks on the 'Negro question'

The resolution of the Comintern dominated discussions inside the Communist Parties, and inevitably the problems that were raised spilt over into the Trotskyist groups that were being formed – and, for our account, particularly in the USA and in South Africa. The first discussion led by Trotsky, was with supporters from the USA who met him in Prinkipo in 1933 to discuss the Comintern's instruction to the CPUS to agitate for an independent Black state in the southern states of America. Trotsky had touched on the problem when he wrote to McKay; in Prinkipo the question was raised again. Yet, despite the sharpness of some of his observations, it is apparent that he still had scant knowledge of the Negroes' position in the USA (believing, for example, that they had their own language), and he did not know that they were paid on a lower scale than White workers, worked longer hours and were allotted the most disagreeable work.

Throughout the recorded discussion Trotsky did not try to place the Blacks inside the political economy of the USA. Instead he concentrated on their political position and supported the demand for self-determination as proposed by the Comintern. He opposed the views of Albert Weisbord, who said that this demand could only appeal to the petty-bourgeoisie, and that the Comintern slogan was only a repetition of the old 'democratic dictatorship of the proletariat and peasantry'. Weisbord thought that Blacks had to be won on a class basis, and proposed demands for 'social, political and economic equality for the Negroes', based on the demand '"equality with Whites" and slogans which flow from this'.

Trotsky, after having the position of Black workers explained to him, accepted the demand for equal rights, but he returned to the Leninist position on the right to national self-determination. He declared that the Blacks (of America and Africa) were a race, but in Africa they were becoming a nation. The American Blacks were at a higher cultural level and would provide leaders for Africa. Discussing the relation between socialists and the American Blacks, he said that it was for Blacks to decide whether they wished to become a nation. But, he insisted, if they wanted self-determination they should get full support. If there was class fraternisation between White and Black workers, then perhaps it would be wrong to propagate this position. However, Trotsky contended: 'the White workers in relation to the Negroes are the oppressors, scoundrels, who persecute the Black and the Yellow, hold them in contempt, and lynch them'.

Asked whether such a slogan would lead to an alliance with the Black petty-bourgeoisie, Trotsky agreed, but said the latter would be bypassed by the militant Black proletariat who, recognising that White communists fight for Black demands, would advance through their own struggle to the proletarian revolution. In concluding the meeting, Trotsky referred to the struggle in Africa. In this case the central problem was with the workers in Europe who held the key to 'real' colonial liberation:

> Without their liberation real colonial liberation is not possible. If the White worker performs the role of the oppressor, he cannot liberate himself much less the colonial peoples. The right of self-determination results; in the final instance, however, it will lead to the struggle against imperialism and to the liberation of the colonial people.

Trotsky had already seen letters sent to the International Secretariat by W. Thibedi, a veteran member of the CPSA who had been expelled and had turned to the opposition for support. He wrote an enthusiastic open letter on the recruitment of Black workers, who, he believed, would form the base of a new revolutionary movement. The praise for a Black recruit (in contrast to a White who might join the opposition) is little less than an embarrassment. The Negro workers, said Trotsky, 'do not and cannot strive to degrade anybody, oppress anybody, or deprive anybody of his rights. They do not seek privileges and cannot rise to the top except on the road to the international revolution'.[8] Although it is possible to see why Trotsky was excited about winning one of the exploited majority, this took little account of the existing class differentiation among Blacks in South Africa, or the actual potential of the man concerned. Thibedi had a long record of service in the CPSA, but had made no known contribution to it programmatically, and the reasons for his expulsion cast doubt on his reliability. Some of the signatories to his letter repudiated the letter, and after a short surge of activity Thibedi's subsequent history is opaque.

In 1935 Trotsky received a set of theses from two contending factions inside the Lenin Club (Left Opposition) in South Africa. Many had been in the Communist Party, and one of their priorities was to develop their criticisms of the new Comintern policy. On the main issue they seemed united. They rejected the slogan of an 'independent native republic' and its corollary, the two-stage revolution in South Africa, in which a bourgeois-democratic state would abolish racial discrimination prior to a socialist transformation. Yet this agreement concealed many differences. The groups differed on many crucial issues, and rejection of the 'Black Republic' slogan did not in itself lead to acceptable alternatives.

Members of the Lenin Club restored the lost tradition of debate inside the left, but their understanding of the problems of South Africa lagged behind the needs of the time. They argued inside the Club as they had once argued inside the CPSA: about the role of the Afrikaners and their possible allegiance in the event of war, the advisability of working clandestinely or openly as a revolutionary movement, the importance of the 'land question' and the advisability of organising trade unions. In trying to find a new programme, the Lenin Club split: one group formed the Workers Party of South Africa (WP) the other became the Communist League and shortly thereafter entered the newly created Socialist Party, including Social-Democrats and Stalinists.

One of the WP papers is devoted exclusively to the land question, and it is this document, entitled the 'Native question' that has remained as the main legacy of those early debates. Yet the thesis of the WP on the 'War question' (quoted below), which at that time was taken as unexceptional by the International Left Opposition, provides a much more rounded position on many questions.

In opposing the Comintern, the members of the WP proposed that the programme of a revolutionary party must start with the dispossession of the Africans from the land. In their thesis they said that 87 per cent of Africans lived on the land. About half of these were in the Reserves (about 7 per cent of the country where land possession was permitted). A further third lived in 'virtual serfdom' as farm labourers (500,000), seasonal farm labourers (700,000) or squatters (500,000). A tiny minority of Whites owned more than 90 per cent of the land. Of these, 11,000 (11 per cent of the total) were farmers with holdings of between 1,000 and 5,000 acres each, amounting to more than half of the country's land. Under these conditions there was no possibility of land reform.

The land question, said the WP, was bound up with the needs of capital. The men in the Reserves were required as workers, and they were 'burdened with heavy taxes ... [and in that way] forced to find work in the mines or on the farms'. On the mines and farms, they said, Africans produced the wealth of South Africa, subject to 'intense exploitation', receiving one-tenth of the wages paid to Whites, whom they outnumbered by 9 to 1 on the gold mines and 17 to 1 on the coal mines. The wages of the Whites would be dragged down to the level of the unskilled workers, unless the entire working class organised to narrow the wage gap. That is, the WP, like the CPSA, failed to see that the division of the working class and the wage differential across the racial divide were built into the method of political control. The preference given to White workers in the mines and industry, the reservation of jobs, higher wages and segregation in housing and social amenities provided the mechanism for atomising the working class. It created a privileged group in the working class which would jealously protect its own position and act as a praetorian guard for capital. Their call for a united working-class movement to fight for the emancipation of labour from capital seemed to be in the best tradition of socialism. However, in calling on White workers to take their place in the fight for 'the removal of all repressive legislation against the Natives and all the other workers', they overstated the role of the Whites, and underestimated the revolutionary potential of the Black workers who had to take the lead in the struggle against discrimination.

Aware of the threat of fascism and the danger of losing the few remaining democratic rights, the WP called on Marxists to find a link between the 'emancipation of the working class and the liberation of the oppressed races, [to throw] ... off the yoke and chains of Capitalism and Imperialism'. Racial oppression would be removed only when the revolutionary movement grasped the national struggle – but without obscuring the class struggle and without pandering to petty-bourgeois Black nationalism. There could be no competition with the ANC in nationalist slogans to win the masses – national liberation could be achieved only through proletarian revolution.

In effect, the WP surrendered its independent thinking and retreated from the position upheld by S. P. Bunting (the former Communist leader, now expelled) in his criticism of the Comintern's new slogan. Proletarian revolution, for the WP, was apparently the task of the White workers alone. The motive force for Africans, they said, would be the demand for land, and this would be followed by the call for national emancipation. Their central programmatic point was encapsulated in a phrase that gained currency (or notoriety) in sections of the left: 'Only the revolution can solve the agrarian question, which is the axis, the alpha and the omega of the revolution'. This transformation would only be effected by the revolutionary working class together with the 'potentially great revolutionary reservoir' of African peasants. However, even this was in doubt. The WP was far from sanguine about the possibility of unifying the workers or of organising the Black rural population, as yet 'untouched by revolutionary propaganda, revolutionary ideas, revolutionary outlook'.

The assertion that the people of the rural areas were peasants was false. The Reserves, as they had said, were little more than a labour reservoir for the mines, the farms and the burgeoning industries. A quarter of a million African labourers worked in the mines, a million Africans were townsmen and the boom that followed South Africa's departure from the gold standard in 1932 would bring more to the towns. This was the proletariat that had to be organised in the coming period, separately from the White workers if necessary.

The entire perspective was flawed. The struggle for land and against 'oppression and exploitation' could be achieved only by the working class in its own struggle for socialism. Precisely what was meant by 'national liberation' was not defined, but it presumably incorporated the demand for 'democratic rights'. The WP, usually so far ahead of other groups in their understanding of the problems of South Africa, had failed to provide the analysis that would inform a future revolutionary cadre.

Trotsky replied, saying he was 'too insufficiently acquainted with the conditions in South Africa' to offer opinions on several practical questions. In those few words he surrendered the right to criticise the basic premises of the WP. In general he accepted the thesis as a valid analysis, but, he wrote, he had to voice disagreement on certain aspects of the draft theses – particularly those which arose from polemical exaggerations in the struggle with the 'national policy of Stalinism'. In so doing he compounded the prevailing confusion.

Dealing with the Black Republic and the land issue, he said:

> Three-quarters of the population of South Africa … is composed of non-Europeans. A victorious revolution is unthinkable without the awakening of the native masses; in its turn it will give them what they are so lacking

today, confidence in their strength, a heightened personal consciousness, a personal growth. Under these conditions the South African Republic will emerge first of all as a 'Black' Republic: this does not exclude, of course, either full equality for Whites or brotherly relations between the two races (which depends entirely upon the conduct of the Whites). But it is entirely obvious that the predominant majority of the population, liberated from slavish dependence, will put a certain imprint on the state.

All struggles had to be seen in the context of imperialist rivalries, and Trotsky linked the issues in South Africa with the necessary overthrow of British imperialism. This could be achieved only through the class struggle, both in South Africa and in Britain: 'The South African possessions of Great Britain form a Dominion only from the point of view of the White minority. From the point of view of the Black majority South Africa is a slave colony.'

In describing South Africa as a slave colony, for any part of the population, Trotsky lent credence to a variant of pluralism which ignored the very point that the WP had made in their thesis on the war question: namely, the centrality of gold in the South African economy, with the creation of a vast army of workers to satisfy the financial and commercial needs of the world economy. The formation of this proletariat, exploited and oppressed, was the feature that had to be stressed by a Marxist theoretician – and not ringing metaphors that ignored economic reality. Consequently, the entire history of Trotskyism in South Africa was directed into a quagmire from which it had difficulty in extricating itself.[9] Such was the inevitable consequence of a Comintern directive that almost destroyed the CPSA and tarnished the groups that tried to establish a new and healthier Marxist tradition. It is my contention that Trotsky erred in his letter and that the correction he alone was capable of offering was not delivered.

However, there was a tension in Trotsky's formulation. Repeating his formulation of 1933, he said that a proletarian party, using the methods of class struggle, would effect a social revolution which also had a national character. 'We have not the slightest reason to close our eyes to this side of the question or to diminish its significance.'

Trotsky raised two further points on which he said the WP thesis was deficient, both tactical rather than substantive. First, he called on the revolutionary party, despite their strictures, to defend the ANC against attacks by the 'White oppressors and their chauvinistic agents in the ranks of the workers' organisations'. It was not incorrect, he said, to enter into episodic agreements with the ANC, while exposing its inability to achieve even its own demands. At all times, however, the revolutionary movement had to retain organisational independence and freedom of political criticism.

Secondly, while agreeing that the national and agrarian questions 'coincided on their bases', and that these questions could be solved only in revolutionary ways, he disagreed with the WP contention that agrarian and not national demands be put first. The struggle for land (an essential ingredient of the struggle for socialism) had to be related to the necessary political and national demands.

The failure by Africans to link the demand for land with that of liberation only reflected political backwardness. The revolutionary movement had to transform the demand for land into a demand for both land and liberty. The agrarian problem had to be made political if there was to be change in the country. For reasons that were mainly tactical, in view of the smallness of the revolutionary party, said Trotsky, the message had to be taken into the rural areas mainly if not exclusively through the medium of the advanced workers.

Trotsky also pinpointed one of the problems that would face the revolutionary movement in South Africa, where, he said, the proletariat consisted of 'backward Black pariahs and a privileged arrogant caste of Whites'. These White workers would have to face the alternative: 'either with British imperialism and with the White bourgeoisie of South Africa, or with Black workers and peasants'. The WP could not reach the White workers and therein lay the difficulty facing the left: if advanced workers had not yet emerged from the ranks of Black labour, who was to take the message to the peasants? For practical and theoretical reasons the small set of intellectuals, isolated from the urban workers and lacking contact with the rural population, had to concentrate their efforts on building a base among the working class. The WP did not attempt this task, nor did the Communist League (the other section which did acknowledge the need for working in the unions). Only in the Transvaal did members of the Left Opposition made a serious effort to organise a Black trade union movement. Through the 1930s a number of Trotskyists established the first viable Black trade unions.[10] These efforts received no support from or mention in the journals of the Cape Town groups.

Ever mindful of the international dimensions of the working-class struggle, Trotsky concluded by looking optimistically to the advantages that would come from co-operation between a Soviet Britain and a socialist South Africa. He also looked forward to the influence that a Soviet South Africa would exercise over the rest of Africa. That was fifty years ago and the working class has suffered serious defeats during that time. But the vision still remains. Only a socialist South Africa can revive hope for an altered southern Africa – in Namibia, Lesotho, Swaziland, Botswana and Zimbabwe, as well as in Mozambique and Malawi – in which Blacks can unite to build a better society.

Trotsky's Final Words on the Negro Question

There was some discussion inside the International Secretariat on the South African thesis, but little was added in the correspondence with Cape Town. Trotsky was in any case preoccupied with events in Europe and in Asia, but there was one last occasion on which he spoke about the Negro question. In April 1939 Trotsky engaged in a discussion with members of the American SWP on the problems they faced in trying to reach the Blacks of America. He had before him a memorandum penned by C. L. R. James, and once again took up the question of self-determination.[11] In the exchanges there is little new light. Once again Trotsky stated his view that, if the Negroes wanted their own state, then it was the task of revolutionaries to support them in their demand.

This was a misreading of the demands of Blacks – whether petty-bourgeois or proletarian – and was inserted into the revolutionary calendar because Trotsky (and members of the SWP) were bewitched by the activities of the Stalinists. The discussion, ultimately, was empty. There was no place for the slogan and it fell away. What is regrettable, if I may repeat the point, is that Trotsky failed to direct discussion to the issues that needed urgent investigation: the specific position of different layers of the working class, the reasons for working-class racism, and their insistence on racial discrimination. Such a discussion would have had its impact wherever revolutionary movements had to face similar problems. It would have directed the training of cadres in South Africa and elsewhere along different lines – and that would have proved invaluable in their attempts at building a revolutionary movement.

Notes

1. Michael Cox, 'The national and colonial question: the first five years of the Comintern, 1919–24,' *Searchlight South Africa*, no. 4, February 1990, discusses the differences between Lenin and Roy and points to the tensions in Lenin's formulations.
2. See *Moscow*, 15 July 1921, and Sheridan Johns, 'The Comintern, South Africa and the Black diaspora', *Review of Politics*, vol. 37, no. 2, 1975. These extracts are taken from the forthcoming biography of D. I. Jones by Gwyn Williams and myself.
3. *International*, 16 September 1921.
4. *Communist Review* (Great Britain), no. 5, September 1922.
5. Reprinted in *The First Five Years of the Comintern*, New York, 1953, vol. 2, pp. 354–6.
6. For a fuller discussion see my article, 'Bunting vs Bukharin: the 'Native Republic' slogan', *Searchlight South Africa*, no. 3, July 1989.
7. This could explain their subsequent silence on events at the sessions at which these resolutions were passed, and their failure to note the opposition voices at the Congress.
8. The letters, signed by several Blacks, were mainly pleas for financial support. There was no discussion of any theoretical issues. The grouping, if it existed, collapsed, although Thibedi said that he had left the CPSA with several trade unions. See Trotsky's response, 'Closer to the proletarians of the "Coloured" races', in George Breitman, ed., *Leon Trotsky on Black Nationalism and Self-Determination*, New York, 1978.
9. The discovery of documents for 1935–39, providing membership lists, theses, correspondence and so on, will make it possible to write an account of the origins of the Trotskyist movement in South Africa.
10. I discuss this in my book *Yours for the Union*, London, 1989.
11. Breitman, *Leon Trotsky*, pp. 33ff.

Part IV

Trotsky and the economic debates
of the 1920s and 1930s

16

Trotsky and NEP

ALEC NOVE

1920–25

Did Trotsky anticipate NEP by a year? In his subsequently published works, and in his autobiography, Trotsky states that he proposed in February 1920 that requisitioning (*prodrazverstka*) be abandoned, that the peasants be allowed to sell freely. The Central Committee turned the idea down, and, as both Deutscher and Knei-Paz point out, Trotsky never returned to his proposal. He continued in fact to be the hardest of the hardliners within War Communism.

There is no need to quote here his well-known and notorious arguments for militarisation of labour, arguments which he extended far beyond the immediacies of 1920, since he saw compulsory labour as necessary throughout the period of transition to socialism: 'If it is true that compulsory labour is unproductive in all circumstances, as the Mensheviks assert, then all our construction-plans are doomed to failure.' This was also when he asserted that:

> the road to socialism lies through the highest concentration of state power (*gosudarstvennost*). Like a light bulb which, before extinguishing itself, flashes brightly, so the state prior to its disappearance takes the form of the dictatorship of the proletariat, i.e. of the most pitiless state, which coercively (*povelitelno*) controls the life of the citizens in all its aspects.[1]

In this last quotation Trotsky anticipates Stalin's view of the coercive role of the state in the period of socialist construction. But presumably none of this excludes the possibility that Trotsky did see the disastrous effects of *prodrazverstka* on agricultural production and on peasant attitudes towards the Soviet regime.

Interestingly, *Argumenty i fakty* (no. 5, 1990) published a note under the title of 'The beginning of the struggle for NEP'. In it the author, S. Pavlyuchenkov, provides evidence that Yu. Larin had prepared a proposal to abolish *prodrazverstka* and put it to the 3rd All-Russian Conference of *sovnarkhozy*, held on 23–29 January 1920. He had the sympathy of Rykov. However, Lenin and Krestinsky strongly opposed even raising the idea, and told Rykov to forbid Larin from proceeding with it. Larin was dismissed from his membership of the presidium of VSNKh (Supreme Council of National Economy). The proposal was in fact adopted by that third conference, but the party leadership refused to recognise it and forbade its publication 'so as to avoid confusion', according to

Pavlyuchenkov. After NEP had been introduced, Larin 'ironically stated that for some comrades the thunder of Kronstadt's guns was needed to awaken them to the need for a new policy'. The article does not mention Trotsky at all. And Trotsky's autobiography does not mention Larin. There is something here to investigate.

Trotsky very foolishly continued his argument with Lenin over the militarisation of labour and of the trade unions even as late as the 10th Congress. But when Lenin proposed the first steps towards NEP at this Congress, Trotsky claimed that he 'accepted them at once. For me they were merely a renewal of the proposals which I had introduced a year before.'[2]

Did Trotsky accept NEP, in the form into which it developed by the end of 1921? Until his expulsion from the Politburo, or perhaps even after that, was he a 'Nepist', as is asserted by Stephen Cohen? Or was he already fighting against the majority on economic issues as early as 1923, as is claimed by Ernest Mandel? Was Knei-Paz right in stating that he 'urged not only the rejection of NEP but a return to the direct path to socialism'.[3] This view has been repeated by a number of Soviet scholars. For example, G. Vodolazov, in the course of an otherwise admirable contribution to the symposium *Osmyslivat Kult* (p. 153) writes of 'the defeat of the attempt to create an administrative-command system on the basis of the conception of primitive socialist accumulation by Trotsky and Preobrazhensky immediately after Lenin's death'. A whole school of Russian nationalists has been presenting Trotsky as an arch-villain who advocated all along the policies which Stalin adopted in 1929–30. Thus, according to V. Belov, 'Stalin was the chief Trotskyist' (*Pravda*, 15 April 1988).

In my view this is wrong. Stephen Cohen is right. Trotsky did indeed disagree with the Politburo majority, with Bukharin, in 1923–5, but at no point did he question the foundations of NEP. His disagreements centred on other matters. Of course he envisaged a socialist future which would be marketless, but in so doing he expressed the virtually unanimous view of Bolsheviks and Marxists of the time. NEP was a transition period, sometimes referred to by Trotsky himself as the 'transition epoch', during which the market was essential. When he expressed concern about the power of the Nep-bourgeoisie, or of potentially capitalist elements in the village, here too he was expressing views held widely in the Party. When he spoke critically at that time about lack of planning, he did not, as is sometimes alleged, counterpoise plan and market. This can be seen vividly in the following quotations:

> For the next period, which is what interests us practically, we shall have a planned state economy, allying itself more and more with the peasant market and, as a result, adapting itself to the latter in the course of its growth ... our success ... will depend in large part upon the degree to which we succeed, by means of an exact knowledge of market conditions and correct economic forecasts, in harmonising state industry with agriculture according to a definite plan ... If the different parts of our state industry (coal, metals, machinery, cotton, cloth etc.) do not mesh with each other ... the costs of production will ... include the expenditures of the most inflated

branches of industry and the final result will be determined by the less developed branches. The present selling crisis is a harsh warning that the peasant market is giving us. ... The correct work of our State Planning Commission is the direct and rational way of approaching successfully the solution of the questions relating to the *smychka* [workers' and peasants' alliance] – not by suppressing the market but on the basis of the market.[4]

All this is from *The New Course*, written in 1923.

In his speech to the 13th Party Congress, on 26 May 1924, Trotsky quoted approvingly a Central Committee resolution to the effect that one can 'serve the cause of *socialist* construction only to the extent that we actually learn to co-ordinate the sectors of the national economy in the course of their constant interaction with one another and with the market',[5] and he went on to deny accusations that he favoured 'exaggerated ideas about the possibilities of planned management of the economy'.[6] A year earlier, at the 12th Party Congress, he spoke of the need to stimulate peasant agriculture, and that to this end one should encourage the peasant to 'get richer' (*stal bogache*).[7] Yes, later on he took exception to Bukharin's 1925 slogan 'enrich yourselves' (*obogashchaites*) and yes, as we shall show, he became conscious of danger from the so-called kulaks. But in these respects too he reflected an attitude widespread in the Party. As such historians as Yuri Afanasiev and Gefter pointed out, was Bolshevik Russia ready to accept NEP?

It is interesting and relevant to note that some of the best recent studies of how NEP ended, such as those by Yuri Goland ('Kak svernuli NEP', *Znamya*, no. 10, 1988, and 'Politika i ekonomika' *Znamya*, no. 3, 1990) stress the evolution of the Party majority, including Stalin, towards positions which conflicted with the logic of NEP, a process which began in 1925 and had nothing to do with Trotsky at all. The same point is made by L. Troparevskaya in *Ekonomika i matematicheskie metody*, no. 6, 1989: referring to 1925–6, she writes: 'the market mechanism towards the end of classical NEP was retreating before the forces of War Communism along the entire front' (p. 1001). In my own article published in *Voprosy istorii*, no. 8, 1989, I listed a number of measures inconsistent with NEP which were adopted in 1926. Clearly, in no sense was Trotsky responsible for them.

In his booklet *Towards Capitalism or Socialism?*, published in August 1925, Trotsky remains wholly within NEP assumptions. True, in discussing agriculture he refers to a 'transition from scattered single peasant establishments to a socialist system of land cultivation', i.e. to the aim to collectivise, but at once he adds that 'this is inconceivable except after passing through a number of stages in techno-logy, economics and culture', a distinctly gradualist approach to which Bukharin could have subscribed.

1926–28

By 1926 Trotsky is in open outright opposition to the Stalin–Bukharin line, and soon teams up with Zinoviev and Kamenev to form the 'united opposition'. As already noted, a number of Soviet publicists consider that they were opposed to

NEP, that in 'turning left' in 1928–9 Stalin 'stole the clothes' of the Left
Opposition. Some Western historians take a similar view. What was Trotsky's
attitude to NEP when in opposition?

First a few words about 'socialism in one country'. At the Follonica conference
on the fortieth anniversary of Trotsky's assassination, I said that Trotsky 'might
well have agreed that, in the absence of revolution in the West, it was possible to
"build" socialism but not to complete the building. Expressing it in terms of
Russian grammar, one could use the imperfective but not the perfective aspect,
stroit not *postroit*.'[8] It therefore gave me some quiet satisfaction to find the
following in the Trotsky Archive. After expressing his opposition to isolationism
and excessive autarky, he continued:

> Obviously the question is not whether we can and whether we must (*i
> dolzhny li*) [these words added by Trotsky in ink] build (*stroit*) socialism in
> the USSR. But in order to *postroit* socialism, i.e. bring our industry to a high
> stage of development and to socialise agriculture on an industrial basis, we
> would need (in the absence of world revolution) not less than roughly a
> quarter of a century.[9]

I agree with Richard Day that 'The operative question for Trotsky was not
whether Russia could build socialism in advance of the international revolution,
but *how* to devise an optimal planning strategy, taking into account both the
existing and the future international division of labour'.[10] Day lays great stress on
the advantages which Trotsky expected to obtain from expanding foreign trade.
True enough, one finds Trotsky writing on 15 January 1926 that entering into the
international division of labour, into 'intensive trade-exchanges with capitalist
countries, we thereby subject our economy to the criteria of world-market productivity and cost'.[11] Then on 15 April 1927 we find him writing:

> The attempt to argue that the inevitable development of our links with the
> world market is for me an argument against the possibility of our socialist
> development is not only false and dishonest, but also meaningless. I dis-
> puted and dispute with theoreticians of an isolated (self-sufficient)
> economy, who abstract from the international factor. I proved and prove
> that our dependence on the world market will grow. The sort of dependency
> which speeds our tempos of development is in our interest ... From this
> follows not lack of faith in socialism, but my total hostility towards the
> philosophy of the pace of the tortoise within the four walls of an autarkic
> economy.[12]

Obviously a kick at Bukharin.

But surely Day is wrong in implying that, in the actual situation of the mid-
1920s, a large increase in foreign trade was feasible. What could Soviet Russia
export? There were only limited amounts of grain and timber available. And the
Left Opposition's peasant policies, of which more in a moment, could hardly be
expected to elicit higher (voluntary) marketings of farm produce.

A word first about the relationship between Trotsky and Preohbrazhensky.
Some of the accusations levelled against both of them are equally false. Thus

neither advocated robbing or impoverishing the peasantry. Preobrazhensky's view, as can be seen by any reader of his *New Economics*, was that accumulation by the socialist sector required unequal exchange, but that this could be achieved painlessly by cutting the costs of state industry and not cutting (or cutting by less) the prices charged, and meanwhile peasant incomes would rise with higher productivity. However, I see considerable differences between their attitudes to the market, and so to NEP. Trotsky, at least from 1922 and after his exile, persistently spoke of the market as necessary for the whole 'transition epoch', frequently relating plan and market. Preobrazhensky was much more inclined to see a life-or-death struggle between the 'law of value' and socialist accumulation, arguing that one must destroy (*pozhirat*, eat up) the other. It is then not a coincidence that when Stalin turned left Preobrazhensky abandoned Trotsky and begged for readmission to the Party. Also Trotsky claimed that he had a policy to deal with the looming crisis of NEP in 1927, whereas Preobrazhensky, in a well-known article published in *Vestnik kommunisticheskoi akademii*, argued that the contradictions were in fact insuperable without world revolution. Whether in fact Trotsky had a viable policy alternative is another question, to be discussed in a moment.

Let us look at his peasant policy. Trotsky shared with nearly all Bolsheviks a negative view of the individual peasantry as a class, which could at any time secrete capitalism. As was noted by both Bolsheviks and non-Bolsheviks at the time, there is a plain contradiction between the urgent need to increase production and marketing and the view that a prosperous peasant is well on the way to becoming a dangerous class enemy.

In 1925, in *Towards Capitalism or Socialism*, Trotsky feared a development of the productive forces that could take the form of 'expansion of the volume of commodity capitalist relations in the village', which 'might be of cataclysmic importance and might shunt our course of development definitely on to the track of capitalism'.[13] On 7 April 1927 we find Trotsky writing: 'From the point of view of the development of the productive forces, a good harvest is absolutely a good thing. From the point of view of socialist development the question is ambiguous ..., since it (the good harvest) could be the base of capitalist accumulation.'[14] He was less insistent than was his then ally Zinoviev on the kulak danger, and it is only fair to add that by 1927 even Bukharin was advocating an 'offensive against the kulak', though doubtless without any notion of liquidating them as a class. However, it is not at all unfair to see the Left Opposition at this time urging the Party leadership to take more severe measures against the so-called kulaks. Yet neither they nor any others in 1927 were advocating forcible mass collectivisation.

The opposition was quick to discern the looming crisis of grain procurements in 1927. They advocated a compulsory grain loan as a short-term expedient. Stalin and his group denied that there was a crisis right through the 15th Party Congress (December 1927), and then resorted to emergency measures reminiscent of *prodrazverstka*. But there had been nothing in the opposition's declared policies which would have helped avert the crisis of NEP.

Certainly not their attitudes to the peasantry. They shared the class approach of nearly all Bolsheviks, which, in the words of Tsipko, caused:

> monstrous strain in a country in which 80 per cent of the population were seen as an obstacle on the path to an ideal society. Because of this the leaders of the Party had to feel that they were in a besieged fortress, not so much because of capitalist encirclement, but rather because they were surrounded by Nepmen, markets, a commodity-and-peasant world.[15]

It is this which enabled Stalin to rally support for his anti-peasant measures. And while the 'left' had not advocated the measures which Stalin took, nothing in their speeches or philosophy prepared the Party members to oppose them. Quite the contrary.

The opposition's policies on industry and on prices were also of questionable relevance. Seeking support from the urban working class, which suffered from low wages and unemployment, they could hardly be expected to come out for wage restraint and higher prices. Trotsky was well aware of the 'goods famine', which was quite apparent at least from the beginning of 1926, and he frequently referred to it. As the author, in 1923, of the phrase 'scissors crisis', he could not but be aware of the importance of the terms of trade between town and village. Bourgeois specialists such as Novozhilov and Kondratiev issued warnings. Trotsky's remedy, as I understand it, was to urge higher investments and also more foreign trade. The latter suffered from an export availability bottleneck, while higher investments required higher savings and some sacrifices in current consumption. Day has argued that, if Trotsky had succeeded in getting a higher investment plan adopted in 1925–6, the resultant flow of goods would have alleviated the goods famine and so avoided the crisis of NEP. I see no evidence for this, for the following reasons.

First, as abundant evidence shows, the comparatively modest attempt to increase the volume of new investment in 1926 was already causing considerable strain on a still weak economy, which had only just recovered from the hunger and destitution of 1921. While the speed-up proposed by Trotsky, and demagogically denounced at the time by Stalin as super-industrialisation, was a mere fraction of what Stalin himself was proposing two or three years later, it was doubtfully consistent with the preservation of NEP. Secondly, productive investments take time to bring forth increased output. And, thirdly, Trotsky advocated higher investments in heavy industry. He pointed out in a memo dated 7 September 1926 that the plans then under discussion (by the so-called OSVOK, the Council for the Restoration of Basic Capital) would still leave output per capita of industrial products in 1929–30 below the level of 1913. This would mean the continuation of goods famine. He then went on: 'whether the industrialisation of a country is proceeding can be seen if there is a relative rise in the share of those sectors which produce means of production'.[16]

So: higher investments, especially in heavy industry, higher wages (in a note dated 6 June 1926 to the politburo, he complains that 'wage rises have been delayed'[17]), stronger measures against kulaks, and no clear challenge to official price policies, although Trotsky shows himself aware of shortages and disequilibria. This does not seem to add up to a coherent policy alternative. But, of course, Trotsky is only one of a great many oppositionists, in many countries, who launch destructive criticisms of government policies. It is also necessary to add that, with all their limitations, Trotsky's and Zinoviev's policies were much less unsound than was Stalin's great leap forward.

One of Trotsky's problems related to the nature of his 'class' analysis. The basis of 'Thermidor' had to be kulaks and Nepmen. The chief enemy therefore had to be the man who, in Trotsky's eyes, was most closely identified with a soft policy towards the new bourgeoisie: that is, Bukharin. Not only did this mean that Trotsky failed to identify the real main enemy. It also meant that he tended to identify progress towards socialism with the extension of state ownership, with the squeezing out of the 'privateer', quite unaware that the growing power of the state over economic life was necessarily accompanied by the growing power of the bureaucracy, and also of Stalin who stood at its head. Later he saw things differently. In exile he wrote of the bureaucracy:

> freeing itself from the supervision of the market and of Soviet democracy ... The innumerable live participants in the economy, state, collective and private, must make known their needs and their relative intensity not only through the statistical compilations of planning commissions but directly though the pressures of demand and supply ... The drafts made in offices must prove their economic rationality through commercial calculation. The economy of the transition period is unthinkable without control by the rouble.[18]

Criticising peasant policies in that same year, he argued that collective farming should be based not on coercion but on personal interest and commercial calculation, adding that 'economically sound collectivisation should lead not to the elimination of NEP but to a gradual reorganisation of its methods'.[19]

Trotsky's view of collectivisation and the five-year plans is not the subject of this paper. I have written elsewhere on this,[20] so I will not pursue the matter further here.

Conclusion

The quite numerous Soviet sources which seek to present Trotsky as an enemy and even the gravedigger of NEP are mistaken. Particularly misleading is the use in this context of quotations from Trotsky of the War Communism period, since at that time his views were shared by Bukharin and indeed, in most respects, by Lenin too. This was well pointed out by Kliamkin in his path-breaking article in *Novy mir*, no. 11, 1987, despite which Trotsky's – and Preobrazhensky's – position continues to be widely misunderstood.

His position must be seen in the context of the fundamental ambiguity of the entire relationship between Bolshevism and NEP, which has been well explored in Tsipko's four articles in *Nauka i zhizn* (nos 11 and 12, 1988, nos 1 and 2, 1989). Lenin's view too was deeply contradictory. Was it the right path or a hateful but necessary retreat? Was it *reculer pour mieux sauter* (in his words, '*chtoby razbegatsa i prygnut vpcred'*? They all saw NEP as a transition period of uncertain length, after which the ruling party would renew the assault on the remaining class enemies and transform the economy, the peasantry and society.

Trotsky cannot be held responsible for the ending of NEP. He was out of power after 1925, and played no part in any of many decisions which led to the crisis of NEP. (The same cannot be said of Bukharin.) Trotsky saw NEP as a stage in a revolutionary process, and he could not envisage the coexistence in the long run of socialism and markets, but in these respects he did not differ from other Bolsheviks. He was indeed more internationalist, less inward looking, than the Politburo majority, but this did not make him into an enemy of NEP. While he was still in the Politburo himself, his ideas on current economic policies differed very little from those of Bukharin. For the reasons advanced above, it seems to me that the policies advocated by the united opposition in 1927 were objectively impractical and represented no solution to the growing crisis within the bounds of NEP – though they did not advocate going beyond these bounds. As Kliamkin was the first to point out in the USSR, Stalin went very much further 'left' than was ever considered possible or desirable by the Left Opposition. I put 'left' in inverted commas because it does seem more than a little perverse to equate the virtual enserfment of the peasant majority of the population with the onward march towards 'socialism'.

Notes

1. L. D. Trotsky, *Sochineniya*, Moscow, 1923–7, vol. 12, p. 161.
2. Trotsky, *My Life*, New York, 1960, p. 466.
3. Baruch Knei-Paz, *The Social and Political Thought of Leon Trotsky*, Oxford, 1978, p. 322.
4. Trotsky, *The New Course* (published as articles in *Pravda* in December 1923 and as a pamphlet early in 1924). The quotations will be found in the chapter 'Planned economy (1042)', and the appendix 'On the "smychka" between town and country' (more precisely, 'On the "smychka" and false rumours'), in *The Challenge of the Left Opposition*, ed. Naomi Allen, New York, 1975, pp. 119, 137–8, 139. [Reference supplied by the editors – TB.]
5. Trotsky, 'Speech to the Thirteenth Congress', in *The Challenge ...*, pp. 155–6.
6. *ibid.* p. 156.
7. 12th Congress of the All-Union Communist Party, 1923, *Stenotchet*, p. 322.
8. Alec Nove, 'Trockij, collectivisation and the five year plan', in *Pensiero e azione politica di Lev Trockij*, ed. Francesca Gori, Florence, 1982, p. 392, where, however, a key line is omitted; reprinted correctly in Nove, *Socialism, Economics and Development*, London, 1986, p. 91.
9. Trotsky Archive, T. 3007, 1926.
10. R. B. Day, *Leon Trotsky and the Politics of Economic Isolation*, Cambridge, 1973, p. 4.
11. Trotsky Archive, T. 2977.
12. *ibid.*, T. 3043
13. *The Challenge ...*, p. 330.

14. Trotsky Archive, T. 2982.
15. *Nauka i zhizn*, no. 12, 1988.
16. Trotsky Achive, T. 2982.
17. *ibid*. T. 2986.
18. *Byulleten oppozitsii*, 1932, p. 8.
19. *Writings of Leon Trotsky, 1932*, ed. George Breitman and Sarah Lovell, New York, 1973, p. 275.
20. In the article cited at note 8 above.

17

Trotsky's conceptions concerning foreign economic relations

AGOTA GUEULLETTE

> Trotsky's grasp of economics was sure; but, unlike Lenin or Bukharin, he did not distinguish himself as an abstract economic theorist ...
>
> Isaac Deutscher, *The Prophet Armed: Trotsky, 1879–1921*, Oxford, 1970, p. 148.

Trotsky's understanding of the imperialist epoch was fundamental to his analysis of the relations that a socialist state could establish with the rest of the world. This was true also of Lenin, Bukharin, Preobrazhensky and other Bolsheviks. At the root of the differences that arose amongst them was the way they saw the further evolution of the capitalist system – in other words, their different conceptions of the theory of imperialism.

Lenin emphasised the 'organisational' aspect of the evolution of capitalism – the strengthening of the role of monopolies, finance capital, the export of capital, and so on. Trotsky assigned secondary importance to these questions. In explaining imperialist expansion by the disequilibrium between productive capacity and effective demand, he in part, accepted Rosa Luxemburg's ideas. For Trotsky and Luxemburg the expansion of foreign trade is synonymous with the search for outlets for goods surplus to consumption in a given capitalist society.

The similarities in their analysis end here, however – even though they predicted the same fate for capitalism. Trotsky did not agree with Luxemburg's view that in a homogeneous capitalist system there could be no foreign trade. On the contrary, he asserted that the lack of political homogeneity, bound up with the existence of national frontiers, national tariffs, etc., constitutes a major obstacle to economic expansion. The tendency of capitalism to expand and to break out of national fetters is, for Trotsky as for Lenin, a positive feature because it makes possible a homogeneous world economy. But it is possible only to speak of tendencies, not finished processes, since national states still exist.

The idea of a 'federation' of the European countries to reduce the constraints on productive forces imposed by the national state was first mentioned by Trotsky in 1909. In 1915 he added that it would need to be a *democratic* federation. Fifteen years later, referring to Lenin, he emphasised that the United States of Europe he envisaged had nothing in common with an 'imperialist Weltmacht':

Needless to say, Lenin rejected the possibility that a *capitalist* United States of Europe could be realized. That was also my approach to the question when I advanced the slogan of the United States of Europe exclusively as a prospective state form of the proletarian dictatorship in Europe.[1]

It follows that there was no similarity between Trotsky's and Bukharin's views on 'pure imperialism'. On the contrary, as Day shows, the difference between them was fundamental: Bukharin thought that the war and the role played by finance capital had created a national state in which planning could eliminate disproportion between different branches of the economy, and in which tariffs and import control could mitigate the impact of world economic forces. For Trotsky proportionality is impossible within one country. In contrast to Hilferding, who assigned a very restricted role to the law of value, Trotsky insisted that it is this law which regulates the interdependent world economy.[2]

After 1915, Trotsky held that the possibility of a United States of Europe was not in contradiction to the law of the unequal development of different countries.

The Theory of Permanent Revolution

The fundamental difference between Lenin and Trotsky lay in their interpretation of uneven development. Lenin, while emphasising how this unevenness was increasing in the imperialist epoch, allowed that revolution in some countries – or even in only one – could be the way in which world revolution began.

Trotsky's approach was quite different. Certainly he did not expect a simultaneous flare-up of the revolutionary movement.[3] As a good dialectician, he emphasised the contradictory nature of the law of uneven development under capitalism. There takes place, he thought, a relative economic levelling between, on the one hand, the different developed countries, and on the other, the advanced and the backward countries as a whole – at the same time as the gap is increasing between one country and another and between one branch of production and another.[4]

The unevenness of development between countries is constantly being renewed; it diminishes, but cannot do away with the growing interdependence of the world's economies. The two fundamental propositions of 'permanent revolution' flow directly from these premises:

> The first proposition [the possibility of the victory of the proletarian revolution in a backward country] is based upon a correct understanding of the law of uneven development. The second [the necessity of a world revolution for the survival of socialism in the backward country] depends upon a correct understanding of the indissolubility of the economic and political ties between capitalist countries.[5]

Trotsky's theory refers to the specific situation of Russia at the beginning of the twentieth century. The purpose of linking economic backwardness to its historical and geographical context was to explain the possibility, in the specific setting of Russia, of combining the bourgeois and the proletarian revolutions. The theory's second tenet indicates the process by which the necessity of the dictatorship of the proletariat could be overcome in a socialist society.

The geographical displacement of the revolution's centre of gravity from West to East, and its economic displacement from developed to backward countries, does not contradict Marx.[6] Like Marx, Trotsky linked economic backwardness and revolutionary socialism. They both established a correlation between economic factors – in this case underdevelopment – and socio-political factors – a proletariat which, even though numerically weak, could constitute a revolutionary class. And they both based their theory on socio-political factors as part of a revolutionary strategy. There, however, the similarity between Marx and Trotsky ends. For Marx there is a delay between the revolutionary phases; for Trotsky, an acceleration. For Marx the bourgeois and proletarian revolutions are separate but connected. Trotsky telescoped them together, though he did not conflate them. In opposition to Marx, who believed in the universality of a capitalism that creates the world in its image, Trotsky emphasised the differentiation that capitalism creates. Whereas Marx's interpretation makes it difficult to explain how a backward country reaches revolutionary maturity, Trotsky, having stressed differentiation, finds it easy.

He conceived a model of development for Russia distinct from that followed by advanced countries. It rests on a particularly pronounced form of the law of uneven development as this applies to backward countries. The coexistence of modern and archaic forms of production, which he was to call, in the 1930s, 'the law of combined development'[7] brings about a dynamic development in the backward counties. It is not a question of a recipe for avoiding the capitalist phase, but rather of showing how industrial modernisation, even of a sectional nature, gives rise to a specific social structure which outstrips Western social forms.

For Trotsky industrialisation did not result from the internal evolution of Tsarist Russia, but was an importation, taking the form of the transfer of capital and technology. This importation, and its absorption, allowed Russia to perform better than the exporting countries without having to go through intermediate phases. But at the same time the rest of the economy remained backward. There was no link between the two parts of the economy. To these economic disparities there corresponded similar ones in the social sphere. The proletariat appeared before the bourgeoisie, which remained small and unimportant. The social structure of agriculture was juxtaposed to that of the classes engaged in industrial production, with nothing in-between. These amalgams in economic and social relations could not last. The fragile social equilibrium was perpetually undermined by the impact of new economic methods that did not originate inside Russian society and so tended to destroy its structure.

The backward condition of the underdeveloped countries, which assures them a certain stability, becomes a factor of instability leading to the appearance of a new mode of production and a new social structure.

Polemicising with Rozkhov, Trotsky said that it is in no way necessary for the preconditions for socialism to be entirely fulfilled before the proletariat exists as a social force. It is enough that 'the development of productive forces has reached the stage at which large enterprises are more productive than small ones',[8] for the industrial structure to create automatically the preconditions for socialism. Trotsky held that large-scale production gave the proletariat a political role independent of its size relative to the total population. A *fortiori*, if the bourgeoisie is as weak as it was in Russia, the proletariat becomes by virtue of its economic position the dynamic force in the fight with the autocracy.

Despite this formulation, alliance with the peasantry is essential during the first phase of the conquest of power. Permanent revolution appears to be tied to two chronologically separated concepts: a national uprising and a class revolution.[9] But Trotsky held the worker-peasant alliance to be only provisional. Tensions are inevitable between the partners because they cannot reach any fundamental agreement on future social objectives. The proletariat did not take the place of the bourgeoisie in order to make the bourgeois revolution, which is only a transitional moment in the uninterrupted revolutionary movement leading to socialism. Since, in Marxist thought, each type of revolution has its own specific social ends, the community of interests uniting the working class and the peasantry breaks up.

The revolutionary dynamism sparked off by the forces within the backward country reaches its peak just at the moment when the permanent (uninterrupted) character of the revolution reveals itself. The advantages of the specific condition of Russia allowed the proletariat to take power; but they became disadvantages when the problem became one of holding on to power, building the new socialist society. Abandoned by its former ally in its social aspirations, the Russian proletariat alone would not succeed in unifying within a modern structure the advanced and the backward elements of the country. The help of its social counterparts in the West would become vital; failing which, the gains achieved would not transcend the aims of the bourgeois revolution. At this precise moment the permanent revolution, engendered by the specific conditions of underdevelopment, would have to go beyond national frontiers to seek support in the capitalist world.

Marxist critics of the theory of permanent revolution are most virulent concerning this crucial point. To be sure, it is not the international expansion of the revolution that is really complained of. It is the reason why Trotsky said that external aid would be necessary: namely, incompatibility between the aims of the workers and those of the peasants. Yet Trotsky only predicted in theory what happened in practice after 1928 – the *forced* collectivisation of the peasantry.

Even though in 1917 (in the 'April Theses') Lenin seemed to rally to the idea of permanent revolution, there remained an essential difference between them. Trotsky's theory rejected Lenin's formula of the dictatorship of the proletariat and the peasantry. Trotsky's refusal to support the sharing of power between workers and peasants was motivated by their social incompatibility. A lasting system of power sharing would have threatened the socialist development of the revolution, since the workers' aspirations went far beyond those of the peasants. A reconciliation between them would therefore be to the detriment of the workers.

As to Trotsky's arguments in favour of an international revolution, economics weighed less with him than fear of the emergence of the forces of counter-revolution. As R. B. Day says: 'external support was thought of as a political balancing factor, intended to compensate for the numerical inferiority of the Russian working class'[10] and bring the revolution to its conclusion. On the other hand, it was in economic factors – particularly the large amount of foreign capital invested in Tsarist Russia – that Trotsky found the basis for the propagation of the revolution in Europe.[11]

Speaking of the 'direct help' of a European socialist state, Trotsky perhaps had in mind material aid such as is nowadays given to an underdeveloped country. Without this help, he did not think that his country could form part of the socialist United States of Europe.

Economic isolation, in the face of the interdependence of the world economy, would be an historic regression compared with the internationalist tendencies of imperialism. Ten years after the October Revolution, Trotsky therefore rejected both Vollmar's notion of the 'isolated socialist state', which depended on peaceful coexistence between the two systems, and the programme of Bukharin who 'proceeds, in his construction of socialism in one country, entirely from the idea of an isolated self-sufficing economy'.[12]

The second fundamental proposition of Trotsky's theory of permanent revolution was thus reaffirmed: it is impossible for a single country to escape from the implications of the economic links established between the capitalist countries. There must be a move towards a *new* political integration (homogenisation) via the world proletarian revolution. In other words, socialism in one backward country could not be achieved, and survive, unless the contradictions between the uneven development and the economic interdependence of the world were resolved in a higher system – namely, universal socialism.

Socialist universality: the theoretical advantages of the international division of labour

As early as 1909 the idea of a federation, similar to that of Switzerland or the USA, was connected in Trotsky's writings with solving the problem of the expansion of productive forces. The economic basis of the United States of Europe (USE) was clearly indicated: it was the international division of labour, already in existence before the world revolution. But he was ambiguous, deliberately or not, on the juridical character of his USE, and it is difficult to be sure of the nature of exchange within this politically unified European body. Would it be exchange between independent states – in this case admitting a certain degree of irrationality – or would it be exchange based on the different economic resources in each region?

In fact, in his publications of 1914 Trotsky wrote of a federation of European socialist countries, independent but linked with each other, which would be able to proceed immediately to 'the socialist organisation of the world economy'. In 1915 he reiterated the idea of the democratic unification of Europe. The participating countries would be politically homogeneous, and this would ensure a harmonious expansion of their productive forces, without the obstacles raised by national frontiers. The slogan of the United States of Europe, launched in the same year by Trotsky, rejects the revolutionary messianism of any one state leading the way to socialism. While declaring in favour of the principle of national self-determination,[13] Trotsky did not abandon the idea of the USE.

His programme, based from the start on the international division of labour, is the antithesis of the Stalin–Bukharin line of building complete socialism first in 'a series of different countries'. This perspective, which envisages 'ready-made blocks', would lead to a unified socialist system in the form of 'a sum total of national-socialist economies';[14] whereas for Trotsky the economic success of the first socialist countries would consist in laying the foundations of the future socialist world economy. In this context Day says very pertinently: 'The operative question for Trotsky was not *whether* Russia could build socialism in advance of the international revolution, but *how* to devise an optimal planning strategy, taking into account both the existing and the future international division of labour.'[15]

As to the functioning of the unified system, Trotsky said that there would not be a huge gap between economic relations before and after the European revolution. Continuity would be assured by maintaining the principle of the international division of labour. Change would take the form of a qualitative improvement in this division, to be achieved by planning, which seems to imply a reorganisation of the productive forces on a supranational scale.

Thanks to free exchange, no longer blocked by frontiers, the backward countries would be able to leap over intermediate phases of development – all the more easily because they had been assimilating the technology of the advanced countries and developing it in the course of the capitalist era. As a result of this acceleration, the backward countries would become increasingly integrated into international exchange. The socialist economic system, established on a world scale, would eliminate the contradiction between productive forces and absorptive capacities typical of capitalism. The location of production, planned according to rational economic criteria, would correspond to the consumption capacity of an integrally socialist world. This network of exchanges would bring about a symbiosis of Russia and Europe.

The Theory of Isolationism

Whereas the theory of permanent revolution implied that, after October 1917, Russia was forging the first link in the new international division of labour in the future world system, other factors intervened which changed Trotsky's attitude and the economic policy he recommended.

Like Lenin and other Bolsheviks, for about two years after 1917 Trotsky believed that European revolution was imminent. But their divergent views on the significance of peace between Russia and Germany signalled a divergence also about Europe. In accordance with his 'law of combined development', Trotsky expected the European revolution to conform to the Russian scenario: that is, to begin in the continent's less developed countries.[16]

The necessity of revolution on the European continent for the survival of socialist Russia and the objective factor of the decline of capitalism were part of the same logic: so long as capitalism persisted, Europe would not provide the necessary aid for recovery in the land of the Soviets.

In Trotsky's view the lack of assistance was due to both political and economic factors. The incompatibility between socialism and capitalism was such that the West would try to achieve by economic means what it could not by military intervention: to crush Soviet power. At most he hoped only for indifference from the capitalist countries.

Trotsky's scepticism about foreign aid was reinforced by the breakdown of international economic equilibrium. He took a negative view of the interdependence of countries, already analysed in his theory of imperialism, because of the contradictions implied in it. The same phenomenon that made Lenin an optimist made Trotsky a pessimist: general poverty in Europe, faced by the plethora of capital and goods in the USA, was working against the established international division of labour. The disequilibrium would probably become worse. As a result of the Treaty of Versailles, the multiplication of national frontiers and tariffs would lead to a fall in international trade.

But the decline of the capitalist world did not follow a straight line. Trotsky took from Marx's trade cycle theory[17] the opinion that economic deterioration in the West might be interrupted by short periods of recovery. This made him amend his initial theory of imperialism because he rejected the idea of a unilateral collapse of the capitalist world.

The concept of economic interdependence between Europe and Russia, which prompted Lenin to make his offers of concessions to foreign capitalists, seemed utopian to Trotsky. Nor did he agree with Lenin that the recovery of Europe would require Russian raw materials. Despite the general interdependence of all countries – which Trotsky never denied – in the political and economic circumstances after the revolution his forecasts were based rather on the political and economic differences between countries.

Apart from their lack of economic interest in trading with Russia, Trotsky feared that another factor also would prevent Western nations from engaging in such activity. The pressure of military considerations could outweigh any businessmen's calculations of long-term profits to be gained from trade with Russia.

Trotsky's theory of imperialism, then, combined with his fear of the renewal of the economic blockade and, above all, of the slowing down of revolutionary movements in Europe, led him to propose an economic policy whereby the country, relying on its own resources, could emerge strengthened from these very unfavourable circumstances.

Substitutes for Foreign Trade under War Communism, 1918–21

Considering, as he did, that Russia could not count on foreign aid, Trotsky was forced to admit the *de facto* isolation of Russia and to elaborate a reconstruction policy in that light. Five years of capital-destroying war and the disorganisation of production meant that the country's stock of machinery had been almost wholly destroyed. This led Trotsky to substitute human labour for capital; in these unfavourable circumstances, the national labour force must undertake the role that foreign capital might have played in the Soviet economy.

It seems that by substituting militarised labour at home for foreign trade Trotsky was seeking a transition from capitalism to socialism peculiar to his own backward country. Given this perspective the militarisation of labour acquired both a quantitative and qualitative significance. The country's lag in development meant that, on the road to socialism, it must manoeuvre around the impasse by way of a sort of pseudo-capitalism. This not only implied independence from foreign machinery and technology, but also demanded that the workers adopt behaviour-patterns for which their past had not prepared them, since Russia had leapt over the usual stages of development.

The militarisation of labour was accompanied by the 'shock' (*udarnost*) system. This strategy concentrated scarce resources at what were regarded as the most important, or the weakest, points of the economy and offered workers material incentives for working at these points. By this violation of the principle of equality Trotsky hoped to be able to effect rapid changes in the distribution of the labour force and thus overcome the shortages which prevented progress on all fronts.

The *udarnost* strategy should have helped, according to Trotsky, to establish proportionality between the different branches and sectors of the national economy. This proportionality was to fulfil the role that foreign trade should have played, and so represented an approach to self-sufficiency in this particular period. Ten years later, in 1930, Trotsky strongly denied that he had been advocating autarky. And, indeed, his policy was in no way derived from isolationist determinism, as was the case with Stalin's a few years later. In the system Trotsky had in mind for the construction of socialism, the militarisation of the labour force was only an interim measure dictated by unfavourable circumstances. Precise proportionality between sectors would dissolve under universal socialism, which was always Trotsky's goal.

Import Policy

The country was not absolutely isolated. Not having opted for autarky in principle, Trotsky was ready to seize every opportunity provided by international events for increasing imports. But, unlike Lenin, he considered these rare occasions as opportunities to be seized and not as precursors of the resumption of normal commercial relations. As trade with the rest of the world developed, Trotsky agreed with Lenin: they must concentrate on buying certain lines of foreign equipment.

Less cautious than Lenin about using gold reserves, Trotsky wanted to use them exclusively to acquire production goods, while Lenin considered also drawing on them for grain in emergencies. All help from foreign capital and technology should, in Trotsky's opinion, be viewed as hypothetical. Being realistic rather than pessimistic, he said: 'in our plan all assumptions, conjectures and hopes are excluded'.[18]

Trotsky's attitude at the beginning of the New Economic Policy

Trotsky on concessions

Trotsky's attitude towards the arguments of advocates of concessions, who made themselves heard many times after 1918, was quite vague until 1925 when he came down on their side. In his desire to break the Western embargo Trotsky, like Lenin, seemed ready to concede certain peripheral areas. Similarly, during the Genoa Conference of 1922 he favoured discussion on concessions – under certain conditions. These were similar to those imposed by Lenin, but Trotsky tried to be more flexible.

From 1925 to 1927 Trotsky recognised that concessions could speed up Soviet development. They could help to 'form scar tissue over certain economic wounds', just as the *udarnost* strategy would clear bottlenecks; but the real take-off in the Russian economy would be assured only by the victory of the European proletariat.[19] Trotsky reaffirmed his faith in permanent revolution. The outside aid that could be obtained occasionally should be devoted exclusively to industry. However, Trotsky did not envisage, in his *udarnost* strategy, giving exclusive priority to heavy industry, as Stalin was shortly to do.

Trotsky's flexibility does not mean that he supported NEP as an alternative to the mobilisation of the country's labour force. In opposition to the views of many Bolsheviks, he did not believe that foreign investment offered a real possibility of substituting capital for labour. Trotsky was not indifferent to the value of foreign capital, but in the existing international economic and political situation, and given the poverty of Russia, it would be utopian and even dangerous to count on a serious contribution from concessions. The failure of the Genoa Conference and the small number of concessions arranged seemed to justify this mistrust.

Trotsky on the advantages of the foreign trade monopoly

In 1921 a debate began between defenders and opponents of the state monopoly of foreign trade. Trotsky was a fervent defender, taking Lenin's side.

Though he saw in national frontiers and tariffs the main obstacles to international interdependence, Trotsky nevertheless still appreciated the protective mechanism which the foreign trade monopoly offered. It seems unlikely that he considered this monopoly in the classical sense, as a protection for infant industry. If he opted for import restrictions it was out of necessity – there being nothing to export. The state's foreign trade monopoly seemed to Trotsky more like the best available planning instrument, and the way to allocate scarce imports in line with priorities defined by the central authority. It is in this sense that one can speak of Trotsky's protectionism.

Trotsky did not deny that he favoured expansion of the socialist sector of the economy, but in 1923 he recognised publicly that the peasants should be granted a degree of market freedom, even to the extent that 'the peasant should become rich'. As Nove says, this does not differ fundamentally from Bukharin's slogan of 1925.[20] Trotsky hoped in this way to increase agricultural production, and thereby agricultural exports, which would finance the importing of equipment. The strict state monopoly of foreign trade should, therefore, be maintained.

Not until 1924 did Trotsky admit some flexibility into this regime. But his coming advocacy of a policy of integration into international economic trends is already foreshadowed here.

From forced isolation to the theory of integration

Mistrustful of foreign investment in 1921, basing primitive socialist accumulation on interior resources in 1923, from 1925 Trotsky deployed all his energies in favour of a policy of integration. This sudden volte-face leads us to ask: had he really two distinct theories, or was it simply the pragmatic adaptation of a single concept to changing circumstances?

Many arguments support the second hypothesis. Trotsky's apparent about-turn seems to be explained essentially by a change in his view of developments in the capitalist world. To justify this change Trotsky amended somewhat his conclusions on the theory of imperialism, mainly with reference to cycles. The absence of cycles in capitalist economic development, he said, is explained by difficulties encountered in expanding markets. He considered capitalism's inability to harmonise exports and production to be Russia's only chance of success. He took up Lenin's old idea even more positively: Europe and the USSR need each other.

Against Stalin's famous division of the world into two camps, Trotsky insisted on the unalterability of the real economic and historical causes of the division of labour between the two politically divided worlds. Intensification of exchange between the two (planned on the Soviet side) was, he held, one of the most certain elements of the division of labour in the future socialist Europe.

In his own country, whose economy had revived in comparison with 1921, Trotsky considered that the advantages of concessions outweighed any threat to socialism. He proposed diversifying relations with the outside world as much as possible, seeing in this diversity a guarantee against the possibility of blockade. This integrationist concept led him to formulate a clear economic strategy, including some quite precise detail. This strategy would guide the USSR, which

> will encounter the greatest difficulties in its progress towards socialism as compared with the proletariat of the advanced countries, who will find it more difficult to seize power, but who, *having seized power long before we have overcome our backwardness*, will not only surpass us but will carry us along so as to bring us towards the point of real socialist construction, on the basis of the highest world technology and international division of labour.[21]

This key passage contains three basic concepts that Trotsky never abandoned: the chance of proletarian revolution occurring first in a backward country, the interdependence of all the countries in the world, and the victory of the world revolution.

In this view of the dialectic of historical evolution it becomes completely logical that capitalism should for a certain time lend aid to socialism. This is Trotsky's suggested solution to the main problem of a backward country: where to find the capital necessary for industrialisation. Foreign capital must complement the indigenous resources where these prove insufficient.

Trotsky rejected the industrialisation policy of favouring only heavy industry. The rhythm of development of a given country is not autonomous, determined only by domestic factors. It is imposed by the pressure of the world market. Not only the speed of growth but also its direction should be in accord with the relations prevailing in the world economy as a whole.

He proposed to exploit the role of foreign trade as an accelerator, and to direct the choice of investments, by means of a system of comparative coefficients. But if a commodity had a low coefficient, this did not automatically mean that it must be imported. Thanks to planning, the state could still invest in producing it, and could appeal to foreign capital to support, even to develop, the weak points in the economy.[22]

Since Trotsky did not confine his coefficient to producer goods, he changed his policy on imports. With his concessions to the consumer he now openly distanced himself from the economic solution proposed by Preobrazhensky. The system of coefficients was not, of course, incompatible with protection of 'infant industries'. But the latter had to be chosen with care, without arbitrary distortion in favour of one particular sector, which was what Stalin's strategy was to amount to.

Trotsky's analysis of how to direct the Soviet economy 'scientifically' during the phase of its 'isolated march' in the hostile capitalist environment attuned perfectly with the political views of the partisan of world socialist revolution. Taken as a whole, his conceptions could only provoke him to violent reaction against the solution of building socialism in one country isolated from the world – even 'at a snail's pace'. He attacked both the 'construction of socialism in one country [based entirely on] the idea of an isolated self-sufficing economy'[23] and the slow pace proposed. Although he criticised Vollmar's idea of 'the isolated socialist state' he found it more convincing than the isolation advocated by Bukharin.

Could Trotsky's criticisms of the Stalin–Bukharin line, developed mainly in exile, be an expression of prejudice? Was his integrationism, based on permanent revolution, a credible substitute for socialism in one country?

In seeking to demonstrate Stalin's fundamental fallacy, Trotsky seems to have taken no special interest in the circumstances which made people choose Stalin's strategy. He examined only one of these circumstances, at least during the years 1923 to 1927. This period of reconstruction, based on 'capital ready to hand, taken from the bourgeoisie',[24] had encouraged the illusion of isolated economic development. The theory of 'socialism in one country' originated in a mistaken interpretation of the real achievements of this period, and in the defeats suffered by communism internationally.

Faced with factual evidence of the failure of the European revolutionary movement, Trotsky remained faithful to the idea of world revolution. But can we conclude that for him permanent revolution was an alternative to 'socialism in one country'? This was Stalin's tactical presentation of the matter, and in the end he persuaded Trotsky himself of it. However, there are two major arguments against this.

First, in Trotsky's eyes, the victory of socialism in Europe would not of itself resolve the problems of socialism in a backward USSR. The building of socialism depended on national and international factors which were interdependent and which operated simultaneously. Secondly, it was Trotsky himself who was fighting for rapid industrialisation and efficient exploitation of internal resources – 'all measures which Stalin himself was eventually to adopt as part of the drive for "socialism in one country"'.[25] Moreover, Trotsky's supporters find some difficulty in reconciling this emphatic demand for industrialisation with his rejection of Stalin's doctrine.[26]

The essential difference between Stalin and Trotsky is not reducible to the opposition between their strategies. The essential difference is the isolation which Stalin's doctrine implied – the antithesis of Trotsky's conception, which was based on the international division of labour. This division, formed during the capitalist era, will prevail for a long time. The world market exercises control over all its component parts – the socialist country and the rest of the world alike. Any attempt to separate these parts would reinforce the political barriers constituted by national frontiers. A socialism built in such a way would be a historical regression in relation even to capitalism. Here we are back with the logic that Trotsky developed in his analysis of imperialism.

Notes

1. L. D. Trotsky, *The Third International After Lenin*, New York, 1957, p. 11.
2. R. B. Day, 'Socialism in one country – new thoughts on an old question', in *Pensiero e axione politica di Lev Trockij*, ed. Francesca Gori, Florence, 1982, vol. 1, pp. 314–19.
3. 'That the international revolution of the proletariat cannot be a simultaneous act, of this there can of course be no dispute at all among grown-up people, after the experience of the October Revolution, achieved by the proletariat of a backward country under pressure of historical necessity, without waiting in the least for the proletariat of the advanced countries "to even out the front". Within these limits, the reference to the law of uneven development is absolutely correct and quite in place.' Trotsky, *The Third International* ..., p. 21.
4. This dialectical conception was to allow him, as we shall see, to adapt his theory of imperialism to the international situation: 'the displacement of the economic centre of the world towards the USA'. 'Report on the world economic crisis and the new tasks of the Communist International', quoted in B. Knei-Paz, *The Social and Political Thought of Leon Trotsky*, London, 1978, p. 317.
5. Trotsky, *The Third International* ..., p. 40.
6. K. Marx, *Oeuvres*, Paris, 1965, vol. 1, p. 194. Knei-Paz points out that the very expression 'permanent revolution' was first used by Marx himself. The idea of continuous revolution, or 'revolution in permanence' had

also appeared in Proudhon. In his *Results and Prospects* Trotsky speaks of 'uninterrupted revolution'. Only in 1908 does he first use the adjective 'permanent'. Knei-Paz, *Social and Political Thought* ..., pp. 152–5.

7. For references to the 'law of combined development' in Trotsky's writings, *ibid.*, p. 89.

8. *Results and Prospects*, quoted *ibid.*, p. 125. Specialists interpret differently Trotsky's appreciation of Russian industry before 1917. Davies thinks he underestimated its strength and dependence on Western capitalism. R. W. Davies, 'Trotsky and the debate on industrialization in the USSR', in *Pensiero e azione* ..., p. 256. Soviet authors share his view. Cf. V. Grinko, N. Mitkin, S. Sopin and S. Shaumian, *Le Parti des bolcheviques en lutte contre le trotskisme (1903 – février 1917)*, Moscow, 1969. The analysis of Knei-Paz tends to show that Trotsky, letting an ambiguity between industrialisation and modernisation float uncorrected, exaggerated the social and political changes accompanying industrial development. Knei-Paz, *Social and Political Thought* ..., pp. 100–6, 168.

9. But this conceptual separation does not enable us to establish a real chronological separation of the different phases of the revolution. A revolution should define itself by its final objectives, not by its intermediary stages. Right through the revolutionary process, stages transcend each other without waiting for the objectives of the previous revolution stage to be achieved. In Trotsky's eyes the leading role of the proletariat in achieving the ends of the agrarian and bourgeois-democratic revolutions entails the possibility of this transcendence. Trotsky, *De la révolution – le cours nouveau, la révolution défigurée, la révolution permanente, la révolution trahie*, Paris, 1963, pp. 293 ff.

10. Day, *Leon Trotsky and the Politics of Economic Isolation*, p. 9.

11. Here again, economic interdependence implies the financial instability of the states of Europe and leads the European proletariat to profit from the political crisis to seize power and help the final stages of the Russian revolutionary movement, *ibid.*, p. 141.

12. Trotsky, *The Third International* ..., p. 44.

13. But by 'the self-determination of nations' Trotsky does not mean the creation of new national states. For him this right is a means permitting these states to participate to the full extent of their wishes in the building of the international socialist world. Deutscher, *Prophet Armed*, p. 237.

14. Trotsky, *The Third International* ..., p. 55.

15. Day, *Leon Trotsky and the Politics of Economic Isolation*, p. 4. Nove rather disagrees with the sentence quoted, because of the exact meaning of the word 'build'. He thinks Trotsky would allow that socialism was *being* built, but in the absence of world revolution it would remain *incompletely* built. Nove, 'Trockij, collectivization and the Five Year Plan', in *Pensiero e azione* ..., p. 392.

16. The chronological order, opposite to the usual Marxist sequence, is explained, says Trotsky, by the nature of modern capitalism which neutralises proletarian militancy in developed countries – a claim strongly criticised in the Soviet literature. See V. Grinko *et al.*, *Le Parti des bolcheviques* ..., p. 291.

17. Marx, 'Contradictions internes de la loi', in *Oeuvres*, II, pp. 1033–41.

18. Day, *Leon Trotsky and the Politics of Economic Isolation*, p. 36.

19. Trotsky, *Voina i revoliutsiia – krushenie vtorogo internatsionala i podgotovka tretego* [*War and Revolution – The collapse of the Second International and the preparation of the Third*],Moscow, 1922, vol. 2, p. 481.

20. Nove, 'Trockij, collectivization ...', in *Pensiero e azione* ..., p. 390.
21. Trotsky, *The Third International* ..., p. 56, emphasis added.
22. Day, *Leon Trotsky and the Politics of Economic Isolation* p. 103.
23. Trotsky, *The Third International* ..., p. 44.
24. *ibid.* p. 253.
25. Knei-Paz, *Social and Political Thought* ..., p. 343.
26. Day, *Leon Trotsky and the Politics of Economic Isolation*, p. 171.

18

Trotsky's political economy of capitalism

HILLEL TICKTIN

L. D. Trotsky was possibly the most dialectical of all Marxist theorists. He wrote on dialectics in a number of places,[1] but it is in his writings as a whole that one sees his dialectical method. It is enough to contrast Trotsky with Bukharin to show the enormous difference between a dialectical Marxist and a mechanical one.[2] But this is really unfair to Trotsky since Bukharin is actually an extreme example of a Marxist who failed to grasp the essence of Marxism.

It is clearer when comparing Trotsky to Lenin. Lenin's political economy is directed to a purpose. He shows the drive inherent in imperialism, leading to war, and then argues that this is part of a declining capitalism. Both the inherent movement in capitalism and its degeneration into finance capitalism are dialectical concepts. What, however, is lacking in Lenin is an attempt to see the contradictions within capitalism and the interpenetration of those contradictions. His original work on the *Decline of Capitalism in Russia* argued convincingly but in unilinear form that the problem with capitalism is not one of markets.[3] He then seems to argue that it is a question of proportionality. Lenin sees contradiction as part of reality, but he sees it as causing 'the decay and transformation' of capitalism, not as the essence of movement itself. He could not therefore interrelate profits, disproportionality and markets. Lenin is right against the Narodniki but wrong otherwise, since it is quite possible that the absence of a market could underdevelop a country. While writers have argued that Lenin changed after reading Hegel,[4] and indeed his work on *Imperialism* is a testament to that fact, he never got as far as Trotsky.

Whereas Trotsky looks for the forces at work, Lenin looks to a way in which those forces can be stopped. For Lenin the dynamic appears to be a one-way street, whereas for Trotsky there is an ebb and flow. Trotsky's approach is shown best in his *History of the Russian Revolution*, but it inspires his other work as well. In particular, his concept of equilibrium not only stands in sharp contrast with that of Bukharin but is the only dialectical description of the term 'equilibrium'. Trotsky describes the dialectic as follows: 'Marx's method is *dialectic*, because it regards both nature and society as they evolve, and evolution itself as the constant struggle of conflicting forces.'[5] Equilibrium for him is thus a temporary containment of conflicting forces.

Trotsky's approach was explicitly organicist. He looked at society as comparable to a living organism, with its own coming into being, maturity and decline. Society has its own laws, which are different not only between societies but also in the embryonic, mature and declining phases of the particular society.[6] This is to be contrasted with the mechanical approach of Bukharin.

The problem with Trotsky's work is not his dialectic but his own dialectical decline. He never produced a political economy, and when he had the time to do so, he could no longer do it. It is, therefore, of some merit to draw out the nature of Trotsky's political economy. This chapter is concerned only with Trotsky's political economy of capitalism. It is not possible to separate his political economy of capitalism and of the USSR entirely, but I have discussed the latter in other papers.[7] Only certain aspects of the question can be tackled here. The central argument is that the concepts of the curve of capitalist development and the transitional epoch are the two key categories that Trotsky uses.

Capitalist equilibrium and revolution

The concept of an equilibrium of forces under capitalism played a crucial role in Trotsky's thought. He saw capitalism constantly trying to assert an equilibrium which is constantly breaking down. This was in direct contrast to Bukharin, who saw the equilibrium as a state of rest. For Trotsky the term was not one of a balance of forces. It was not derived from the metaphor of the physicist's balance, with two substances being weighed against each other. Instead his concept involved the view that there are contradictory self-moving forces opposing each other, which are part of the society. As long as they can interact and not overwhelm each other they move into and out of equilibrium. Equilibrium from this point of view is a state which is constantly being reached and broken until one or other of the poles of the contradiction loses its power and fails. How?

For Trotsky a revolution could occur either on an upturn, when the workers acquire confidence after previous defeats, or after a series of defeats and partial victories. Unlike other Marxists, Trotsky was specific about the conditions for working-class consciousness. Capitalism, for Trotsky, goes on until it is overthrown.

In 1922 Trotsky produced a statement which is remarkable for its prescience. Posing the question, 'where are the guarantees that capitalism will not restore its equilibrium through cyclical oscillations?', he replied, 'There are no guarantees and there can be none.' He went on:

> If we cancel out the revolutionary nature of the working class and its struggle and the work of the Communist Party and of the trade unions ... and take instead the objective mechanics of capitalism, then we could say: 'Naturally, failing the intervention of the working class, failing its struggle, its resistance, its self-defence and its offensives – failing all this, capitalism will restore its own equilibrium, not the old but a new equilibrium; it will establish the domination of the old Anglo-American world in which the entire economy will pass into the hands of these countries and there will be

a temporary alliance between the United States and Great Britain, but presently this equilibrium will once again be disrupted.[8]

Trotsky's view of capitalism at the 3rd Congress of the Comintern

Trotsky's best discussion of political economy is in his speech to the 3rd Congress of the Comintern. In that speech he described the way in which the bourgeoisie had recouped and stabilised capitalism. From his understanding of contemporary capitalism he was led to put forward the theory of capitalist development, later taken up from him by Kondratiev, in the form of a long-term cycle. It is, however, quite clear that Trotsky was putting it forward because it was part of his understanding of capitalist stabilisation of that time. At the centre of his analysis is the category of accumulation, which is determined in large part by the political perception of the bourgeoisie. In other words, the capitalist class will not invest in productive capital unless it is guaranteed control over the working class. It is the job of the capitalist state to ensure this result. The working class requires some form of disciplining such as wars and counter-revolution. Accumulation, then, appears as a result of subjective and objective events.

Trotsky is the only Marxist theorist to put the subjective into political economy. He stands in stark contrast to theorists like Paul Mattick and Henryk Grossman who in their own ways tend to objectivise economic laws. Capitalism, for them, will come to a natural end. Trotsky did not theorise this point, he simply used it. He is not counterpoising his own Marxism to that of Marx, but simply using Marxism in his own way. When Rosdolsky quotes Marx to the effect that capital constitutes its own barrier, Trotsky would not dissent. Indeed, his later work makes that abundantly clear.[9] What Trotsky did was to add a new dimension to political economy by arguing that the movement of capital has to be seen as part of the class struggle and not just as an unconscious movement of rates of profit. On the other hand, he does not go the whole way to the point where all movements of capital are to be seen as a conspiratorial form, as some modern-day theorists have done.[10]

In contrast to those theorists, Trotsky was looking at the control over capital rather than the form of control over labour. Obviously both approaches have their own validity. Nor is there any evidence that Trotsky would have denied the forms of control over the labour process. I take up this question below. He saw the form of capital itself and the struggle over its control as crucial. In other words, he adopted Lenin's formulation of finance capital as the modern form of capital.[11] The class struggle took on forms which originated from the subjective actions of the capitalist class, but then became part of objective developments. He was also arguing that the bourgeoisie needs a clear vehicle for its investment. It will not invest when it expects to have negative profits through obstacles deriving directly or indirectly from working-class opposition.

Trotsky, however, did not discuss the nature of accumulation itself. He provides no discussion of the falling rate of profit, and – though he did refer to the disproportionalities developing in capitalism and the problem of the market, or underconsumption – he never produced an explanation of crisis. His discussion is more one of a general political economy, focused on the antagonisms between countries and between labour and capital. Trotsky's perspective is much more one of looking at the nature of capitalist equilibrium and its disruption. 'To understand the mechanism whereby various aspects of the economy are brought into a state of relative balance, is to discover the objective laws of capitalism.'

The problem with Trotsky's analysis is that it remained at too general a level to be called a detailed political economy; but there is enough said to be able to construct one on the basis of his approach.

Interestingly, he did lay out the possibility of a new equilibrium in which the capitalist class would recoup and there would be an upswing over decades.[12] His political economy was really based entirely on the developmental theory, popularised by Mandel as the long-wave theory. Most people do not realise its importance to his analysis, simply regarding it as a part of his viewpoint. In fact it is central to his overall theory.

The curve of capitalist development

Trotsky's argument on the development of capitalism was based on the view that there is an overall tendency to decline or boom over periods longer than the immediate trade cycle. He specifically alluded to the underlying causation. This could be wars, revolutions or more technical causes like expansion overseas and the introduction of new technology. At this point the question is which of these two sets of causes is primary, or whether they are co-equal.

In fact, he considered the exogenous and usually political causes as primary.[13] Richard Day has already discussed this question by contrasting Mandel and Kondratiev with Trotsky. Whereas for Kondratiev the technical developments play an independent role, for Trotsky they play a dependent role. In a remarkable rehabilitation of an old debate, Day has shown conclusively that Ernest Mandel's interpretation based on the theory of the long wave is incorrect.[14]

Kondratiev argued that there were long cycles, ultimately based on a relation between savings and technology. Mandel, however, tries to marry the technological argument with one of 'exogenous' shocks. He asserts that there were three technological revolutions beginning with steam, through electricity and ending with the electronic/nuclear age.[15] This would mean that there were indeed long waves of development, whatever the initial driving force. Trotsky did not assert more than that there had been upturns and downturns, and he associated them very clearly with political events. The conclusive argument is probably the length of time of Trotsky's illustrative curve. His x-axis has ninety years without providing an upturn. At the time he wrote, it implied that only one curve had really ever existed. Alternatively, one might argue that there could be more if one projected capitalist development before Napoleon and took the post-Second World War years as the beginning of a new period. In such a case, however, it would be more proper to use Trotsky's usual terminology of epochs.

We can explicate the political economy as follows. Surplus value is extracted, reinvested and so turned into capital in distinct periods. In the upturn the extracted surplus value is turned into productive capital, but in the downturn it is not. How could it not be? It can be turned, for instance, into finance capital and so circulating capital, and hence can act parasitically on productive capital. Trotsky accepted the role of finance capital, giving it explicit prominence.[16] In other words, the 'curve of capitalist development' would then be dependent on the extent of accumulation in productive capital.

The concept is also bound up with the decline of capitalism. He argued that, as capitalism developed, it expanded the productive forces, but 'In the epoch of capitalist decline, the productive forces are decomposing, as has been by and large the case in the epoch which began after the war, which has endured to this very day and which will continue to endure for a long time to come.'[17]

The overall argument can now be put together. Developing capitalism tended to have long-term boom periods. A declining capitalism would have long-term downturns. In both kinds of capitalism the other part of the curve can be present, but there are special reasons to explain it. Imperialism, for instance, explains the upturn at the end of the last century, while the boom period during and after the Second World War can also be explained by the war, and the post-war equilibrium which established control over the working class. Nonetheless, it is impossible to avoid the conclusion that the curve, which Trotsky discussed over the period from 1789, relates to both the organic evolution of capitalism and causes internal to accumulation. Most particularly, the capitalist class accumulates in a way and at particular periods which will ensure its returns. Curiously, this is a kind of mirror image of Keynesian subjectivism in relation to liquidity preference and the animal spirits of the stock exchange. As I have argued, there is a deliberate injection of the subjective view of the capitalist class.

The subjective aspect opens the way to the argument that the capitalist class may not understand its real interests; or, alternatively, may understand the epoch better than the workers. As a result, the leadership of the working class becomes absolutely crucial in the transitional epoch. Trotsky did argue that the problem is one of leadership, though he did not actually draw the connection made above. It is, however, inescapable.

Another conclusion applicable to the present time must also be drawn. The capitalist equilibrium is established when the class relations are favourable to the capitalist class over a period of time. Then a boom period can ensue. Clearly, a declining capitalism will find it more and more difficult to establish such an equilibrium. Hence it might be concluded that the capitalist class might fail to reach such a state and there could then be long-term stagnation. In other words, the increasing strength of the working class might compel the capitalist class to avoid productive investment. The downswing might then not find an end.

It has been argued that there is no evidence of a long wave. There is now a considerable literature on the subject. Trotsky was not arguing, of course, for the kind of automatic movement often implied in the use of the term 'wave', but on Trotsky's argument, the evidence is amenable to mathematical modelling. The question is whether there is a period of relatively low accumulation followed by a period of relatively high levels of accumulation. The last seventy years quite clearly show precisely that tendency. The depression is followed by a war, a period of reconstruction and relatively high growth, followed by a period of relatively low growth with mass unemployment. Of course, if you look at some global average you might come to any conclusion, but it contradicts Marxism and common sense to do so. The point would be to choose the determining productive capital in the world and chart its course. Before 1920 or so that would mean concentrating on Britain; after that period on the United States. In fact, Trotsky took the United Kingdom as his particular case. It is easy to show that odd countries bucked the trend, but that is neither here nor there.

The point would then be to look at crucial companies. For the United States one might look at Ford or General Motors. (Again there is little point in looking at some general average. One could average out high profits in the big companies and very low profits in the small companies and come to some absurd conclusion.) If the determining companies experienced observable trends in accumulation, the case will be proven. What makes the statistical analysis very difficult is that bourgeois categories are not the same as Marxist ones.

Nonetheless, it should be clear that Trotsky's argument was not one of long cycles or waves of generalised upturn and downturn, but rather an organicist reading of economic history in which a capitalism in decline will tend to have an overall decline in its economy unless counter-measures are taken. In Trotsky's terms, if an equilibrium can be established in favour of the capitalist class then there can be an upturn, but once the equilibrium breaks down, the system itself begins to crash.

The whole question arose out of Trotsky's and the Bolsheviks' need to understand their own situation in the world economy, so that in the end Trotsky was really saying that cycles are neither here nor there. What is critical is whether the capitalist class can find a new strategy for maintaining and expanding capital. He answered that question in the negative for the 1920s (but argued that Marx had been wrong in 1848 because he did not understand that capitalism was on a generally rising tendency):

> If the capitalist world stood now before the possibility of a new organic boom, there would be a new economic equilibrium, as the basis for the further development of the economic forces, and this would signify that we were finished as a socialist state.'[18]

My interpretation seems to be closer to Trotsky's actual thinking of the time. But it is not surprising that Kondratiev and Mandel should have taken him up differently because Trotsky did not spell out his own theory. The problem with Kondratiev and Mandel is not that they have introduced a technological component, but that they have made that component play either a primary role (Kondratiev) or at least a fundamental role (Mandel) in the movement of capital. As a result they are able to see cycles – Mandel calls them waves to differentiate his own view – which must have some necessity of their own. These waves must go up and go down, and so they constitute a similar mechanism to the crisis. It is not at all clear that Trotsky would have wanted to argue that case. Put differently, the economic crisis does have an automaticity about it, such that, if the workers do not take power, equilibrium is restored through a reduction in wages and depreciation of capital. Trotsky's downward movement has no necessary reason to end. If it does come to an end, this will be related to a particular new class equilibrium – such as imperialism, Stalinism and fascism. No one can say that such so-called exogenous events are unlimited. I have referred to the downturn because Trotsky argued that the almost cataclysmic events of the early 1920s were part of the overall decline of capitalism.

There is no reason why the word 'wave' should not be used as Mandel has done, as long as it is clear that the analogy with water or light is limited to a single wave. Alternatively, the waves could be regarded as empirical forms of the past, which have no necessary movement into the future. One could just as well, however, use an analogy with a man who had achieved his goal in life, and then started to decline. There would be an upturn during his mature period and a downturn as he entered his late middle age. This might be followed by another upturn as the old man found a new equilibrium by entering a more rewarding job, but his powers would have clearly diminished. His influence might grow, but his ability could only decline, and in time, whatever upsurges he might have, the decline could only become more and more important. It appears to me that Trotsky's crucial perspective is one of a declining capitalism which was desperately seeking a way out of its old age. At certain periods it was able to find a temporary alleviation through imperialism, fascism, war and Stalinism/cold war, but the palliatives become ever more useless over time.

Trotsky and crisis

The logic of the curve theory seems to lead to the view that the regular crisis is a secondary phenomenon. On the other hand, the driving causes of both are the same. Trotsky took the view that markets and disproportionality play crucial roles in the economy.[19] He argued that fixed capital is critical in crisis, but that since Marx had written only hints on the subject, Hilferding had pieced it together.[20] Preobrazhensky, Lenin and Trotsky say little about the falling rate of profit. Trotsky, however, was insistent that crises are in the nature of capitalism and that a depression is necessarily followed by a boom, until the working class itself takes power.

This leads to the conclusion that Trotsky saw capitalism as a system whose contradictions necessarily led it into crises, but those crises would tend to get worse in periods of decline and to be less important in periods of boom. The key concept remains one of crisis, but the evolution of capitalism determines its depth and importance. The logic of Trotsky's position leads to the argument that crises must grow deeper under capitalism, but not in a unilinear way.

Capitalism in the introduction to Capital

Perhaps the most extensive exposition of Trotsky's views is set forth in his introduction to the Fawcett abridged edition of *Capital*,[21] put together by Otto Ruhle. Trotsky's introduction puts *Capital* in the context of the world depression of the 1930s. His own outline of Marxist political economy comes across as rigid and mechanical, in sharp contrast with his own dialectical work of the 1920s. He supports the view that capitalism will collapse and was indeed already collapsing. He was also of the opinion that there is a theory of increasing misery which was validated by the empirical situation of the time. Even if these views were correct, they should have been argued out and theorised and not simply buttressed by empirical evidence. The contrast between this dogmatic attitude to Marxist political economy and his own earlier views makes it impossible to synthesise his later work with his earlier speeches, despite the common thread of basic Marxist positions.

Trotsky was insistent that socialism is not merely possible but inevitable. Clearly, if there is a necessary development of human history and the world is not destroyed then Trotsky was right. He glossed over, however, the whole question of working-class defeat and what would happen if the working class were defeated over a very long period of time. It looks very much as if Trotsky did not want to admit that the October Revolution had been defeated, even if he argued that there had been a counter-revolution. The point is that if the revolution had been defeated than there would be not just a transitional epoch but an epoch of defeat. That would then mean that it was necessary to retrench and hold out for as long as the epoch of defeat itself lasted. It would mean that ways would have had to be devised of organising a strategic retreat for the left.

Of course, the left at that time was small. Yet there were many disparate groups and isolated left-wing anti-Stalinist intellectuals. If it was an epoch of defeat then the task would be to find a minimum common programme in order to conserve forces. On the other hand, if it was a temporary defeat about to be undone within a few years, as Trotsky clearly believed, then the task became one of founding a pure socialist organisation in order to tackle the coming working-class upsurge. The cataclysmic view buttressed Trotsky's perception of the political tasks of the time.

His statements, then, make more sense if we understand the assumptions outlined above. The terminal crisis of capitalism would, he thought, necessarily involve a disintegrating society, and a falling standard of living – if for no other reason than that the capitalist class would cease to accumulate if it could see no future for itself.

The problem is that Trotsky was wrong in his assessment of Stalinism and so in the nature of the epoch. Although he had seen the great importance of the subjective, he now relied on the mechanical movement of objective categories because the subjective intervention of the working class had been defeated. He still argued that the subjective was all important, but he failed to see that new objective categories had formed. Stalinism and social-democracy were not just subjective doctrines. They had become an objective reality which constituted the main obstacle to change. Trotsky's argument was that they were subjective realities which would be defeated. His implicit view was that they would be defeated by the movement of objective categories, which would lead to the formation of new parties and new leaders, and so to a new subjective reality to replace the old. Because he did not anticipate a whole epoch of defeat, he was not able to sketch out the underlying laws of contemporary capitalism.

Today, when Stalinism and social-democracy are dying, the subjective, paradoxically, becomes again all important. The enormous obstacles that have stood in the way of the proletariat for the last seventy years are being swept away without anything being put in their place. The bourgeoisie is playing the tune that Stalinism is Marxism, and the only feasible socialism, for all it is worth. The speed of the socialist recovery will now depend on the ability of socialists to put forward a credible revolutionary programme.

Imperialism

Trotsky's concept of imperialism seems to be restricted to the view that the forces of production outgrow national boundaries, and hence that capitalism has to expand.[22] The national state becomes increasingly otiose and, indeed, a barrier to production itself. He did not flesh this out, although it is possible to see that his argument is different from that of Bukharin and Lenin.

Because he was a dialectical thinker, he was not led into the Bukharinist simplicities of a supra-capitalism. Trotsky argued that there are the two forces at work, the national and the international. The necessity of the development of capital drives it to go beyond national boundaries, but on the other hand not all industry does so, while the nation-state itself continues to exist and hinder the internationalist drive of modern industry. This may be seen in his description of the problems of Europe and the need for a United States of Europe.[23] He argued that, while the forces of production demand an international base, they are not able to obtain it. Hence there is a conflict between nation-states to establish the new international order.[24]

His description of the mechanism of imperialism was closely linked to his theory of combined and uneven development. He argued that capitalism had developed unevenly, and hence the more developed countries are quickly able to exploit the less developed. This process starts with the origins of capitalism itself.[25] His view was, therefore, close to that of Luxemburg in seeing imperialism and capitalism as one entity, and differed from Lenin who saw imperialism as a particular stage of capitalism. On the other hand, he adopted both the concepts of monopoly and finance capital from Hilferding and Lenin, but he did not apply them to the theory of imperialism.

For Trotsky, then, imperialism consists of the exploitation of one country by another. It is the exaction of tribute, which is used by the metropolitan country to build up its productive forces at the expense, therefore, of the colonial world.[26] At this point there is a problem, since he appears to be arguing that imperialism represents the movement of capital in its embryonic phases as well as in its declining phases. The argument that the forces of production have gone beyond the nation-state is only sustainable in the late phase of capitalism. The lacuna in his argument can be made good by using the same divisions for imperialism as for capitalism, of early, mature and declining phases. Therefore a declining imperialism is one in which expansion beyond the borders of the nation-state is necessitated because the forces of production have outgrown their national boundaries, whereas a rising imperialism goes beyond its national borders because the uneven development of national economies has permitted a more dynamic capital to exploit other less developed economies on a national basis. In the first instance, the nation-state is in a process of disintegration, whereas, in the second, it is in the process of formation. Indeed, we find Trotsky using another definition of imperialism which fits this description. In 1939 he defined imperialism as the expansionist policy of finance capital.[27]

The less developed country is then subject both to the law of combined development and to permanent revolution. In the first instance, it is enabled to skip economic stages by using the most advanced technique with all its social and political consequences, and in the second it finds that it cannot consummate its own bourgeois-democratic revolution. Trotsky specifically pointed to the lack of an agrarian revolution in underdeveloped countries of his time.[28]

There has been a considerable debate around the continued applicability of permanent revolution given the anti-colonial revolution and the relative success of the so-called national liberation movements. For our purpose the whole argument is subsumed into one on the general nature of the transitional epoch. It is in this period that attempts to consummate the bourgeois-democratic revolution have been linked to the failed proletarian revolution and so to Stalinism.

The transitional epoch

The concept of the transitional epoch was Trotsky's own. I have discussed the concept in relation to the USSR in a previous paper.[29] Trotsky argued that social-democracy had saved capitalism, and that a transitional epoch between capitalism and socialism had evolved.[30] Earlier his view was that 'the epoch beginning with the First World War and our revolution is the epoch of the socialist revolution'.[31] Preobrazhensky and Trotsky discussed the transitional period in the USSR, but the content of the transitional epoch for the world is another matter. It would not be going too far to state that the category of the transitional epoch is Trotsky's crucial theoretical innovation. It contrasts with the Stalinist view of a general crisis of capitalism and the coexistence of two social systems.

Trotsky did not produce a political economy of the transitional epoch, but it may be pieced together. In the first place, it is a period when capitalism has been overthrown in a part of the world, without the introduction of socialism itself. In the second place, capitalism continues to decline. In the third place, the subjective aspect plays a critical role as the leaders of both social-democracy and

Stalinism are seen as saving capitalism during this period. It may therefore be seen as the period during which the old order is objectively declining but the revolutionary forces of the working class have yet to defeat the old ruling class. It is, therefore, a period of partial victories and defeats. 'It is impossible to say how long the proletarian revolution will endure from its beginning to its termination: it is the question of an entire historical epoch.'[32]

In a sense it was an extension of the concept of permanent revolution. For Trotsky the revolution could be consummated only when all the partial victories of the working class were made permanent through world revolution. The original concept of permanent revolution involved a combination of two aspects. On the one hand, the revolution proceeds from one anti-government class to another – from the industrial bourgeoisie to the petite-bourgeoisie and then from the petite-bourgeoisie to the working class. On the other hand, the demands of the workers begin from limited forms of pressure, which are conceded, to more important and global programmatic demands. Both aspects can be seen at work during the transitional epoch. The old landlords are swept away with agrarian reform, industry is expanded, nationalisation is extended, unemployment is reduced and the standard of living is raised, but all these victories are constantly under threat because they undermine the capitalist system.

Trotsky did not take the next step and argue that the transitional epoch was one in which the decline of capitalism would also involve the increasing socialisation of production. Logically this would lead to the reduction of the sphere of operation of the law of value. There would then be a conflict between increasing degrees of organisation of production and society on the one hand, and an increasingly beleaguered and transmuted law of value on the other. Burnham, Shachtman and Victor Serge all pointed to aspects of this change, but in a primitive and sociological form, to which Trotsky reacted negatively because they appeared to be arguing that the administrators were actually taking over, whereas the law of value had clearly not been superseded.

The word 'epoch' is used to denote a period of time during which a specific correlation of forces evolves to its natural end. Trotsky saw capitalism and socialism as distinct modes of production, with their own laws and hence their own organic natures. They cannot be mixed. The evolution from one to the other involves the complete elimination of the form of the old mode of production, exchange value, and its replacement by the new form, planning. If the two are placed together then they have the disadvantages of both systems and the advantages of neither.[33] Hence the theory of the transition period. The evolution of the forces of the working class to the point of victory ushers in the transition period as opposed to the transitional epoch.

The transitional period to socialism, Trotsky thought, would involve the gradual, irreversible elimination of the market under the direction of the working class. Whether this is true remains today an unanswered question. Crucial aspects of it were discussed during the period of NEP and later – notably the reconcilability of plan and market, the inherent drives involved in this process and whether it is indeed reversible.[34] The political economy of the transition period, however, is study in itself.

The point to be drawn out here is how this reinforces the previous discussion on Trotsky's organicism. He saw the market as part of capitalism, even if it had to be used for a temporary period, standing in total conflict with planning and democracy. Trotsky did not spell out any of the problems, as Preobrazhensky did, but there is no mistaking his approach. The two systems – capitalism and socialism – cannot be mixed.

Fascism

Trotsky's understanding of fascism remains unsurpassed. Whereas the Stalinists insisted on regarding it simply as the rule of monopoly capital by force, after they had moved towards the popular front, Trotsky stressed the importance of the petite-bourgeoisie and the ability of the fascists to mobilise them. On this basis, where there was no petite-bourgeoisie, there would be no fascism. For Trotsky fascism was a specific phenomenon, whereas for the Stalinists it was a natural outcome of capitalism. Had the German Communist Party heeded Trotsky and joined with the Social-Democratic Party to halt Hitler, it is very probable that Hitler would not have come to power. In addition, many of Hitler's inventions – from the one-party state to the role of the Führer – had already been introduced by Stalin. The Stalinists, then, refused to introduce into the discussion of fascism two vital questions: Stalinism itself, and the role of the petite-bourgeoisie. Trotsky used the concept of 'totalitarian' to apply to both states. Obviously the Stalinists, in explaining fascism, could not use such a term. The Stalinist view of fascism has remained extremely influential down to the present day.

When one turns to the specific economic attitude that Trotsky took to fascism the picture is less clear. He saw fascism as a political formation which emerges and takes power in a period of declining capitalism: 'The Fascist regime which merely reduces to the utmost the limits of decline and reaction inherent in any imperialist capitalism, became indispensable when the degeneration of capitalism blotted out the possibility of maintaining illusions about a rise in the proletariat's standard of living'.[35] From this point of view, fascism is a means of maintaining the rate of profit by raising the rate of exploitation. For Trotsky, the bourgeoisie of the 'imperialist democracies' had to concede either to the aristocracy of labour, or else to the fascists, who would club the proletariat in order to force down wages.

Trotsky did not synthesise his earlier work on fascism with his remarks on its political economy; but the argument was that, in a period of capitalist collapse, with declining incomes and consequent instability, force is required to control the working class and restore profitability. 'The last word in the disintegration of monopolistic capitalism is *Fascism*.'[36] Such force can only be introduced if there is a mass basis in the population for the regime and if the alternative, socialism, is discredited or impotent. Trotsky's argument would have been more complete if he had envisaged options other than fascism and the New Deal. It may be that Trotsky did not want to introduce complications into his introduction to *Capital*, but it is more likely that he wrote the introduction, under the stress of exile, without the necessary books and with constant organisational and financial problems.

At all events, Trotsky argued that capitalism was in a state of terminal crisis, with disintegration setting in, and had turned to fascism in the less well-endowed developed countries, and to the New Deal type of reformism in the wealthier countries. If we project the argument on to a theoretical plane and away from the context of the 1930s then it would have to be argued that capitalism can maintain itself only by depressing wages when in the midst of a depression. This view coincides with that of the bourgeois economists, particularly, though not exclusively, with the doctrines of the monetarists. Wages then can be forced down either by directly smashing the organisations of the working class or by dividing the workers sufficiently to demoralise the entire class. Today it is difficult to see any way that the capitalist class could actually employ either means to drive down wages in the developed countries. The reason lies in the necessary precondition for fascism, so well identified by Trotsky: the existence of a mass petite-bourgeoisie. Both the peasantry and the small entrepreneur have declined in importance. The application of force in the developed country would now have no mass support.

The simple application of force to an industrialised country cannot achieve very much in political-economic terms. If anything it would tend to speed up the organisation of opposition to capitalism and it would very likely fail to secure a change in class relations at the level of the factory. Of course, a Pinochet solution is always possible; but that is the final solution, the liquidation of modern industry in order to maintain control. It is not really an option for more than one or two countries as the ruling class of the particular country must have an alternative country in which to invest its capital. Hitler did not liquidate industry. On the contrary, he built it up and reintroduced full employment. The success of fascism was its ability to use force to restore capital, even if it was at a price to the capitalist class.

Trotsky's conception of fascism, then, was specific to his time. He explained the success of fascism and its concrete historical role. He did not, however, actually make all the necessary connections; and he did not discuss the contradictions of fascism *per se*, as opposed to the general contradictions of capitalism.

Yet those contradictions are clear enough in his writings. On the one hand, the fascists needed the support of the petite-bourgeoisie, while, on the other, their measures tended to destroy that very layer. The fascist drive raised the rate of profit and developed industry, but that led to an increasingly powerful working class demanding a better deal. They were forced to war and a controlled economy, but continued to rule by force, so that the nature of production necessarily suffered. The quality of German goods deteriorated. Fascism was a temporary solution predicated on capitalism finding an alternative form of continued existence.

The labour process and Taylorism

In the past twenty years it has become fashionable to look at the form of control over labour as a key element in the domination over the worker. In this respect Taylorism is seen as playing an historic role. Both Lenin and Trotsky welcomed the use of Taylorist methods in the early USSR, although both indicated that such methods were not in any way socialist. This apparent contradiction is seen by some[37] as playing a determining role in the formation of Stalinism. In the case of Trotsky, it is also alleged that his support for the militarisation of labour and his opposition to the right to strike show his anti-worker attitude.

These arguments are useful only as a background to a discussion of Trotsky's views of labour. Lenin and Trotsky both opposed Bogdanov and workerism.[38] In 1902 Lenin, in *What is to be Done*, had explicitly attacked workerism, and he remained consistent. Trotsky criticised Bogdanov for precisely this attitude. Along with most Marxists he argued that the worker has no culture to preserve, only a slave culture which must be overthrown. The working class takes power in order to abolish itself. The form of labour is abstract labour, which is the very expression of capitalist domination and hence must be sloughed off. There are no positive values on the side of labour. Taylorism, in this context, serves to reinforce abstract labour. Hence the working class must explode abstract labour, and so Taylorism, on taking power. Such is the logic of the argument, although Trotsky did not anywhere argue in that form.

Workers who have not become the masters of the economy remain workers. There is therefore a transition period during which the worker must shift from being an object to becoming the subject. If he simply refuses to work or works badly, the whole economy suffers and he cannot reach his goal of becoming the regulator of the economy itself. Hence the worker must remain the abstract labourer until such time as he can control the economy and then, being the master of the economy itself, he will have an incentive to work in a rational and socially planned way. He cannot, however, master production until production has reached a level sufficient to supply the basic needs of society. Until that time, even with the highest level of democracy, the worker will remain dominated by the machine. Hence it is in the interests of the worker to function in a disciplined manner until such time as it becomes a self-discipline. That is why Trotsky took such an apparently harsh attitude to the workers. If we start from the labour theory of value then it follows that the nature of production depends precisely on the nature of labour and hence on the form of labour.

He argued concretely that the crucial question to be overcome is poverty. This can be done only on the basis of:

> mechanisation and automation, the finished expression of which is the conveyor. The monotony of labour is compensated for by its reduced duration and its increased easiness. There will always be branches of industry in society that demand personal creativity, and those who find their calling in production will make their way to them.[39]

In other words, while the economy must be run on the principle of the conveyor, the worker gains by having a higher standard of living, improved work conditions, fewer hours of work and more creative labour.

From this point of view, Stalinism and Bogdanovism appeared as the false friend of the worker. They accepted the culture of the worker even if that means that workers work slowly and badly and their standard of living is consequently low. Trotsky was no voluntarist or Maoist. The mastery of production through self-discipline could be achieved only when collective discipline replaced external discipline.

Conclusion

The form which has existed for the last fifty years is based on the disciplining of the workers through Stalinism, social-democracy and the constant threat of a return to fascism and depression. It has permitted an unprecedented growth of industry and so an upturn in the 'long wave'.

Trotsky's political economy could not foresee the future and it did not describe all the contradictions of the time. But it is the best that was written. Its dialectical nature, its insights, hints and pregnant beginnings provide the basis for a modern political economy; one based on a theory of the decline of capitalism which, by distinguishing between the terminal crisis Trotsky was describing and the decline of the law of value, creates the conditions for an understanding of the conversion of laws of motion into laws of transition.

Notes

1. Leon Trotsky, 'Philosophical tendencies of bureaucratism', in *The Challenge of the Left Opposition, 1928–1929*, ed. Naomi Allen, New York, 1981, pp. 389ff; 'Dialectics and the immutability of the syllogism', *The Writings of Leon Trotsky*, ed. Naomi Allen and George Breitman, New York, 1973, pp. 399ff. His replies to Shachtman and Burnham in the collection *In Defence of Marxism*, London, 1966, are of course replete with paragraphs discussing aspects of the dialectic. See too Philip Pomper, *Trotsky, Notebooks of 1933–35*, New York, 1986.
2. Trotsky, 'Who is leading the Comintern today?' in *The Challenge ...*, p. 203. Trotsky interprets Lenin's testament on Bukharin as effectively meaning that Bukharin was not a Marxist theoretician. Richard Day, 'Dialectical method in the political writings of Lenin and Bukharin', *Canadian Journal of Political Science*, vol. 9, no. 2, June 1976, pp. 244–60.
3. V. I. Lenin, 'Razvitie kapitalizma v Rossii' ['Development of capitalism in Russia'], *Polnoe sobranie sochinenii*, vol. 3, Moscow, 1958, p. 48.
4. M. Lowy, 'From the great logic of Hegel to the Finland Station in Petrograd', *Critique*, vol. 6, pp. 5–15. Lowy shows that Lenin adopted a more dialectical viewpoint after writing his philosophical notebooks. He argues that this then permitted him to agree with Trotsky's permanent revolution. There can be no doubt about Lenin's understanding of Hegel and Marxist dialectics from that point onwards (1915), but his writing never took on the necessary theoretical form or depth, consonant with such an understanding.

5. Trotsky, 'Karl Marx', in his *The Living Thoughts of Karl Marx*, 3rd edn, London, 1946, p. 5.

6. 'Just as the operation of the laws of physiology yields different results in a growing organism from those in a dying one, so the economic laws of Marxist economy assert themselves differently in a developing and a disintegrating capitalism.' Trotsky, *Living Thoughts*, p. 19.

7. H. H. Ticktin, 'Trotsky and the social forces leading to bureaucracy', in *Pensiero e azione di Lev Trockij*, ed. Francesca Gori, Florence, 1982, pp. 451–67; Ticktin, 'Trotsky's political economy of the USSR', *forthcoming* (ms. available from the author).

8. Trotsky, 'Report on the fifth anniversary of the October Revolution and the Fourth World Congress of the Communist International. October 20, 1922', in *The First Five Years of the Communist International*, vol. 2, New York, 1953, p. 201.

9. See Trotsky, 'Karl Marx', in *Living Thoughts*.

10. See, as representative of this approach, Leo Tronti, 'Workers and capital, the labour process and class strategies', *Conference of Socialist Economists*, London, 1976. He argues that collective bargaining and the labour contract 'are more relevant in this respect than just the birth of finance capital, the various "stages" of imperialism, the so called "ages" of monopolies. Here we have the *labor history of capital* which is its actual history, and in front of which everything else is ideological legend, a dream of visionaries, the unconscious ability to mislead, or the wanted will to error on the part of the weak subaltern intellectuals.' (pp. 125–6). The contrast with Trotsky could not be more complete.

11. Trotsky, 'Manifesto of the Communist International to the workers of the world'. Capital is seen as finance capital, with all the consequences which follow. 'If the complete subjection of the state power to the power of finance capital had led mankind into the imperialist slaughter, then through this slaughter finance capital had succeeded in militarizing not only the state but also itself', in *First Five Years ...*, New York, 1945, vol. 1, p. 22.

12. He put forward the conception in many places after the initial speech at the 3rd Congress of Comintern.
    (a) 'Report on the world economic crisis and the new tasks of the Communist International', *ibid.*, pp. 199–213.
    (b) 'Report on the fifth anniversary of the October Revolution and the Fourth World Congress of the Communist International. October 20, 1922', in *First Five Years ...*, vol. 2, New York, 1953, p. 187.
    (c) 'The curve of capitalist development', in Trotsky, *Problems of Everyday Life*, New York, 1973, pp. 273ff.
    (d) Trotsky, 'K voprosu o tendentsiakh razvitiya mirovogo khoziaistva', *Planovoe khoziaistvo*, no. 1, 1926, pp. 188–91.

13. 'The acquisition by capitalism of new countries and continents, the discovery of new natural resources, and, in the wake of these, such major facts of "superstructural" order as wars and revolutions, determine the character and the replacement of ascending, stagnating, or declining epochs of capitalist development.' Trotsky, 'The curve of capitalist development', in *Problems of Everyday Life*, p. 277.

14. R. B. Day, 'The theory of the long wave, Kondratiev, Trotsky, Mandel', *New Left Review*, vol. 99, Sept.–Oct. 1976, pp. 67–92, esp. p. 82.

15. Ernest Mandel, *The Long Waves of Capitalist Development*, Cambridge, 1980.

16. Trotsky, 'Manifesto of the Communist International', in *First Five Years* ..., vol. 1.
17. 'Report on the fifth anniversary of the October Revolution and the Fourth World Congress of the Communist International. October 20, 1922,' in *First Five Years* ..., Vol. 2, p. 199.
18. Trotsky, 'K voprosu,' p. 199.
19. Trotsky, 'Report on the world economic crisis and the new tasks of the Communist International', in *First Five Years* ..., vol. 1, pp. 199–213. He looks there at the problem of consumption and the disproportions between sectors and countries.
20. Trotsky 'K voprosu', p. 188.
21. Trotsky, 'Karl Marx,' in *Living Thoughts* ...
22. 'Imperialist wars are nothing else than the detonation of the productive forces against the state borders, which have come to be too confining for them.' *ibid.*, p. 44.
23. Trotsky, *Europe vs America: Two speeches on imperialism*, New York, 1971, p. 61.
24. 'The programme of so-called autarchy has nothing to do with going back to a self-sufficient circumscribed economy. It only means that the national base is being made ready for a new war.' Trotsky, 'Karl Marx', in *Living Thoughts* ..., p. 44.
25. *ibid*, pp. 41ff.
26. *ibid.*
27. Trotsky, 'Again and once more again on the nature of the USSR, Oct. 18, 1939', in *In Defence of Marxism*, p. 31.
28. *ibid.*, p. 49.
29. Ticktin, 'Trotsky's political economy of the USSR', *forthcoming.*
30. Trotsky, *The Revolution Betrayed*, London, 1937, p. 62.
31. Trotsky, 'Platform of the opposition', *Challenge of the Left Opposition, 1926–1927*, New York, 1980, p. 373.
32. Trotsky, 'Report on the fifth anniversary of the October Revolution and the Fourth World Congress of the Communist International. October 20, 1922', in *First Five Years*, vol. 2, p. 187.
33. Ticktin, 'Trotsky's political economy of the USSR', *forthcoming.*
34. Trotsky, *First Five Years* ..., vol. 2, p. 218.
35. Trotsky, 'Karl Marx', in *Living Thoughts*, p. 16.
36. *ibid.*, p. 10.
37. Reinhart Kossler and Mammo Muchie, 'American dreams and Soviet realities: socialism and Taylorism. A reply to Chris Nyland', *Capital and Class*, vol. 40, spring 1990, pp. 61–88. This article argues very persuasively that Taylorism was introduced early on in the USSR. The authors, however, assume an unbroken development of socialism in one country and never consider the essential Lenin/Trotsky argument that the base for an advance elsewhere in the world had to be maintained. Nor do they really consider Lenin's and Trotsky's critiques of Fordism and Taylorism.
38. Trotsky, 'Leninism and workers' clubs', in *Problems of Everyday Life*, p. 317.
39. Trotsky, 'Culture and socialism', *ibid.*, p. 244.

Part V

Conclusion

19

Trotsky's future: an essay in conclusion

TERRY BROTHERSTONE

Trotsky was a giant, certainly a giant of the twentieth century. There have been other giants but Trotsky's situation was unique ... Nobody of his stature has ever been reduced to zero in his own place, in his own nation, in his own culture. Stalin almost succeeded in wiping Trotsky out of history. The fact that this is now ending is of course long overdue. But it is enthusiastically to be welcomed ...[1]

These words were spoken by George Kline, professor of philosophy at Bryn Mawr College, Pennsylvania. He was participating in the concluding plenary session of the conference 'Trotsky after fifty years', from which the essays in this book derive. Kline, as his article included in our section 'Approaches to Trotsky' makes clear, is no supporter of the ideas of Lev Davidovich. This makes his judgement on Trotsky's significance the more striking, the more appropriate to head a short conclusion, particularly since it is in the nature of this conclusion that it is also a beginning.

What is beginning, in my view, is a new stage in the study of Trotsky, his role in twentieth century history, his ideas and his significance. Herein lies the central importance of this volume. No single reader could approve of everything in it. The collection is deliberately eclectic, the viewpoints of the contributors diverse. One of our authors, Philip Pomper, for example, has recently written of another, Pierre Broué, that his biography of Trotsky is 'the most scholarly and uptodate ... a significant achievement'. But he goes on: 'one might have bones to pick with [Broué's] larger framework: his faith in Marxism-Leninism, his sense of Trotsky's heritage, and his belief in the relevance of Trotsky's ideas in this new era'.[2] Broué, in response, might well object to the phrase 'faith in Marxism-Leninism', with its irredeemably Stalinist associations, and deny that any such thing should be ascribed to him. If so, this would be but one indication that discussions about Trotsky must now go back to first principles, even to the definition of what language is appropriate.

This is not, however, to advocate empirical paralysis while theoretical terms are fought over. This volume also illustrates, I think, that there is a certain virtue in that essential quality of Anglo-Saxon scholarship: getting on with the job of making research experiences. This may seem an odd thing to say in an essay on Trotsky. No one was more penetrating than he on the limitations of empiricism. Polemicising in 1940 against James Burnham – soon to desert the Fourth International, then to become a key figure in a superficial but influential trend in academic sociology, and much later to be a supporter of ultra-right presidential hopeful, Barry Goldwater – Trotsky wrote of that way of thinking in which:

> History becomes transformed into a series of exceptional incidents; politics becomes transformed into a series of improvisations ... [This is] the disintegration of Marxism, the disintegration of theoretical thought, the disintegration of politics into its constituent elements ... Empiricism and its foster-brother, impressionism, dominate from top to bottom.[3]

But counterpoising the capacity of Marxism to grasp theoretically a contradictory, ever-changing world to empiricism, with its fixed categories and tendency to keep its eye on only one thing at a time, is not the same as denigrating empirical work. Much that has gone on in the name of Marxism during the long period in which Stalinism and Marxism have been so mischievously confused has suffered from this error. It was not one which Trotsky made. For him dialectics was no substitute for the discovery of, and attention to, historical detail. One of his most succinct remarks on the relationship between dialectics and empirical precision came, appropriately enough for our purposes, in an historical discussion – and one on the central question of the rise of Stalinism. C. L. R. James had written on the history of the Left Opposition, and Trotsky discussed his work with him and others in April 1939:

> In parts [said Trotsky] the manuscript is very perspicacious, but I have noticed the same fault that I have noticed in [James's] *World Revolution* – a very good book – and that is a lack of dialectical approach, Anglo-Saxon empiricism, and formalism which is only the reverse of empiricism.
>
> C. L. R. James makes his whole approach to the subject depend on one date – the appearance of Stalin's theory of socialism in a single country – April 1924. But the theory appeared in October 1924. This makes the whole structure false ...[4]

Through a wrong date – the product of the sort of concealed preconception which, in empiricism, tends to fill the vacuum left by the neglect of conscious theory – a whole structure of carefully assembled facts had been made to imply the opposite of the truth. Stalinism was made to seem primarily the creation of Stalin's perverted thought processes, rather than the outcome of a definite set of historical circumstances which came together to place almost intolerable pressures on revolutionary theory and dialectical method. Marxism, Trotsky was indicating, lapses into empiricism and impressionism not through too great a concern for the facts, but through slovenliness with regard to the theory – abstracted from the cumulative analysis of previous 'facts' – which guides how new facts are approached and understood.

What, then, is the relationship of this eclectic book, which contains a good deal that is opposed to Trotsky's theory and practice, to the method which

Trotsky advocated and to his life's work?

One commentary on the conference at which almost all these papers were first delivered has remarked that 'One "blank spot" (to use a popular Soviet term) was the question of the Fourth International, which ... Trotsky considered to be his most important political work'.[5] Not only is the criticism a fair one, appropriately made in a journal, *Revolutionary History*, which provides an invaluable service by devoting itself to the much neglected subject of the history of the Trotskyist movement; it is also worth commenting on for two reasons. First, it reminds us of Trotsky's own assessment of his life, confided to his diary on 25 March 1935:

> I still think that the work in which I am engaged now, despite its extremely insufficient and fragmentary nature, is the most important work of my life – more important than 1917, more important than the Civil War or any other ...
>
> Had I not been present in 1917 in Petersburg, the October Revolution would still have taken place – *on the condition that Lenin was present and in command* ... If Lenin had not been in Petersburg, I doubt whether I [alone] could have managed to overcome the resistance of the Bolshevik leaders. The struggle with 'Trotskyism' (i.e. with the proletarian revolution) would have commenced in May, 1917, and the outcome of the revolution would have been in question. But I repeat, granted the presence of Lenin the October Revolution would have been victorious anyway. The same could by and large be said about the Civil War, although in its first period ... Lenin wavered and was beset by doubts. But this was undoubtedly a passing mood which he probably never even admitted to anyone but me.
>
> Thus I cannot speak of the indispensability of my work, even about the period from 1917 to 1921. But now my work is 'indispensable' in the full sense of the word ... The collapse of the two Internationals has posed a problem which none of the leaders of these Internationals is at all equipped to solve. The vicissitudes of my personal fate have confronted me with this problem and armed me with important experience in dealing with it. There is now no one except me to carry out the mission of arming a new generation with the revolutionary method over the heads of the leaders of the Second and Third International. And I am in complete agreement with Lenin (and Turgenev) that the worst vice is to be more than 55 years old! I need at least about five more years of uninterrupted work to ensure the succession.[6]

Secondly, our *Revolutionary History* critics point us to the truth, obvious but worth stating, that this most certainly is not a 'Trotskyist' book, neither in a scholarly nor, *a fortiori*, in a political sense.

Many contributors, I am sure, share the scepticism of Paul Dukes's introductory implication that Trotskyism derives, in the main, from the reverence of 'followers' for a leader who wore the mantle of the October Revolution while maintaining what Dukes – with what, from the point of view of his co-editor, looks like immoderate understatement – calls an 'avoidance of the over-simplifications and distortions of Stalinist "Marxism-Leninism"'.[7] Pomper's disclaimer of the 'relevance of Trotsky's ideas in this new era' has already been quoted. Alec Nove, too, has written of Broué's informative, 'valuable' and 'elegantly written' Trotsky biography that it raises 'a whole number of critical questions', not the least of them being: 'How important *was* Trotsky after all?'[8] The implied answer is: 'Not very!' Given Trotsky's own assessment of the importance of the Fourth International, the manifold and still, to all but a small circle, apparently incomprehensible splits it has witnessed since it was deprived of his guidance, and the fact that, as our introductory essay puts it, socialism itself 'is widely discerned as on the retreat throughout the world',[9] there will be many readers, no doubt, who find themselves in tune with these reservations.

Yet there are other attitudes expressed in this book too. Baruch Hirson, in a far from uncritical assessment of Trotsky's attitude to Black nationalism, speaks of the 'vision' which 'still remains' that 'Only a socialist South Africa can revive hope for an altered southern Africa ... in which Blacks can unite to build a better society'.[10] If I read him correctly, Hirson sees it as important to mount a critique of Trotsky's thinking from the standpoint that, if the continuity of the socialist vision is to be re-established in the minds of a mass audience, the basic ideas which Trotsky fought and died for – in a way that no other comparable figure did – have to be made to live, to be real and relevant, in the greatly changed – but not fundamentally transformed – world of today. Sergei Kudriashov's point of view is different again – that of a young Soviet scholar able to come to terms for the first time with the possibility of openly studying one of the major founders of the Soviet republic. He reaches the striking conclusion that:

> if by Bolshevism we understand profession of the ideas of historical and dialectical materialism, struggle for the interests of the oppressed, devotion to the idea of proletarian revolution and dictatorship of the proletariat, and honesty in struggle against ideological opponents, then, at the end of the 1930s, Trotsky was a greater Bolshevik than the whole of the CPSU(B).[11]

The point about this book, then, is not that it asks who is, and who is not, a Trotskyist – or, for that matter, an anti-Trotskyist. Neither does it set out to discover what Trotskyism means today. Yet there can be no meaningful definition of Trotskyism which does not include the fact that the term came to take on a positive identity – one with which relatively small but significant numbers of courageous people were proud to claim for themselves – only in opposition to Stalinism. It was the rise of Stalinism that created the necessity for something called 'Trotskyism'. And the coherence, the unity (the dialectical unity, if you like) of this very varied book comes from a recognition that it is possible because of the disintegration of Stalinism – or what is orthodoxly, if misleadingly, called 'communism' – in Eastern Europe. With regard to the conference, this was recognised, in their different ways, by North American, Western European, Eastern European and Soviet – and by pro-Trotskyist, anti-Trotskyist and non-Trotskyist – contributors alike. When a discussion like this can take place about a uniquely controversial 'giant' of the twentieth century, it clarifies, as nothing else could in quite the same way, that we are living in a new and very challenging period.

There is space for only a few quotations to reinforce the point. Hirson, recalling his contribution to the final session of the conference, has written:

> I [said] how good it was to meet with persons from the other side of the 'curtain'. Whatever our differences there was now the possibility of a dialogue with people cut off from us for so long. Also, at last, we could hope that their access to the archives would provide us with material to fill in the gaps in our knowledge of the earlier revolutionary period.[12]

'The Stalin era', he went on 'had a profound affect' on those attracted to Trotsky's ideas, many of whom came out of Stalinist parties and brought with them a miseducation which helped block the development of Marxism, or even a proper understanding of it. The GPU terror reached deep into the Trotskyist movement, making creative theoretical work almost impossible. Trotsky himself was profoundly affected by the blows struck against his family and his supporters – the former so movingly described in this volume by Valery Bronstein – and by his own enforced isolation.

Following up Hirson's point, Cyril Smith spoke of the 'terrible conditions under which [Trotsky's] ideas were developed' in the 1930s, when, according to many accounts, he would often 'in the morning ... say to [his wife] Natalia, "Well, we're still alive today!"' Smith spoke specifically as a Trotskyist, not as an historian, and had initially called into question whether a discussion about Trotsky in an academic context could be meaningful at all – given that, for Lev Davidovich, theory and political practice were inseparable. He concluded, however, by commenting that, after forty years in the Trotskyist movement, he had learnt (or re-learnt) two things at the conference: first, how necessary it was to study Trotsky's ideas in their development, not as a fixed and static body of thought; and, secondly, the importance of seeing how they developed in a changing – and usually unfavourable – historical context.[13]

These comments were not, I think, a soft-headed concession by a revolutionary Marxist to academic liberalism, engendered perhaps by the bonhomie born of a must unusual conjuncture – a week of uninterrupted sunshine in Aberdeen. Rather they point to two important aspects of the truth which might otherwise have gone unremarked at the conference.

First is the simple fact that Stalin did *not* succeed 'in wiping Trotsky out of history', and that this was due, not to divine intervention, but to a very human struggle. However imperfect, confused and sometimes seriously distorted their efforts may often have been, the courageous defiance of Trotskyists in the face of both Stalinist and capitalist repressions has been a major factor in preserving a continuity of basic knowledge about Trotsky on which, in the new circumstances of the 1990s, historians can now build. If sunlight is now, indeed, to fall upon previously darkened archives, it is important that scholars, as they bask in it, do not forget these bitter, and often fatal, struggles.

Secondly, Smith's remarks prompt the thought that the conference, and this volume, have a broader significance which derives, contradictorily, from their own necessary limitations, from what it would have been impossible to accomplish within the confines of one pioneering set of seminars or one book. Trotsky as an historical figure is inseparable from the October Revolution, which, the efforts of revisionist historians notwithstanding, is likely to retain its status as *a* – if not, indeed *the* – central event of the twentieth century. The reappraisal of Trotsky implies a re-examination of every aspect of this event – its origins, its theoretical inspiration, its practical conduct, its international reverberations, its historiography, its degeneration, and the struggle against that degeneration based on a confidence, certainly so far as Trotsky was concerned, in world socialist revolution. This is not the place to attempt to indicate even a selection of the vast and growing academic and political literature which exists to aid this task. But it is perhaps the occasion to suggest that it is a task which goes beyond historical retrospection *per se* to the most crucial questions of our own age.

This is, of course, a personal point of view. It is encouraged, however, by a positive account of the Aberdeen conference by Sergei Kudriashov in *Voprosy istorii KPSS*.[14] He comments that its value was to an important extent a product of the way in which it set out not simply to discuss Trotsky historically, but also to evaluate his heritage from both a Soviet and an international point of view. A number of the liveliest debates, he observes, took place in the specifically economic stream of seminars (made possible by the generosity of the Nuffield Foundation), some of the differences of opinion in which will be clear from the papers by Alec Nove, Agota Gueullette and Hillel Ticktin. The Trotskyists present, remarks Kudriashev, played an important role in some of these debates – particularly those which sought to evaluate Trotsky's economic views from the standpoint of today's problems – in that their scepticism at what they see as 'market euphoria' in the USSR helped to stimulate productive controversy.[15] Once again the unity and integrity of the discussion came not from arriving at agreed solutions, but from the remarkable degree to which it was possible for scholars coming from quite different starting points to define important questions.

This is, I think, what R. V. Daniels meant when he spoke of 'how the thinking in this conference has converged' on 'the central problem of Trotsky's ambiguity, ambivalence, contradiction, in some central personal and political questions'. He referred particularly to Trotsky's relationship to Lenin, to the Bolshevik Party, to the revolution and to the possibility of achieving socialism in Russia. In all these respects the study of Trotsky raises central questions, key contradictions. The very magnitude of Trotsky's personality in so many fields of achievement in Daniels' view led him, at almost every turn, to appear as either an isolated or a dominant individual, rather than being simply a part of the general story. For this reason, Daniels concluded, the different episodes in Trotsky's life provide 'tremendous stimulation for future inquiry ... into the whole problem of what the further study of Trotsky's successes and failures may tell us about the ... evolution of the Soviet phenonemon'.[16]

This book, then, is offered as a working tool, a stimulation to further study, a publication as important for those things in it which are provisional, speculative and even may be proved wrong, as for the many new things it contributes to knowledge which will stand the test of time. As editors – even if we had been arrogant enough to believe that we could do so – we have not seen it as our task to point the reader to what she or he should agree with, or have reservations about. Each reader will make up her or his mind about that. Nor have we tried to select contributions that might lead to some synthesised conclusion about Trotsky, despite the fact that more than fifty years have now elapsed since his assassination. It will not have escaped attention that, if we had set out with such a goal, we would have had great difficulties, not least because we would not have been able to agree between ourselves. One of us holds that the future significance of Trotsky will be determined in the struggle of the oppressed for a truly human world; the other that the world has changed too much for his ideas to be of direct relevance to the achievement of that desirable end. It has not been necessary to resolve that basic difference between us in order to agree that the importance of Trotsky in academic study and intellectual discourse is only beginning to be internationally recognised. In this recognition lies the unifying claim of this book to the reader's attention.

Notes

1. Trotsky conference tapes, 4 August 1991 (in the possession of T. Brotherstone, University of Aberdeen, Department of History, Kings College, Old Aberdeen, AB9 2UB). Cited hereafter as ATCT.
2. Review of Broué's *Trotsky* by Pomper in *American Historical Review*, vol. 96, 1990–1, pp. 567–8.
3. L. D. Trotsky, *In Defence of Marxism*, London, 1966, pp. 114–5.
4. *Writings of Leon Trotsky 1938–39*, New York, 1969, ed. Naomi Allen and George Breitman, p. 260
5. Paul Flewers and Barry Buitekant, 'Work in progress: Trotsky after 50 years', *Revolutionary History*, vol. 3, no. 3, spring, 1991, p. 45.
6. *Trotsky's Diary in Exile*, Cambridge, Mass., and London, 1976, foreword by Jean van Heijenoort, pp. 46–7.
7. *supra*, p. 6.
8. Review of Broué's *Trotsky* by Alec Nove ('Blinkers and blunders'), *Times Literary Supplement*, 10 March 1989.
9. *supra*, p. 6.
10. *supra*, p. 189.
11. *supra*, p. 95.
12. Letter to T. Brotherstone (unfortunately, Hirson's original spoken contribution coincided with our only tape-recorder breakdown of the conference).
13. ATCT, 4 Aug. 1990.
14. *Voprosy istorii KPSS* no. 12, 1990, pp. 144–7.
15. ATCT, 3 Aug. 1990 (p.m., seminar B, both sessions).
16. ATCT, 4 Aug. 1990.

Index